JOHN

EVANGELIST & INTERPRETER

Stephen S. Smalley

InterVarsity Press
Downers Grove, Illinois

InterVarsity Press
P.O. Box 1400, Downers Grove, IL 60515
World Wide Web: www.ivpress.com
E-mail: mail@ivpress.com

Second edition ©Stephen Smalley 1998
First edition ©1978 The Paternoster Press

Published in the United States of America by InterVarsity Press, Downers Grove, Illinois, with permission from Paternoster Publishing, Carlisle, U.K.

InterVarsity Press® is the book-publishing division of InterVarsity Christian Fellowship/USA®, a student movement active on campus at hundreds of universities, colleges and schools of nursing in the United States of America, and a member movement of the International Fellowship of Evangelical Students. For information about local and regional activities, write Public Relations Dept., InterVarsity Christian Fellowship/USA, 6400 Schroeder Rd., P.O. Box 7895, Madison, WI 53707-7895.

Cover illustration: Roberta Polfus

ISBN 0-8308-1514-7

Printed in the United States of America

Library of Congress Cataloging-in-Publication Data

Smalley, Stephen S.
  John, evangelist and interpreter/Stephen S. Smalley.
    p.   cm.—(New Testament profiles)
  Originally published: Exeter: Peternoster Press, 1978
  Includes bibliographical references and index.
  ISBN 0-8308-1514-7 (pbk.: alk. paper)
    1. Bible.   N.T. John—Criticism, interpretation, etc.   I. Title.
  II. Series.
  BS2615.2.S58   1998
  226.5'06—dc21   98-20199
                                                                                          CIP

21	20	19	18	17	16	15	14	13	12	11	10	9	8	7	6	5	4	3	2	1
15	14	13	12	11	10	09	08	07	06	05	04	03	02	01	00	99	98			

CONTENTS

Prologue to First Edition   xi
Prologue to Second Edition   xiii
Abbreviations   xv

1. JOHN AMONG THE EVANGELISTS   1
   The Gospel of John   1
   The Puzzle and its History   2
   A consensus reached   3
   (a) Zahn to Windisch   3
   (b) The question of authorship   5
   A New Consensus   6
   The New Consensus Eroded   9
   Conclusion   12

2. JOHN'S TRADITION   14
   Literary Evidence   14
   (a) Similarities   14
       Narrative material   15
           The feeding of the five thousand   15
           The anointing at Bethany   17
           Conclusions   18
       Discourse material   19
           Conclusions   22
       Summary   23
   (b) Differences   23
       John the Baptist   24
       Chronology   25
       Christology   28
       The teaching of Jesus   29
       The miracles of Jesus   31
   Summary and conclusions   31
   Further Evidence   32
   (a) From manuscripts   32
   (b) From background research   33
   (c) From Qumran   33
       John the Baptist   36
   (d) From topography   37
   Conclusions   40
   The Gospel Tradition   41
   Conclusion   43

3. JOHN'S BACKGROUND   45
        John's Background   46
        (a) Greek influence   46
            Philosophy   46
            Religion   48
                The Mystery religions   49
                Mandean literature   49
                Hermetic literature   52
                Gnosticism   54
                Bultmann's view   56
                Conclusions   61
            Philo   61
            Conclusions   64
        (b) Jewish influence   64
            The slant of the Gospel   65
            The Gospel's original language   66
            John's use of the Old Testament   68
            John and Rabbinic Judaism   70
            John and Non-conformist Judaism   72
            Conclusions   74

4. JOHN AND JOHN'S GOSPEL   75
        External Evidence   75
        (a) John and Ephesus   77
            Conclusion   79
        (b) John the Elder   80
        Internal Evidence   82
        The beloved disciple   82
            John the apostle   83
            John Mark   85
            Lazarus   85
            The ideal disciple   86
            Other disciples   87
                John 1:41   87
                John 18:15–16   87
                John 19:35   88
            The disciple witness   88
        Conclusion   89
        The Date of the Gospel   90

5. JOHN'S SOURCES   94
        John's Sources   95
        The problem   95
            Conclusion   98
        The solutions   98
            (a) The author's method   99
            (b) Displacements   100

(c) Sources   101
    Rudolf Bultmann's theory   101
    Signs sources   104
    Discourse sources   108
    Passion sources   112
(d) Editions   114
Conclusion   119

6   JOHN'S COMPOSITION   121
   Narrative Criticism   121
   Literary Approaches to John   122
   R.A. Culpepper   122
   Other Johannine literary critics   124
   Conclusions   126
   Disadvantages   127
   Advantages   127
   Our Own Approach   128
   John's centre   128
   The signs, discourses and sayings   129
      The signs   129
      The discourses   132
      The 'I am' sayings   133
   Prologue and epilogue   135
      John 1   135
      John 21   139
      Conclusions   140

7. JOHN'S GOSPEL DRAMA   141
   The Play   142
   The Introduction (John 1)   142
   Act One (John 2–12)   142
      The signs   143
      The discourses   146
   Act Two (John 13–20)   149
   The Epilogue (John 21)   152
   Conclusion   153
   The Origin of John's Gospel   155

8. JOHN'S PURPOSE   159
   Earlier Suggestions   159
   (a) To replace, interpret or supplement the synoptic Gospels 159
   (b) To restate the Christian gospel in Hellenised terms   160
   (c) As polemic or apology   161
      Polemic against the Baptist sect   161
      Polemic concerning the sacramental teaching of the church   164
      Polemic concerning the eschatological teaching of the church 166
      Polemic against heresy   169
   (d) For liturgical use   172
   The Aim of the Gospel   174

'Seeing and believing'   175
John's Audience   177
(a) Unbelieving Jews   177
(b) Diaspora Jewish-Christians   179
(c) Christians   180
(d) The Johannine Church   181
Provenance   186

9. JOHN: EVANGELIST   187
   John as Evangelist   188
   John's Kerygma   190
   John and Paul   193
   John and Mark   195
   Conclusions   199
   John and History   199
   (a) History and tradition in Acts   201
   (b) History and tradition in the Gospels   204
      What are the Gospels?   205
      Did it happen?   207
         History behind the signs   211
         History behind the discourses   223
   Conclusion   229

10. JOHN: INTERPRETER   230
    Salvation in the Fourth Gospel   231
    The Sacramental Dimension of the Fourth Gospel   232
    Symbolism and sacrament   234
    The Christology of the Fourth Gospel   238
    (a) Son of man   240
    (b) Logos   243
    (c) Son (of God)   244
    (d) Christ (Messiah)   245
    Glorification in the Fourth Gospel   248
    (a) Omission   251
    (b) Emphasis   251
    (c) Addition   252
    John's theology of the cross   252
    Spirit and Church in the Fourth Gospel   256
    The Paraclete   257
       Who is the Paraclete?   257
       What does the Paraclete do?   260
    The church   263
    Church and Spirit   264
    Eschatology in the Fourth Gospel   265
    Present eschatology   265
    Future eschatology   268
    Conclusion   269
    John's Interpretation   271

EPILOGUE   273
    Why is John Different?   273
    John for Today   276
    John's balance   276
    Conclusions   282

Bibliography   284

Index of Modern Authors   307
Indexof Subjects   312
Index of Ancient Sources   325

THIS BOOK IS STILL FOR SUE

in her memory

PROLOGUE TO THE FIRST EDITION

The Gospel of John is a source of endless fascination for the student of the New Testament. Its problems deserve and receive constant investigation, and yet its secrets show no sign of being fully discovered. This is not surprising, since – in Luther's phrase – its incomparably 'simple words' are at the same time 'inexpressible words'.

This book is offered as one further attempt to sound the Johannine depths. It is intended primarily for theological students; but others may find it useful, if only as a stimulus to further discussion and investigation.

Some indication of the scope and outline of the following pages may be in place at the start. In the first two chapters we shall try to assess the present drift of the debate about the Fourth Gospel, especially in the light of the 'new look' on John and in the wake of the recent finds at Qumran and Nag Hammadi, which have helped us to know more about the background to Christianity at its beginning and in its subsequent progress. For this purpose we shall investigate the crucial matters of the tradition, background and authorship of John's Gospel. Then we shall look at the way the Gospel has been built up, and the purpose behind its composition. Finally, we shall consider the extent to which John as an evangelist is in touch with a common Christian tradition, and also the nature of his special contribution to that tradition as an interpreter.

Many books about John have been written, and many remain to be written. The present volume does not pretend to be in any sense a final word, and it will probably raise as many questions as it tries to answer. For example, the thesis of this book is that John's Gospel is indebted to an independent and basically historical tradition which the evangelist has interpreted in his own way. But it may be felt by some that if the Fourth Gospel contains both history and theology, the real nature of John's 'history' requires more detailed clarification than space has permitted here. Similarly, the relation of my discussion about John to the issues of biblical inspiration and authority demands a treatment which it has not been able to receive in these pages. Equally, my frankly literary analysis of John may well prove unacceptable to those of my readers whose sensitivities are more linguistically inclined.

This does not mean, I hope, that we have toiled all night and taken nothing; but rather that there is still room for all of us to put out further into the deep and let down our nets. If this book has charted the course of current studies in the Fourth Gospel with any degree of accuracy, and thrown out occasional buoys as markers for future voyages in Johannine waters, it will have gone a considerable way towards fulfilling its purpose.

My continuing interest in John was inspired originally by Mr P. Gardner-Smith and Dr John A.T. Robinson, both of whom taught me theology at Cambridge. I gladly acknowledge my very considerable debt to them, and to many others whose names appear in this book, especially Professor C.F.D. Moule and Professor Raymond E. Brown. I am also grateful to the large number of students and friends at Cambridge, Ibadan and Manchester, who over the years have stimulated my thinking about 'John', and deepened my understanding of him. Finally, I owe more than I can say, in the production of this volume, to the encouragement and help of my family, my head of department at Manchester (Professor F.F. Bruce, who read the manuscript and made many valuable suggestions for its improvement), my publishers, and Miss Gillian Shepherd, who typed the manuscript with her customary generosity and efficiency. My greatest debt, of course, is recorded in the dedication.

Manchester   STEPHEN S. SMALLEY

The Feast of St John the Evangelist, 1975

PROLOGUE TO THE SECOND EDITION

There has been great movement in Johannine studies since this book first appeared in 1978. First, a reassessment has taken place of the relationship between John's tradition and that of the other evangelists. Second, and more significantly, a literary approach to the Fourth Gospel has firmly taken its place alongside the historical and theological methods of interpreting the Johannine text. It therefore seemed right to take proper account of these two major developments in the study of John, by devoting new chapters to each of the topics, as well as by revising extensively the notes and bibliography.

The percipient reader will notice that at some points I have modified, and even altered, stances which I adopted in the first edition of this book. But I have maintained without question my belief, argued in the earlier version, that John's Gospel should be analysed as a sustained piece of dramatic writing; and I owe my continuing sensitivity to the literary character of the Fourth Gospel to the fact that I read English as well as Theology at Cambridge. All three avenues of exploration, the historical, theological and literary, are together, it seems to me, essential means of mapping the endlessly fascinating Johannine territory.

My thinking about John – his Revelation, Gospel and Letters – has been enriched over the past nineteen years by many scholars and friends whose work has inspired my own, as well as by the students whom I taught at Coventry, and those whom I now teach in Chester; and I am grateful to them all. I owe more than I can say to Diane Jackson, who typed the manuscript with such patience and cheerfulness; and I am also appreciative of the consistent welcome afforded to me by the staff of St Deiniol's Library, where the bulk of my work on this new edition was undertaken.

The dedication of this volume remains the same: not now from the perspective of time, but of eternity.

Chester   STEPHEN SMALLEY

Easter Day, 1997

ABBREVIATIONS

1. GENERAL

AB	Anchor Bible Series
AGSU	Arbeiten zur Geschichte des antiken Judentums und des Urchristentums
AnBib	Analecta Biblica Series
ANCL	Ante-Nicene Christian Library
BAL	The Bible and Liberation Series
BDSR	Biblioteca di Scienze Religiose
BET	Beiträge zur biblischen Exegese und Theologie
BETL	Bibliotheca Ephemeridum Theologicarum Lovaniensium
BI	Biblical Interpretation Series
BJRL	*Bulletin of the John Rylands Library*
BNTC	Black's New Testament Commentary Series
BWANT	Beiträge zur Wissenschaft vom Alten und Neuen Testament
BZ (NF)	*Biblische Zeitschrift* (Neue Folge)
CBET	Contributions to Biblical Exegesis and Theology Series
CBQ	*Catholic Biblical Quarterly*
ConBNT	Coniectanea Biblica, New Testament Series
DB (S)	L. Pirot, *et al.* (ed.), *Dictionnaire de la Bible* (Supplément) (Paris: Letouzey, 1928–)
EQ	*Evangelical Quarterly*
EvT	*Evangelische Theologie*
ExpT	*Expository Times*
FRLANT (ns)	Forschungen zur Religion und Literatur des Alten und Neuen Testaments (new series)
Hennecke	E. Hennecke, *New Testament Apocrypha*, ed. R.McL. Wilson, 2 vols. (London: Lutterworth Press, 1963 and 1965)
HNT	Handbuch zum Neuen Testament, ed. H. Lietzmann and G. Bornkamm
HS	Hermeneia Series

HTCNT	Herder's Theological Commentary on the New Testament Series
HTFG	C.H. Dodd, *Historical Tradition in the Fourth Gospel* (Cambridge: Cambridge University Press, 1963)
HTR	*Harvard Theological Review*
IBT	Interpreting Biblical Texts Series
IFG	C.H. Dodd, *The Interpretation of the Fourth Gospel* (Cambridge: Cambridge University Press, 1953)
Int	*Interpretation*
IRT	Issues in Religion and Theology Series
JBL	*Journal of Biblical Literature*
JSNT	*Journal for the Study of the New Testament*
JSNTS	Journal for the Study of the New Testament Supplement Series
JTS (ns)	*Journal of Theological Studies* (new series)
LPT	Library of Philosophy and Theology Series
Migne, *PG*	Migne, *Patrologia Graeca*
NCB	New Century Bible Series
NIGTC	New International Greek Testament Commentary Series
NovT	*Novum Testamentum*
NovT Sup	Novum Testamentum Supplement Series
NRSV	New Revised Standard Version
NTL	New Testament Library Series (SCM Press)
NTR	New Testament Readings Series
NTS	*New Testament Studies*
NTT	New Testament Theology Series
NTTS	New Testament Tools and Studies Series
par.	parallel verse(s)
PGC	The Pelican Gospel Commentaries Series
RB	*Revue Biblique*
RechBib	Recherches Bibliques
RevT	*Revue Thomiste*
RGG	K. Galling (ed.), *Die Religion in Geschichte und Gegenwart*, 3rd edn., 7 vols. (Tübingen: Mohr-Siebeck, 1957–65)
RNT	Reading the New Testament Series
RQ	*Revue de Qumran*
RSR	Recherches de Science Religieuse
SANT	Studien zum Alten und Neuen Testament
SBLDS	Society of Biblical Literature Dissertation Series
SBLMS	Society of Biblical Literature Monograph Series
SBS	Stuttgarter Bibelstudien

SBT	Studies in Biblical Theology Series, 1 and 2 (SCM Press)
SE	*Studia Evangelica (= TU)*
SJLA	Studies in Judaism in Late Antiquity
SJT	*Scottish Journal of Theology*
SNTA	Studiorum Novi Testamenti Auxilia
SNTSMS	Society for New Testament Studies Monograph Series
SNTW	Studies of the New Testament and its World Series
StudT	*Studia Theologica*
TBC	Torch Bible Commentary Series
ThZ	*Theologische Zeitschrift*
TNTC	Tyndale New Testament Commentaries Series
TPINTC	Trinity Press International New Testament Commentary Series
TR (NF)	*Theologische Rundschau* (Neue Folge)
TU	*Texte und Untersuchungen zur Geschichte der altchristlichen Literatur*
TynB	*Tyndale Bulletin*
UNT	Untersuchungen zum Neuen Testament
VF	*Verkündingung und Forschung* (Theologischer Jahresbericht)
WBC	Word Biblical Commentary Series
WF	Wege der Forschung
WMANT	Wissenschaftliche Monographien zum Alten und Neuen Testament
WUNT	Wissenschaftliche Untersuchungen zum Neuen Testament
ZNW	*Zeitschrift für die neutestamentliche Wissenschaft und die Kunde der älteren Kirche*
ZTK	*Zeitschrift für Theologie und Kirche*

2. DEAD SEA SCROLLS

CD	Zadokite Damascus Rule
1QH	Hymns of Thanksgiving
1QM	War of the Sons of Light against the Sons of Darkness
1QS	The Community Rule

3. ANCIENT WRITERS

Eusebius	*HE*	*Historia Ecclesiastica*
Ignatius	*Eph*	*To the Ephesians*
	Mag	*To the Magnesians*
	Philad	*To the Philadelphians*

Irenaeus	*AH*	*Adversus Haereses*
Josephus	*Ant*	*Antiquities*
	Bell Jud	*Bellum Judaicum*
Philo	*De agric*	*De Agricultura*
	De conf	*De Confusione Linguarum*
	De fuga	*De Fuga et Inventione*
	De migr	*De Migratione Abrahami*
	De opific	*De Opificio Mundi*
	De praem	*De Praemiis et Poenis*
	De spec leg	*De Specialibus Legibus* (I–IV)
	Quod det	*Quod Deterius Potiori insidiari soleat*

1

JOHN AMONG THE EVANGELISTS

Outside the new Testament various documents bear the name of John. The most famous is the legendary Acts of John, which belongs to the early third century AD and purports to give information about the life and work of the apostle.[1] But other fragments exist, mostly of a gnostic character, which claim some connection with John: an apocryphon, various apocalypses and mysteries, a dialogue between John and Jesus, and even an unknown Gospel with Johannine elements.[2]

The links between this literature and the documents within the New Testament which carry the name of John are not easy to determine, and provide a fascinating area for research. This is not our present task, which is the more concentrated but no less exciting one of taking a fresh look at the Gospel of John.

Of the five New Testament books which tradition associates with John (the Revelation, the Gospel and the three Letters), none has provoked such interest or caused such constant reappraisal as the Fourth Gospel.[3] In recent decades the reassessment of John's place among the evangelists, in particular, has become rapid and wide-ranging. It will therefore be useful to begin this study with an historical overview, to put in context our own approach to that mercurial topic. We can then move on to a closer look at the Gospel itself.

THE GOSPEL OF JOHN

All four Gospels in the New Testament tell the story of Jesus. He is the central character in each; and the evangelists together are concerned to present, in their different ways, the good news about Jesus: in terms of who he was, what he said and what he did.

But if we take a synoptic view of the four Gospels, it soon becomes apparent that the first three (Mark, Matthew and Luke) are closer

1. For the text of the *Acta Ioannis* see Hennecke 2, pp. 188–259.
2. See Hennecke 1, pp. 94–97.
3. This title, 'the *Fourth* Gospel', will serve for the moment as a description of John's testimony. But, as we shall see, its use can be the result of questionable presuppositions on the part of critics, and imply less than accurate conclusions. *Cf.* J.A.T. Robinson, *The Priority of John*, ed. J.F. Coakley (London: SCM Press, 1985), pp. 1–35. Similarly, the use in this book of 'John' for the evangelist and his Gospel, like the expression '*fourth* evangelist' itself, should not be construed as prejudging the authorship issue.

together than any one of them is to John. Compare, for example, Mark and Matthew. These two Gospels are firmly related to each other; and the reason for this is that most of the content of Mark is taken over and used by the writer of Matthew.[4] Similarly Luke, perhaps at a second stage, incorporates a good deal of Marcan material in his Gospel.[5]

However, when Mark is placed alongside John, the picture changes sharply.[6] While there are obvious parallels, clear differences immediately appear. First, the portrait of John the Baptist differs in the two Gospels. Second, the length and geographical location of the ministry of Jesus vary in the evangelists' accounts. Third, the presentation of Jesus as Messiah is not the same in John as it is in Mark. Fourth, the teaching of Jesus, both in its manner and content, assumes a different character in the Marcan and Johannine traditions. Fifth, the record of the miraculous deeds of Jesus does not accord in the two Gospels.

These differences should not be exaggerated; nor should they be allowed to drive too sharp a wedge between the basic traditions upon which John and Mark, and the other Gospel writers, drew. In due course we shall look in more detail at the variations which have just been listed, and see that, as it happens, they can all be qualified.[7] We shall also be examining arguments to suggest that, in any case, all four evangelists drew in some way upon a common Christian witness to the story of Jesus.[8]

So what exactly is the relationship between John and the other three Gospels? This question has provided a puzzle for students of the New Testament down the ages. The four documents are alike, and yet not alike. In that case, how – if at all – do they fit together? We can now look at some of the answers which have been given to that question over the years, and more especially in twentieth-century Johannine scholarship.

THE PUZZLE AND ITS HISTORY

The description by Clement of Alexandria, at the turn of the third century AD, of John's Gospel as a 'spiritual' version of the other three,[9]

4. *Cf.* P. Perkins, *Reading the New Testament: An Introduction*, 2nd edn. (London: Geoffrey Chapman, 1988), pp. 214–19. Such a conclusion, of course, presupposes the priority of Mark.

5. V. Taylor, *Behind the Third Gospel: A Study of the Proto-Luke Hypothesis* (Oxford: Clarendon Press, 1926), pp. 126–143, 184.

6. By looking at Mark and John, we are comparing *two* underlying traditions, since Mark is followed so closely by Matthew and Luke. The strength of the comparison, that is to say, is one in relation to one, *not* John's single witness over and against the ultimately triple testimony of the synoptic writers.

7. See below, pp. 23–32.

8. Below, pp. 41–44. For this section see further D.M. Smith, *John Among the Gospels: The Relationship in Twentieth-Century Research* (Minneapolis: Fortress Press, 1992), pp. 2–6.

9. Quoted in Eusebius, *HE* 6.14.7.

suggests a felt need early on to defend the alternative nature of John's writing. Similarly, Eusebius of Caesarea, roughly a century later, implausibly tried to explain the special character of John's work by arguing that the first three evangelists tell the story of Jesus *after* the imprisonment of John the Baptist, while the fourth evangelist draws for his record on those events which happened *before* that time.[10] Origen, writing in the early part of the third century AD, accepts that there are 'discrepancies' between John and the other Gospels, especially in their accounts of the early years of the ministry of Jesus.[11] But because these differences cannot be harmonised when they are read literally and historically, Origen claims, they must be 'solved analogically': that is, they are to be interpreted spiritually.[12]

These initial attempts to address the perceived problem, that John and the synoptic writers seem not to be at one in their versions of the Jesus tradition, embraced a fundamental assumption: that the writer of the Fourth Gospel knew the other three, and used them in his own composition. That presupposition has also characterised critical scholarship from its rise in the middle of the nineteenth century,[13] until the earlier part of the twentieth.

A CONSENSUS REACHED

(a) From Zahn to Windisch

Johannine studies at the beginning of the twentieth century were dominated by scholarly names such as those of Theodore Zahn, Adolf Jülicher and James Moffatt. All three authors, in their introductions to the literature of the New Testament,[14] reflect the then prevailing view that the writer of the Fourth Gospel had access to the work of the synoptic evangelists, and to some extent utilised their material.[15] In

10. *HE* 3.24.7–14.

11. Origen, *Commentary on the Gospel of John* 10:2–3 (ANCL, additional volume, pp. 382–83); also 10:15–16 (ANCL, pp. 391–95), on the placing of the cleansing of the temple.

12. *Ibid.*, 10:2 (ANCL, p. 382). See further Smith, *John Among the Gospels*, pp. 6–10.

13. Modern biblical criticism essentially began with the *Life of Jesus* (1835–36) by D.F. Strauss, who discounted the historical basis of the Jesus tradition, and the subsequent diachronic investigation of the New Testament by the Tübingen school in Germany. See H. Harris, *The Tübingen School* (Oxford: Clarendon Press, 1975), esp. pp. 181–262.

14. T. Zahn, *Introduction to the New Testament*, vol. 3 (Edinburgh: T. and T. Clark, 1909), pp. 254–98, esp. 264; A. Jülicher, *An Introduction to the New Testament* (London: Smith Elder, 1904), pp. 396–97; J. Moffatt, *An Introduction to the Literature of the New Testament*, 3rd edn. (Edinburgh: T. and T. Clark, 1918), pp. 533–47, esp. 533–34, 546.

15. Moffatt, *Introduction*, is cautious in his approach, taking for granted that John's Gospel presupposes the synoptic tradition, but acknowledging the need to establish the actual use of 'any or all' of the other Gospels (p. 533).

subsequent years Burnett Hillman Streeter[16] from Great Britain, and Benjamin Bacon[17] from America, greatly influenced the development of this discussion in the English-speaking world.

Streeter's name is usually associated with his standard defence of the priority of Mark's Gospel, and an apparently definitive explanation of what he called the 'four-document hypothesis'.[18] But he also argued compellingly for the use of Mark and Luke (or Proto-Luke) in the composition of John's Gospel.[19] By adopting this stance, however, Streeter identified an inherent problem: why should the fourth evangelist depart from the synoptic tradition when there is no theological reason for him to do so?[20] In raising this question, Streeter anticipated later research on John's relation to the other Gospels.[21]

Bacon's study[22] adopts a similar critical position. John 'practically ignores' Matthew, and makes Mark as modified by Luke the basis of his composition.[23] Two notable points emerge in Bacon's approach: first his conclusion that the writer of the Fourth Gospel used 'every available shred of Mark' creatively, and in his own way;[24] and second, his claim that John was influenced by Paul's handling of the Christian good news.[25]

However, in all this, as Moody Smith points out,[26] Bacon does not seriously consider the possibility that it could be easier to account for the similarities between John and the synoptists by arguing that John wrote independently of them, than to explain the variations (some of which Bacon ignores) on the assumption that the fourth evangelist knew and used them. To this issue we shall return.[27]

The problematic nature of John's relationship to the other three Gospels has a bearing on the purpose of the Fourth Gospel, which we

16. B.H. Streeter, *The Four Gospels: A Study of Origins*, 2nd edn. (London and New York: Macmillan, 1930). The first edition appeared in 1924.

17. B.W. Bacon, *The Fourth Gospel in Research and Debate*, 2nd edn. (London and Leipzig: T. Fisher Unwin, 1918).

18. Streeter, *Four Gospels*, pp. 150–331, esp. 223–70. See also below, pp. 42–43.

19. *Ibid.*, pp. 393–426, esp. 416–17.

20. Streeter's answer invokes the authority of the fourth evangelist over Mark and Luke, neither of whom was an eyewitness (pp. 417–18).

21. See the treatment of P. Gardner-Smith's work below, pp. 6–7 and n. 35; also 14–19.

22. Bacon, *Fourth Gospel*, pp. 356–84.

23. *Ibid.*, pp. 368–70.

24. *Ibid.*, p. 381. According to Bacon, Johannine discourse material, and not only the narrative sections, depended on the synoptic tradition. See *ibid.*, pp. 379–80 (John 5 develops the doctrinal implications of Mark 2:1–3:6); on this point see also B.W. Bacon, *The Gospel of the Hellenists,* ed. C.H. Kraeling (New York: Henry Holt, 1933), pp. 183–92.

25. *Ibid.*, p. 368. Bacon subsequently modified his belief that Pauline theology was a formative principle underlying John's writing. *Cf.* Bacon, *Hellenists*, pp. 335–44. On John and Paul see below, 193–95.

26. *Cf.* Smith, *John among the Gospels*, pp. 18–19, esp. 19.

27. See below, pp. 23–32.

shall be considering in due course.[28] For if it is argued that John wrote with the synoptic Gospels (in some sense) before him, then it is possible to claim that the fourth evangelist was in one way or another developing and even correcting the witness of the other evangelists. The work of Hans Windisch[29] occupies a significant place in this particular discussion, and marks a departure from the scholarly consensus reached by the end of the first quarter of the twentieth century. For (as we shall discover) Windisch, while accepting that John knew the synoptic Gospels, believed that he *ignored* them, and fully intended to displace them. The Fourth Gospel, on this showing, is a piece of theological polemic, aimed distinctively at opposing gnostic and Jewish interpretations of the Christian message.

(b) The question of authorship

Relevant to any enquiry into the origin of the Fourth Gospel, and the relationship between its tradition and that of the synoptics, is the question of *authorship*. In what sense can John's Gospel be said to belong to (the apostle) John? If the work is indeed apostolic, and Jewish, it can be regarded as 'historical'; and in that case the apparent conflict between the Johannine and synoptic traditions presents a difficulty. But if it is taken as a 'theological' interpretation of the other Gospels, it can easily be classified as non-apostolic and Hellenistic.

At the turn of the twentieth century scholarly opinion was clearly divided between these two views. Conservatives like B.F. Westcott maintained that the Fourth Gospel was mainly if not entirely the work of the apostle John;[30] whereas radicals such as A. Loisy regarded the Gospel as an unhistorical, theological reconstruction of the synoptic Gospels unconnected with the apostle.[31]

Another aspect of the authorship issue concerned the cultural background of John's Gospel. In the early years of the twentieth century, and under the influence of the religio-historical method of biblical exegesis, the fashion was to describe the Gospel as merely a late stage in the process of hellenising the Christian good news. The leading proponent of this view was Otto Pfleiderer, who believed that the New Testament

28. See chapter 8.

29. H. Windisch, *Johannes und die Synoptiker: Wollte der vierte Evangelist die älteren Evangelien ergänzen oder ersetzen?* UNT 12 (Leipzig: J.C. Hinrichs, 1926), pp. 1–40. For a detailed summary of Windisch's argument, in a work which has not been translated, see Smith, *John Among the Gospels*, pp. 19–31.

30. B.F. Westcott, *The Gospel According to St John* (London: James Clarke, 1958), pp. v–xxxii. The original edition was published in 1880.

31. A. Loisy, *Le quatrième Évangile*, 2nd edn. (Paris: Picard et Fils, 1921), pp. 1–150. W. Sanday, *The Criticism of the Fourth Gospel* (Oxford: Clarendon Press, 1905), pp. 25–32, describes the position of Loisy with reference to the apostolicity and historicity of the Fourth Gospel as one of 'uncompromising rejection'.

was a product of its age and should be interpreted as such. He concluded that John's Gospel did not belong 'to the historical books of primitive Christianity, but to its Hellenistic, doctrinal writings'.[32]

By the 1920s a reaction had set in against a preoccupation with the supposedly Greek character of the Fourth Gospel. The conservative scholar Adolf Schlatter had already published a study of John which suggested that the setting of this Gospel was essentially Jewish.[33] Writing out of an expert knowledge of the Semitic background to the ethos and language of the New Testament, Schlatter argued that much of the alleged Hellenism of the Fourth Gospel had parallels in Jewish writing, and that the Palestinian character of the Gospel could best be explained if its writer were a Palestinian Jew. In 1922 C.F. Burney, an Old Testament Professor at Oxford, carried on and developed Schlatter's position in a book which set out to demonstrate not merely that John was indebted to a Jewish background, but also that it was originally written in Aramaic.[34] Few today would endorse this view; but at the time it was a healthy reminder that the history of religions school had not spoken the last word on the Fourth Gospel, the origin of which was still open to debate.

A NEW CONSENSUS

We have observed that the history of the interpretation of the Fourth Gospel, from the end of the nineteenth century to the beginning of the twentieth, was preoccupied with two leading assumptions. First, that the historical nature of John's tradition could be determined by solving the question of the Gospel's authorship; and second, that the fourth evangelist knew and used the synoptic Gospels in the composition of his work. Both of those claims have been challenged in more recent Johannine scholarship; and the effects have been profound. Let us take the issue of Johannine dependence first, and set the scene.

In 1938 a small but significant study of the relation between the synoptic and Johannine traditions appeared under the title of *Saint John*

32. O. Pfleiderer, *Primitive Christianity: Its Writings and Teachings in Their Historical Connections*, vol. 4 (London: Williams and Norgate, 1911), p. 2; see pp. 1–80, 129–53.

33. A. Schlatter, 'Die Sprache und Heimat des vierten Evangelisten' in K. Rengstorf (ed.), *Johannes und sein Evangelium*, WF 82 (Darmstadt: Wissenschaftliche Buchgesellschaft, 1973), pp. 28–201.

34. C.F. Burney, *The Aramaic Origin of the Fourth Gospel* (Oxford: Clarendon Press, 1922), esp. pp. 126–52. S.C. Neill and N.T. Wright, *The Interpretation of the New Testament 1861–1986*, 2nd edn. (Oxford and New York: Oxford University Press, 1988), pp. 335–47, offer a useful section on the history of the interpretation of John's Gospel. In the course of it, the suggestion is made that Dr Israel Abrahams of Cambridge (a Reader in Rabbinics, and an orthodox Jew) was among the first at that time (1923 or 1924) to assert that 'the Fourth Gospel is the most Jewish of the four' (p. 338).

and the Synoptic Gospels.[35] It was written by Percival Gardner-Smith of Cambridge, and is in many ways an anticipation of later research on John. On purely literary grounds, it challenged the accepted view that the Gospel of John depended on the other three; and it did so by reviewing the similarities between the Gospels, as well as the differences between them.

The method of this writer is important. Earlier critics, he maintains, emphasised the correspondences between the synoptic and Johannine traditions, and then attempted to explain their divergences. Gardner-Smith's own view is that the Fourth Gospel should be taken as it stands, and the similarities and dissimilarities between it and the other Gospels noted simultaneously.[36] The result of his analysis is very revealing, and leads him to conclude that John may well provide an 'independent authority' for the life of Jesus.[37]

> If in the Fourth Gospel we have a survival of a type of first century Christianity which owed nothing to synoptic developments, and which originated in quite a different intellectual atmosphere, its historical value may be very great indeed.[38]

The abiding influence of Gardner-Smith's work was considerable; and its repercussions were being felt in the international world of Johannine scholarship in a relatively short time. In 1945, for example, a weighty article by the American scholar Erwin Goodenough, 'John a Primitive Gospel', took issue with Gardner-Smith's conclusions about the origins of the Fourth Gospel, but also developed the case for John's independence from the synoptic Gospels.[39]

In the middle years of the twentieth century, two leading Johannine scholars moved this case forward in such a dominant way that it became possible to speak of a new consensus of academic opinion. In the first of his two major volumes on John's Gospel,[40] C.H. Dodd acknowledged

35. Originally published by Cambridge University Press, Gardner-Smith's book has been reprinted under the same title, *Saint John and the Synoptic Gospels* (Weston-super-Mare: Readersoft, 1992). References are to the new publication. For a reassessment of the important influence of Gardner-Smith on Johannine studies in the mid-twentieth century see J. Verheyden, 'P. Gardner-Smith and "The Turn of the Tide" ' in A. Denaux (ed.), *John and the Synoptics*, BETL 101 (Leuven: Leuven University Press and Peeters, 1992), pp. 423–52.

36. *Ibid.*, p. iii.

37. *Ibid.*, p. 46. But note also the anticipation of this conclusion in A.E. Brooke's commentary on John in A.S. Peake (ed.), *A Commentary on the Bible* (London and Edinburgh: T.C. and E.C. Jack, 1920), pp. 743–65, esp. 743–44.

38. Gardner-Smith, *John*, p. 46.

39. E.R. Goodenough, 'John a Primitive Gospel', *JBL* 64 (1945), pp. 145–82. See n.1 on p. 145; and *cf.* pp. 169–78 for Goodenough's 'positive arguments' for an early dating of the Fourth Gospel.

40. C.H. Dodd, *The Interpretation of the Fourth Gospel* (Cambridge: Cambridge University Press, 1953), p. 449 and n.2 (= *IFG*).

his indebtedness to Gardner-Smith's book, and cautiously proposed that the fourth evangelist worked independently of other written Gospels. An appendix to this volume, devoted to a consideration of the Fourth Gospel's historical aspect,[41] sets out an agenda which Dodd addressed in his later book on that subject.[42]

In his monograph, *Historical Tradition in the Fourth Gospel*, Dodd used a form critical approach to make a careful and detailed examination of the text of the Gospel. On that basis, Dodd felt able to conclude that behind the Gospel of John there lies 'an ancient tradition independent of the other gospels', meriting serious attention as a contribution to our historical knowledge about Jesus.[43]

The other writer whose scholarship helped to shape Johannine studies decisively in the mid-twentieth century is John Robinson, who in 1957 gave a paper to an Oxford Conference on the Gospels, entitled 'The New Look on the Fourth Gospel'.[44] Such was the appeal of his phrase, 'the new look', and to such an extent did it strike chords in the scholarly arena, that it came to be widely used as a description of the progress of the debate about John's Gospel at that time.

In his lecture, Robinson suggested that if a new look on John existed, it could be distinguished from an 'old look'. He therefore set out what he regarded as the five presuppositions belonging to critical orthodoxy in the first half of the twentieth century, so far as the interpretation of John's Gospel was concerned, and tried to demonstrate that each was in need of re-examination, and in the process of it.

The five presuppositions listed by Robinson are as follows: (i) That the fourth evangelist is dependent on sources, including at least one of the synoptic Gospels. (ii) That his background differs from that of the tradition he reports. (iii) That his work is a serious witness not to the Jesus of history but to the Christ of faith. (iv) That he reflects the latest stage of theological development in first-century Christianity. (v) That he is neither the apostle John nor an eyewitness.[45]

41. *Ibid.*, pp. 444–53.

42. C.H. Dodd, *Historical Tradition in the Fourth Gospel* (Cambridge: Cambridge University Press, 1963) (= *HTFG*).

43. *Ibid.*, p. 423; see also 423–32.

44. J.A.T. Robinson, 'The New Look on the Fourth Gospel' in *idem, Twelve New Testament Studies*, SBT (London: SCM Press, 1962), pp. 94–106. For work from the same period, following Robinson's line, see A.J.B. Higgins, *The Historicity of the Fourth Gospel* (London: Lutterworth Press, 1960); R.H. Fuller, *The New Testament in Current Study: Some Trends in the Years 1941–1962* (London: SCM Press, 1963), pp. 114–44; S.S. Smalley, 'New Light on the Fourth Gospel', *TynB* 17 (1966), pp. 35–62; A.M. Hunter, *According to John: A New Look at the Fourth Gospel* (London: SCM Press, 1968). Robinson regards the discovery of the Dead Sea Scrolls as a catalyst in bringing together the ideas about John's Gospel which eventually produced 'new look' language. So Robinson, *Priority*, pp. 37–38. See below, pp. 33–36.

45. Robinson, 'New Look', p. 95.

The most crucial of these assumptions mentioned by Robinson, as indicated already, is the first. Once it is allowed that John to any extent depends on the synoptic Gospels, it follows that the only way to account for the differences between the synoptic and Johannine traditions when they are in conflict is to say that the fourth evangelist has altered his material to suit his own purposes. Having said that, the other assumptions follow. For particular reasons of writing, the evangelist (it may be claimed) cuts loose from the tradition to which he is presumably indebted, and theologises the 'history' he is interpreting. He does this in a developed manner for a late, primarily Hellenistic audience, by which time any eyewitness links have disappeared. In other words, as Robinson himself points out,[46] the effect of adopting the 'old look' on the Fourth Gospel is essentially to separate the evangelist from his tradition. It is to oppose Johannine history and theology, and to make the second superior to the first. On the contrary, Robinson argued that John took history seriously, and that he is 'often remarkably primitive in his witness' – theological, as well as historical.[47] For Robinson, the assumption of dependence remained unproven.

Robinson's work provided a benchmark in Johannine scholarship at the time. Not only did he, like Dodd, drive all students of John's Gospel back to the text; he also showed that the issue of authorship, while still important, had receded behind the fresh look that was being taken at the nature of the basic Johannine tradition. If light can be thrown on the derivation of John's material, the question of who was responsible for the presentation and shaping of the tradition will fall into place, and may be investigated with more assurance.[48]

THE NEW CONSENSUS ERODED

We shall come back to the character of John's material, and how it originated, in a moment. Meanwhile, it will be useful to bring further up to date the progress of the debate about John's relationship to the synoptic writers. We have seen the pendulum swing, in the course of the twentieth century, from theories of complete dependence to complete independence. It is probably true to say that the latter part of the century provided evidence for taking up a more balanced, mediating solution to the problem.

46. *Ibid.*
47. *Ibid.*, p. 102.
48. See further, for a refinement of his position, Robinson, *Priority*, esp. pp. 36–122. Robinson came to believe not only that the tradition behind the Fourth Gospel was primitive, but also that it stemmed directly (around AD 65) from the apostle John himself. As a result, his Gospel could 'take us as far back to source as any other', if not a good deal further (p. 122). *Cf.* in addition J.A.T. Robinson, *Redating the New Testament* (London: SCM Press, 1976), pp. 254–311, esp. 307.

It has to be said that, in any case, there were scholars along the way who were not persuaded by the claim that John used his own sources, independently of the other three evangelists. Dissenting voices were heard in the magisterial commentaries written, for example, by R.H. Lightfoot and Kingsley Barrett, both of whom accept that John depended on the synoptic Gospels to some extent.[49] Nevertheless, mainstream commentaries, such as those of Raymond Brown,[50] Rudolf Schnackenburg,[51] Rudolf Bultmann,[52] and Ernst Haenchen[53] adopted the basic stance of independence, without necessarily arguing as a result for the historicity of the Johannine tradition.[54] It is worth pointing out, however, because it will be seen to be relevant later,[55] that in each case the commentators cited above, as being identified with the new consensus (the independence of John's sources), were also being cautious, and were prepared to consider that the fourth evangelist was in touch with Christian traditions, both oral and written, which lay in common *behind* the final version of the synoptic Gospels.[56]

Meanwhile, another feature in Johannine studies, emerging in the second half of the twentieth century, deserves some mention. Scholarly attention was given to the frequent points of contact between the Third and Fourth Gospels; and this led to the supposition that the fourth evangelist's material was closer to Luke than to Mark.[57]

49. See R.H. Lightfoot, *St John's Gospel: A Commentary*, ed. C.F. Evans (Oxford: Clarendon Press, 1956), pp. 26–42, esp. 29 (= Lightfoot), who claims that John knew all three synoptic Gospels; C.K. Barrett, *The Gospel According to St John*, 2nd edn. (London: SPCK, 1978), pp. 15–18, 42–54 (= Barrett), who argues that the fourth evangelist was familiar with Mark, and probably – to a lesser degree – with Luke as well.

50. R.E. Brown, *The Gospel According to John*, 2 vols. AB 29 and 29a (London: Geoffrey Chapman, 1971) (= Brown); see Brown 1, pp. xliv–xlvii, esp. lxv. Similarly, in Great Britain, B. Lindars, *The Gospel of John*, NCB (London: Oliphants, 1972) (= Lindars).

51. R. Schnackenburg, *The Gospel According to St John*, 3 vols. HTCNT (London: Burns and Oates, 1968–82) (= Schnackenburg); see Schnackenburg 1, pp. 26–43.

52. R. Bultmann, *The Gospel of John: A Commentary* (Oxford: Basil Blackwell, 1971) (= Bultmann); see pp. 3–5: John 'leaves aside' synoptic material, treats the Christian tradition with freedom, 'takes traditions that have come from outside Christianity', and reconstructs redactionally on a larger scale than the synoptists (p. 5).

53. E. Haenchen, *John 1* and *John 2*, ed. R.W. Funk and U. Busse, HS (Philadelphia: Fortress Press, 1984) (= Haenchen); see Haenchen, *John 1*, pp. 74–78, esp. 75.

54. This is true of Haenchen. According to him, the evangelist drew rather on a primitive gospel with a non-synoptic character. *Cf.* Haenchen, *John 1*, pp. 75–77, esp. 76; also Smith, *John Among the Gospels*, p. 67.

55. See below, pp. 12–13, 41–44..

56. *Cf.* Schnackenburg 1, p. 42, where 'cross-currents' are mentioned as connecting underlying Johannine and synoptic traditions.

57. Smith, *John Among the Gospels*, pp. 85–110, calls this a 'parallel consensus'; but such a description hardly seems warranted.

Certainly, the association between Luke and John, especially in the passion narrative, often appears to be close.[58] Given the parallels between the two Gospels, John Bailey published in 1963 a study of the traditions common to Luke and John, in which he proposed that John used the third Gospel, as well as underlying material common to both authors, in the composition of his work.[59] Bailey also claimed that John knew Mark. As it happens, the connections between John and Luke had been explored much earlier, but with different conclusions. Julius Schniewind in 1914,[60] and the American F.C. Grant in 1937,[61] both addressed these correspondences; but neither believed that the evidence pointed to John's dependence on Luke!

A final twist in this story is provided by such scholars as F. Lamar Cribbs, who maintained in 1971 that the association can be reversed: the connections between Luke and John suggest that Luke depends on an early form of John, and not the reverse.[62] Such thinking is becoming more familiar.[63]

58.   Luke and John are alone, for example, in their mention of such characters as Mary and Martha (Luke 10:38–42; John 11:1–44; 12:1–8); in their witness to speculation about the messianic status of John the Baptist (Luke 3:15; John 1:20); and in their indirect, rather than direct, reports of the baptism of Jesus (Luke 3:21–22; John 1:32–34). In their passion and resurrection narratives, John and Luke show even closer agreement. So in Luke's account of the Roman trial of Jesus, Pilate protests three times, rather than two (Mark, Matt.), the innocence of Jesus (Luke 23:4, 14–16, 22; John 18:38; 19:4,6); and after the resurrection John and Luke are the only evangelists to speak of Jesus eating with his disciples, and showing them his wounded hands and feet (Luke 24:36–43; John 21:9–15, 20:20).

59.   J.A. Bailey, *The Traditions Common to the Gospels of Luke and John*, NovT Sup 7 (Leiden: E.J. Brill, 1963), esp. pp. 103–116. On the other side note P. Parker, 'Luke and the Fourth Evangelist', *NTS* 9 (1962–63), pp. 317–36, who argues that the similarities between Luke and John can be explained in terms of a shared oral tradition (enshrined in preaching and debate); whereas the variations cannot be accounted for on the assumption of direct literary relationship (p. 333).

60.   J. Schniewind, *Die Parallelperikopen bei Lukas und Johannes* (Hildesheim: G. Olms, 1914/1958), esp. pp. 95–100.

61.   F.C. Grant, 'Was the Author of John Dependent Upon the Gospel of Luke?', *JBL* 56 (1937), pp. 285–307.

62.   F.L. Cribbs, 'St Luke and the Johannine tradition', *JBL* 90 (1971), pp. 422–50, esp. 445. According to Cribbs, for example, Luke closely follows Mark and Matthew in pericopes which he shares with those two evangelists alone, but moves in the direction of the Johannine tradition when his material overlaps with all three of his co-evangelists (p. 426).

63.   See R. Morgan, 'Which was the Fourth Gospel? The Order of the Gospels and the Unity of Scripture', *JSNT* 54 (1993–94), pp. 3-28; also B. Shellard, 'The Relationship of Luke and John: A Fresh Look at an Old Problem', *JTS* (ns) 46 (1995), pp. 71–98. See also A. Dauer, *Johannes und Lukas* (Würzburg: Echter, 1984).

CONCLUSION

If we speak of the 'erosion' of a consensus in the later part of the twentieth century, it is because scholars have been taking a more balanced, median position on the dependence/independence issue, and doing so with needed caution. The important commentary on the Fourth Gospel written by M.-E. Boismard, which appeared in 1977,[64] is symptomatic of the ambivalence which began some time ago to characterise the debate about Johannine origins. In a complex study of sources, Boismard argues for an independent Johannine source or tradition; but at the same time he claims that both the fourth evangelist and his redactor were in touch with the synoptic Gospels as such. Frans Neirynck, in a major work of scholarship published in 1979,[65] criticised Boismard's theories, and was able to do so not least because their very complexity made them vulnerable. More importantly, Neirynck arrived at the firm conclusion that John took the synoptic Gospels as his starting-point. The result is simplicity itself: John knew Matthew and Luke, and redacted them for his own purposes. Neirynk's work needs to be considered with great seriousness; but we seem almost to have come full circle.

The massive commentary on the Fourth Gospel by George Beasley-Murray, published in 1987,[66] probably represents very fairly the stage reached in the discussion about John among the evangelists, at least in the English-speaking world, towards the end of the twentieth century. Beasley-Murray's own position is median. He therefore agrees with Moody Smith, whose own considerable contribution to this debate has been balanced but incisive,[67] that while John's dependence on the synoptists is not a necessary thesis for the exegesis of his Gospel, the document probably did not come to birth in isolation from the work of the other three evangelists.[68] In principle, that is to

---

64. M.-E. Boismard et A. Lamouille, *L'Évangile de Jean* (Paris: Edition du Cerf, 1977).

65. F. Neirynck, *et al., Jean et les Synoptiques: Examen critique de l'exégèse de M.-E. Boismard,* BETL 49 (Leuven: Leuven University Press, 1979), pp. 23–39.

66. G. R. Beasley-Murray, *John,* WBC 36 (Waco: Word Books, 1987) (= Beasley-Murray).

67. See Smith, *John Among the Gospels,* esp. pp. 177–93 ('Retrospect and Prospect'); also the collection of articles published as D.M. Smith, *Johannine Christianity: Essays on its Setting, Sources and Theology* (Edinburgh: T. and T. Clark, 1987), in particular his discussion, 'John and the Synoptics: Some Dimensions of the Problem', *ibid.,* pp. 145–72. Note further the whole section on John and the Synoptics in *ibid.,* pp. 97–172; also D.M. Smith, *The Theology of the Gospel of John,* NTT (Cambridge and New York: Cambridge University Press, 1995), pp. 20–22, 62–65, 77–78.

68. Beasley-Murray, *John,* pp. xxxv–xxxvii, esp. xxxvii.

say, the mode of John's relationship to the synoptic Gospels *remains open.*[69]

Granted that this openness is important we can now move, in the next chapter, to examine the nature of John's tradition for ourselves. If the result is broadly the same as in the first edition of the present book, this is not because careful reflection on the part of the author has not taken place; but rather that his basic conviction has been softened, without being shaken.

69. For further literature on this whole area of discussion see the listings in J. Blinzler, *Johannes und die Synoptiker : Ein Forschungsbericht*, SBS 5 (Stuttgart: Katholisches Bibelwerk, 1965); H. Thyen, 'Aus der Literatur zum Johannesevangelium', *TR* (NF) 39 (1974–75), pp. 1–69, 222–52, 289–330, and *TR* (NF) 42 (1977), pp. 211–70. See also R. Kysar, *The Fourth Evangelist and His Gospel: An Examination of Contemporary Scholarship* (Minneapolis: Augsburg Publishing House, 1975), pp. 54–66; F. Neirynck, 'John and the Synoptics' in M. de Jonge (ed.), *L'Évangile de Jean: Sources, rédaction, théologie*, BETL 44 (Leuven: Leuven University Press, 1977), pp. 73–106; B. de Solages, *Jean et les Synoptiques* (Leiden: E. J. Brill, 1979); J. Becker, 'Aus der Literatur zum Johannesevangelium (1978–80)', *TR* (NF) 47 (1982), pp. 279–301, 305–347, esp. 289–94; S.S. Smalley, 'Keeping up with Recent Studies: XII. St John's Gospel', *ExpT* 97 (1985–86), pp. 102–108; P. Borgen and F. Neirynck, 'John and the Synoptics' in D.L. Dungan (ed.), *The Interrelations of the Gospels*, BETL 95 (Leuven: Leuven University Press and Peeters, 1990), pp. 408–458; F. Neirynck, 'John and the Synoptics 1975–1990' in Denaux (ed.), *John and the Synoptics*, pp. 3–62; J.D.G. Dunn, 'John and the Synoptics as a Theological Question' in R.A. Culpepper and C.C. Black (ed.), *Exploring the Gospel of John: In Honor of D. Moody Smith* (Louisville: Westminster John Knox Press, 1996), pp. 301–313.

2

JOHN'S TRADITION

In this chapter we shall be investigating the character of John's tradition in more detail, and sifting carefully the evidence for the independence or otherwise of his sources. On that basis, we can assess the extent to which the Johannine basis for the story of Jesus may be regarded as historical.

We have seen that one way of examining the relationship between John's Gospel and the other three, in terms of their shared or independent traditions, is by means of a straight literary comparison. This was the method used by Percival Gardner-Smith; and we have noted its results.[1] Before we take account of further evidence beyond the Gospels themselves, therefore, let us look at the four documents as they stand, to discover if any clues emerge about the origin of the Jesus tradition which is preserved in each case.

LITERARY EVIDENCE

Any reader of the four Gospels is struck by the differences, and yet similarities, between them; and in the previous chapter we took account of the way in which this puzzle has been addressed in the ongoing study of the Fourth Gospel itself. Let us now begin our own investigation with a consideration of the obvious similarities which exist between all four Gospels.

(a) Similarities

All the Gospels have this in common, that they are a proclamation of the gospel of Jesus Christ. The evangelists write from different backgrounds to different audiences and with different intentions. Yet the aim they share is essentially and similarly evangelistic.[2] To this end, moreover, they draw on a common tradition, which must eventually run back to the words and actions of Jesus himself, as well as to the report about

1. See above, pp. 6–9.
2. *Cf.* C.F.D. Moule, 'The Intention of the Evangelists', in *idem, The Phenomenon of the New Testament: An Inquiry Into the Implications of Certain Features of the New Testament*, SBT (2) 1 (London: SCM Press, 1967), pp. 100–114.

these by the first Christian disciples. They all tell us about the beginning and progress of the ministry of Jesus, about his teaching and miracles, about the controversy between himself and the Jews, and about the passion and resurrection.

The various critical disciplines which are used in any serious contemporary study of the Gospels (source criticism, form criticism, redaction criticism and narrative criticism[3]) tell us, however, that we can go back only so far in recovering the origins of this tradition, and the actual words that Jesus spoke. The narrative and discourse material of the Gospels in their present form has been preserved and interpreted at an earlier, substructural level. This material has been influenced by various settings (mostly Palestinian and Hellenistic, or a mixture of both),[4] and shaped by the contribution of the evangelists themselves and their predecessors. As a result, we cannot take for granted the origin of the material in John's Gospel, or in any of the Gospels. We must examine carefully the sources used, and how these have been handled. As we do so, we can follow Gardner-Smith's lead,[5] and see what happens when narrative and discourse material in John is placed alongside parallel accounts in the synoptic tradition. We begin with two examples of common narrative material.

Narrative material

The feeding of the five thousand
It is manifestly true that when narrative material in the Fourth Gospel and the Synoptics overlaps, significant differences emerge, even if the same tradition evidently underlies each version. A familiar example of this is the miracle of the feeding of the five thousand, which appears in all four Gospels.[6] Obviously the four accounts stem ultimately from the same tradition; although the situation is complicated to some extent by the fact that Mark and Matthew each carry two accounts of a multiplication miracle, one for five thousand and a second for four thousand

3. See further I.H. Marshall (ed.), *New Testament Interpretation: Essays in Principles and Methods* (Exeter: Paternoster Press, 1977/1985); also R.A. Burridge, *What are the Gospels? A Comparison with Graeco-Roman Biography*, SNTSMS 70 (Cambridge: Cambridge University Press, 1992), esp. pp. 26–54 and (on John) pp. 220–39; *idem, Four Gospels, One Jesus? A Symbolic Reading* (London: SPCK, 1994), esp. the introductory material at pp. 1–32; J.B. Green (ed.), *Hearing the New Testament: Strategies for Interpretation* (Carlisle: Paternoster Press, 1995). See further below, chapter 7, for a consideration of the literary approach to John's Gospel.
4. *Cf.* I.H. Marshall, 'Palestinian and Hellenistic Christianity: Some Critical Comments', *NTS* 19 (1972–73), pp. 271–87; R.E. Brown, 'Not Jewish Christianity and Gentile Christianity but Types of Jewish /Gentile Christianity', *CBQ* 45 (1983), pp. 74–79.
5. See above, p.7.
6. John 6:1–15 = Mark 6:32–44 = Matt. 14:13–21 = Luke 9:10–17.

people. But when the versions are analysed, it becomes difficult to say with any certainty that John has derived his report from the other Gospels. On the contrary, the real probability exists that his tradition is independent. We may compare John and Mark in particular.

(i) The *introduction*, for a start, differs. Mark places the incident after the missionary tour of the disciples, and beside the lake (6:34); although, as with John, his geography is not exact. John thinks of Jesus as performing this miracle in the hills (6:3)[7] and introduces it with the vague chronological note μετὰ ταῦτα ('after this', 6:1).

(ii) The *motivation* for performing the miracle also differs. In Mark it is late in the day, and the disciples take the initiative in suggesting that the crowds should be given food because they have stayed too long with Jesus to buy their own. John sees the sign as taking place before the evening (6:16), and in this Gospel Jesus himself initiates the event (verse 5).

(iii) Differences also appear in the *conduct* of the miracle. In Mark's account no disciples are named, they provide the loaves and fish, and for the greater part of the narrative there is very little dialogue. John's version, on the other hand, includes the naming of Philip and Andrew, the food is provided by a boy (6:9), and there is a considerable exchange of dialogue between Jesus and the disciples. Almost the only point of contact between John and Mark here is the phrase 'two hundred denarii worth of bread' (διακοσίων δηναρίων ἄρτοι; nominative in John 6:7, but accusative in Mark 6:37). However, this is just the kind of memorable phrase which would have become fixed in the tradition, and so appear in any version of the miracle. Furthermore, the meal itself is differently described in the two accounts. According to Mark, Jesus commanded the crowds to sit down by companies on the green grass (6:39);[8] whereas John simply says that 'there was grass in the place', and that Jesus ordered the people to sit down (ἀναδεσεῖν, 6:10, rather than the synoptic ἀνακλιθῆναι). John's account also contains phrases which some regard as eucharistic in their shading[9] ('Jesus took the loaves, and gave thanks and distributed them', verse 11). The synoptic account has a similar

7. Dodd, *HTFG*, pp. 199–200, regards the accounts in Mark (6:35–44; 8:1–8) as a duplication, stemming from two independent versions of the miracle tradition at the pre-canonical stage. See the whole section, pp. 196–222. Brown 1, pp. 237–38, accepts as a 'probable hypothesis' that Mark and Matthew give us two accounts of the same multiplication, but hesitates to claim that one account is more primitive than the other. *Cf.* E. Haenchen, 'Johanneische Probleme', *ZTK* 56 (1959), pp. 19–54, esp. 31–34 (the version in Mark 8 is older); also Haenchen, *John 1*, pp. 273–77.

8. Matt. 15:29 sets the feeding of the four thousand in the hills; but it is unlikely that John was indebted to Matthew for this detail, which might well have become attached to the Matthean account by assimilation within the oral tradition. *Cf.* Gardner-Smith, *John*, p. 14.

9. So Brown 1, pp. 246–49; Beasley-Murray, p. 88.

colouring, including the mention of the fraction (6:41); but the vocabulary shifts (John has εὐχαριστήσας, 'gave thanks', 6:11; whereas the corresponding verb in Mark is εὐλόγησεν, 6:41 par.).

(iv)   Again, there are variations in the reports of the *conclusion* to the miracle. Mark says that the disciples of their own accord collected the fragments of bread and fish, and he mentions the number of participants as the emphatic final comment (6:44). In John, Jesus commands the disciples to collect the fragments (6:12), and only pieces of bread are then gathered up (verse 13). The number of people involved was mentioned earlier (verse 10).

(v)   Finally, the *outcome* of this miracle differs in Mark and John. In Mark, Jesus dismisses the crowd and his disciples and goes into the hills to pray (6:45–46). The effect of the sign in the Fourth Gospel is dramatically different. There (6:14–15) the people react with wonder at the advent of 'the prophet', and wish to make him king. It is in order to escape their attentions that Jesus simply withdraws to the hills by himself.

The anointing at Bethany

As a second example of the literary relationship between John and the Synoptics, we may consider the anointing of Jesus at Bethany. This appears in John, Mark and Matthew;[10] although there is a story in Luke (7:36–50) of a penitent sinner washing and anointing the feet of Jesus, which seems to be related. Luke's account, which is set in Galilee, certainly contains echoes of the Bethany anointing, even to the use of the phrase καὶ ταῖς θριξὶν τῆς κεφαλῆς αὐτῆς ἐξέμασσεν (lit., 'and she wiped them [his feet] with the hair of her head', Luke 7:38; *cf.* John 12:3). But it obviously describes a different occasion, and stems from an independent source. In Luke the emphasis is on the forgiveness of sin, and anointing as such is not central to the incident; whereas in John there is no mention of forgiveness, and even if there is possibly an anticipation here of the *Pedilavium* (Footwashing) in John 13, the action of the woman is understood above all as pointing towards the death of Jesus.[11]

Assuming, then, that on this occasion we are comparing John's tradition of the anointing with that in Mark and Matthew, we find that the variations as well as the correspondences are impressive.

(i)   John places the incident at Bethany, as do Mark and Matthew. But John makes no reference to the fact, recorded in the other two Gospels, that the company was assembled in the house of Simon the leper. John alone tells us also that Martha served the meal preceding the

10.   John 12:1–8; Mark 14:3–9 = Matt. 26:6–13.
11.   See further Lindars, pp. 412–15; also T.L. Brodie, *The Gospel According to John: A Literary and Theological Commentary* (New York and Oxford: Oxford University Press, 1993), p. 408 (= Brodie).

anointing (12:2), which may if anything indicate that he thought of the house as hers. Only John, inevitably, mentions the presence of Lazarus, who appears only in the Fourth Gospel.[12]

(ii)   John names the woman who anointed Jesus as Mary (12:3), presumably the sister of Martha. In the synoptic accounts the woman is not named.

(iii)   John describes the ointment used for the anointing in terms which reflect the narration of this event by Mark and Matthew. He speaks of μύρου νάρδου πιστικῆς ('perfume made of pure nard', 12:3; cf. Mark 14:3), and refers to its value as 'costly' (πολυτίμου, verse 3; cf. Mark 14:3, πολυτελοῦς). But the weight of the ointment is specified uniquely by John as one pound (verse 3). The other Gospels simply mention 'an alabaster jar of ointment'.

(iv)   John tells us that Mary anointed the *feet* of Jesus (verse 3), and wiped his feet with her hair (cf. Luke 7:38). In Mark and Matthew the woman anoints his *head*.

(v)   Like the other evangelists, John mentions a protest that was made over the woman's action; it might have been sold τριακοσίων δηναρίων ('for three hundred denarii'), and given to the poor (12:5; cf.: Mark 14:5, adding ἐπάνω ['more than'], and using δηναρίων τριακοσίων). But John records that it was Judas Iscariot who protested, whereas Mark has 'some' (14:4) and Matthew 'the disciples' (26:8).

(vi)   All three evangelists mention that Jesus replied to this challenge, and in each case the reply contains common elements: the command to leave the woman alone, the reference to his burial and the allusion to the poor being ever-present. But the drift of the reply in the two traditions is quite different. The synoptic version suggests that the woman's action has anticipated the burial of Jesus, and he promises that her devotion will be remembered. The form of the reply in the Fourth Gospel seems to imply that, although the burial of Jesus had been foreshadowed by the woman's action, the anointing at the actual time of his burial would be carried out by the same woman and with the remainder of the ointment.[13]

Conclusions

We have examined two samples of Gospel narrative material which

---

12.   The parable of Lazarus and Dives (Luke 16) does not provide us, as in John, with a figure in real life.

13.   So Gardner-Smith, *John*, p. 23; also J.H. Bernard, *A Critical and Exegetical Commentary on the Gospel According to St John*, vol. 2 (Edinburgh: T. and T. Clark, 1928), p. 421 (= Bernard). There are problems, however, if this exegesis is followed. One is the fact that the woman apparently used all the ointment at the time of the anointing at Bethany. Another is that, although John (not Mark) records an anointing of the body of Jesus after the crucifixion, this is carried out by Joseph of Arimathea with Nicodemus. (But cf. John 20:1; and according to Mark 16:1 women came to the tomb for the express purpose of anointing the body of Jesus.) It may be that in the interpretation of this incident

appear in both the Johannine and synoptic traditions. In both cases it is clear that, despite the similarities between the two versions, there are real differences. In the report of the feeding miracle and the anointing, as in many other instances, features appear which cannot all be explained on theological grounds: details of names, for example, and descriptions of place.

For those who believe that John depended for his material on the synoptic Gospels, and rewrote their 'history' from a 'theological' point of view,[14] this is a difficulty. Assuming that John wrote with the other Gospels before him, the only reason for altering the facts as already recorded (unless we regard the fourth evangelist as a completely arbitrary writer), is in the interests of his own theological interpretation and developed understanding. But we have seen evidence to suggest that this will not explain at all satisfactorily the Johannine variations in narrative material which both traditions have in common. One conclusion is, therefore, that John's tradition is independent at these points (and, by implication, at others; because if he knew the synoptic Gospels at one point he could have used them at all points). As Gardner-Smith says, the burden of proof lies with those critics who maintain that John knew the Synoptics, when there is considerable evidence pointing in the other direction.[15]

Discourse Material

Before we leave this discussion, it will be necessary to give some attention to the similarities between the Johannine and synoptic traditions which appear in discourse material. This area is less straightforward to analyse since, for a start, sayings are more prone than

the Johannine and synoptic traditions are in the end closer together than might appear, especially if John 12:7 means 'it was to keep the ointment for my (anticipated) burial (that it was not sold)'. John understands, in other words, that (as in Mark) a prophetic act has been performed. See Lindars, p. 418; also Barrett (pp. 413–14), who inclines to the view that τηρεῖν ('to keep') in John 12:7 means 'remember' (that the anointing has already taken place), or 'observe' (the last rites now, against the day of burial). See further on the anointing *HTFG*, pp. 162–73; also Brown 1, pp. 449–54, who argues that behind the reports of anointing in the four Gospels lie two separate incidents, one in Galilee and one in Bethany, and that John's version represents a form of the second into which have been incorporated details from the Lucan form of the first. Brown believes in addition that the Johannine account of the anointing is close to the earliest tradition about it, especially in view of the appearance of Judas in the narrative (pp. 452–53). For this whole section, on the feeding of the five thousand and the anointing at Bethany, see Gardner-Smith, *John*, pp. 14–16, 21–24.

14. We shall consider later the relation between history and theology in John; see below, esp. pp. 199–229.

15. Gardner-Smith, *John*, p. 24; see also pp. 43–47. Against this view see Lightfoot, pp. 26–42, esp. 28–33.

descriptions of events to a shift of meaning and reapplication to new situations. We shall pursue this point further when we come to look more closely (in chapter 5) at the sources of the discourse material in John's Gospel.

Nevertheless, it is possible to detect easily in the Fourth Gospel sayings which may be classified as 'synoptic' in character; although such a description is in fact tendentious if it implies that John necessarily derived such sayings directly and exclusively from the synoptic Gospels. For when material of this kind overlaps between the Gospels, it is equally possible to suggest that John is in touch with the same basic Christian tradition, but that he receives it for his Gospel independently of the others, and then uses it in his own way.

We have sayings of this type, for example, in the material concerning John the Baptist, where John 1:27 ('the one who is coming after me; I am not worthy to untie the thong of his sandal') clearly echoes the words of the Baptist reported in the synoptic Gospels.[16] However, John has caught this logion in a distinctive form. Thus he uses the term ἄξιος '(not) worthy (to untie)' with a ἵνα ('that') clause, where the other evangelists have ἱκανός ('worthy'), with an infinitive. When Luke repeats this saying in Acts 13:25 he seems to be following the tradition accessible to John, and not the one beneath his own Gospel; for the phrase ἄξιος (λῦσαι) reappears there. One reasonable explanation of these variations is to suggest that John derived this saying from the early Christian tradition about the Baptist independently of the other evangelists.[17]

Similarly, at John 1:42 we are given the fourth evangelist's version of the naming of Peter, which appears in Matthew at the time of the confession at Caesarea Philippi (Matt. 16:18). The tradition is manifestly the same, but the context differs. It cannot be said even so that one evangelist is more accurate than another at this point, or that John is necessarily secondary; since it seems that the *logion* was fixed in the Gospel tradition, but not its original *setting*.[18]

The 'Son of man' saying at John 1:51 (heaven opened, and the angels of God ascending and descending upon the Son of man) is hardly synoptic in character, despite points of contact with Mark 14:62 par. (the Son of man 'coming with the clouds of heaven'). John may be drawing on his own primitive christological tradition here, as normatively for the

16. Mark 1:7 = Matt. 3:11 = Luke 3:16.
17. *Cf.* Schnackenburg 1, p. 34. He thinks that John's version of the synoptic phrase, 'more powerful than I' (ἰσχυρότερος, Mark 1:7 par.) appears in John 1:15, 30 ('he who comes after me ranks ahead of me, because he was before me'). We find the same combination of common tradition and independence, no doubt, in John 1:33 (*cf.* verses 26, 31), referring to the contrast between baptism in water and Spirit.
18. *Cf.* Mark 3:16; note also Matt. 16:19 = 18:18 = John 20:23. The naming does not appear in Mark's account of the confession (Mark 8:27–30).

Son of man logia in his Gospel.[19] However, the saying in John 2:19
('destroy this temple, and in three days I will raise it up') is without doubt
in touch with the tradition which reappears in the synoptic Gospels.[20]
Once more, John evidently knows a tradition about the destruction and
rebuilding of the temple current in primitive Christianity. But his derivation and use of that tradition is special to him, so that he attributes
the saying directly to Jesus, and refers it to the actual body of Jesus. Thus
in John 2 it bears a developed theological significance; and the 'temple
of Jesus' becomes the mid-term between the temple of the Israelites and
the Christian temple, the church (cf. 1 Cor. 3:16–17; 6:19).

In John 4:44 there occurs a logion with clear synoptic affinities: the
comment, 'a prophet has no honour in his own country'. Once more
John's version reveals a measure of freedom when it is compared with
the other Gospels.[21] In the first place the wording differs somewhat, and
the whole saying is briefer than it is in Mark (although similar in length
to the versions in Matthew and Luke). Secondly, the context of this
saying is not the same in the Fourth Gospel. The synoptists place it in
the setting of the rejection of Jesus when he teaches in the synagogue of
his 'own country' (Galilee, Mark 6:1 par.; Luke has 'Nazareth'[22]). John,
by contrast, includes the proverbial comment about a prophet having no
honour in his own country[23] when Jesus is on his way from Judea
through Samaria to Galilee. John's application of the saying is perhaps
secondary, since apparently he takes it to refer to the desire which Jesus
then showed to escape from the glare of publicity.[24] But the saying itself
no doubt comes from a very early tradition, which John has received on
his own.

The passion narrative in John's Gospel contains a number of words
of Jesus which have links with similar sayings in the synoptic Gospels.
John 13:21, for example ('one of you will betray me'), appears in an
identical form in Mark 14:18 = Matt. 26:21. But the Marcan version

19. Cf. S.S. Smalley, 'The Johannine Son of Man Sayings', NTS 15 (1968–69), pp.
278–301, esp. 287–89. For a different view see B. Lindars, Jesus Son of Man: A Fresh
Examination of the Son of Man Sayings in the Gospels in the Light of Recent Research
(London: SPCK, 1983), pp. 27–28, 147–50. See further D. Burkett, The Son of Man in the
Gospel of John, JSNTS 56 (Sheffield: JSOT Press, 1991), pp. 112–19.

20. Mark 14:58 = Matt. 26:61; Mark 15:29 = Matt. 27:40.

21. Mark 6:4 = Matt. 13:57 = Luke 4:24.

22. Luke 4:16.

23. This saying possesses the character of a well-known proverb, and was used in
Jewish literature (although not identically) of Moses. See D. Daube, The New Testament
and Rabbinic Judaism (London: Athlone Press, 1956), pp. 9–11.

24. As it stands, John 4:44 is in any case difficult. Lindars (pp. 200–201) takes the
ὅσρί ς ('country', or 'territory') mentioned to refer to Jerusalem. Thus John maintains
the recurring theme in this Gospel that, when Jesus came to his real home (the religious
and cultural centre of Judaism), his own people did not receive him (p. 201; cf. John 1:11).

includes a phrase from Psalm 41:9, 'one who is eating with me'. This verse from Psalm 41 is quoted specifically, although not fully, at John 13:18, where it appears in a non-Septuagintal form. The suggestion from such evidence is that the fourth evangelist in this passage is drawing directly from an early testimony tradition,[25] parallel to but independent of Mark. On the other hand, the saying in Mark 14:20 = Matt. 26:23 (the traitor is one 'dipping [bread] in the same dish with me'), which becomes an action in John (13:26), while a variation of the same tradition, cannot be used as proof of Johannine independence. It could be argued in this case that John knew Mark, and altered his account in the dramatic interests of the introduction to his passion narrative. However, the 'cock-crow' saying of Jesus in John 13:38 appears in all four Gospels,[26] and approximates most closely to the form in Luke. Since there are good reasons for believing on other grounds that John and Luke independently shared a common tradition, this kind of parallelism need not surprise us; rather, it will fit into the general pattern of Johannine freedom from the synoptists for which we are arguing.[27]

Conclusions

Other logia in the Fourth Gospel may appear to be borrowed from the synoptic Gospels, particularly when the same saying appears in a different context. This is true, for instance, of John 12:25[28] (the word about losing and saving life) and the 'cup' saying in 18:11*b*.[29] Even if John has handled these sayings (and indeed all the 'synoptic-type' discourse material) in his own way, and tinted them with his own theological outlook, as we shall see, we are not compelled to believe that he must have derived them directly from the synoptic Gospels. As with John's narrative material, although in some cases admittedly less obviously, the best explanation of the form in which 'synoptic-type' sayings occur in the Gospel is to say that the Johannine and

25. *Cf.* B. Lindars, *New Testament Apologetic: The Doctrinal Significance of the Old Testament Quotations* (London: SCM Press, 1961), pp. 98–99.

26. Mark 14:30 = Matt. 26:34 = Luke 22:34.

27. See Bailey, *Traditions*. However, Bailey's thesis maintains that John knew Luke, and drew in part on his Gospel and in part on traditions which, although related, came independently to them both (*cf.* pp. 115–16). See also M. Wilcox, 'The Composition of John 13:21–30' in E.E. Ellis and M. Wilcox (ed.), *Neotestamentica et Semitica: Studies in Honour of Matthew Black* (Edinburgh: T. and T. Clark, 1969), pp. 143–56, an essay which argues for John's literary independence of the synoptic tradition in this section of the betrayal story. Lindars (pp. 430–31) regards the words of Jesus which appear in John 12:27 ('now is my soul troubled . . .') as a Johannine composition which depends on a variant form of the synoptic Gethsemane tradition.

28. *Cf.* Mark 8:35 = Matt. 10:39 = Luke 17:33.

29. *Cf.* Mark 10:38 = Matt. 20:22.

synoptic traditions coincided at this point, rather than that John knew the Synoptics.[30]

Summary

There are similarities, then, between St John and the synoptic Gospels in their narrative and discourse material. These need not surprise us. To go no further, the material they use concerns Jesus of Nazareth. But when the similarities are closely examined, and differences in the presentation of the same tradition emerge, we do not have to argue exclusively for literary dependence. The independent use of a common tradition by John and the other evangelists may fit the facts better. Such an explanation will also remove the need to charge John with being 'content wantonly to contradict the testimony of "standard" works in matters dogmatically indifferent'.[31]

So far it has been suggested that in one respect, that of the similarities between John and the other Gospels, there is reason to suppose that John did not rewrite the Synoptics but was rather preserving in his own way a Christian tradition parallel to theirs. Moreover, there are already indications that the Johannine version of the Jesus tradition is not necessarily to be regarded as historically *unreliable* because it is independent, but rather the reverse. We can now go on to explore the question of the literary inter-relation of the four Gospels in terms of the differences between them.

(b) Differences

It is obvious that, despite the resemblances between the Johannine and synoptic traditions, real differences are also involved which seem to set John apart from the other Gospels. Only John, for example, presents us with a portrait of John the Baptist[32] which repudiates any identification with Elijah. Only John tells us that Jesus cleansed the temple at the outset of his ministry rather than at the end of it, and that he died on the day of preparation for the Passover, rather than on Passover itself. Only John suggests that Jesus was known and confessed as Messiah from the beginning of the ministry. John alone indicates that Jesus' method of teaching was to use extended sermons rather than short sayings and

30. See for this section Schnackenburg 1, pp. 34–37. See also C.H. Dodd, 'Some Johannine "Herrnworte" with Parallels in the Synoptic Gospels', *NTS* 2 (1955–56), pp. 75–86, where Dodd examines four specimen sayings of Jesus in the Fourth Gospel which have parallels in the Synoptics (John 13:16; 12:25; 13:20; 20:23), and concludes that there is a high degree of probability that John has here transmitted independently 'a special form of the common oral tradition' (p. 86).

31. Gardner-Smith, *John*, p. 45.

32. The synoptic writers use the name of John the Baptist (Baptiser) in this form (*cf.* Mark 1:4; Matt. 3:1; Luke 7:20). The fourth evangelist, by contrast, uses simply 'John' throughout (*e.g.* John 1:19).

parables. John's selection of the miracles (signs) performed by Jesus, also, differs from that of the other three evangelists.[33]

These certainly appear to be large and striking divergences. What is their origin? If John knew the synoptic Gospels, the answer is that he departed from them, and introduced his own material or interpretations, for theological reasons. But this need not be the only explanation and conclusion. It could still be that John was writing independently of the other evangelists, and drawing on a tradition which all four held in common. This view increases in likelihood, moreover, if we discover that the differences between the Johannine and synoptic traditions are not in fact as major as at first appeared. We can examine the variations just mentioned to see the position for ourselves more clearly.

John the Baptist

The portrait of John the Baptist, which the fourth evangelist gives us, appears to be very different from that in the synoptic Gospels. In John's Gospel the figure of the Baptist is played down, until he becomes simply 'a voice crying in the wilderness' (1:23).[34] Moreover, whereas the synoptic tradition clearly identifies John with Elijah (*redivivus*),[35] and even reflects the apparent confusion in the popular mind between John and Jesus,[36] no such high estimate appears in the Fourth Gospel. There John the Baptist explicitly denies that he is either the Christ (John 1:20) or Elijah (verse 21*a*), or a prophetic figure of any kind (verse 21*b*). In the Johannine record, then, John the Baptist is no more than a herald (but *cf.* 1:31), even if he is a 'man sent from God' (1:6); while in the synoptic account he is an Elijah-figure ushering in the messianic age, even if the least in the kingdom is greater than he (Matt. 11:11 = Luke 7:28).

These variations are intriguing; but they need not suggest that the fourth evangelist is altering an earlier tradition. On the contrary, it is probably in John's Gospel that we have the most primitive tradition of all preserved, and possibly even one that derived ultimately from the Baptist himself. Later reflection no doubt caused the estimate of John the Baptist to be heightened, particularly once the riddle of his identity had been solved: *he* was Elijah, and *Jesus* was the Christ. At first, however, this identification was not clear; and the Baptist himself gave no real support to it because, perhaps, he thought of himself as an Elijah-figure, a herald of the new age, without believing himself to be Elijah *redivivus*. This accords exactly with the denial in John's Gospel that the Baptist was Elijah or the Christ. On the other hand, the Synoptists echo a later and developing Baptist tradition. We can see this enhancing process at work even within the synoptic Gospels

---

33. See also above, pp. 2–3.
34. Although Mark 1:3 par. maintains the 'voice' allusion (from Isa. 40:3).
35. Matt. 11:14; 17:10–13; Luke 1:17.
36. Luke 3:15. The synoptic presentation of John the Baptist is heightened in Luke by the parallel accounts of the birth and infancy of John and Jesus, Luke 1–2.

themselves. After the transfiguration, for example, the disciples ask Jesus about Elijah to come, and Jesus replies that Elijah has already come (implying therefore that he himself is Messiah). In Mark 'Elijah' is left unidentified, whereas in Matthew (presumably written later) Elijah is named as John the Baptist.[37]

The relationship of the Baptist to the Qumran community is not certain; but even if he were an associate rather than a full member, he could have been influenced by its theology and outlook. Thus, if the Qumranic elements in the Fourth Gospel, which we shall be considering further on in this chapter, derive from the Baptist (and even if the writer(s) of the Fourth Gospel also knew of the Qumran sect, this is not impossible), there is all the more reason to believe that the Johannine tradition about John the Baptist came originally from the man himself. We shall return to this point.[38]

Chronology

John's chronology certainly looks distinctive. According to him, Jesus cleanses the temple at the beginning of his ministry, and over a period of at least three years[39] goes several times from Galilee in the north of

37. See further J.A.T. Robinson, 'Elijah, John and Jesus: An Essay in Detection' in *idem, Twelve New Testament Studies*, pp. 28–52. It is possible that the synoptic and Johannine traditions are closer together than has been suggested, however, since the Elijah figure may be differently understood in each. There was a tradition in Judaism in which messianic associations clustered around Elijah (see Daube, *Rabbinic Judaism*, pp. 21–22, on the 'throne of Elijah'). If this can be traced to the New Testament period, it becomes understandable that John the Baptist should in the Fourth Gospel deny that he was Elijah (Messiah), and simply say that he was a (messianic) forerunner, in the spirit of Isa. 40:3 rather than Mal. 3:1. The synoptic Gospels, on the other hand, identify John the Baptist with Elijah, but they do not say that Elijah is a forerunner; there, he is a suffering 'restorer' (Matt. 17:11–13, *cf.* Mal. 4:5; Luke 1:17). See also W. Wink, *John the Baptist in the Gospel Tradition*, SNTSMS 7 (Cambridge: Cambridge University Press, 1968), pp. 87–106, who claims that the Fourth Gospel 'Christianises' the role of the Baptist as a witness so that, like any Christian, he is at once humbled (in self-denial) and exalted (in the proclamation of Jesus); see esp. p. 106.

38. See below, pp. 33–37. See further J.A.T. Robinson, 'The Baptism of John and the Qumran Community: Testing a Hypothesis in *idem, Twelve New Testament Studies*, pp. 11–27; and, on the other side, claiming that there was no connection between the Baptist and Qumran, H.H. Rowley, 'The Baptism of John and the Qumran Sect' in A.J.B. Higgins (ed.), *New Testament Essays: Studies in Memory of Thomas Walter Manson 1893–1958* (Manchester: Manchester University Press, 1959), pp. 218–29, esp. 222. Note also C.H.H. Scobie, *John the Baptist* (London: SCM Press, 1964), pp. 207–208; P. Benoit, 'Qumran et le Nouveau Testament', *NTS* 7 (1960–61), pp. 276–96, esp. 279–81 (there were relations 'of some kind' between the Precursor and the Qumran community; p. 280).

39. Three Passover festivals are mentioned in John (2:13; 6:4; 11:55). It is just possible that the 'feast of the Jews' mentioned at 5:1 (although the best MS reading is '*a* feast', ἑορτὴ τῶν Ιουδαίων) is also Passover; so M.-J. Lagrange, *L'Évangile selon Saint Jean* (Paris: Gabalda, 1948), pp. 131–32 (= Lagrange). In this case a further year may have been involved in the length of the ministry of Jesus.

Palestine to Jerusalem in the south; whereas the Synoptists suggest that there was virtually only one progress to Jerusalem, for the cleansing of the temple and the passion, and that the entire ministry of Jesus occupied the space of no more than a year or so. Furthermore, the chronology of the events of passion week itself differs in the two traditions, so that there is a variation of 24 hours in their report of the crucifixion of Jesus.

It is important to recall that neither John nor the synoptic Gospels are 'biographies' of the life of Jesus, designed to give us details of his movements such as might appear in a modern travel agent's itinerary. This was the classic mistake of the liberal writers of 'Lives of Jesus' in the 19th century.[40] As a result, we need not expect, nor do we have, an exact correspondence in the chronology of the Gospels, either of the events themselves or of the order in which they occurred. Furthermore, it is quite likely that the ministry of Jesus took longer than any of the evangelists imply.[41] For Jesus to have established his reputation as a prophetic teacher and healer, and to have called forth the response that he did from John the Baptist and the first disciples as swiftly as the records suggest, it seems necessary for a ministry of some kind to have been in progress beforehand. The evangelists all *select* their material; and this means that inevitably they contract their time-scale (notably in the case of Mark), and give us the highlights of the Jesus story rather than every detail of every moment.[42] John is therefore quite likely to be *nearer* than his colleagues to the truth about the length of the ministry of Jesus, and about the journeyings between north and south Palestine, even if his outline of the itineraries is not always crystal clear.

The placing of the cleansing of the temple in John (2:13–22) is more difficult, since if necessary this can be explained on theological grounds. Here it seems is a dramatic illustration, at the very outset of the Gospel, of the fact that Jesus the Messiah has by his advent fulfilled and replaced Judaism. The cleansing also provides a telling reinforcement of the same truth acted out immediately beforehand, in the Johannine sign of 'water into wine' at Cana (John 2:1–11). For these reasons it might be argued that the fourth evangelist has shifted this incident from its synoptic setting at the end of the ministry, where it precipitates the arrest and death of Jesus.[43] If we allow the possibility that the Johannine tradition

40. See F.F. Bruce, 'The History of New Testament Study', in Marshall, *Interpretation*, pp. 21–59, esp. 39–41.

41. *Cf.* D.H. Smith, 'Concerning the Duration of the Ministry of Jesus', *ExpT* 76 (1964–65), pp. 114–16.

42. But see Burridge, *What are the Gospels?*, who seeks to demonstrate that the genre of these documents is a form of ancient biography. See esp. the conclusions and implications set out at pp. 240–59.

43. Mark 11:15–19 par. This is the view taken by Barrett, pp. 194–97, esp. 195; also Lindars, pp. 135–37. There is a link between the traditions, however, since the liturgical context in both is Passover.

is independent, however, we need no longer assume that John is inevitably secondary and unhistorical. Unless there were originally two cleansings, which is unlikely, it is in fact an open question as to whether John *or the Synoptists* made the alteration in chronology. Theological incentive notwithstanding, a case may still be made for John's accuracy in placing this incident.[44]

The chronology of the passion events is a complex issue in Gospel studies. The crux lies in the date of the last supper, and therefore of the death of Jesus. In John's narrative the crucifixion takes place on 14 Nisan, the day before the Passover (*cf.* John 18:28), whereas the other Gospels[45] state clearly that the last supper was the Passover meal. In the synoptic tradition, then, the evening on which the last supper was shared, and the following day when the crucifixion was carried out, were 15 Nisan, the feast of the Passover itself.

Again, it could be argued that John is here theologising the synoptic tradition, which he knew and used. For if Jesus is represented as dying on the day of the preparation for the Passover, then his death coincides with the slaughter of the sacrificial Passover lambs; and this is theologically suitable in a Gospel which uniquely designates Jesus 'the Lamb of God' (John 1:29, 36). But other explanations, which favour the historical character of the Johannine chronology, are equally plausible. It is possible that different calendars were being followed by the two traditions; and the distinguished work of Mlle Jaubert on the *Jubilees* calendar has shown that a second Jewish (solar) calendar, dating from the Babylonian exile, was in fact used by the Qumran community in the first century AD.[46] Jaubert argues that Jesus and his disciples used this calendar, according to which Passover always fell on a Wednesday, causing the Passover meal itself to take place on Tuesday evening. If the last supper (= Passover) was held on Tuesday and the crucifixion of Jesus was carried out on Friday, the eve of the official Jewish Passover, as John says, this allows time on the Wednesday and Thursday for the legal hearings and the condemnation of Jesus. (As it stands, the synoptic chronology seems

44. But see J. Marsh, *The Gospel of St John*, PGC (Harmondsworth: Pelican Books, 1968), pp. 157–65 (= Marsh), who believes that John knew the synoptic tradition, and deliberately altered it to make its deeper theological meaning more available to his own readers (pp. 162–63). For a persuasive argument that John's placing of the temple cleansing is original, and that Mark and the other evangelists have edited their tradition, see J.A.T. Robinson, ' "His Witness is True": A Test of the Johannine Claims' in E. Bammel and C.F.D. Moule (ed.), *Jesus and the Politics of His Day* (Cambridge and New York: Cambridge University Press, 1984), pp. 453–76. Robinson notes the reference to John the Baptist at Mark 11:30-32 par., which would be in place in the early Johannine setting, but not in the Marcan.

45. *Cf.* Mark 14:12 par.

46. A. Jaubert, *The Date of the Last Supper* (New York: Alba, 1965). See the critique of Mlle Jaubert's essay by P. Benoit, *Jesus and the Gospel*, vol. 1 (London: Darton, Longman and Todd, 1973), pp. 87–93.

to be impossibly condensed.) Given that both traditions telescope the events of the last hours of Jesus, and that none of the Gospel writers is concerned solely with an exact chronology, this theory will account for the synoptic evidence that the last supper was a passover meal and also for the Johannine witness that Jesus died on the day of preparation for the Passover. An alternative explanation, favoured by Raymond Brown, is that the synoptic tradition of the last supper has involved a simplification, so that 'a meal with Passover characteristics has become a Passover meal'.[47]

Neither of these proposed solutions to the chronological conflicts in John and the Synoptics over the dating of the crucifixion can be said to be conclusive; but at least they demonstrate that the old argument of Johannine theologising is not the only way of accounting for the differences. Equally, these may arise from an independent use of the same basic tradition, possibly reflecting variation within it before the Gospels came to birth.

Christology

The unfolding of the identity of Jesus in the synoptic and Johannine traditions also differs markedly. In the synoptic Gospels Jesus is only gradually known and confessed as Messiah. The turning-point occurs in Peter's confession at Caesarea Philippi (Mark 8:27-30), which forms the watershed of Mark's Gospel. After this, Jesus concentrates his attention on the instruction of the Twelve rather than of the crowds in general, and reveals the nature of his Messiahship in terms of the person and work of the Son of man.[48] In the Fourth Gospel, on the other hand, Jesus is identified as Messiah from the outset. The call of the first disciples includes the announcement of Andrew to Peter, 'we have found the Messiah' (John 1:41). This is followed by the naming of Peter (verse 42), which, as we have seen, recalls the confession scene at Caesarea Philippi in the synoptic tradition. Moreover, this messianic designation of Jesus is only one of a cluster of titles (such as Son of God and King of Israel, verse 49) which appear in the first chapter of John to form a christological commentary of a very developed nature.

47. R.E. Brown, 'The Problem of Historicity in John' in *idem*, *New Testament Essays* (London: Geoffrey Chapman, 1967), pp. 143–67 (148); for an analysis of Jaubert's thesis see *ibid.*, pp. 160–67. In the light of the work of J. Jeremias, *The Eucharistic Words of Jesus*, 2nd edn. (London: SCM Press, 1966), it seems difficult to deny that the last supper was a Passover meal: see, however, the critique of Jeremias' position by J.A. Baker, 'The "Institution" Narratives and the Christian Eucharist' in I.T. Ramsey *et al.*, *Thinking about the Eucharist* (London: SCM Press, 1972), pp. 38–58, esp. 38–45.

48. *Cf.* Mark 8:31, *et al.* T.W. Manson, *The Teaching of Jesus*, 2nd edn. (Cambridge: Cambridge University Press, 1935), believes that the watershed is marked by the use of the phrase 'kingdom of God' in the teaching of Jesus before Peter's confession, and the expression 'Son of man' afterwards. See, for example, pp. 213–15, 234–36.

But again, this variation should not be exaggerated. For on the other side we may set the fact that the synoptic tradition itself is ambivalent about the moment when the identity of Jesus became most clear to the disciples. Matthew, for example, does not give to the Caesarea Philippi incident the same climactic significance as Mark;[49] this is obvious from the fact that an important confession by the disciples has already taken place just before this, when they worship Jesus as Son of God after the stilling of the storm (Matt. 14:33). There are those who have argued that the so-called 'messianic secret' is in any case a dogmatic intrusion into the tradition, to account for the absence of pre-resurrection faith in the Messiahship of Jesus.[50] At the same time, John has his own version of the 'secret' of the identity of Jesus. Even if he is known to disciples at the beginning of the ministry, he is hidden to those without the eye of faith, who cannot 'see' (a favourite Johannine term) that Jesus is the Christ. So the Jews in the Fourth Gospel still ask whether Jesus is really Messiah or not (John 10:24); and, when he is rejected by non-believers, he is described symbolically (and not only literally) as 'hidden' from them (8:59; 12:36).[51]

The teaching of Jesus

A further difference between the synoptic and Johannine traditions, already mentioned, concerns the style in which the teaching of Jesus is presented in the Gospels. John's Gospel consists largely of leisurely discourses delivered by Jesus to his opponents or to his disciples, or (as in chapter 6) both. The parables, especially the kingdom parables, which are such a feature of the other Gospels, do not appear. Conversely, the sermon-type of address is largely missing from the Synoptics, which

49. See O. Cullmann, *Peter – Disciple, Apostle, Martyr: A Historical and Theological Study*, 2nd edn. (London: SCM Press, 1962), pp. 180–81; also R.E. Brown, K. P. Donfried and J. Reumann (ed.), *Peter in the New Testament* (London: Geoffrey Chapman, 1974), pp. 83–101.

50. So W. Wrede, *The Messianic Secret* (London: James Clarke, 1971), esp. pp. 115–49; also R.P. Martin, *Mark: Evangelist and Theologian* (Exeter: Paternoster Press, 1972), pp. 40–41. E. Best, *Mark: The Gospel as Story*, SNTW (Edinburgh: T. and T. Clark, 1983), pp. 84–85, shows that discipleship is more in view at Mark 8:27–9:1 than Messiahship.

51. *Cf.* John 1:26; 7:27; also 20:28–31, where sight and faith (and therefore their opposites) are made synonymous. See further, on the christology of the synoptic and Johannine traditions, C.H. Dodd, 'The Portrait of Jesus in John and in the Synoptics' in W.R. Farmer, C.F.D. Moule and R. R. Niebuhr (ed.), *Christian History and Interpretation: Studies Presented to John Knox* (Cambridge: Cambridge University Press, 1967), pp. 183–98. Dodd maintains that the (christological) portrait of Jesus in the two traditions supports the view that 'John worked from an early tradition independent of the synoptics but having much in common with the tradition they followed' (p. 195). On the basis of John 5:19–30, Dodd shows that the picture of the personality and work of Jesus which we have in the Fourth Gospel corresponds closely to the picture offered by the synoptists; only the idiom differs (p. 194).

nevertheless abound in parabolic teaching. Even the language differs in the Johannine version of the dominical message. Terms such as 'love', 'truth' and 'knowing' are used frequently in the Fourth Gospel, but not by the other witnesses; whereas the typical synoptic categories of 'preaching' and 'miracle' (δύναμις, rather than σημεῖον, 'sign'), for example, are not to be found in John at all.

This variation is real; but it should not be overlooked that parables, even if not the synoptic parables (of the kingdom) themselves, are present in John. The fourth evangelist preserves several brief parables of his own in the midst of his discourse material, which sometimes act as a 'text' to a sermon. There is the parable of the father and the apprenticed son, for example, in John 5:19–20a;[52] and also the famous parable of the good shepherd and the sheep (10:1–5).[53] At the same time, the synoptic tradition is not unfamiliar with the form of an extended address on the part of Jesus: for example, the Sermon on the Mount/Plain (Matt. 5–7, Luke 6:17–49), and the eschatological discourse in Mark 13 par.[54] Equally John's sophisticated style and language, which are no doubt shaped to some extent by his intention in writing this Gospel in the first place, are his own;[55] just as the other evangelists use their individual, and possibly more traditional, diction.

While the two traditions stand apart, then, in the basic shape they give to the teaching of Jesus, this need not mean inevitably that John's material is altogether secondary, or completely detached from underlying sources which are common to all the Gospels. The fourth evangelist may still be editing primitive discourse material, derived from his own sources rather than from the synoptic Gospels. His editorial activity results in a different appearance being given to the teaching of Jesus in his Gospel; but his independent use of primitive tradition creates links in form as well as content between the Johannine and synoptic versions of that teaching.[56]

52. *Cf.* C.H. Dodd, 'A Hidden Parable in the Fourth Gospel' in *idem, More New Testament Studies* (Manchester: Manchester University Press, 1968), pp. 30–40.

53. It is referred to in John 10:6 as a παροιμία ('figure', 'parable'). See further J.A.T. Robinson, 'The Parable of the Shepherd (John 10:1–5)' in *idem, Twelve New Testament Studies*, pp. 67–75. Robinson argues that this passage contains a fusion of two initially separate parables. A.M. Hunter, *John*, pp. 78–89, lists ten certain examples of parables in the Fourth Gospel, and three possible instances: the Father's house (John 14:2–3); the true vine (15:1–2); and the footwashing (13:1–15).

54. If indeed Mark 13 par. began life as a connected dominical discourse. See further the arguments for and against this view presented by G.R. Beasley-Murray, *A Commentary on Mark Thirteen* (London and New York: Macmillan, 1957).

55. Beasley-Murray, *John*, pp. xli–xlii (*cf.* pp. xxxviii–xliii), believes that the fourth evangelist's *preaching* also influenced the style and composition of his Gospel.

56. See further below, pp. 114–120, 155–156. For a defence of the historical reliability of John's account of the teaching of Jesus see P.W. Ensor, *Jesus and His 'Works': The Johannine Sayings in Historical Perspective*, WUNT 2.85 (Tübingen: Mohr – Paul Siebeck, 1996).

The miracles of Jesus

The Christian tradition presented by the synoptic writers differs from John's version, finally, in its record of the miraculous deeds performed by Jesus. For only once, as we have seen,[57] is the same miracle narrated in all four Gospels; and that is the account of the feeding of the five thousand (Mark 6:32–44 par.; John 6:1–15). Otherwise, John's reported miracles are to be found in his Gospel alone. Furthermore, John treats his miracles distinctively. He uses the term 'sign' (σημεῖον) to describe them; and in each case he draws out their meaning, their significance, by means of an explanatory discourse, to which may be attached one of the 'I am' sayings of Jesus.[58]

Once more, however, balance is necessary. Although it is true that John's signs are almost entirely his own selection,[59] those he does hand on are similar in *kind* to the synoptic list, even to incidents of raising people from the dead.[60] If John's handling of the signs of Jesus is special to him, moreover, this is the result of his particular theological and literary stance. He explores the meaning of the signs, which in John evoke faith rather than presuppose it,[61] in the light of his understanding of the nature of Jesus; and he does so by presenting the miracles dramatically.[62] In the process John may well be tapping his own sources, and moving on theologically from the synoptic account. But this need not mean that he is being unhistorical in his witness, or departing altogether from a Christian tradition which is ultimately held in common.

Summary and conclusions

We may now summarise our investigation of the literary relationship between St John and the synoptic Gospels. (a) The similarities between the two traditions should not be exaggerated so that the differences are obscured; and the differences should not be exaggerated so that the similarities are forgotten. (b) The similarities need not prove that John knew and merely reshuffled the synoptic Gospels; and the differences need not mean that he is out of touch with their tradition.

John does of course use material of his own (which we shall call JA), just as do the Synoptists (especially Matthew and Luke). Like the other evangelists, again, he reshapes all his material in accordance with his

57 See above, pp. 15–17.
58. See further below, pp. 129–35.
59. Note John 20:30!
60. See John 11:1–44 (the raising of Lazarus) and Luke 7:11–17 (the son of a widow, raised to life at Nain).
61. *Cf.* Brodie, pp. 63–64.
62. For a fuller treatment of the Johannine signs from the viewpoint of the fourth evangelist's (sacramental) theology, and his narrative method, see below, pp. 143–46, 234–38. Note also Schnackenburg 1, pp. 154–56.

theological outlook on the tradition. But this is not the same as saying that everything in the Fourth Gospel which does not correspond to the synoptic tradition must be regarded as late Johannine theological invention. We can now reckon seriously with the possibility that the Fourth Gospel, including John's special material, is grounded in historical tradition when it *departs* from the Synoptics, *as well as* when it overlaps with them. Thus such notorious narratives as the raising of Lazarus in John 11 need no longer be viewed automatically as a fictional composition, in which the fourth evangelist has woven together different pieces of synoptic material.[63] It can as well derive from a primitive and reliable source, even if John has used it distinctively to throw light on his understanding of the passion and resurrection of Jesus.[64] On this showing John preserves in JA material worthy of the same kind of respect that we would give to material from the other equally independent sources behind the Gospel tradition, Mark, Q, M and L.[65]

FURTHER EVIDENCE

So far we have considered the nature of John's tradition exclusively in terms of the literary relationship between the Fourth Gospel and the other Gospels. In so doing we have seen good reason to realise the importance of the trail of Johannine independence blazed by Mr Gardner-Smith. The conclusion we have reached, that John's Gospel is likely to contain historically valuable sources which have not been derived from the synoptic Gospels, has since 1938 received support from other directions. We can now consider this fresh evidence.

(a) From manuscripts

Attempts to assign a late, second-century date, to the Fourth Gospel have been made difficult if not impossible by the discovery in Egypt of a papyrus manuscript known as the Rylands Papyrus 457 (P52), which contains a section of John 18 and can be dated AD 135–50.[66] A second papyrus (Egerton Papyrus 2), which may use John, also dates from c. AD

---

63. So A. Richardson, *The Gospel According to St John*, TBC (London: SCM Press, 1959), pp. 137–39 (= Richardson).

64. *Cf.* Brown 1, pp. 428–30. Lindars (pp. 383–86) believes that the Lazarus story is a 'fine composition' by John on the basis of an otherwise unknown tradition of the raising of a man from death by Jesus. This, he argues, has been fused with the story of Martha and Mary (located in Bethany, because of the anointing), and related theologically by John to the passion narrative. See also Schnackenburg 2, pp. 340–46.

65. For this whole section see further Brown, 'Historicity'; also R.E. Brown, 'John and the Synoptic Gospels: A Comparison' in *idem*, *Essays*, pp. 192–213.

66. See K. Aland, 'Neue Neutestamentliche Papyri II', *NTS* 9 (1962–63), p. 307.

150. (There are two other early MSS containing parts of John, the Bodmer Papyri II and XV, P66 and P75; but these cannot be dated earlier than AD 200, or a little before.) The existence of P52 (and Egerton Papyrus 2), suggests that John must have been written at the very latest by the beginning of the second century AD, and probably earlier.

(b) From background research

An earlier date is in fact made likely by recent research into the supposed Hellenism of John's Gospel, and into its probable Jewish background. We shall return to this point in detail.[67] Meanwhile we may notice that if the results of this research confirm that John's tradition is essentially Jewish and indeed Palestinian in character, there is less reason than ever to separate the origins of the Fourth Gospel from a primitive Christian tradition, parallel to that found beneath the synoptic Gospels.

(c) From Qumran

The discovery of the Dead Sea Scrolls at Khirbet Qumran in 1945 or 1947 has thrown new and fascinating light on the question of the derivation of John's Gospel. For these documents have made it plain that before the Christian era began a literary setting existed in which Jewish and Greek, even 'pre-gnostic', religious ideas were combined in a way that once was thought to be unique to John and of a later date (the end of the first century AD, or beyond).

The links between the Scrolls and our Gospel are numerous, and they have often been discussed.[68] There are, to begin with, obvious literary parallels. These are particularly evident in the *Manual of Discipline* (or *Community Rule*), the best manuscript of which was discovered in cave 1; although they also exist in other documents from Qumran. The opening column of the *Rule*, for example, refers to 'practising truth', and loving the 'sons of light' while rejecting the 'sons of darkness', in a way that is reminiscent of the Fourth Gospel.[69] Again, the concept of knowledge in association with the existence and activity of God, and human-

---

67. See below, chapter 3.

68. From a wealth of literature see W.F. Albright, 'Recent Discoveries in Palestine and the Gospel of St John' in W.D. Davies and D. Daube (ed.), *The Background of the New Testament and its Eschatology: In Honour of Charles Harold Dodd* (Cambridge: Cambridge University Press, 1956), pp. 153–71; R.E. Brown, 'The Qumran Scrolls and the Johannine Gospel and Epistles', in *idem, Essays*, pp. 102–131; Hunter, *John*, pp. 27–33.

69. Compare 1QS 1.5, 9–10 with John 3:21; 12:35–36. Note also 1QS 5.19–21; and further the description of God as perfect light (1QH 18.29), which can be associated with the self-designation of Jesus as 'the light of the world' (John 8:12). For translations of the text of the Scrolls see G. Vermes, *The Dead Sea Scrolls in English*, 4th edn. (London: Penguin Books, 1995); F.G. Martínez, *The Dead Sea Scrolls Translated: The Qumran Texts in English* (Leiden: E.J. Brill, 1994).

ity's relationship to him, is present in both the *Rule* and John.[70] Similarly, the Scrolls and the Fourth Gospel both contain references to the wisdom of God, and his enlightenment of the worshipper (and initiant) in answer to (covenant) faith.[71] Even the title of the *War* Scroll (1QM), *The War of the Sons of Light and the Sons of Darkness* (in Vermes, *The War Rule*), has a Johannine ring about it;[72] although its apocalyptic content approximates more closely to the ethos of the Revelation than to the Gospel of John.

Points of contact between the Qumran documents and John exist, then, in their use of terminology which occurs in Jewish literature and indeed in the Old Testament, but also has a Greek flavour (and will reappear in the later literature of thoroughgoing gnosticism).[73] This is in itself significant. But contact exists at a deeper level still. The crucial resemblance between the outlook of this Essene-type community and the Fourth Gospel lies in what Professor Raymond Brown has called the 'modified dualism' which characterises both.[74]

There is present in the Qumran documents the notion of a struggle between truth and perversity, light and darkness, good and evil, in which everyone is involved. The opposing forces in each case are ruled by the appropriate spirit. The source of this thought is not absolutely certain; although the suggestion of Iranian mythology, which could have influenced Judaism in Mesopotamia after the captivity, seems very likely.[75] Certainly it is not derived from the Old Testament. But whatever its source, the character of this dualist thinking in the Scrolls is restrained; it is not thoroughgoing, as in the literature of second-century Greek gnosticism.[76]

There is first no sense, as in gnostic thought, of equally powerful forces

70. Compare 1QS 3.15, and generally columns 3 and 4, with John 1:2 (17:3), *et al. Cf.* also 1QS 7.26–27.

71. Compare 1QH 9.23–24 with John 3:33–36 (5:31–32); also 1QH 17.26–28 and John 12:44–50 (16:25–27).

72. Note esp. 1QM 1.1–17.

73. But notice the common indebtedness of the Scrolls and John to characteristic Jewish notions, such as the eschatological appearance of the 'prophet like Moses' (Deut. 18:18). See 1QS 9.9–11 and John 5:46; 6:14; 7:40. Note further W.A. Meeks, *The Prophet-King: Moses Traditions and the Johannine Christology*, NovT Sup 14 (Leiden: E.J. Brill, 1967), esp. pp. 164–75.

74. Brown, 'Qumran Scrolls', pp. 105–20. Brown also mentions (pp. 123–27) the correspondences occurring in the use of the concepts of brotherly love (*cf.* 1QS 1.9 and John 13:34–35), and living water (*cf.* CD B19.33–35 and John 4:14).

75. *Cf.* K.G. Kuhn, 'Die Palästina gefundenen hebräischen Texte und das Neue Testament', *ZTK* 47 (1950), pp. 192–211, esp. 209–210.

76. See further R.McL. Wilson, *Gnosis and the New Testament* (Oxford: Blackwell, 1968), pp. 1–30, esp. 11–13. On gnosticism generally see further below, pp. 54–61; also F.F. Bruce, *New Testament History*, revised edn. (London and Glasgow: Pickering and Inglis, 1982), pp. 394–99; C.C. Rowland, *The Open Heaven: A Study of Apocalyptic in Judaism and Early Christianity* (London: SPCK, 1982), pp. 249, 337–38.

of good and evil being locked in a struggle, the outcome of which is uncertain. Under the influence of Jewish monotheism to this extent, the principle of God's sovereignty prevails in the Qumran literature. Even if the battle rages, the victory of God and of good is assured. Furthermore, the arrival of that victory is not far off, as the *War* Scroll makes plain. Secondly, whereas the dualism of Greek metaphysical thinking may be described as physical and substantial, the literal conflict of opposing powers, the modified dualism which appears in Qumranic literature has to do with the conflict between good and evil; it is *ethical*, and not physical.

We are not far here from the world of John. The fourth evangelist also colours his work with a restrained dualism.[77] He is also aware of the opposition of light and darkness, good and evil (John 12:35–36); and he also knows that the final outcome of this struggle lies in the victory of God in Christ, and involves a judgment which has already begun (3:18–19). As in Qumranic thought, John's dualism is not physical but monotheistic, ethical and eschatological.

There are differences, of course, between the *milieux* of the fourth evangelist and the men of Qumran, despite this dualist overlap. To go no further, the Fourth Gospel is a Christian document and the Scrolls are Jewish. For John, the coming of Christ makes all the difference. It is not just that he sees the end as already upon us, whereas in the *War* Scroll (for example) it is still in the apocalyptic future. There is a more fundamental separation. In John's theology salvation is achieved, not through the Law as interpreted by the community of Qumran, but through the Word made flesh; and the final victory is gained, not through the intervention of an angel of light, but by the victorious Messiah, Jesus. He is identified with the truth of which the Scrolls speak, and for which the Qumran community was searching (John 14:6). John's Gospel teaches clearly that knowledge of the truth derives uniquely from the knowledge of God through Christ and by the Spirit.[78]

Nevertheless, despite these differences, the overlap between the Scrolls and the Fourth Gospel is supremely important for our purpose of examining the nature of John's tradition. For it demonstrates excitingly what has already been guessed from the literary evidence, that a setting and even a date for the tradition behind John's Gospel can be provided which is much closer to the origins of Christianity than had previously been thought possible. The Jewish-Greek ideas which pervade the Gospel of John need not stem from a late Hellenistic environment; they can as easily derive from a Qumranic background, where as early as the turn of the first century AD they were, to some extent, already a feature. This

---

77. *Cf.* S.S. Smalley, 'Diversity and Development in John', *NTS* 17 (1970–71), pp. 278–79.

78. John 17:3; 15:26; 16:13.

need not surprise us, when we recall that the Jews of Palestine had been subject to Graeco-Roman influence for many years before the opening of the New Testament era.[79]

John the Baptist

We may return briefly at this point to the possible relation between John the Baptist and the Qumran community, and the implications of this association, if any, for the nature of John's tradition.

There are links between the Baptist and Qumran in terms of their religious outlook and intention. Both John and the Qumran sectarians withdrew to the desert (cf. Mark 1:4), to escape the political pressures exerted by their Jewish colleagues, and give themselves to spiritual activities. Both regarded their mission as one of heralding the way of the Lord, even if the nature of this preparation was differently conceived;[80] and both used the same text from the Old Testament (Isa. 40:3) to describe and support their divinely-appointed role.[81] Both practised baptism, or at least (in the case of Qumran) initiatory lustration of some kind.[82] And with this washing was linked in both cases an eschatological message of judgment and forthcoming messianic renewal in the Spirit.[83]

Important as these connections may be, they do not establish conclusively that John the Baptist was a Qumran initiant. It is evident from the brief witness of the New Testament to him that ultimately he was an independent figure, with his own following (cf. Matt. 11:2, et al.) and his own preaching. At most, John would have known about the community and been influenced by its ideas. But given such an association, several fascinating possibilities emerge which bear on our subject.

In this case, the Qumran community is the single link between John the Baptist and the Jewish-Greek thought-forms present in the Fourth Gospel which once seemed so Hellenistic and late. It may well be therefore that the source of the Qumranic, Jewish-Hellenistic features in

79. See further on the subject of this section J.H. Charlesworth (ed.) John and Qumran (London: Geoffrey Chapman, 1972); G. Vermes, The Dead Sea Scrolls: Qumran in Perspective, 3rd edn. (London: SCM Press, 1994); J.C. VanderKam, The Dead Sea Scrolls Today (Grand Rapids: Eerdmans and London: SPCK, 1994). Note also K.G. Kuhn 'Johannesevangelium und Qumrantexte' in Neotestamentica et Patristica: In Honour of O. Cullmann, NovT Sup 6 (Leiden: E.J. Brill, 1962), pp. 111–22; Robinson, Redating, p. 284; J.H. Charlesworth, 'The Dead Sea Scrolls and the Gospel according to John' in Culpepper and Black (ed.), Exploring John, pp. 65–97.

80. Preparation for the messianic age in Qumran was understood to mean a return to a more determined devotion to the law of Moses (cf. 1QS 5.7–9, et al.).

81. Cf. John 1:23; 1QS 8.12–14.

82. Cf. Scobie, Baptist, pp. 102–110.

83. Cf. John 1:26-27, 33; 1QS 4.20–22.

the Gospel of John was John the Baptist himself, who was no doubt close to the disciples of Jesus (some of whom, including perhaps John the Apostle, were originally his), and could have influenced and informed the Johannine tradition in its early stages. Moreover, it is possible that the distinctive tradition about John the Baptist belonging to John's Gospel[84] derives from the Baptist himself. Historically and theologically, the portrait of John the Baptist given to us by the fourth evangelist can be accounted for easily if common ground existed between the Baptist and the Qumran community, and if the Baptist himself were responsible for that portrait.[85] This is supported by the fact that the early chapters of the Fourth Gospel (John 1–3) seem to depend on an independent and historical witness, since they contain topographical and other details about the ministry of John the Baptist which have no particular theological point, and need not otherwise have been included.[86]

Admittedly this is not the only way of accounting for the features which are common to the Gospel of John and the Dead Sea Scrolls. There is no reason, for example, why literary and theological characteristics of this kind could not have come into primitive Christianity from less sectarian sources, such as the group of priests spoken of in Acts 6:7 who were 'obedient to the faith', and who might have been influenced by the teaching of Qumran (itself a priestly community). But if John the Baptist *is* the link, this must affect our estimate of the reliability both of the tradition about him in the Fourth Gospel, and indeed of the Johannine tradition as a whole.

(d)   From topography

A final piece of evidence remains, which may help to throw light on the character of the tradition behind the Fourth Gospel, especially when that Gospel is compared to the Synoptics. This has to do with John's topography, and the relevance to this of archaeological excavation.

There are several place names in John's Gospel which do not appear in the synoptic Gospels. Some of these places, such as the pool of

---

84. See above, pp. 24–25.

85. Note the distinctive way in which, according to the fourth evangelist, John the Baptist acts as he does to *reveal* and not merely to herald the Messiah (John 1:31; *cf.* 1 QS 4.20–23). *Cf.* also the common reference in the traditions of the Baptist, according to the Fourth Gospel and Qumran, to the figure of the 'prophet like Moses' (John 1:19, 25; *cf.* 1QS 9.11).

86. *Cf.* John 1:28; 3:23. See further Robinson, 'Baptism of John', esp. pp. 24–27; also *HTFG*, pp. 248–301. Dodd makes the point that the narrative about John the Baptist at Aenon (John 3:22–30) is remarkably non-Johannine in style and theology, and shows affinity with traditional forms known from the other Gospels. 'It is highly probable,' he concludes, 'that we are here in touch with pre-canonical tradition' (p. 287). *Cf.* also the literature cited in n. 38.

Siloam[87] (John 9:7) and the Kidron valley (18:1), can be seen by any visitor to Jerusalem today. The fact that John alone refers to them does not therefore mean that their existence needs to be questioned. Other place names given by John are less easily identifiable, however, and might cause his accuracy to be questioned. This is true, for example, of 'Bethany beyond the Jordan' (1:28), which has not been located; and 'Solomon's portico' (10:23; cf. Acts 3:11) which, since it was part of the temple when it was destroyed, cannot be found.[88]

Nevertheless, recent archaeological excavation has confirmed the existence of a number of places mentioned by John which might otherwise be attributed to his inventive genius. If John's accuracy is therefore vindicated on the occasions when it can be tested, we have less reason to doubt his topographical reliability when it cannot be established.

Two of the most important sites in Jerusalem to have been excavated fairly recently are the pool of Bethesda (John 5:2) and the Pavement (19:13). Until excavation began in 1878 on the Bethesda site, near what is today called St Stephen's Gate[89] in the old city of Jerusalem, no knowledge of this pool existed outside the Fourth Gospel. The fact that it had 'five porticoes', moreover, could have meant that John was using allegory or symbolism freely, and that he simply invented the name Bethesda[90] to provide a setting for his sign. But the excavations have put a different light on the matter. The first stage, completed in 1931–32, uncovered two tank-like pools, separated by a wall of rock; these are now to be seen very close to the Crusader church of St Anne. It was thought at first that here was the Bethesda pool itself; and this impression was confirmed by the fact that a Byzantine church was built on the site, partly over the tanks (supported by eight columns, which still stand more or less intact), and partly on the solid ground. Fresh discoveries, however, have convinced the White Fathers in charge of the excavations that the

87.   But there is a reference at Luke 13:4 to 'the tower in Siloam'. John's reference to Siloam is manifestly historical, despite the symbolism he draws from the etymology of the name ('which means Sent').

88.   But see Josephus, *Ant* 20.9.7, who refers to temple 'cloisters' built by Solomon. Note also the identification of 'Aenon near Salim' in John 3:23 (as a village in the region of Shechem) by Albright, 'Recent Discoveries', p. 159; see also Bruce, *History*, p. 152. *Cf.* Hunter, *John*, p. 51.

89.   The 'sheep gate' mentioned in John 5:2 was situated north-east of the temple, and close to the present St Stephen's Gate. There is a problem in the text at this point, however, in that some MSS make ἐπὶ τῇ ὀροβατικῇ ('[by the] sheep [gate]') and κολυμβήθρα ('[a] pool') agree. Lindars, pp. 211–12, thinks that this, more difficult, reading is correct, and that it should be taken to mean 'by the sheep pool, a *place* called. . . '. But 'sheep *gate*' is the correct interpretation, and this was added in to the text later.

90.   For a discussion of the evidence, and a proposal that this is the correct version of the name (rather than Bethzatha or Bethsaida), particularly in the light of information from the copper scroll of Qumran, see D.J. Wieand, 'John V.2 and the Pool of Bethesda', *NTS* 12 (1965–66), pp. 392–404, esp. 392–95. But see also Lindars, pp. 212–13.

site of the healing of the sick man in John 5 was located in shallower pools adjacent to the tanks, and was once associated with the pagan cult of healing presided over by the god Aesculapius. The inference is, in fact, that a pagan sanctuary and probably an Aesculapian temple stood on this site originally.

This makes considerably more sense of the situation. It would have been easier to immerse invalids in a shallow pool than a deep tank; and once the sign mentioned in John 5 had occurred, the holy place would naturally be preserved by building a church over it as an effective reminder that Christ *the* healer had appeared. Here is impressive support for the historicity of the tradition in John 5.[91]

The other site of interest for our purposes is the place where Jesus was tried and condemned by Pilate. John tells us that this was at a place called the Pavement (*Lithostrotos*), in Hebrew (Aramaic) *Gabbatha* (John 19:13). The debate about the exact location of this site continues. Père Benoit favours Herod's palace, on the western side of Jerusalem, partly on the grounds that according to Josephus this was the headquarters of a successor to Pilate, the barbarous Gessius Florus.[92] But nothing like a 'pavement' has been discovered there. On the other hand, beneath the Antonia fortress in the north-west corner of the temple area, the excavations of Fr L.H. Vincent have revealed a paved court made up of massive blocks of stone which may well have been the Roman governor's temporary praetorium, and a suitable place for its location. The real problem in this case is whether the excavated pavement formed part of the Antonia in the time of Jesus.[93] But in any case John's unique reference to this site is evidently historical; and even if we still cannot be sure where *Gabbatha* was to be found, we can be fairly certain that the fourth evangelist was in touch with early tradition when he referred to it.

Before we leave the evidence of John's topography, it will be instructive to consider for a moment the appearance of actual place names in the Fourth Gospel, quite apart from the support given to the existence of these places by archaeology.

John uses several place names (such as Jerusalem, Bethany, Jordan and Galilee) which are common to all the Gospels. His Gospel also

91. See further the important study by J. Jeremias, *The Rediscovery of Bethesda: John 5.2* (Louisville: Southern Baptist Theological Seminary, 1966). *Cf.* also P. Benoit, 'Découvertes archéologiques autour de la piscine de Béthesda', in P.W. Lapp (ed.), *Jerusalem through the Ages* (Jerusalem: Israel Exploration Society, 1968), pp. 48–57; C. Kopp, *The Holy Places of the Gospels* (Freiburg im Breisgau: Herder and London: Nelson, 1963), pp. 305–313; and B.E. Schein, *Following the Way: The Setting of John's Gospel* (Minneapolis: Augsburg Publishing House, 1980), pp. 87–91, 206–209.

92. Josephus, *Bell Jud* 2.14.8. *Cf.* P. Benoit, 'Praetorium, Lithostroton and Gabbatha' in *idem, Jesus and the Gospel*, vol. 1 (London: Darton, Longman and Todd, 1973), pp. 167–88.

93. *Cf.* Kopp, *Holy Places,* pp. 370–73; also Brown 2, pp. 881–82. See further P. Benoit, 'L'Antonia d' Hérode le Grand et le Forum Oriental d' Aelia Capitolina', *HTR* 64 (1971), pp. 135–67, where the conclusions of Vincent are disputed.

contains names which he alone uses. In addition to those already mentioned (the pool of Siloam, the Kidron valley, Bethany beyond the Jordan, Solomon's portico, Aenon near Salim, Bethesda and Gabbatha), there are Cana, Tiberias (and the Sea of Tiberias), Sychar and Ephraim. With Luke only he shares Samaria. From this evidence C.H. Dodd concludes that the setting of John's basic tradition was not only Palestinian, and therefore (we may add) close to the origins of the Jesus story, but also located in Jerusalem and the south rather than in Galilee and the north.[94] For, as Dodd points out,[95] Cana in Galilee is the only place in northern Palestine known to John but not to the other evangelists, and a large range of northern place names present in the synoptic Gospels (such as Decapolis, Caesarea Philippi and the territory of Tyre and Sidon) cannot be found in the Fourth Gospel. Similarly, although John's Gospel lacks the Judean names Bethphage, Gethsemane and (in Luke only) Emmaus, it includes no less than nine southern place names unknown to the other Gospel writers.[96]

Conclusions

The topography of the Fourth Gospel bears, as we shall see in the next chapter, on the issue of the background to John's Gospel. But the purpose in alluding to it here has been to indicate one further reason for entertaining seriously the possibility that the Fourth Gospel rests on and preserves a tradition that was shaped in a Jewish-Christian environment at a fairly early date.[97]

Establishing the accuracy of the fourth evangelist's reference to sites or localities does not by itself, of course, guarantee the historical authenticity of the events he places there. But at least it suggests that John is not being purely fanciful in his narrative information when he refers to locations for it which can be verified; particularly since the reliability of such information would be open to question by eye witnesses who were still around when the Fourth Gospel was being written, and who would know the sites mentioned. On the contrary, the traditional elements in

94. *HTFG*, pp. 244–45.
95. *Ibid.*, p. 245.
96. John's use of *personal* names is as interesting as his use of place names, and may have a bearing on the nature of the tradition beneath the Gospel. Note the use of (i) synoptic names in a synoptic context (*e.g.* Andrew and Philip in John 6:5–9, and Peter in 18:10); (ii) synoptic names in a Johannine setting (*e.g.* Philip in John 14:8–9; and perhaps also Judas in 14:22); (iii) Johannine names in a synoptic context (Malchus at 18:10); (iv) Johannine names in a Johannine account (Nicodemus, John 3; 19:39; and Lazarus, John 11;12:1–2). If the fourth evangelist knew the other Gospels, the main reasons for adding or dropping or relocating names would presumably have been literary and theological. Yet these motives alone cannot account for the personal, any more than the geographical, references that are unique to the Fourth Gospel.
97. *Cf: HTFG*, p. 426.

John's topography may well indicate traditional and indeed historical elements in the reports associated with it, even if in the end these have been theologically treated. Again, we shall return to the main issue involved here: the relation between history and theology in John.[98]

The additional evidence we have been considering, from manuscripts, background research, and Qumran, as well as from topography, points to a conclusion similar to that derived from a literary comparison between John and the Synoptics. There are good reasons for believing that the fourth evangelist did not know or use the synoptic Gospels, as we now have them, but drew independently on a tradition parallel to theirs.

Much has happened since Gardner-Smith in 1938 challenged the dependence of John on the Synoptics. He was in fact ahead of his time; and subsequent evidence, such as the discoveries at Qumran, has confirmed his opinion rather than undermined it. We can now see that his monograph was an unexpectedly important pebble thrown into the theological pool; and indeed it has produced ripples which have rocked the critical boats ever since.

There are many implications for the Fourth Gospel arising from the presupposition of Johannine independence, and we shall be considering these in due course. For if John did not depend on the synoptic tradition through the synoptic Gospels, but used his own equally valuable sources, this will obviously affect the view we take of the historicity, composition and indeed authorship of the Gospel. But not only are there implications for John; there are also implications for the Gospel tradition as a whole. It will be useful to draw these out before we move on to consider the Fourth Gospel by itself in more detail.

THE GOSPEL TRADITION

(i) If the Johannine tradition is independent, its claim to be historically valuable is high. This means that the Fourth Gospel can no longer be disregarded in any study of the Gospels, but must be taken into one purview with the Synoptics.[99] It is no longer possible to say that the Synoptics are 'history', and John is 'theology', so that when John disagrees with the other Gospels he must always be wrong.[100] All four

98. See below, pp. 199–229.

99. The reluctance to do this is still evident in New Testament scholarship. In A.J.B. Higgins, *Jesus and the Son of Man* (London: Lutterworth Press, 1964), for example, the relevance of the Johannine tradition to the subject of the Son of man sayings is easily dismissed (pp. 153, 182). *Cf.* Smalley, 'Johannine Son of Man', pp. 278–81.

100. However, when there is a conflict between the traditions, and there are arguments for Johannine accuracy, it is necessary to face the implications of this for the reliability of the synoptic Gospels. Note the strictures to this end in the review by D.E. Nineham of A.M. Hunter's book, *According to John* (1968), in *SJT* 22 (1969), pp. 374–76.

Gospels are theological as well as historical, historical as well as theological; although we still have to consider what 'historical' means in the total context of John.[101] Thus John's record of the Jesus tradition, for all its theological shaping, may well be in general terms as accurate as the synoptic record, and at times even more reliable.

(ii)   If there are connections between the synoptic and Johannine traditions these, on the assumption of Johannine independence, are in the 'underground'. They remind us not of borrowing from one Gospel to another, but of a common, primitive Christian tradition shared by all the evangelists; even if at times John's sources approximate remarkably to those used by the other Gospel writers, especially Luke.[102] In this sense, only, John is 'among the synoptists'.[103]

(iii)   If this conclusion about the nature of John's tradition is correct, and the Fourth Gospel has indeed emerged in a fresh light, the discipline of Gospel criticism as a whole will be affected. It means that critical methods can now be applied to John as to the other Gospels objectively, without presupposing from the outset that the Johannine tradition must necessarily be secondary and inferior. We have reached the stage, in fact, when the expression 'the synoptic problem' is no longer adequate as a description of the analytical task facing students of the Gospels. For if there is a 'problem' belonging to the Gospels, it belongs to them all, and not just to the first three. The phrase 'the problem of the four Gospels' is perhaps a better designation for the key issue in Gospel origins: the relation of the Gospels to each other.

The problem of the four Gospels, moreover, can no longer be solved exclusively by the famous 'four document hypothesis' associated with the name of B.H. Streeter.[104] Even that phrase needs modifying, as we now recognise, into the 'four *source* hypothesis'.[105] If John is brought into the picture, as now he must be, we can go further and boldly rename one solution to the problem of the Gospel sources, the '*six* source

101.   *Cf.* Mark 1:1; John 20:31, *et al.* Note also C.F.D. Moule's reminder ('Intention'), that evangelism in some form was the primary aim of all the evangelists. On history and theology in John see below, chapter 9.

102.   *Cf.* Bailey, *Traditions.* Also Parker, 'Luke', pp. 317–36. See above, pp. 10–11.

103.   See J.A.T. Robinson, 'The Place of the Fourth Gospel', in P. Gardner-Smith (ed.), *The Roads Converge* (London: Edward Arnold, 1963), pp 49–74, esp. 73–74; also *idem, Priority*, pp. 33–35. For a study which, unusually, considers the theological implications of the relationship between the Johannine and synoptic traditions see J.D.G. Dunn, 'John and the Synoptics as a Theological Question' in Culpepper and Black (ed.), *Exploring John*, pp. 301–313.

104.   Streeter, *Four Gospels*, pp. 223–70.

105.   Source criticism is still a live issue, and no one answer satisfies all the critics. For a survey, and further bibliography, see D. Wenham, 'Source Criticism' in Marshall (ed.), *Interpretation*, pp. 139–52, 376–77. For source-critical approaches to John's Gospel see below, chapter 5.

hypothesis'. For the sources belonging to the substructure of the Gospels then include not only Mark, Q, M and L, but also JA (as we have designated John's own material) and Jl (John's version of material parallel to the synoptic tradition).

My own solution to the relationship between John's Gospel and the other three, and therefore between the Johannine and synoptic traditions, can therefore be represented in diagrammatic form like this (where T stands for the origin of the Jesus tradition):

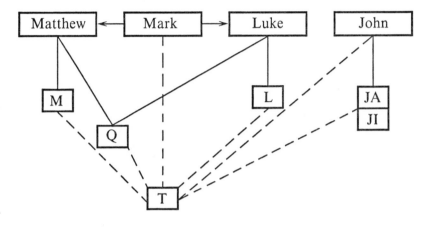

CONCLUSION

We have been considering so far in this book the nature of the tradition upon which John depended for the composition of his Gospel. Our investigations have shown that tradition is now regarded as a more important issue than authorship in Johannine research, and that there is evidence pointing in the direction of the literary independence and historical reliability of John's basic material. However, balance is needed. As we have noticed, in the past 100 years or so the scholarly consensus about the relation of the Johannine to the synoptic tradition has moved from a position of 'complete dependence', to one of 'complete independence', to a solution somewhere between those two extremes.

It is still unlikely, in my view, that the fourth evangelist knew the first three Gospels as we have received them, especially as the latter originated from geographical centres other than Ephesus.[106] On the other hand, it is quite possible that John was able to tap into common sources of

106. Traditionally Mark was written at Rome, and Matthew at Antioch. The provenance of Luke is conjectural; but Caesarea and Achaia are possibilities. See C.F. Evans, *Saint Luke*, TPINTC (London: SCM Press and Philadelphia: Trinity Press International, 1990), p. 15.

Christian tradition circulating in Asia Minor, and even Palestine, at the time. So, for example, there may be links in the underground between the traditions concerning the apostle Peter preserved, apparently independently, by both John and Matthew.[107]

It will be fascinating to discover where the study of John's Gospel, and in particular its underlying tradition, will lead us in the twenty-first century. Meanwhile, we can proceed in the next chapter to consider the background and authorship of this document. Which John wrote the Gospel, and – a prior question – what was his background?

---

107.   See Matt. 14:28–31; 16:17–19; 17:24–27; and John 13–20; 21, *et passim*. For the presentation of this Petrine material in Matthew and John see Brown *et al.*, *Peter*, pp. 75–107, 129–47.

3

JOHN'S BACKGROUND

In an earlier section of this book we noticed that, since roughly the middle of the twentieth century, two assumptions previously made by critics of the Fourth Gospel have been challenged: first, that a solution to the authorship question can determine the origin, apostolic or otherwise, of the Johannine tradition; and second, that there is a relationship of literary dependence between John and the synoptic Gospels.[1] We have dealt with the dependence issue in the previous chapter; we can now address the problem of authorship.

For the claim that to concentrate on the nature of John's underlying tradition is a more crucial exercise than discovering who wrote this Gospel, if we are to discover the true character of the document, does not allow us to dismiss completely an enquiry into its authorship. We still need to know who was responsible in the first place for the traditional sources which may be found in this Gospel, and whether 'John' had any connection with them. We need to know this not only because the answers to such questions are of obvious and immediate interest to any student of the New Testament, but also because they will help us to determine still more positively the character of the Johannine tradition, and the extent of its historicity. For if it can be shown that John's Gospel is in any real sense apostolic, in that it was in origin associated with John the apostle, our view of John and our estimate of its witness to the Jesus tradition must clearly be affected profoundly. One important result of the recent research into the Fourth Gospel which has been undertaken, and the sometimes surprising results to which it has given rise, is that such an investigation is seen to be both timely and valid.

Who then was John? We have spoken many times already of 'John's Gospel'. In what sense, if any, was it really John's; and in any case which John are we discussing? The best way to answer questions about the origin and authorship of the Fourth Gospel is to examine its background. To this we now turn, in the present chapter. In the next, we shall try to discover who actually wrote this Gospel.

---

1. See above, pp. 2–9.

JOHN'S BACKGROUND

To determine the background of the Gospel of John is a complex task. To begin with, we must establish which particular background we are investigating: the setting, so far as this can be discovered, of the basic Johannine tradition underlying the Gospel; the environment of the author (or authors) of the document; or the background of its immediate audience.[2]

As soon as we have made such distinctions, however, we are faced with the further problem of holding these backgrounds apart when characterising the setting of John's material. It is not easy, for example, to separate the background of the fourth evangelist from that of his readers, especially since we have not yet decided how the Fourth Gospel was written, and whether more than one hand or different stages of composition (or both) were involved. We shall be on firm ground, however, if we seek to identify the fundamental background of John's Gospel, and allow this to inform us about the environment in which John's tradition (as already discussed) took shape. This information will then tell us something more about the context in which the Fourth Gospel was written, and eventually about those for whom it was first written.

A further complexity involved in this task is inherent in the very nature of the background to John's Gospel. A cursory glance at this Gospel is sufficient to convince the reader that most probably more than one ethos can be discovered within it. We shall now look at the various strands it contains. For convenience we shall consider first the possible Greek and then the possible Jewish influence on John; although it is of great importance to remember at the outset the extent to which inevitably Judaism and Hellenism overlapped during the first century AD.[3]

(a) Greek influence

Philosophy

Earlier writers on John, such as E.A. Abbott,[4] located the background of the Gospel primarily in Hellenism. It is true, of course, that the Fourth Gospel contains language and ideas belonging to the derived forms of

2. *Cf.* Robinson, 'New Look', pp. 98–99.

3. See further M. Hengel, *Judaism and Hellenism: Studies in Their Encounter in Palestine During the Early Hellenistic Period*, 2 vols. (London: SCM Press, 1974), esp. 1. pp.107–254.

4. *Cf.* E.A. Abbott, *Notes on New Testament Criticism: Diatessarica*, vol. 7, (London: A. and C. Black, 1907), p. 6, where he discusses the influence of Epictetus on John. See also Moffatt, *Introduction*, pp. 522–25, who sees the main currents flowing through John's Gospel, apart from the Old Testament, as Paulinism, Jewish Alexandrian philosophy and Stoicism.

Platonism and Stoicism which were typical of the Mediterranean world in the first century AD. But it is necessary to look at these carefully before concluding that John was profoundly influenced by such systems of philosophical thought.

We may first examine briefly the character of Platonic and Stoic thinking, and then test the extent of John's dependence on this. By the time that John's Gospel came to be written, the pure classical philosophy of the Hellenic golden age (the fifth century BC, when Plato lived) had become tainted by eclectic, Hellenistic thought. Platonism, and the school which Plato had founded, known as the Academy, survived until the sixth century AD, and its influence was great. At the opening of the New Testament period, however, instruction in the philosophical schools mostly involved the teaching of rhetoric, and Platonic ways of thought had become sceptical. Nevertheless, the chief ideas in Plato's philosophy persisted. These centred in the typically Greek, dualist contrast between the invisible, 'real' world beyond time (above), and its inferior copy in this world of time (below). Allied to this basic conception, and deriving from it, is the further contrast between humanity's superior mind and inferior flesh, and the notion of perfection as the mind is released by contemplation from its material confines in order to unite with true reality in God.

Stoicism owed its origin to Zeno (335-263 BC), who came to Athens from Cyprus in 313 BC and attended the Academy. The Stoics were committed to the search for stability rather than salvation, and emphasised the importance of the *logos*. This term could mean either indwelling reason or outgoing expression, and described both God and the universe. On the Stoic view, the *logos* was expressed in the material world in such a way that God was to the world what the soul was to the human body. The result of this world-view was an obviously pantheistic outlook, in which the soul of a person and the 'soul' of the universe (the mind of God) discover kinship when anyone lives according to reason.

Can we find elements of either Platonic or Stoic thought in John? First, John's Gospel is distinctive in that it attributes to the evangelist and to Jesus reference to a series of contrasts. John speaks of the difference between the one 'from above' and 'of the earth' (John 3:31); and Jesus says to the Jews, 'You are from below, I am from above' (8:23). Similarly Jesus, in speaking to Nicodemus, distinguishes between flesh and spirit (3:6), and introduces the same contrast when replying to criticism from his disciples (6:63). These contrasts, between 'above' and 'below', and flesh and spirit, almost certainly stem from a Platonic world-view, in which (as we have seen) the ideal world above was set over against the inferior, shadowy forms of it on earth. But such notions were common in the Graeco-Roman world of the New Testament period, and had long influenced Judaism. There is no reason to suppose that John was heavily dependent on Platonism because his Gospel shows familiarity with occasional ideas which were current coinage in the Jewish-Hellenistic environment of the day, and shared indeed by other New Testament writers.[5]

The same is true of any attempt to prove that John leans heavily on Stoic patterns of thought, because of his *Logos* ('Word') terminology in the prologue (John 1:1, *et al.*). The composition of the first chapter of John's Gospel is in any case a matter for debate, as we shall discover later.[6] But this apart, the use of a popular Stoic concept by the fourth evangelist cannot by itself prove that he was himself a Stoic, or even derived the *Logos* idea from Stoicism. First, he uses the term differently, since the notion of the Word incarnate is far from the Stoic idea of *logos* as the mind of God.[7] Second, we need not look further than the Old Testament, including its Wisdom literature, although this was itself influenced by Hellenistic ideas, to find a source for John's use of the concept of the Word of God.[8] Knowing John as we do already, it is probable that this was his natural and primary source, and that any Stoic associations attaching to the term Logos would merely help to appeal to the understanding of his Greek readers.[9]

Religion

The possible influence on the Fourth Gospel of Hellenism, whether or not this was transmitted through the Judaism of the time, does not end with Greek philosophy. The fourth evangelist and his readers were also surrounded in their day by a Mediterranean world in which syncretistic, pagan religions, themselves influenced by the orient, flourished. The further away from Palestine John's tradition is located, moreover, the more likely it is for pressures from this source to have been exerted upon it.

What were these possible religious influences, and to what extent can the background of John's Gospel be regarded as having been shaped by them? We can examine four.

5. *Cf.* Heb 8:5; 10:1. The contrast between flesh and spirit is present even in the Old Testament; *cf.* Isa. 31:3.

6. See below, pp. 135–39, 142.

7. See Brown 1, pp. 519–24.

8. *Cf.* Gen. l; Deut. 32:46–47; Psa. 33:6; 107:20; Prov. 8:22–31; Wisdom 16:12, 26, *et al.* See also J.T. Sanders, *The New Testament Christological Hymns: Their Historical Religious Background*, SNTSMS 15 (Cambridge: Cambridge University Press, 1971), pp. 29–57, who believes that John's prologue is a further stage in 'the progressive hypostatization of the Word in *Judaism*, constantly under influence from foreign religions' (p. 56, italics mine).

9. For a fuller description of the Greek philosophical schools, which formed part of the setting of early Christianity, see Bruce, *History*, pp. 39–52.

The mystery religions

Although Rudolf Schnackenburg claims that mystery religions 'need hardly be considered' in this context,[10] it is not possible to dismiss quite so easily the apparent connections between contemporary pagan cults of initiation, using the myth of a saviour god,[11] and the Fourth Gospel. As Kingsley Barrett points out,[12] they share the ideas of initiation by divine rebirth (John 1:12; 3:3, 5), and of spiritual life achieved by sacramental eating and drinking (6:51, 53). Nevertheless, the differences between the world of John and these cults (the Greek Eleusian mysteries, for example, or those of Adonis in Syria, Isis in Egypt and Mithras in Persia) are real. Despite superficial parallels, these Hellenistic myths remained myths. The Jesus of St John, in contrast to the cultic saviour figures, becomes incarnate in flesh and blood (John 1:14); his ethos is not ultimately mythical, but genuinely historical. It is doubtful if in the end the Fourth Gospel overlapped at all with the religious outlook of the Greek mysteries.

Mandean literature

The work of Reitzenstein[13] and Bultmann[14] on the literature of the Mandeans, in the earlier part of this century, resulted in a theory which is relevant to our subject. This theory maintained that the formulation of Christian doctrine, particularly in its Johannine and gnostic versions, was influenced by a pre-Christian Mandean myth at the heart of which lay the Iranian redemption mystery. The theory also suggested that John the Baptist was responsible for the formation of Mandean myth and ritual, and that the Mandeans themselves were the successors of the Baptist sect allegedly referred to in Acts (cf. Acts 18:24–19:7).[15]

We know about the Mandean sect from a small community still living today in Iraq and Iran. Their writings, principally the *Ginza* ('Treasure') and the *Book of John* (both collections of tractates), are a varied assortment of literary types, the teaching of which has affinities with a Manichean type of dualism. Mandean doctrine, inasfar as it is unified,

10. Schnackenburg 1, p. 135.

11. See further R. Reitzenstein, *Die hellenistischen Mysterienreligionen: nach ihren Grundgedanken und Wirkungen* (Darmstadt: Wissenschaftliche Buchgesellschaft, 1966), which deals in the first place with Paul's background. *Cf.* also Neill and Wright, *Interpretation*, pp. 168–73.

12. Barrett, pp. 36–39.

13. R. Reitzenstein, *Das mandäische Buch des Herrn der Grösse und die Evangelienüberlieferung* (Heidelberg: Akademie der Wissenschaften, 1919).

14. R. Bultmann, 'Die Bedeutung der neuerschlossenen mandäischen und manichäischen Quellen für das Verständnis des Johannesevangeliums', *ZNW* 24 (1925), pp. 100–146; also Bultmann, pp. 25–31 *et passim* (on the 'gnostic' background to the term *logos* in John).

15. See C.H. Dodd, *The Interpretation of the Fourth Gospel* (Cambridge: Cambridge University Press, 1953), pp. 115–30, esp. 120–21 (= *IFG*).

may be regarded as gnostic in character. It involves a central myth, described already, of salvation by the escape of the soul from the body. Preparation for this escape consists of the proper performance of a baptismal ritual.

The literature of the Mandeans as it currently exists (and since the discovery in 1947 of the Coptic gnostic texts from Nag Hammadi, this has undergone considerable reappraisal) cannot be dated as a collection much before AD 700, since the *Ginza* and the *Book of John* contain allusions to Mohammed and the Islamic faith, stemming from the period of the Muslim conquest. No doubt some of the writings come from an earlier period but, as with the origin of Mandaism itself, we can only speculate about this. If the origins of Mandaism are in fact pre-Christian, as Reitzenstein and Bultmann argue, then the parallels which can be drawn between Mandean thought and John are obviously important for any investigation of the background to the Fourth Gospel.[16]

The most likely point of contact between the Fourth Gospel and the literature of the Mandeans lies in the existence among the gnostics of a so-called 'redeemer myth'. In Mandaism this takes the form of a divine being (the most important is Manda d'Hayye = 'Knowledge of Life'), who descends into the lower realms, conquers the powers of darkness and victoriously ascends to the realm of light. His action thereby guarantees to the faithful the living efficacy of their myth and ritual.

In Johannine Christianity similar ideas are present. The descent of a redeemer and his ascent to glory,[17] the language of light and life,[18] the contrast between truth and error,[19] and between the 'upper' and 'lower' worlds,[20] are all familiar to us from the Fourth Gospel. But John's interpretation of these concepts differs from the Mandean, particularly as it involves a Jewish-Christian understanding of historical reality and salvation which cannot be said to characterise the gnostic, speculative world-view, and does not need Mandaism to explain it.[21] Similarly, the association between John the Baptist and the Mandean sect suggested

16.   An earlier translator and editor of the Mandean texts was M. Lidzbarski who, in his introductions to the *Ginza* and the *Book of John*, maintained the theory also propounded by Reitzenstein and Bultmann that John was influenced by Mandaism. See the literature cited in *IFG*, p. 115 n. 1. W. Bauer's commentary on the Fourth Gospel, *Das Johannesevangelium*, 3rd edn., HNT 6 (Tübingen: Mohr-Siebeck, 1933) (= Bauer), also anticipated Bultmann's work in its conclusion that the Mandean texts should be used to interpret John.

17.   *Cf.* John 3:13.

18.   *Cf.* John 1:4.

19.   *Cf.* John 14:6; 18:37–38.

20.   *Cf.* John 17:16; also 1 John 2:15–17.

21.   E. Percy, *Untersuchungen über den Ursprung der johanneischen Theologie, zugleich ein Beitrag zur Frage nach der Enstehung des Gnostizismus* (Lund: C.W.K. Gleerup, 1939), argued along these lines against the view that the theology of John derives from a Mandean-gnostic background.

by Lidzbarski and others, and indeed the survival of a Baptist sect, which forms a necessary part of their theory about John the Baptist's responsibility for Mandean forms of religion, lacks the support of historical evidence. John the Baptist's appearance in the literature of Mandaism adds nothing to our knowledge of him from the New Testament, and need not carry the significance that some Mandean scholars would give to it.

When we compare the Mandean texts and John, then, sufficient distance lies between them to prevent us concluding immediately that Mandaism influenced the background of the Fourth Gospel. But the decisive factor, as already suggested, is that of chronology. The pre-Christian origin of Mandaism and the Mandean texts proposed by Lidzbarski, Reitzenstein and Bultmann, upon which their theory of John's indebtedness to Mandean thought depends, was challenged at an early date. E. Peterson, for example, argued that the Mandean sect did not emerge until the eighth century AD;[22] and F.C. Burkitt also believed that the origin of the sect was late because its members knew the Syriac Peshitta.[23] More recently, the outstanding Mandean scholar Lady E.S. Drower has reasserted the thesis that Mandaism derives from a pre-Christian period;[24] although this has in turn been questioned in a study of Mandean origins by E.M. Yamauchi.[25] A further point of distinction between the Mandean texts and primitive Christianity (as well as Qumran), pointed out by Yamauchi, lies in the significance that baptism has for each: the one is magical, and the other ethical.[26] He therefore regards Mandaism, on this and other grounds, as post-Christian in origin.

Sufficient has been said to indicate that, despite the superficial parallels existing between John and Mandean thought, neither the content of the Mandean literature nor the uncertain date of the actual texts can lead us to conclude that Mandaism is of any real importance for the study of the background to the Fourth Gospel.[27]

22. E. Peterson, 'Urchristentum und Mandäismus', *ZNW* 27 (1928), pp. 55–98.

23. F.C. Burkitt, *Church and Gnosis* (Cambridge: Cambridge University Press, 1932), pp. 92–122, esp. pp. 120–22.

24. For a bibliography of E.S. Drower's work on the Mandean texts see E.M. Yamauchi, *Gnostic Ethics and Mandaean Origins* (Cambridge: Harvard University Press and London: Oxford University Press, 1970), pp. 95–96. For the question of origins see in particular E.S. Drower's fascinating study, *The Mandeans of Iraq and Iran: Their Cults, Customs, Magic Legends and Folklore* (Oxford: Clarendon Press, 1937, and Leiden: E.J. Brill, 1962), esp. pp. 1–16.

25. Yamauchi, *Ethics*, esp. pp. 85–89.

26. *Ibid.*, pp. 83–85. *Cf. The Baptism of Hibil-Ziwa*, in the edition of E.S. Drower, *The Haran Gawaita and The Baptism of Hibil-Ziwa* (Studi e Testi 176, Vatican City: Biblioteca Apostolica Vaticana, 1953), pp. 31–32.

27. See further *IFG*, pp. 129–30; Schnackenburg 1, pp. 138–43. For an English translation of the Mandean texts see W. Foerster (ed.), *Gnosis*, ed. R.McL. Wilson, vol. 2 (Oxford: Clarendon Press, 1974), pp. 148–317.

Hermetic literature

Another link between John and Hellenistic religion has been sought and found in the *Hermetica*. The *Corpus Hermeticum* is a collection of writings produced in Egypt (probably), mostly during the second and third centuries AD; although the occasional tractate may date from the first century. These writings, gnostic in character, deal with religious subjects from a philosophical point of view, the philosophy in question being a mixture of Platonic and Stoic thought. They take the form of dialogues between Hermes (Trismegistus)[28] and his sons, and include discussions about the means of salvation, through the knowledge of God, and the ethical human demands involved in this. The various books, which appeared originally in Greek, breathe an atmosphere of pantheism and gnosticism.[29]

Study of the Hermetic literature has shown that there are possible affinities between these documents and the Fourth Gospel, especially in the dualist treatises I (*Poimandres*) and XIII (*De Regeneratione*).[30] Once again, there are obvious resemblances in language and thought. The ideas of light and life (associated), truth, knowledge and 'sight' are present in both. *Poimandres* contains a concept of the *logos* which shares in creation, and links together the spiritual and material realms.[31] Treatise XIII, as its title suggests, concerns the new birth of the initiate who receives knowledge and therefore redemption through revelation; as a result, that person becomes a child of God and is even 'deified'.[32]

In view of the date of the Hermetic corpus, it is impossible for John to have been dependent on this literature as it stands. But it is still possible for the ideas which were eventually incorporated into the written form of the *Hermetica* to have been in circulation in the Mediterranean world at a much earlier date, and to have influenced the writing of the Fourth Gospel. To establish this, however, it would be necessary to demonstrate a real community of thought between John and the Hermetic corpus; and it is not easy to do this. It is in any case difficult to apply the terms 'gnostic' and 'dualist' to the Fourth Gospel without considerable qualification. But apart from this, close examination reveals once more that the Johannine theology of salvation involves terms and ideas which may appear superficially to resemble those used in the cosmogony and soteriology of the

28.   He was a legendary sage of ancient Egypt, deified posthumously as Hermes (that is, the god Thoth); hence the name of the corpus.

29.   See the standard edition of the *Hermetica* in A.D. Nock and A.-J. Festugière, *Corpus Hermeticum*, 4 vols. (Paris: L'Association Guillaume Budé, 1945–54).

30.   Note the parallels listed in *IFG*, pp. 34–35 (the first *libellus*), 50–51 (the thirteenth). See the whole section on the *Hermetica* in *IFG*, pp. 10–53.

31.   *Cf. Poimandres* i.5–6. In i.6 the actual phrase, Λόγος υἱὸς θεοῦ ('Word, son of [a] god') appears. See further C.H. Dodd, *The Bible and the Greeks* (London: Hodder and Stoughton, 1935), pp. 99–209.

32.   *Cf. De Regeneratione* xiii.2, 10.

Hermetica, but in the end differ markedly from them. Thus the *logos* of the *Poimandres*, while sharing with John 1 a background in Genesis 1, has less to do with the revelation of God than with a cosmic *logos*, answering to that contained in the human soul.[33] Similarly, the ideas of regeneration present in the thirteenth *libellus* of the corpus do not coincide with the Johannine view of revelation and eternal life. For John the way of rebirth is not by a gnostic vision, but by 'seeing' (= believing) that Jesus of Nazareth is the Christ (John 20:31) and receiving life through his name. Again, while the language of John would at times have appealed to Greek readers nurtured in a background similar to that of the *Hermetica*, there are important variations between the two writings in their terminology. John, perhaps deliberately, omits the term γνῶσις ('knowledge') altogether; and several typically Hellenistic ideas are present in the Hermetic treatises which do not appear in the Fourth Gospel.[34]

The result of investigations such as these has led C.H. Dodd to suggest that the Hermetic writings 'represent a type of religious thought akin to one side of Johannine thought, without any substantial borrowing on one side or the other'.[35] Dodd believes that there was no direct Christian influence on the *Hermetica*,[36] but still regards this literature as valuable for interpreting John.[37] However, there are (as Dodd himself admits)[38] striking contrasts between the Fourth Gospel and the Hermetic corpus in their outlook and theology. To go no further, one is Christian and the other pagan-gnostic. At the same time, the points of contact appear so superficial that any real indebtedness on John's part to Hermetic thought must be ruled out.

33. *Cf. Poimandres* i.6–32. See Schnackenburg 1, p. 137.

34. Schnackenburg, 1, p. 138, lists (ἀθανασία ('immortality'); αἴσθησις ('insight'); δημιουργέω ('create'); εἰκών ('image'); ἰδέα ('appearance'); and νοῦς ('mind'). All but the third and fifth of these terms are in fact used elsewhere in the New Testament; although not, of course, in a typically Hellenistic way. John's omission of the key term γνῶσις ('knowledge') need not necessarily mean that he was consciously detaching his ideas from those of Greek gnosticism; after all, he still uses the verb γινώσκειν ('to know'). It might just as readily reflect the influence on Johannine Greek of the Semitic tendency to use verbs wherever possible in place of the cognate noun (*cf.* the frequent use of the verb πιστεύειν ['to believe'], against the absence of πίστις ['faith'] in the Fourth Gospel). But for John rebirth is still personal and moral, rather than purely intellectual, and involves commitment to Jesus as the Christ (*cf.* John 3:16–18, *et al.*). As such, it seems to represent a different world from the gnostic.

35. *IFG*, p. 53.

36. *Ibid.*, pp. 33, 52–53; against F.-M. Braun, 'Hermétisme et Johannisme', *RevT* 55 (1955), pp. 22–42; 259–99; also F.-M. Braun, *Jean le théologien: les grandes traditions d'Israël et l'accord des écritures selon le quatrième évangile* (Paris: J. Gabalda, 1964), pp. 253–300 (= *JT*).

37. *IFG*, p. 53.

38. *Ibid.*

Gnosticism
The literature we have so far surveyed in order to discover the extent of possible Hellenistic influence on John's background (the Mandean texts and the *Corpus Hermeticum*) has prompted the use of the term 'gnostic' to describe the character of its world of ideas. We must now come closer to the subject of gnosticism in relation to the Fourth Gospel, and define its meaning.

The term 'gnosticism' is used to describe a wide range of religious movements which, during the first Christian centuries, sought to provide an answer to the basic problem of people and the world by concentrating on salvation through a secret *gnosis*, or 'knowledge'. Gnosticism is in fact more a climate of thought than a religious system; and whereas the early fathers saw gnostic movements solely as heretical corruptions of Christianity, modern scholarship views gnosticism as a religious and philosophical outlook which may be completely independent of Christianity. It is true to say, however, that not all scholars agree about the origins of gnosticism (whether its sources are pre-Christian, and indeed Jewish, as well as Christian), or even about its precise definition. For this very reason it is important to be flexible in any approach to this subject; and even if, for the sake of convenience, we shall here consider gnosticism in connection with possible Hellenistic influences on the Fourth Gospel, this does not imply that gnosticism is to be regarded as a purely Greek phenomenon.

The flowering of Christian gnosticism took place during the second century AD, in the sophisticated and developed systems of such thinkers as Basilides and Valentinus. Its ideas were known to us once solely from the writings of the early church fathers, who opposed gnostic teaching. But the discovery at Chenoboskion of the Nag Hammadi library has now made it possible to become acquainted with second-century gnosticism directly, especially from such important documents as *The Gospel of Truth*[39] and *The Gospel according to Thomas*.[40] We are therefore in a better position than ever to compare the thought of the gnostics with that of John.

Christian gnosticism in its developed form is entirely intellectual and speculative. Using mythical ideas which drew on a (mostly Greek) philosophical background, it was an attempt to express the Christian gospel in terms which would be appreciated by those who were nurtured in a Hellenistic environment. A cursory glance at *The Gospel of Truth* is sufficient, however, to show how far gnostic Christianity travelled eventually from its apostolic and New Testament origins.

39.   See K. Grobel (ed.), *The Gospel of Truth: A Valentinian Meditation on the Gospel* (London: A. and C. Black, 1960).

40.   See A. Guillaumont *et al.* (ed.), *The Gospel According to Thomas: The Coptic Text Established and Translated* (Leiden: E.J. Brill and London: Collins, 1959).

According to A.D. Nock, in his valuable article on this subject,[41] gnosticism has three characteristics which were all to be found in the world in which it took its rise: a preoccupation with the problem of evil, a sense of alienation from the human environment, and a desire for special knowledge. We can see these in any of the gnostic systems.

Basic to the outlook of the gnostics was a dualistic view of the world, in which the upper world of spirit or mind contrasted with the lower world of evil matter. Creation took place when God wound himself down through a series of intermediary creators (*demiurges*), sometimes as many as 365 (one for each day of the year). The gnostic salvation myth begins with the pre-existent figure of the good Original Man (*Urmensch*), who was divided into small particles of light which, as human souls, descended into an evil world. Deliverance from material existence was possible, however, because a heavenly redeemer brought from the upper world a *gnosis* which could be acquired by the initiant through revelation. Those who accepted this could be released from bondage, and could then wind themselves up to the heavenly sphere of light by a series of mediators.[42]

This simplified summary fails to do justice to the complexity of the gnostic systems in their varied and final forms. The point in drawing attention here to the broad outlines of this kind of thinking is to show how easy it was for the presentation of the Christian gospel, with its superficially similar religious content, to be influenced by gnosticism, especially when that gospel was cradled in a Hellenistic environment. But long before this, gnostic antecedents of an equivalent philosophical character existed which might have influenced the expression of apostolic Christianity, and even the message of Jesus himself. These earlier forms of gnostic thought, which perhaps also characterised Judaism and Qumran, have been labelled 'pre-gnosticism'.[43] We know from parts of the New Testament outside John's Gospel that gnosticising tendencies[44] of some kind were a feature of primitive Christianity. Paul was forced to resist such inclinations in Corinth, Colossae and

41. A.D. Nock, 'Gnosticism', in Z. Stuart (ed.), *Arthur Darby Nock: Essays on Religion and the Ancient World*, vol. 2 (Oxford: Clarendon Press, 1972), pp. 940–59 (see 940–42).

42. See further Brown 1, p. liv; also S.S. Smalley, *Thunder and Love: John's Revelation and John's Community* (Milton Keynes: Nelson Word, 1994), pp. 84–86.

43. So B. Reicke, 'Traces of Gnosticism in the Dead Sea Scrolls?', *NTS* 1 (1954–55), pp. 137–41 (esp. 141).

44. In view of the confusion surrounding the use of the term 'gnosticism', and its varied applications, it is perhaps better to use a non-pejorative term of this kind when discussing the relation between such tendencies and the literature of the New Testament. *Cf.* the cautionary essay by J. Munck, 'The New Testament and Gnosticism', in W. Klassen and G.F. Snyder (ed.), *Current Issues in New Testament Interpretation: Essays in Honor of Otto A. Piper* (London: SCM Press, 1962), pp. 224–38; see also *StudT* 15 (1961), pp. 181–95.

probably Ephesus.[45] The community behind the Letters of John seems to have been beset by problems of heterodoxy with both Jewish and Hellenistic antecedents; but those certainly included a docetic understanding of the person of Christ, gnosticising in character.[46] Perhaps the Fourth Gospel itself, assuming that it was not influenced by later forms of Christian gnosticism, was also subject to tendencies of this kind.[47] We shall now consider that possibility.

Bultmann's view

The so-called 'history of religions' school of biblical scholarship, beginning with Richard Reitzenstein[48] and Wilhelm Bousset,[49] and followed by Rudolf Bultmann[50] and his pupils, favours the view that 'pre-gnosticism' was an eclectic tradition of thought which infiltrated Judaism and Hellenistic paganism, as well as Christianity, from the orient (perhaps from Iranian or Babylonian mythology). If the mystery religions provided one way of salvation for the occupants of the

45. *Cf.* 1 Cor. 1:22–23; 8:11–12; Col. 1:16, 19–20; 2:1–3, 8; Eph. 3:3–4, 4, 19. For a study of this point with reference to the writing of Paul's Corinthian correspondence see W. Schmithals, *Gnosticism in Corinth: An Investigation of the Letters to the Corinthians* (New York and Nashville: Abingdon, 1971). The suggestion that gnosticising tendencies were current in the New Testament period, and were resisted by the New Testament authors, is not modern. One early writer to take this view was the seventeenth-century English divine, Henry Hammond, in an essay entitled 'De Antichristo'. See H. Hammond, *Dissertationes Quatuor* (London: J. Flesher, 1651), pp. 1–51. He regarded the gnostics as opponents of Christ who were referred to as such in all parts of the New Testament, especially (within the Johannine corpus) 1 John and the Apocalypse. For the view that gnosticising tendencies were *not* a problem for those addressed in Colossians see M.D. Hooker, 'Were there False Teachers in Colossae?', in B. Lindars and S.S. Smalley (ed.), *Christ and Spirit in the New Testament: Studies in Honour of Charles Francis Digby Moule* (Cambridge: Cambridge University Press, 1973), pp. 315–31.

46. See 1 John 4:1–3; 2 John 7. *Cf.* H. Hammond, *A Paraphrase and Annotations upon all the Books of the New Testament: Briefly Explaining all the Difficult Places Thereof*, 5th edn. (London: J. Maycock and M. Flesher, 1681), pp. 822–41. See also J.L. Houlden, *A Commentary on the Johannine Epistles*, BNTC (London: A. and C. Black and New York: Harper and Row, 1973), pp. 1–22. For the view that 1 John was written in the light of more than one heretically-inclined christological understanding see S.S. Smalley, *1,2,3 John*, WBC 51 (Waco: Word Books, 1984), pp. xxiii–xxxii.

47. Hammond, *Paraphrase*, does not appear to find gnosticism widely present or attacked in John's Gospel; but see his comment (pp. 323–24) on John 19:35.

48. See notes 11 and 13.

49. See his seminal work: W. Bousset, *Die Hauptprobleme der Gnosis*, FRLANT 10 (Göttingen: Vandenhoeck & Ruprecht, 1907).

50. See esp. R. Bultmann, *Primitive Christianity in its Contemporary Setting* (London and New York: Thames and Hudson, 1956), pp. 162–71; also R. Bultmann, *Gnosis* (London: A. and C. Black, 1952). See further Bultmann, pp. 7–9; also W.G. Kümmel, *The New Testament: The History of the Investigation of its Problems*, NTL (London: SCM Press, 1973), pp. 342–62, esp. 350–54.

Mediterranean world at the turn of the first century AD, then gnosticism provided the other.[51]

According to Bultmann, the thought of John was shaped by oriental gnosticism in this primitive form, rather than being derived from Hellenistic Judaism as represented by Philo,[52] or Hellenistic paganism as delineated by the *Hermetica*. The *gnosis* to which (in Bultmann's view) John was indebted, as distinct from the more developed, Hellenised *gnosis* already mentioned, manifests among other things a dualism which is restrained. This may have been the result of association with Judaism, and the Old Testament doctrine of God's ultimate sovereignty over creation and the powers of evil.[53]

Bultmann believes that the fourth evangelist was himself a one-time gnostic, concerned to restate the kerygma in gnostic categories which had been Christianised.[54] For the Gospel discourses, it is maintained therefore, John used a source which was gnostic in tendency. (We shall return to this point in more detail, when in chapter 5 we consider the sources of the Johannine discourses.)[55] In the formation of the discourse material, Bultmann sees the fourth evangelist as dependent above all on the 'redeemer myth', a form of which has already been described. John, he believes, attached the myth of a heavenly redeemer to the historical person of Jesus, who existed before time (John 1:1–2), became incarnate (1:14) as the light of the world (8:12), and returned in glory to the Father (13:1, 31–32) to become the way to him (14:6).[56]

Support for this reconstructed gnosticism in John is found by Bultmann from the Mandean literature already discussed, and also from the *Odes of Solomon*, a second-century collection of 42 songs which contain echoes of the Fourth Gospel in their thought and language. The *Odes* were either Jewish in origin and then revised by Christians,[57] or of

51. But see R.McL. Wilson, *The Gnostic Problem: A Study of the Relations between Hellenistic Judaism and the Gnostic Heresy* (London: A.R. Mowbray, 1958), p. 225, who claims that the gnostic redeemer figure is merely a 'radical interpretation of the Christian Jesus in terms of current belief'. See also E.M. Yamauchi, *Pre-Christian Gnosticism: A Survey of the Proposed Evidence* (London: Tyndale Press, 1973), and the literature cited below. See further Fuller, *New Testament in Current Study*, pp. 132–33.

52. See further on Philo below, pp. 61–64.

53. *Cf.* Brown 1, p. liv.

54. Similarly F.C. Grant, *The Gospels: Their Origin and Their Growth* (London: Faber and Faber, 1957), pp. 154–79 esp. 159–60.

55. See below pp. 108–112.

56. See Bultmann, pp. 19–83 (on the prologue), *et al.* Bultmann also sees the *differences* between gnostic and Johannine theology, however (p. 9). He maintains that John's dualism varies, for example, in that it is non-cosmic; so that at this point the fourth evangelist becomes anti-gnostic in his presentation of the redeemer myth.

57. This suggestion is made more likely when the *Odes* are compared with the *Hodayoth* (the thanksgiving hymns) from Qumran. See Schnackenburg 1, pp. 143–44. See also J. Carmignac, 'Les affinités qumraniennes de la onzième Ode de Salomon', *RQ* 3 (1961–62), pp. 71–102.

Jewish-Christian derivation in the first place. They are generally regarded as gnostic in character,[58] including once more the mythological
concept of a heavenly redeemer figure. The relation, if any, between the
Odes and John is still the subject of considerable debate;[59] but if there is
dependence at all, it is arguable that the *Odes* are influenced by the
Fourth Gospel rather than the reverse.[60]

The view of John's background taken by Rudolf Bultmann is in fact
open to question at several points. In the first place, as we have discovered already when comparing John with the Mandean and Hermetic
literature, it is difficult to regard John as 'gnostic' in any real sense. His
basic, Christian outlook differs from the mythical, philosophical approach of gnosticism and its earlier (oriental or other) manifestations.
The fourth evangelist not only has a real concern for the historical basis
of salvation; he also has what gnosticism lacks: a theology of salvation
which involves deliverance from sin by means of a cross.[61] For John,
salvation does not mean a rescue from ignorance achieved by secretly
imparted knowledge; it means the revelation and glorification of Jesus,
the Christ and the one mediator, whose saving work is received by faith.[62]
The Johannine soteriology is historical and christocentric; that of the
gnostics is mythical and speculative. His dualism is ethical; theirs, even
in modified versions, substantial. However many parallels may be drawn
between John's Gospel and the supposed gnosticising tendencies of his
day, therefore, it cannot be maintained that John was deeply influenced
by gnostic thought-forms, or indebted to them for his theology. The two
are literally worlds apart. At most it might be argued that John wrote
with gnostic tendencies in mind, in order to oppose them; although, as
we shall see, even this is questionable.[63]

The second doubt which can be expressed in connection with Bultmann's position arises from the first. It is that the Fourth Gospel itself
refuses to settle into a consistently gnostic mould. The evangelist's
sacramental theology, for example, not to mention his distinctive escha-

58. On the other side see J. Daniélou, art. 'Odes de Salomon', in *DB*(S) 6 (1960) cols.
677–84; see also J.H. Charlesworth, 'The Odes of Solomon – not Gnostic', *CBQ* 31 (1969),
pp. 357–69.

59. *Cf.* F.-M. Braun, *Jean le théologien et son évangile dans l'église ancienne* (Paris: J.
Gabalda, 1959), pp. 224–51. For the relation between the *Odes* and the prologue to the
Fourth Gospel see Brown 1, p. 21 (the *Odes* are possibly dependent on John).

60. *Cf.* Schnackenburg 1, p. 145. For a definitive edition of the *Odes* see J.H.
Charlesworth (ed.), *The Odes of Solomon* (Oxford: Clarendon Press, 1973). For a study
which argues that the *Odes* and John's Gospel derive from the same religious environment,
without interdependence, see J.H. Charlesworth and R.A. Culpepper, 'The Odes of
Solomon and the Gospel of John', *CBQ* 35 (1973), pp. 298–322.

61. John 12:31–36, *et al.*

62. John 20:31.

63. See below, pp. 169–72. R.McL. Wilson, *Gnosis*, also questions the gnostic character of John. *Cf.* J.M. Lieu, 'Gnosticism and the Gospel of John', *ExpT* 90 (1978–79), pp.

tology, cannot be regarded as in any sense gnostic.[64] In both cases John's outlook arises from the fact that he regards history, since the moment of the incarnation, as invaded by eternity; so that the material can now *express* the spiritual. When the fourth evangelist, then, is describing bread as mediating life,[65] or time as conveying judgment,[66] he is speaking unashamedly as a Christian for whom the Word has become flesh. A true gnostic, who viewed material things as evil, could never do this. Small wonder, then, that Bultmann finds considerable difficulty when he tries to interpret John in uniformly gnostic terms.[67] Even the early gnostics themselves found this a problem.[68]

Thirdly, our brief examination of the Mandean literature and the *Odes of Solomon*, both of which are used by Bultmann as further evidence for a pre-Christian gnosticism which may have influenced the background of John's Gospel, has shown that in neither case is it clear that John could have been dependent on these texts or the thought they embody. On the contrary, it is on balance more likely that they themselves looked back to the Fourth Gospel.

Finally, and perhaps most damagingly of all to Bultmann's thesis, there is no evidence to suggest that the eclectic elements which were fused in the developed Christian gnosticism of the second century AD, and indeed produced the later gnostic systems by this very amalgamation, were joined together at the start of the first century in such a way that they could have provided a single pattern of pre-gnostic thought (a redeemer myth, indeed) to shape John's outlook. The gnostic myth in its final form is a synthesis of ideas from different sources and *milieux*; and the discovery of one idea at a primitive stage need not imply familiarity with the others. Without such a coming together of intellectual notions at an early date, however, we do not have a pre-Christian or even Christian gnosis on which the Fourth Gospel could draw. A.D. Nock maintains that the documents discovered at Nag Hammadi confirm the impression we already have from the Fathers that gnosticism was regarded in the second century as 'a Christian heresy with roots in speculative thought'.[69] But the shaping of what R.E. Brown calls 'proto-gnostic attitudes and elements'[70] into a body of thought took

---

64. *Cf.* O. Cullmann, *Early Christian Worship*, SBT (London: SCM Press, 1953), pp. 37–119, which is a plea for a sacramental interpretation of John's thought in the strict sense. But see S.S. Smalley, 'Liturgy and Sacrament in the Fourth Gospel', *EQ* 29 (1957), pp. 159–70. *Cf.* also A. Corell, *Consummatum Est: Eschatology and Church in the Gospel of St John* (London: SPCK, 1958), esp. pp. 44–112. See further below, pp. 232–38.

65. John 6:51.

66. John 3:18–19.

67. *Cf.* Neill and Wright, *Interpretation*, pp. 331–33.

68. *Cf.* M.F. Wiles, *The Spiritual Gospel: The Interpretation of the Fourth Gospel in the Early Church* (Cambridge: Cambridge University Press, 1960), p. 107.

69. Nock, 'Gnosticism', p. 956.

70. Brown 1, p. lv.

place later rather than earlier; and the evidence which survives strongly suggests that the impetus was provided by the claims made for Jesus Christ himself.[71]

Bultmann's ideas about a setting for John, then, cannot be accepted without question; for there is insufficient evidence to claim that the fourth evangelist wrote against a background of gnostic-type thought, even if he used terms and ideas which appealed, and would appeal increasingly, to a Greek audience.[72]

As it happens, the shadow of Bultmann still looms large. The work of Ernst Käsemann on the Fourth Gospel is in many ways allied to Bultmann's position. In *The Testament of Jesus*,[73] Käsemann maintains that the christology of John is docetic and therefore, in that respect, heretical.[74] The incarnation for the fourth evangelist, he believes, is apparent rather than real, and does not involve total entry into human existence (p. 65). As a result, the origin of John's Gospel is to be traced, in Käsemann's view, to an independent (perhaps Syrian) community where the Christian tradition had 'to some extent run wild' (p. 36). John therefore writes a document which is to prepare the way for a gnostic proclamation of the gospel, 'or else already stands under its influence', in the setting of a conventicle with gnosticising tendencies (p. 73).

The position of Käsemann is open to as many questions as that of Bultmann. First, Käsemann's view that John's Gospel was removed from the mainstream of early catholicism means that he gives to John a late date, without deciding what exactly is meant by 'gnosticism' at that time, or whether John could have been influenced by it. Secondly, this writer does not take seriously the possibility of an independent and historical Johannine tradition beneath the Fourth Gospel, which, while interpreted theologically, could preserve a reliable basic account of the

71. C. Colpe, 'Mandäer' in *RGG* 4 (1960) cols. 709–712, doubts if the 'redeemer myth' we have been discussing was pre-Christian. See also Schnackenburg 1, pp. 543–57 (excursus 6, on 'The Gnostic Myth of the Redeemer and the Johannine Christology').

72. Although the primitive gnosticism which influenced John, according to Bultmann, ultimately derived (in his view) from an oriental setting, its Hellenistic affinities would be apparent. However, Bultmann himself (pp. 9–12) believes that John wrote – at the turn of the first century AD – to convince *Syrian* adherents of gnostic circles as to the truth of the gospel. *Cf.* further C.K. Barrett, *The Gospel of John and Judaism* (London: SPCK, 1975), p. 7. Barrett draws attention to the circularity of Bultmann's position, which uses John's Gospel to reconstruct its gnostic background, and then uses this *gnosis* (supposedly reworked by the evangelist) to explain the Gospel. For a general assessment of Bultmann's interpretation of John's Gospel see D.A. Carson, *The Gospel According to John* (Leicester: Inter-Varsity Press and Grand Rapids: Eerdmans, 1991), pp. 31–33.

73. E. Käsemann, *The Testament of Jesus: A Study of the Gospel of John in the Light of Chapter 17*, NTL (London: SCM Press and Philadelphia: Fortress Press, 1968).

74. It is doubtful, however, whether the terms 'orthodoxy' and 'heresy' can be applied to the teaching of John's Gospel at the time when it was written; *cf.* Smalley, 'Diversity', pp. 276–92.

message of Jesus. Thirdly, Käsemann's study draws conclusions about the whole of the Fourth Gospel on the basis of what may be regarded as its later strands: notably the prologue, and the prayer of Jesus in John 17. This side-steps the issue of the composition and edition of the Fourth Gospel, which we shall be considering later.[75] Finally, Käsemann's version of John's christology is decidedly unbalanced. While elements in the Johannine portrait of Jesus are capable of a docetic interpretation if taken by themselves, the total effect can scarcely be regarded as one of 'divinity without humanity'. With the inescapably *human* elements in John's christology every examination candidate is familiar.[76]

Once again, therefore, we must conclude that the attempt to brand the fourth evangelist and his tradition as 'gnostic' is unfounded.[77]

Conclusions

Nothing we have examined so far under the heading of 'gnosticism' has forced us to the conclusion that ideas of this kind – pre-gnostic or gnostic, oriental or Hellenistic – exercised any deep influence on the background to the Fourth Gospel. The same may be said about the intellectual content of the Mandean and Hermetic literature, and about the mystery religions. Before we leave the subject of a possible Greek religious background for John, however, we must examine one further likely influence from Hellenistic *Judaism*. That is Philo.[78]

Philo

The eclectic thought of the Jewish writer Philo of Alexandria (*c.* 20 BC–*c.* AD 50) combined elements from both Judaism and current philosophical systems: notably Platonism and Stoicism. Philo's work was an attempt to express his understanding of Judaism in Hellenistic categories, and shows how deeply he was influenced by the piety of the Old Testament, as well as the religious outlook of the Greek thinkers.[79]

75. See below, chapter 5, and pp.155–57.

76. See the appreciative critique of Käsemann's book by G. Bornkamm, 'Zur Interpretation des Johannes-Evangeliums: Eine Auseinandersetzung mit Ernst Käsemanns Schrift "Jesu letzter Wille nach Johannes 17" ', *EvT* 28 (1968), pp. 8–25. Note also S.S. Smalley, 'The Testament of Jesus: Another Look', *SE* 6 (1973), pp. 495–501 .

77. See also below, pp. 169–72. For gnosticism in general see further Foerster, *Gnosis*, esp. vol. 1; also P. Perkins, *Gnosticism and the New Testament* (Minneapolis: Fortress Press, 1993). For gnosticism in relation to John see further *IFG*, pp. 97–114, esp. 112-14; Perkins, *Gnosticism*, pp. 109–142.

78. 'Hellenistic Judaism' is a useful description of the Jewish-Greek synthesis typical of the Mediterranean world in the first century AD; but always it leaves open the question of level, and the measure of the Jewish and Greek elements combined.

79. *IFG*, pp. 60–61. See the whole chapter on Philo in *IFG*, pp. 54–73. Dodd maintains that Philo was able to reconcile these two religious ways, the Jewish and the Greek, up to a point; but he believes that 'in the end they remain unassimilated' (p. 61).

Affinities between this writer and John are easy to suggest. For both, the knowledge of God is our chief end. As with the Hermetists, to know God is to be a child of God;[80] although for Philo rebirth does not mean, as in the *Hermetica*, divinisation. The knowledge of God, the search for reality and immortality, is represented by Philo in Platonic terms as the passage from the visible and changing world of matter to the invisible and real world of absolute being. At one moment this is achieved by mystical awareness;[81] at another, by faith of which Abraham is the leading exemplar.[82]

In addition to Platonist doctrine of this kind, Philo draws on the Stoic concept of the *logos*. Although his view of this is complex, it seems clear that for Philo the *logos* is the means of the world's creation and ordering, and also the link between the world and God. The *logos* is equated with the heavenly (true) Man, and also with the real person indwelling each human soul. Humanity thus possesses kinship with the universal *logos*, and can rise by communion with it to a knowledge of God.[83]

Apparent links between Philo and John's Gospel have already begun to emerge. The fourth evangelist also presents eternal life as something which derives from the knowledge of God (John 17:3); and, like Philo, he uses a doctrine of the *Logos* to express his theology of salvation (1:1–14). Furthermore, John employs terms and concepts (such as (ἀληθινός, 'true') in a way that is apparently Philonic.[84] But at the same time there are differences, both in the absence from John of leading concepts belonging to normative Hellenistic Judaism,[85] and also in the way John uses ideas which he appears to have in common with Philo. For example, both writers are indebted for their idea of the *Logos* (in one direction, at least) to the figure of Σοφία ('Wisdom') in the Wisdom literature of Judaism,[86] as well as to the Old Testament in

80. *De conf* 145.
81. *De praem* 45.
82. *De migr* 1–6.
83. *De spec leg* 4.14.
84. *Cf.* John 8:40; 14:6, *et al.* and Philo, *Quod det* 22 (using τοῦ πρὸς ἀλήθειαν ἄνθρωπος, '[the name] for the real person').
85. Schnackenburg 1, p. 125, lists ἀθανασία ('immortality'), ἀρετή ('excellence'), ἀφθαρσία ('incorruption'), εἰκών ('image'), εὐδαιμονία ('prosperity') and εὐσέβεια ('piety').
86. *Cf.* Prov. 8:22–31; Sirach 24. In the Wisdom figure of Jewish thought, we can in fact discover the assimilation of Judaism and Hellenism long before Philo. Perhaps deliberately, John avoids the use of the actual term σοφία ('wisdom') in his Gospel, just as he avoids employing the noun γνῶσις ('knowledge'). But see B. Witherington, III, *John's Wisdom: A Commentary on the Fourth Gospel* (Cambridge: The Lutterworth Press and Louisville: Westminster John Knox Press, 1995) (= Witherington), who claims that the fourth evangelist's thought (in and beyond the prologue [John 1]) was deeply affected by Jewish Wisdom literature. Hence the title of this volume. For Witherington's comments on John's *Logos* theology see *ibid.*, esp. pp. 47–59.

general.[87] But the Johannine theology of the Word of God is anchored in scripture and in history in a way that Philo's philosophical interpretation ultimately could never be. Similarly, the use of categories in the Fourth Gospel such as 'true' or 'truth' — as in the vine imagery of John 15:1 — involves a metaphorical rather than, as in Philo, an allegorical process of thought.

Philo was much given to allegorical exegesis, by means of which he was able to bring the narratives of the Pentateuch into line with his homiletic and evangelistic purposes. Thus, Law and *logos* for Philo were closely associated. This could also be regarded as a Johannine approach, until it is recalled that John rarely allegorises the Old Testament. Instead, he uses images and explanations to restate and reapply Old Testament themes in their Christian setting.[88]

To what extent, then, may it be said that the fourth evangelist is dependent on Hellenistic Judaism as represented by Philo? C.H. Dodd thinks that there is a 'remarkable resemblance' between the range of ideas in Philo and in the Fourth Gospel,[89] despite differences which are evident at the same time: the *Logos* for John becomes incarnate, for example, while in Philo the *logos* remains impersonal. Kingsley Barrett is also positive in his view of John's alignment with Philonic thought.[90]

Can we be so sure? Certain factors seem to argue in the other direction. (i) We do not know whether Philo was known and read in first-century Palestine. (ii) John never shows literary dependence on Philo. (iii) If there is common ground between these writers, it is likely to be the result of their mutual indebtedness to a Jewish background. In any case, probably neither John nor Philo was the first to reflect on the *Logos* in a way that brought together both a Jewish and a Greek understanding of this concept. Although we now have no literary evidence of it, both writers may well represent the culmination of a long history of such thought.[91] (iv) As we have seen, terms and ideas which have Hellenistic associations and are shared by Philo and John are used very differently in both, and presuppose radically different starting-points. The fourth evangelist's approach is Christian and historical, whereas Philo's is Jewish and philosophical. (v) The two writers stand far apart also in method. Philo's

---

87. *Cf. De opific* 26–71 and John 1:1–18, both running back to Gen. 1.

88. See below, pp. 68–70. Dodd, *IFG*, pp. 55–58, sees an affinity between John and Philo not in the use of allegory as such, but in their common attraction to symbolism. He points to the symbols of the divine as light (John 1:9 and *De migr* 40), the fountain of water (John 4:10, 14 and *De fuga* 197–98), and the shepherd (John 10:1–18 and *De agric* 50–53). *Cf.* Psa. 27:1; Jer. 2:13; Ezek. 34:15. However, once more there are limitations to these parallels, arising from the non-philosophical ethos of John's theology.

89. *IFG*, p. 73.

90. Barrett, pp. 40–41.

91. So R. McL. Wilson, 'Philo and the Fourth Gospel', *ExpT* 65 (1953–54), pp. 47–49, esp. 47–48.

insistent allegorising differs, as we shall see, from the interpretation of Old Testament scripture present in the Fourth Gospel. We may therefore conclude that it is doubtful whether Philo and John do more than share a common Jewish-Hellenistic background. There are no real reasons for supposing on any count that John was influenced by Philo himself, or by the intellectual ethos which Philo represents.[92]

Conclusions

Consideration of a possible Greek background for the fourth evangelist and his tradition has led us to the conclusion that neither seems to be influenced by Hellenism beyond that which belonged to normative Judaism at the time; and this mixture of Judaism and Hellenism can be taken for granted, in view of the classical influences to which Palestine had been subjected for many years preceding the New Testament era. In this case, the Hellenistic affinities in John's Gospel, of which we have taken note along the way, may be said to represent an appeal to any Greek or Jewish-Greek readers of the Fourth Gospel in its final form, rather than indicating a primary indebtedness to Hellenism on the part of John or his tradition.

Support for this conclusion, in a positive direction, has been supplied by the more recent investigations into possible Jewish influences on John's background of which mention has already been made. Our consideration of Hellenistic Judaism as exemplified by Philo has provided a bridge to this subject, which we shall now examine in more detail.[93]

(b) Jewish influence

Earlier in the twentieth century, as we have already seen, the associations between the Fourth Gospel and Judaism were reassessed, and the belief that John derived from a purely Hellenistic ethos was challenged. The position represented by Pfleiderer, for example, was reversed in the work of Schlatter and Burney.[94]

92. On Philo and John see further A.W. Argyle, 'Philo and the Fourth Gospel', *ExpT* 63 (1951–52), pp. 385–86 (the resemblances are not coincidental); also *JT*, pp. 296–98. On Philo generally see A.D. Nock, 'Philo and Hellenistic Philosophy', in Stewart (ed.), *Nock* 2, pp. 559–65; also P. Borgen, 'Philo of Alexandria' in M.E. Stone (ed.), *Jewish Writings of the Second Temple Period* (Assen: Van Gorcum and Philadelphia: Fortress Press, 1984), pp. 233–82.

93. For the possible Greek background to John see further A.D. Nock, 'Early Gentile Christianity and its Hellenistic Background' in Stewart (ed.), *Nock*, 1, pp. 49–133 (esp. Part 1). But see also P. Borgen, 'The Gospel of John and Hellenism: Some Observations' in Culpepper and Black (ed.), *Exploring John*, pp. 98–123, esp. 116 ('it is difficult to identify direct Hellenistic influence on John from outside of Judaism').

94. See above, pp. 5–6.

The discovery of the Dead Sea Scrolls, combined with evidence from archaeology, and the likelihood suggested by literary criticism that John's tradition is probably independent of the synoptic and therefore historically valuable, has reopened this question. Increasingly it is being suggested that the fundamental background to John's tradition and thought is Palestinian and Jewish, rather than Asian and Hellenistic. Palestinian Judaism at the time of Jesus was diverse;[95] and, as Raymond Brown points out, this may account for some of the diversity in John's own thought.[96] We shall now consider five features belonging to the Fourth Gospel which reflect this variety, and may support the view that John's background is more Jewish than Greek.

The slant of the Gospel

J.B. Lightfoot, writing on the evidence for the authenticity and genuineness of St John's Gospel, declared it as his belief that the writer of the Gospel was a Hebrew and probably a contemporary. He argued this from the knowledge which the fourth evangelist shows of the Jewish language, of Jewish ideas and traditions, and of the external facts of the Jewish people. Lightfoot's conclusion was that, with the possible exception of the Apocalypse, St John is 'the most Hebraic book in the New Testament'.[97]

This is evident at once from the Jewish slant of the Fourth Gospel, quite apart from its other Jewish features which we shall study in due course. John Robinson, taking up Lightfoot's point, has reminded us that the tone of this Gospel is not anti-Semitic, in spite of the fact that 'the Jews' consistently appear in John as the enemies of Jesus and as responsible for his death.[98] On the contrary, the Fourth Gospel, in Robinson's opinion, 'reveals an unremitting concentration on Judaism'.[99] Jesus himself, for example, is presented as a Jew, rejected by his own people when he came to them.[100] Moreover, the world of John is

95. Cf. J. Bonsirven, *Palestinian Judaism in the Time of Jesus Christ* (New York: Holt, Rinehart and Winston, 1964); also Hengel, *Judaism and Hellenism*. See further W. Foerster, *Palestinian Judaism in New Testament Times* (Edinburgh and London: Oliver and Boyd, 1964).

96. Brown 1, p. lix.

97. J.B. Lightfoot, *Biblical Essays* (London and New York: Macmillan, 1893), pp. 125–93, esp. 135.

98. J.A.T. Robinson, 'The Destination and Purpose of St John's Gospel' in *idem*, *Twelve New Testament Studies*, pp. 107–125 (108–109). On this point see M.W.G. Stibbe, *John's Gospel*, NTR (London and New York: Routledge, 1994), pp. 107–131, esp. 129–31, who identifies the supposedly anti-Semitic debate in John 8 as satire against *apostasy*, and not against Judaism.

99. *Ibid.*, p. 112.

100. John 4:9; 1:11; 18:35.

a Jewish world; Gentiles as a group seldom appear.[101] And it is to (diaspora) Jews, and the crisis of Judaism, that the gospel of Jesus the Messiah is brought. This does not mean, of course, that John is simply restating the case for Judaism uncritically and in exclusive terms. For him Jesus is the true Israel, through whom Judaism is transformed and universalised. But it is still the Jewish rather than the Gentile problem which engages John's attention; so that, for example, all the controversies in this Gospel take place in a Jewish – and no doubt Palestinian – context.[102]

Whether or not we accept the details of this estimate of the character of John's Gospel, and of the Jewish perspective which governs the presentation of his material, it cannot be denied that, apart from the figure of Jesus, the Jews play a crucial role in the Johannine drama. Because of this alone, it is more likely that the Fourth Gospel will breathe a Jewish rather than a Greek atmosphere; and we find that this is in fact the case. We do not need to go far into the Gospel before we find ourselves fundamentally distanced from the world of Greek and oriental mythology. That this is not a subjective impression, moreover, is indicated by further Jewish characteristics belonging to John.

The Gospel's original language

It is possible that behind the composition of the Fourth Gospel lie sources, for the discourse material in particular, which were originally written in Aramaic rather than Greek, or were at least open to the influence of Semitic language. This is a complex issue, and one on which scholars are divided; but it will be relevant to mention it at this point.

It is likely that when he taught Jesus normally spoke Aramaic, which was the conversational language among Jews of Palestine in his day. Possibly he also used Hebrew on occasions, since this was found in written and spoken form among the educated.[103] If Aramaic were his chief language, this has obvious implications for the preservation of the Jesus tradition in all its forms. The Greek of the Gospels will then, and in any case, have been influenced in a Semitic direction, since both the words of Jesus himself which the Gospels contain, and

101. Similarly Brown 1, p. 466, thinks that 'the Greeks' of John 12:20–21 were perhaps proselytes, rather than Gentiles as such, or Greek-speaking Jews. But see below, p. 149 and n. 54. Beasley-Murray, p. 211, believes that the Greeks who asked to 'see Jesus' in John 12 were Gentiles, representing the first fruits of the Gentile world.

102. *Cf.* Robinson, 'Destination', pp. 115–16. Robinson's further conclusions, on this basis, about the intention of the evangelist will be considered later (see below, pp. 177–79.).

103. *Cf.* J. Barr, 'Which Language did Jesus Speak? Some Remarks of a Semitist', *BJRL* 53 (1970–71), pp. 9–29. (The language was probably Aramaic, but the question is still an open one.)

the work of those who handed on and wrote down the tradition about Jesus, came to birth in this environment. The Greek of the Septuagint, which the evangelists use at times for their Old Testament quotations, was also shaped in diaspora Judaism.

Semitic influence on the language of the Fourth Gospel, then, as of the other Gospels, is undoubted. In the case of John, however, opinion has varied as to the extent of this influence.[104] Earlier discussion suggested on syntactical grounds that the whole Gospel was originally written in Aramaic, and later translated into Greek. This was the position, for example, of C.F. Burney[105] and C.C. Torrey,[106] who point out in John the presence of Aramaisms,[107] confused Greek (becoming clear when retranslated into Aramaic), Old Testament quotations from the Hebrew, and the fact that the Johannine prologue and discourses can be translated easily into good Aramaic poetry. These arguments are not equally weighty.[108] The presence of Aramaisms in the Fourth Gospel, for example, or anywhere in the Gospels, need not prove a totally Aramaic original.[109]

The claim of an Aramaic origination for John has been challenged by J. Bonsirven, who argues that Burney's supposed Aramaisms all belonged to *koinē* (common dialect) Greek.[110] Other scholars have suggested an Aramaic background to John, but more cautiously. Matthew Black, for example, believes it possible that John used an Aramaic sayings-tradition, which he incorporated into his Gospel, written in Greek. He finds evidence to support this from 'mistranslated' Greek in the Fourth Gospel, and Greek textual variants which may be said to represent two different translations of the Aramaic original.[111] M.-E. Boismard is equally cautious. He finds further examples of the 'textual variants' phenomenon to which Black draws

104. See the useful survey of S. Brown, 'From Burney to Black: The Fourth Gospel and the Aramaic Question', *CBQ* 26 (1964), pp. 323–39.

105. Burney, *Aramaic Origin*, p. 3, *et passim*.

106. C.C. Torrey, *Our Translated Gospels: Some of the Evidence* (London: Hodder and Stoughton, 1937), p. ix, *et passim*. Torrey argues (p. 121) that John was translated nearly a generation after its composition.

107. *Cf.* also *HTFG*, pp. 424–25, where Dodd cites the example of John's use in 19:18 (at the crucifixion) of the Semitism ἐντεῦθεν καὶ ἐντεῦθεν ('[the others were on] either side [of Jesus]'; lit., 'from here and from there') for the Greek idiom ἐκ δεξιῶν . . . ἐκ ἀριστερῶν ('on the right . . . on the left', as in Mark 15:27).

108. See Brown 1, p. cxxx.

109. Bultmann, pp. 18 and 52 n. 2, *et passim*, discovers an Aramaic original only for the source which he posits for the Johannine prologue and discourses.

110. J. Bonsirven, 'Les aramaïsmes de S. Jean L'Évangéliste?' *Biblica* 30 (1949), pp. 405–32.

111. M. Black, *An Aramaic Approach to the Gospels and Acts*, 3rd edn. (Oxford: Clarendon Press, 1967), pp. 272–74.

attention, and also suggests that John's Old Testament quotations are drawn from the Aramaic Targums.[112]
Few would be prepared to accept Burney's theory of an Aramaic origination for the whole of John. It is very likely, however, that Semitic influence was exercised on John's sources, which may well run back to Aramaic originals in part at least.[113] If so, this has important significance for the Jewish-Palestinian background to John's tradition which we are investigating; and, from the point of view of language, it makes it probable.

John's use of the Old Testament

John quotes directly from the Old Testament less frequently than the other evangelists, but his use of the Old Testament is theologically significant, and relevant to our present study.

Kingsley Barrett claims that the Old Testament forms an 'essential element in the background of the Fourth Gospel'.[114] He shows that John normally uses the Septuagint when citing the Old Testament, but occasionally translates directly from the Hebrew with which he is clearly familiar. Moreover, rather than employing messianic *testimonia* ('testimonies')[115] as proof-texts, the fourth evangelist (in Barret's view) possesses such a comprehensive knowledge of the Old Testament that he can use his testimonies theologically, incorporating in his material testimony themes (based on Old Testament ideas) which can appear, and often do so, without any direct reference to an Old Testament passage.[116] In

112. M.-E. Boismard, 'Importance de critique textuelle pour établir l'origine araméenne du quatrième évangile', in *idem et al., L'Évangile de Jean: Études et problèmes,* RechBib 3 (Bruges: Desclée de Brouwer, 1958), pp. 41–57.

113. Although, as Barnabas Lindars points out, it is not clear even then whether such sources were still in Aramaic when John used them. See Lindars, p. 44. Lindars also suggests that although John wrote 'good, if not very stylish, Greek', this was probably not his first language. And since, according to Lindars, John's stylistic limitations are to be found in all parts of the Gospel, this (in his view) 'weakens the theory of multiple written sources, some of which might have been in Aramaic' (pp. 44–45).

114. Barrett, p. 30.

115. These were quotations from the Old Testament, assembled by the early church and possibly extant in collections, to provide evidence that the Messiah of God would come, and that in Jesus he had come.

116. See Barrett, pp. 29–30. He gives as one example the implied reference to Isa. 29:13 at John 7:19–24; 18:28, *et al. (cf.* Mark 7:6–7). Barrett assumes that John knew Mark, and therefore argues that John 'develops' the synoptic use of the Old Testament here by applying a proof-text, which in the Marcan tradition referred to a specific hypocritical action (ceremonial cleansing), to the general need for a proper response to Jesus (p. 30). We may accept this assessment of John's overall approach to the Old Testament without being committed to Barrett's view of John's sources. See further C.K. Barrett's earlier article, 'The Old Testament in the Fourth Gospel,' *JTS* 48 (1947), pp. 155–69.

addition to this subtle use of Old Testament material, the fourth evangelist, it may be claimed, uses extensive Jewish symbolism to demonstrate the notion of fulfilment, as in the allegories of the shepherd (John 10:1–16) and the vine (15:1–6).[117]

The work of F.-M. Braun and C.H. Dodd is also important in connection with John's use of the Old Testament. Braun picks up the point just noted about John's thematic treatment of the Old Testament, and shows that the Fourth Gospel as a whole reflects the major streams of Jewish theological thought and expectation.[118] The promised advent of the true Messiah, Prophet, Servant and King of Israel comes to fulfilment in Jesus, whom John presents as the Christ.[119] Dodd, for his part, believes that the precise selection of *testimonia* from the Old Testament by the fourth evangelist reveals a primitive interpretation of the person and work of Christ, akin to that of the synoptic tradition but independent of it.[120] He argues that John selected his testimonies, when these occur,[121] according to that early interpretation, rather than selecting the *testimonia* and then giving them his own interpretation.

Finally, on this topic, E.D. Freed's study of the quotations from the Old Testament in John's Gospel[122] is of interest, because it argues that the fourth evangelist's use of the Old Testament reveals a thorough training in Jewish tradition and in the scriptures of Judaism. Freed regards the Fourth Gospel as a theological rather than historical document; yet he is nevertheless convinced that the actual form of Old Testament quotation by the evangelist is not the result of memory work, but of close attention to the written text.[123]

117. On the shepherd image see J. Beutler and R.T. Fortna (ed.), *The Shepherd Discourse of John 10 and its Context*, SNTSMS 67 (Cambridge and New York: Cambridge University Press, 1991) esp. pp. 53–74, 94–115. On the vine allegory see Carson, pp. 510–24. For both metaphors see M.W.G. Stibbe, *John*, Readings (Sheffield: JSOT Press, 1993), pp. 113–16, 161–63.

118. *JT*. pp. 3–45.

119. See also the study of the Moses/Exodus motif in John, obviously relevant to this present discussion, in T.F. Glasson, *Moses in the Fourth Gospel*, SBT 1 (London: SCM Press, 1963) esp. pp. 15–32. *Cf.* further R.H. Smith, 'Exodus Typology in the Fourth Gospel', *JBL* 81 (1962), pp. 329–42, who sees the signs of Moses in Egypt as the background to the signs in the Fourth Gospel.

120. *HTFG*. pp. 31–49, esp. the conclusions on pp. 45–47. John uses nine testimonies, five of which are non-Marcan. See *ibid.*, pp. 33-34.

121. John's use of explicit *testimonia* is in any case restrained, and most evident in the passion narrative.

122. E.D. Freed, *Old Testament Quotations in the Gospel of John*, NovT Sup 11 (Leiden: E.J. Brill, 1965).

123. See further Lindars, p. 438 (commenting on John 12:40), for a suggested example of the fourth evangelist's indebtedness to a Palestinian (non-LXX) form of the text of the Old Testament. But *cf.* C. Goodwin, 'How Did John Treat His Sources?', *JBL* 73 (1954), pp. 61–75, who maintains that John's variations from the LXX are the result of free quotation from memory.

The implication of these lines of research for any study of the Johannine tradition is clear. John's knowledge of the Old Testament was both wide and deep. He knew it well, and used it in a way that demonstrates a profound understanding of its thematic contents, as well as (possibly) a primitive interpretation of its testimonies. None of this proves, of course, that the fundamental background of the writer and his tradition was Judaism of the Palestinian variety; especially since the Septuagint (a pre-Christian, Greek version of the Old Testament), which he used, was known outside Palestine. All that we can say with certainty is that John appears to have been in the first place a good Jew who knew his Old Testament intimately, as well he might. Nevertheless, the evangelist's acquaintance with the Jewish scriptures appears to be strikingly close, and to have influenced markedly the presentation of his tradition about Jesus. Moreover, there is nothing to show that John's dependence on the Old Testament did *not* arise from Palestinian Judaism originally, especially if it can be shown that his variations from the Septuagint[124] stem not from quotation by memory (Goodwin against Freed), but from the citation of the Palestinian Targums.[125] On balance, therefore, it is likely that John's use of the Old Testament can be used to support the view that the Johannine ethos is basically more Jewish than Greek.[126]

John and Rabbinic Judaism

A further direction in which the connection between the Fourth Gospel and Judaism may be explored involves the literature of the rabbis: the Targum traditions, the Mishnah, Talmud and *Midrashim*.[127] Here we are on difficult and sometimes speculative ground, because the rabbinic documents are not easy to date. They belong to the Christian period, and often preserve early, even pre-Christian, material. But we can never be certain that rabbinic parallels in the Gospel of John echo first-century Jewish thought.[128]

124. *E.g.* at John 19:37, quoting Zech. 12:10 (*cf.* Rev. 1:7).

125. So Brown 1, p. lxi. The 'Targums' were interpretative paraphrases of the Old Testament in Aramaic, made when Hebrew ceased to be the normative medium of speech among the Jews.

126. For a further study of John's use of the Old Testament, with special reference to the Old Testament basis of John's distinctive christology, see G. Reim, *Studien zum alttestamentlichen Hintergrund des Johannesevangeliums*, SNTSMS 22 (Cambridge: Cambridge University Press, 1974), esp. pp. 247–61.

127. *Cf.* J.W. Bowker, *The Targums and Rabbinic Literature: An Introduction to Jewish Interpretations of Scripture* (Cambridge: Cambridge University Press, 1969). The Mishnah is a Jewish law code, completed by *c.* AD 200; the Talmud contains systematic commentaries on the Mishnah; the *Midrashim* are interpretative commentaries on Old Testament scriptures.

128. *Cf.* Brown 1, p. lxi.

Nevertheless, when an examination of the Fourth Gospel is undertaken from this standpoint, obvious similarities between Johannine and rabbinic ideas appear to emerge. Lindars (p. 37) cites the argument in John 5:17 ('My Father is working still, and I am working'), since this includes a point in the contemporary Jewish debate about sabbath observance;[129] the 'bread of life' discourse in John 6, which not only follows the homiletic form of the *midrashim* but also finds its centre in the rabbinic equation of manna and Law, and uses a particular rabbinic argument;[130] the notion of the 'hidden Messiah' (John 7:27), which is known only from rabbinic sources; and the rabbinic style of John 8.[131]

This kind of Jewish influence on the Fourth Gospel suggests at least that its author 'had personal contact with Jewish and Christian discussions'.[132] But we may go further, and conclude with Brown that the influence can be most easily explained if its origins lay in Palestinian Judaism, with which John himself was familiar.[133] Again, the significance of this thesis for John's background is obvious.

129. See the whole passage, John 5:9b–18.

130. John 6:45. See the distinguished and seminal work on this chapter by Peder Borgen, *Bread from Heaven: An Exegetical Study of the Concept of Manna in the Gospel of John and the Writings of Philo*, NovT Sup 10 (Leiden: E.J. Brill, 1965), pp. 59–98, 147–92. It is quite possible that the rabbinic homilectic format, employing a pesher (interpretative) technique, also underlies other parts of the Fourth Gospel. For a study of the proposed rabbinic background to the 'agency' motif in the Fourth Gospel with reference to Jesus, particularly evident in the farewell discourse (*cf.* John 14:9–11, *et al.*), see also P. Borgen, 'God's Agent in the Fourth Gospel' in J. Neusner (ed.), *Religions in Antiquity* (Leiden: E.J. Brill, 1968), pp. 137–48. In this area see further P. Borgen 'Observations on the Targumic Character of the Prologue of John', *NTS* 16 (1969–70), pp. 288–95.

131. See further *IFG*, pp. 74–97; also D. Daube, *Rabbinic Judaism*, pp. 36–51 (on the feeding in John 6), *et al*. The important work of H.L. Strack and P. Billerbeck, *Kommentar zum Neuen Testament aus Talmud und Midrash*, 2nd edn., vol. 2 (München: C.H. Beck, 1956), pp. 302–587, is obviously relevant to this topic; see also H. Odeberg, *The Fourth Gospel: Interpreted in Its Relation to Contemporaneous Religious Currents in Palestine and the Hellenistic-Oriental World* (Amsterdam: B.R. Grüner, 1968; originally published in 1929), p. 5 *et passim*. Note further the (questionable) thesis of A.E. Guilding, *The Fourth Gospel and Jewish Worship: A Study of the Relation of St John's Gospel to the Ancient Jewish Lectionary System* (Oxford: Clarendon Press, 1960), that the discourses of Jesus in John given at festival times are suggested by the synagogue lections which belong to those feasts. Barrett (pp. 31–34, esp. 32–33) suggests further instances of John's knowledge of rabbinic ideas, including the processes of criminal and religious law (*e.g.* John 8:17; 7:22–23). He also distinguishes between the streams of rabbinic and Jewish apocalyptic thought in the first Christian century (virtually the successors of the legal and prophetic parts of the Old Testament), and significantly claims for John a similar familiarity with apocalyptic (*e.g.* the use of the expression 'Son of man' in association with future judgment at John 5:27).

132. Lindars, p. 37. *Cf.* J.W. Bowker, 'The Origin and Purpose of St John's Gospel', *NTS* 11 (1964–65) pp. 398–408.

133. Brown 1, p. lxii.

John and Non-conformist Judaism

A final area to be investigated for evidence of possible Jewish influence on the background to the Fourth Gospel is that of sectarian Judaism. Under this heading we shall first consider briefly the likelihood of connections between John and Qumran; although, as we have already considered this point in some detail during our discussion of the Johannine tradition,[134] there is no need to do more than marshal the relevant conclusions here.

The affinities between John's Gospel and the Dead Sea Scrolls outside the Old Testament, on which both depend, are obviously of great interest. As we have noticed, there are real differences between the Qumran sectaries – who seem to have been Essenic in outlook, if not actually Essenes – and the early Christians.[135] But at the same time there are striking points of contact, notably in the attitude taken by both towards prophecy (fulfilled in the history of their own community), eschatology and scriptural interpretation.[136] Above all, the similarity of language and even ideas exhibited by the Fourth Gospel and the Scrolls – for example, the modified (ethical) dualism[137] they share, and their mutual emphasis on brotherly love within the community[138] – reveal an early setting previously unknown in Judaism itself, where Hellenistic thinking lay intertwined with Jewish.[139]

None of this, as R.E. Brown shows,[140] suggests that the Fourth Gospel depends directly on the literature from Qumran. But it seems clear that

134. See above, pp. 33–37.
135. See p. 35.
136. *Cf.* Lindars, pp. 37–38.
137. The dualism of the Fourth Gospel and the Scrolls is regularly expressed by means of pairs of opposites, especially 'light and darkness' (a clear contrast in the literature of Qumram, and a leading motif in John) and 'truth and error' (although falsehood occurs in the Scrolls, and not in John except by implication; but *cf.* John 8:44, 55). John's description of the devil as 'the father of lies' (8:44), and the Holy Spirit as the Spirit of truth (14:17, *et al.*), reminds us of reference in the *Community Rule* to the contest between the Spirit of Error (Angel of Darkness) and the Spirit of Truth (Angel of Light); *cf.* 1QS 3.17–26. See also O. Böcher, *Der johanneische Dualismus im Zusammenhang des nachbiblischen Judentums* (Gütersloh: Gerd Mohn, 1965), who regards John's dualism as closer to the apocalyptic and sectarian thought of Judaism than to dualist ideas in any Greek sources (see *e.g.* pp. 25–27).
138. *E.g.* John 13:34, compared with 1QS 5.1–7.
139. See further J.H. Charlesworth, 'A Critical Comparison of the Dualism in 1QS III.13–IV.26 and the "Dualism" Contained in the Fourth Gospel', *NTS* 15 (1968–69), pp. 389–418; note esp. 414–15. On the other side see H.M. Teeple, 'Qumran and the Origin of the Fourth Gospel', *NovT* 4 (1960), pp. 6–25, who argues that the author of John was a Gentile with Jewish traits, and that the Qumranic affinities such as those we have noticed prove nothing about the Palestinian background to the Fourth Gospel.
140. Brown 1, p. lxiii.

John was familiar with Qumranic patterns of thought, and may even have been influenced by the sect itself: either through personal contact, or through John the Baptist.[141] It is otherwise difficult to account for the proximity of John's Gospel to the Scrolls, and for the fact that certain features in both afford a parallel closer than that which exists in any other Jewish or Greek non-Christian literature of the time or earlier. John's relation to sectarian Judaism as exemplified by Qumran, then, helps to fill in the picture so far as the Jewish influence on his background is concerned.

It has been suggested further in this connection by Oscar Cullmann[142] that John was himself a non-conformist Jewish-Christian, and in fact a Hellenist. Cullmann suggests that the 'Hellenists' mentioned in Acts 6:1, whose identity has often been debated, were Jews (or Jewish-Christians) of sectarian outlook who were noted for their outspoken opposition to the temple, and linked with the Qumran community.[143] To their ranks, Cullmann maintains, belonged before their conversion (possibly) Stephen,[144] and the authors of John's Gospel and Hebrews. This would explain, for example, the 'hostility' towards the temple implicit in John 4:21-24 (*cf.* 2:13-22, the cleansing of the temple). Also, and more importantly, if Cullmann is right we do not need to regard John's background as non-Palestinian and his tradition as secondary merely because these are further removed than the synoptic Gospels from 'official Judaism'.[145] Once more the evidence points in the direction of a Jewish rather than a Greek background as basic to John.[146]

141. See above, pp. 36–37.

142. O. Cullmann, 'A New Approach to the Interpretation of the Fourth Gospel', *ExpT* 71 (1959–60), pp. 8–12 and 39–43. See also *idem, The Johannine Circle: A Study in the Origin of the Gospel of John*, NTL (London: SCM Press, 1976).

143. There was also an attitude of resistance to the Jewish temple present in the sect of Qumran; *cf.* CD 6.

144. See the further suggestion by A. Spiro, 'Stephen's Samaritan Background' in J. Munck, *The Acts of the Apostles*, revised by W.F. Albright and C.S. Mann, AB 31 (Garden City: Doubleday, 1967), pp. 285–300.

145. Cullmann, 'New Approach', p. 43.

146. It has also been proposed that John was familiar with the thought and ideas of the Samaritans (*cf.* 4:20–25), and even wrote his Gospel either to win or to instruct Samaritan converts. See the literature cited in Lindars, p. 37 n. But, as Lindars mentions, this suggestion is 'highly speculative'; John's familiarity with Samaritanism need not have been greater than that characteristic of any Jew, just as his knowledge of Qumran *need* not have been greater than that derived from Judaism in general (p. 38). See also C.H.H. Scobie, 'The Origins and Development of Samaritan Christianity', *NTS* 19 (1972–73), pp. 390–414, esp. 401–408; J.D. Purvis, 'The Fourth Gospel and the Samaritans', *NovT* 17 (1975), pp. 161–90; Beasley-Murray, pp. lxiii–lxv (Samaritanism appears to be 'one of the sources that fed the Johannine reservoir' [p. lxv]).

Conclusions

Our consideration of the Jewish influence on the background to the Fourth Gospel leads us to the conclusion that John's ethos is at root more in touch with Judaism than Hellenism; and this reinforces the similar result reached by an investigation of the possible Greek influences exercised on John. We need not attempt to deny *any* influence from Hellenism on the Johannine tradition, or on its authorship; but if we accept the description of John's background as 'Jewish-Hellenistic', which clearly it is, we must also recognise that the contact with Judaism is primary.[147] The Hellenistic features of the Fourth Gospel tell us more about its final audience, that is to say, than about the background of its author or its tradition. We shall return to this point.[148]

Needless to say, the chief influence on John is in the end neither Jewish nor Jewish-Hellenistic, but Christian.[149] The fourth evangelist is in the first place a Christian writer: and, as we shall see, as much in touch with the apostolic tradition as any other New Testament author. But the writer comes out of his own environment; and we have seen reason to believe that both John and his tradition originated from a setting of (Palestinian) Judaism. If we are looking for the identity of the writer of the Fourth Gospel, we shall not be wasting our time if we search that area first.

We have carefully considered the likely background to the Gospel of John and its tradition, and therefore, presumably, of its author.[150] But we have not yet seen if it is possible to discover who was responsible for the Gospel as it now stands, or whether the tradition that John the apostle had a hand in its composition is still acceptable. Was John involved; and, if so, what was the precise identity of the 'John' in question? We shall address this issue in the next chapter.

---

147.   See further *IFG*, p. 453; J.A.T. Robinson, 'Destination', p. 116; D. Guthrie, *New Testament Introduction*, 4th edn. (Leicester: Inter-Varsity Press and Downers Grove: Apollos, 1990), pp. 261–63, 339–40. Note also Barrett, *John and Judaism*, who examines carefully the *nature* of the Jewish background to John, and its precise relation to the Fourth Gospel; see esp. pp. 40–76. W.D. Davies, 'Reflections on Aspects of the Jewish Background of the Gospel of John' in Culpepper and Black (ed.), *Exploring the Gospel of John*, pp. 43–64, esp. 59, believes that the fourth evangelist set out to engage 'all the essential elements in the Judaism of his day', and to *challenge* them in the name of Christ.

148.   See below, pp. 181–85; also Carson, pp. 58–63.

149.   So L.L. Morris, *The Gospel According to John*, 2nd edn. (Grand Rapids: Eerdmans, 1995), pp. 58–59 (= Morris).

150.   We have yet to discuss the relevance of this background to the nature of John's immediate audience. On this point see below, pp. 177–85.

4

JOHN AND JOHN'S GOSPEL

Already in this book we have used the name 'John' more than once in association with the Fourth Gospel, and also indeed in relation to the Apocalypse and 1, 2, 3 John.[1] It appears that 'John' was a popular name in the early church, as it is today.[2] When the designation is used traditionally to describe the writer of this Gospel, therefore,[3] we need to identify carefully the 'John' in question, if we are to learn more fully about its author.

In any discussion of authorship, the normal method of procedure is to sift the evidence available to us from outside the work itself, and then to examine the clues which are provided by the document from within. So we begin with the external evidence.

EXTERNAL EVIDENCE

Christian tradition since the second century AD has associated the Fourth Gospel with the apostle John. The first clear witness is provided by Irenaeus, who became Bishop of Lyons in AD 177.

In his letter to Florinus,[4] a gnostic Roman presbyter, Irenaeus claims direct contact with the apostle John through the aged Polycarp, Bishop of Smyrna. In terms which are very revealing as a description of the transmission of the Jesus tradition, Irenaeus reminds Florinus of their early days together, and of the way in which they were instructed by Polycarp. Apparently Polycarp was in the habit of discoursing to them about both the teaching and miracles of Jesus, as these were handed on by John and 'the others who had seen the Lord' with whom Polycarp had been associated. Not only was Polycarp's recollection of this eyewitness evidence about Jesus clear, and 'in harmony with the scriptures'; Irenaeus tells Florinus that he also remembered the events of that time more vividly than he did 'those of recent years'.[5]

---

1. See above, pp. 1–3, 14, *et passim*.
2. So John the apostle, John Baptist, John Mark, *et al.*.
3. The author is not named as John in the Fourth Gospel; although the Revelation is given to John, by tradition 'the Divine' (Rev. 1:1, 4, 9; 22:8), and an 'elder' (John) writes 2 and 3 John (2 John 1; 3 John 1).
4. Quoted in Eusebius, *HE* 5.20.4–8.
5. *Ibid.* 5.20.5.

In two important passages of his work *Against Heresies*, Irenaeus also tells us that the elders associated with John the disciple of the Lord in Asia testify that John, who remained among them until the time of Trajan,[6] delivered the gospel to them;[7] and that the church in Ephesus, where John remained until the time of Trajan, is a truthful witness of the apostolic tradition.[8] The church historian Eusebius (*c.* AD 260–340) cites the second passage again, and more fully; and in this extended quotation it emerges that the authority of Irenaeus for saying these things is once more the trustworthy Polycarp, who received directly from the apostles the truth transmitted by the church.[9]

The link between Irenaeus and Polycarp is a significant backcloth to the vital further piece of information given in the third book of *Against Heresies*, where Irenaeus tells us that 'John, the disciple of the Lord', who at the last supper reclined on the bosom of Jesus, 'gave out' (ἐξέδωκε) the gospel at Ephesus after the other Gospels had been written.[10] The collective witness of Irenaeus is therefore unambiguous. On the basis of contact with the apostle John through Bishop Polycarp, the single intermediary, it is plain in the view of Irenaeus that John the son of Zebedee was the beloved disciple, and that he published his Gospel at Ephesus in his old age.

We must now examine the authority of the tradition which Irenaeus preserves, about the authorship and origin of the Fourth Gospel, by looking at the support which this tradition receives in the early church. An important piece of evidence in this connection is provided by Poly-crates, who was Bishop of Ephesus from AD 189–98. Writing to Victor, Bishop of Rome, Polycrates refers to John, among the great lights who have fallen asleep in Asia, as a witness and teacher, who reclined on the bosom of the Lord, was a 'priest',[11] and died at Ephesus.[12] Here again the connection is made between John and the beloved disciple and Ephesus. Clement of Alexandria (AD 150–211) perpetuates this tradition in his famous reference to John composing a 'spiritual gospel',[13] and in the legend about John entrusting to a bishop a youth who turned robber, contained in the document *Quis dives salvetur?*[14]

6. Emperor of Rome AD 98–117.
7. *AH* 2.22.5; quoted, although not completely, at *HE* 3.23.3.
8. *AH* 3.3.4; quoted *HE* 3.23.4.
9. *HE* 4.14.3–8.
10. *AH* 3.1.1, quoted *HE* 5.8.4.
11. The precise meaning of this description of John is obscure, unless it refers to the apostle's share in the priesthood of all believers.
12. See *HE* 3.31.3 (*cf.* 5.24.2–3).
13. Quoted *HE* 4.14.7.
14. *Quis dives* 42.1–15. *Cf.* also *HE* 3.23.5–19, where the quotation from Clement connects John with Ephesus, and Patmos indeed, but says nothing about his association with the Fourth Gospel.

Three other early witnesses may be mentioned at this point, because they all subscribe to the apostolic authorship of the Fourth Gospel, without mentioning any link with Ephesus. The so-called anti-Marcionite Prologue to John speaks of the Gospel of John as revealed to the churches by John while still alive. But the contents of this document, like its date (AD 160–80?), are suspect. It refers to Papias as a disciple of John, and claims that he wrote down the Gospel at John's dictation. It also mentions that the heretical Marcion himself was 'rejected by John'. But clearly these statements, and the relationship they imply between the apostle John and either Papias or Marcion, cannot be correct; so that the evidence of the Prologue as a whole must therefore be treated with great care.

The Muratorian Canon, an annotated list of New Testament documents which was discovered in 1740 and belongs originally to the last quarter of the second century, contains some interesting comments on the composition of the Fourth Gospel. Although it refers categorically to the Gospel as the work of 'John, one of the disciples', it goes on to describe the contents of the Gospel as revealed to all the apostles, but written down by John at Andrew's direction. In other words, the difference between John's Gospel and the rest should present no problem to the believer. Since the reference to the apostolic authorship of John is incidental to the point being made, and indeed only tenuously supports John's connection with the Fourth Gospel, the evidence of the Muratorian Canon cannot for our purposes be rated very highly.

Thirdly Ptolemaeus, a mid-second-century disciple of the gnostic teacher Valentinus, accepted the apostolic authorship of the Fourth Gospel. But once again such attestation must be regarded with caution, since we know that the gnostic thinkers of the second century found John's Gospel a happy hunting-ground for beliefs similar to their own, and were only too ready to invoke the apostle's authority in support of their heretical systems.

The early evidence so far considered in our search for a link, as maintained by Irenaeus, between the apostle John and the composition of the Fourth Gospel, seems not to be uniform, nor always completely reliable. We may now consider some further witnesses, particularly any who may associate John with Ephesus.

(a) John and Ephesus

It would be valuable if some early evidence could be found to help us establish the eventual fate of John the apostle, in particular his residence in Ephesus, and thus the likelihood of his connection in any way with the writing of the Fourth Gospel. But this is not easy to discover. The New Testament itself, for example, does not associate John with Ephesus: not even the Apocalypse, which contains a letter to the church in that city (Rev. 2:1–7).[15] Equally surprising is the fact that Paul's speech to the Ephesian elders at Miletus (Acts 20:18–35) makes no mention of John's presence in Ephesus; although perhaps it could be argued that this was not called for directly. The omission of John's name from Ephesians itself is also noteworthy; although probably this was a circular letter addressed to other churches besides Ephesus. On the other hand, Galatians (2:9) puts John in Jerusalem; although admittedly this does not mean that he stayed there indefinitely.

Beyond the New Testament we have the witness of Clement of Rome, writing to Corinth *c.* AD 96, who does not refer to John at all. Possibly, however, this implies that he, and the other apostles, had died by then;[16] and this could still be consistent with the possibility that John was responsible for the Fourth Gospel at Ephesus in his old age. At the same time Ignatius, whose letters may be dated *c.* AD 107–115, is also silent about the apostle John; and even if this is understandable in the majority of his letters, it is very hard to explain when he is writing to Ephesus itself – particularly since he mentions the association between Paul and the Ephesians.[17] This is all the more strange in view of the fact that John and Ignatius are close in thought, outlook and even vocabulary; although this proximity need not imply more than dependence upon a similar Christian tradition, and does not prove literary association.

Three other second-century writers may be cited in this context. Papias mentions John, without connecting him with Asia.[18] Polycarp, writing briefly to the Philippians, does not refer to the apostle at all; which is surprising in view of the testimony of Irenaeus already considered linking Polycarp and the apostle. Justin Martyr claims that the Revelation was written by the apostle John,[19] without attributing the Fourth Gospel, which he possibly knew, to him.

All these further witnesses, then, remain inconclusive about John's connection with either the Fourth Gospel itself or Ephesus. One document earlier than Irenaeus, however, claims very definitely that John lived at Ephesus. The so-called *Acts of John*, written by Leucius Charinus *c.* AD 150–60,[20] tells us that John ministered in Asia, including Ephesus.

15. The link between Revelation and the remainder of the Johannine corpus is in any case an open question. For a defence of its proximity to the Fourth Gospel, and therefore to 1,2,3 John, see Smalley, *Thunder and Love*, esp. pp. 57–73. Nevertheless, the Apocalypse clearly belongs to Asia (*cf.* Rev. 1:9–11).

16. See esp. 1 Clement 42, 44.

17. Ignatius, *Eph* 12.2. In a later, interpolated, edition of the Ignatian letters, made when the tradition of John's authorship of the Fourth Gospel had been established, John the apostle *is* mentioned in *Ephesians* (11).

18. Eusebius, *HE* 3.39. 3–4.

19. *Dial Trypho* 81. See J.N. Sanders, *The Fourth Gospel in the Early Church: Its Origin and Influence on Christian Theology up to Irenaeus* (Cambridge: Cambridge University Press, 1943), pp. 27–32.

20. Hennecke 2, pp. 215–58.

But although this document shows that a link between the apostle John and Asia Minor was not considered unlikely, too much reliance cannot be placed on the historical value of the work, which is manifestly legendary, and originated in a gnostic setting.

The tradition initiated by Irenaeus about John's connection with the Fourth Gospel and Ephesus is not only lacking in strong early support; it is also perhaps countered by another tradition about John's fate, that he was martyred with his brother James under Herod Agrippa I.[21] This may be reflected in Mark 10:39,[22] the prediction by Jesus that the sons of Zebedee would be baptised with their Lord's baptism. However, this verse by itself does not prove that the martyrdom of John took place with that of James, and before Mark was written;[23] it merely points towards his death at some future time.

Clearer, but still inconclusive, evidence of a belief that the apostle John was martyred at the same time as James is provided by the historian Philip of Side (c. AD 450), whose later epitomist quotes Papias as referring to the simultaneous deaths of James and John 'the divine' at the hands of the Jews.[24] A Syrian martyrology from Edessa (c. AD 411), and possibly the Calendar of Carthage (c. AD 505), also commemorate John and James as if they died in the same way, and perhaps together.[25] Finally, Georgius Monachus (Hamartolus), in the ninth century, refers to both Mark 10:39 and Papias in terms which evidently perpetuate the view that John died with his brother.[26]

External witness to the early martyrdom of John thus exists; but it rests on a doubtful exegesis of Mark 10:39, and is unimpressive.[27]

Conclusion

It is time to draw together some of the threads of evidence which we have just examined, concerning John's association with the Fourth Gospel. External attestation to the apostolic authorship of the Gospel is neither strong nor uniform before Irenaeus. Those early witnesses, who might reasonably be expected to mention a link between the apostle and the Gospel, are at times completely silent on the point; and it is difficult

21. *Cf.* Barrett, pp. 103–104. See Acts 12:2.

22. *Cf.* Matt. 20:22–23.

23. So Barrett, p. 104.

24. *Cf.* C. de Boor, *Neue Fragmente des Papias, Hegesippus und Pierius, TU* 5 (1888–89), p. 170.

25. *Cf.* H. Lietzmann, *The Three Oldest Martyrologies* (Cambridge: Deighton Bell, 1904), p. 9; see also p. 7 (under 27 December).

26. *Chronicle* 3.134.1, according to one MS (*cf.* PG 110, cols 522–26).

27. *Cf. HTFG,* p. 12. See also J.H. Bernard, 'The Traditions as to the Death of John, the Son of Zebedee' in *idem, Studia Sacra* (London and New York: Hodder and Stoughton, 1917), pp. 260–84.

to find a clear consensus of opinion at any time about the eventual fate of John, and whether or not he could have produced a Gospel late in his life at Ephesus, as Irenaeus maintains he did. By the time of Irenaeus writers such as Theophilus of Antioch[28] are assigning the Fourth Gospel to John, without saying explicitly that he was an apostle; although only shortly before this Justin and Melito, Bishop of Sardis, allude to the Fourth Gospel in such an indirect manner as to suggest that they did not regard it as apostolic.[29]

We shall seek to interpret these facts in due course. Meanwhile, we must give some attention to a figure other than the apostle John who makes an early appearance in connection with the writing of the Fourth Gospel: John the Elder.

(b) John the Elder

The crucial witness in the case of John the Elder is Papias, Bishop of Hierapolis, during the earlier part of the second century AD. In a famous extract from his *Expositions of the Lord's Oracles*,[30] Papias tells us that he was concerned to hand on, with his interpretations, the command-ments of the Lord which he had carefully learned from 'the elders'; for he regarded the living tradition as more profitable than the written. So he discovered from any followers of the elders he chanced to meet what the elders said about Jesus. Papias then lists two such groups of inform-ants, both containing the name of John. The first consists of Andrew, Peter, Philip, Thomas, James, John, Matthew 'or any disciple of the Lord' (ἤ τις ἕτερος τῶν τοῦ κυρίου μαθητῶν); the second contains simply the names of Aristion and 'the elder John' (ὁ πρεσβύτερος Ἰωάννης).

To see what was made of this double reference by Papias to 'John', we must notice the fact that some early Christian fathers found it difficult to accept the Revelation to John as the work of John the apostle, particularly because of its millenarian view of the last things (*cf.* Rev. 20:1–15).[31] But equally they were reluctant to say that it was pseudony-mous; so they looked round for another John who could have been its author. Dionysius of Alexandria, who died *c.* AD 265, drew attention to the presence of two tombs at Ephesus, both of which purported to be the burial place of John; although doubtless there were many tombs and many Johns in Ephesus. On this basis Dionysius claimed that such a second John existed, who could have been responsible for the Revelation.

---

28.   *Cf.* Theophilus, *ad Autolycum* 2.22 (*c.* AD 180). He calls John 'inspired'.

29.   Justin, *Dial Trypho* 63; Melito, *Homily* (on the passion) 95, *et al.* We have already noticed (above, pp. 57–58) that the *Odes of Solomon* do not yield conclusive evidence about the knowledge or use of John's Gospel in the early church.

30.   Quoted *HE* 3.39.3–4,7.

31.   See further Smalley, *Thunder and Love*, p. 38.

32.   *HE* 3.39.5–6.

Eusebius[32] followed him, and mistakenly discovered the other John in the Papias tradition already quoted. He regarded 'the elder John', who is mentioned in the second group of informants, as a separate figure, called him John the Elder, and also ascribed the Apocalypse to him. But it is very likely that Papias was originally referring to the *same* John, the apostle, in both lists. In the first case he groups him with the disciples who had died, and in the second case – as a senior, an 'elder' – with those, in this instance Aristion, who still lived. In this connection it is worth recalling that in the New Testament the disciples of Jesus were also called elders[33] (and indeed apostles), and that Papias himself refers earlier in the same passage to the disciples, including John, as 'elders'.[34] In the context of a discussion about the transmission of authentic, dominical tradition, it is not surprising therefore that Papias should use the term 'elder' (πρεσβύτερος) to describe his apostolic authorities. We do not have to follow Eusebius, and on this flimsy basis invent a second (Elder) John, who can then be regarded as responsible for the Apocalypse or indeed any part of the Johannine corpus. Even if it can be proved that John the Elder existed, it certainly cannot be established that he lived at Ephesus, or that he was connected at all with the composition of the Fourth Gospel.[35] There may be difficulties in the way of associating the apostle John directly with any of the Johannine documents; but it is possible, as we shall see, to account for these difficulties without resorting to the hypothetical figure of the Elder John, and assigning the authorship of these documents to him.

33. *Cf.* 1 Pet. 1:1; 5:1. See further J.R.W. Stott, *The Epistles of John: An Introduction and Commentary*, TNTC (Leicester: Inter-Varsity Press and Grand Rapids: Eerdmans, 1964), pp. 35–41.

34. The use of the term ὁ πρεσβύτερος ('the elder') in 2 John 1 and 3 John 1 is not conclusive evidence for the identity of the writer of either the Letters or Gospel of John. See Houlden, *Commentary*, pp. 4–6, who argues that 'the elder' in 2 and 3 John is not a personal name, but a title for the guardian of tradition in the Johannine church. Houlden (p. 38) also maintains that the Johannine Gospel and Letters are unlikely to have come from the same hand.

35. *Cf.* Barrett, pp. 105–109, esp. 109; *HTFG*, pp. 16–17. See also G.H.C. MacGregor, *The Gospel of John* (London: Hodder and Stoughton, 1928), pp. l–lxviii, who takes the view that the fourth evangelist was 'John the Elder of Ephesus', a younger contemporary of the beloved disciple (perhaps John the apostle), upon whose witness the Elder depended. On the other side see Lightfoot (p. 7), claiming that our knowledge of the Elder is non-existent; see also Carson, p. 70. R.A. Culpepper, *John, the Son of Zebedee: The Life of a Legend* (Columbia: University of South Carolina Press, 1994), pp. 297–307, subscribes to the view that John the Elder is an 'elusive ghost' (p. 298), who will not be laid to rest. Culpepper surveys recent scholarship on this subject, including the work of M. Hengel, *The Johannine Question* (London: SCM Press and Philadelphia: Trinity Press International, 1989). Hengel not only argues for the existence of John the Elder, but also regards him as the mastermind behind the Johannine corpus. See Hengel, *Question*, esp. pp. 124–35.

INTERNAL EVIDENCE

Before we make any concluding suggestions about the authorship of the Fourth Gospel, we must consider help that may be offered by the evidence of the Gospel itself.

No one is named in the text as the writer of this Gospel; although the beloved disciple, to whom we shall return, is referred to in John 21:24 as the one 'who has written these things'. This phrase is problematic, however, like the identity of the beloved disciple himself; and, as we shall see, John 21:24 cannot be appealed to as an unambiguous answer to the authorship question. Possibly the anonymity of the work is deliberate, and the writer has 'burnt himself out' of the Gospel in order to concentrate his readers' attention on the main subject.[36] Whatever the reason, the traditional ascription of the authorship of the Fourth Gospel to John the son of Zebedee is unsupported by any explicit reference in the Gospel either to him or to his brother.[37] Since we are looking for an eyewitness as the author, in accordance both with tradition and the character of John's Gospel which has already been discussed, these facts constitute a difficulty.

Certain disciples appear in the course of the Fourth Gospel without being named, however; and we must now investigate their identity to see if any of them may be associated with the authorship of this document. We begin with the so-called 'beloved disciple', referred to in the tradition of Irenaeus as the author of the Gospel of John, and identified as the apostle himself.

The Beloved Disciple

The 'disciple whom Jesus loved' is mentioned five times in John's Gospel, and not at all in the other Gospels. He appears only in the closing section of John, from the beginning of the passion narrative onwards.

(a) *John 13:23.* The disciple whom Jesus loved lies 'close to the breast of Jesus' during John's equivalent of the last supper: here, the Footwashing. Peter beckons to this disciple to ask for information about the betrayer of Jesus (13:24–25).

(b) *John 19:26–27.* The disciple loved by Jesus stands with Mary near the cross of Jesus at the crucifixion. This disciple and Mary are commended to each other by the Lord.

36. So E.C. Hoskyns, *The Fourth Gospel*, ed. F.N. Davey, 2nd edn. (London: Faber and Faber, 1947), p. 19 (= Hoskyns).

37. There is a vague allusion to οἱ τοῦ Ζεβεδαίου ('the sons [lit. those] of Zebedee') at John 21:2; but that is all. The only John mentioned by name in the Fourth Gospel is the Baptist (John 1:6, and elsewhere); but, while he may have influenced the Johannine tradition, there is no reason to connect him with the authorship of the Fourth Gospel as a whole. See above, pp. 36–37, 72–73.

(c) *John 20:2–10.* Peter and 'the other disciple',[38] the one whom Jesus loved,[39] discover the empty tomb. The 'other' disciple 'sees and believes' (in the resurrection, verse 8).

(d) *John 21:7, 20–23.* The disciple whom Jesus loved is involved with Peter in the sign of the catch of 153 fish, and recognises the risen Christ as Lord. He also (verses 20–21) follows Jesus and Peter, and hears his eventual fate, giving rise to the rumour that he would not die, discussed.

(e) *John 21:24.* A final reference, which does not use the phrase 'beloved disciple', but points clearly to him, claims that the same disciple (of John 21) is 'bearing witness to these things' and 'has written these things'. His testimony is endorsed as 'true'.

Can we interpret this information to discover the identity of the beloved disciple, and eventually his part (if any) in the composition of John's Gospel? There are at least four possible candidates.

John the apostle

The beloved disciple in the Fourth Gospel seems to fulfil the role assigned to John the apostle in the synoptic Gospels. He is present at the Johannine equivalent of the last supper, and is likely therefore to have been one of the Twelve. He is associated with Simon Peter, and with Peter appears to be close to Jesus himself; just as in the synoptic tradition Peter, (James) and John belong to the 'inner group' of disciples.[40] The beloved disciple is also of sufficient standing and intimacy with the family of Jesus to be entrusted with the care of the Lord's mother.[41] These details, combined with the further fact that John the son of Zebedee is not mentioned by name in the Fourth Gospel, except in the vague allusion at 21:2, make it likely that it is he who should be identified with the disciple whom Jesus loved. This suggestion is reinforced when we recall that the other leading members of the Twelve (notably Peter) *are* named; and, more importantly, that the beloved disciple acts as a witness to the

---

38. The precision of this reference (the Greek is τὸν ἄλλον μαθητήν) suggests that the fourth evangelist is here taking over a recapitulatory phrase from his source.

39. The word translated 'loved', on this single occasion, uses the verb φιλεῖν, rather than ἀγαπᾶν. Possibly this change is again due to John's source. See Schnackenburg 3, pp. 309–310.

40. *Cf.* Mark 9:2, *et al.* Peter and John also worked together, according to Acts (3:1; 8:14–15, *et al*), in the early days of the church's history.

41. John 19:27. It is even possible that the apostle John was related to Jesus. So Brown 1, pp. 14–15; 2, pp. 904–906. This suggestion depends on the identification of Salome as John's mother and the sister of Mary the mother of Jesus (*cf.* John 19:25; Mark 16:1). If it be accepted, the connection between the beloved disciple and John becomes even more likely. However, in view of Mark 14:50 ('all the disciples deserted him and fled'), it is strange to find one of them so near the cross; but *cf.* John 16:32. In any case, as with Peter, the initial flight was only temporary.

Jesus tradition, as John himself at some point obviously would have done, in this Gospel.[42]

There are, however, difficulties in the way of associating the beloved disciple with John the apostle, and therefore (as in the tradition) with the fourth evangelist.[43] Chief among these are the following.

(a) Despite the commendation of Mary to the beloved disciple by Jesus on the cross, according to Acts 1:14 Mary is mentioned in company with the brothers of Jesus, and not with John.[44] However, John is in fact mentioned with other disciples in the previous verse of Acts (1:13), and we are told that 'all these' devoted themselves to prayer *with Mary* and the brothers of Jesus (verse 14).

(b) The sons of Zebedee were from Galilee, whereas the Fourth Gospel concentrates on the Jerusalem ministry of Jesus. However, this does not mean that the beloved disciple knew nothing of the ministry of Jesus in Galilee, which is in any case the location from time to time of the Johannine tradition (John 1:43, *et al.;* and notably John 21).

(c) According to the synoptic Gospels, the apostle John was present both at the transfiguration of Jesus and during his agony in Gethsemane (Mark 9:2; 14:32–33 par.); but neither of these important incidents is related as such in the Fourth Gospel. However, John's particular theological perspective, which sees glory and victory over (real) temptation as constant features in the life of the incarnate Word of God, would by itself account for these omissions. Furthermore, elements of the synoptic accounts of both the transfiguration and the agony do in fact appear in John.[45]

(d) Finally, according to Acts 4:13 John was 'uneducated' (ἀγράμματος); and this is hardly a suitable description for the author of the Fourth Gospel, if the beloved disciple is to be identified with John as the fourth evangelist. However, quite apart from the ambiguity of the word 'uneducated' as a description of John, the 'author' of the Fourth Gospel, as we shall see in a moment, is not necessarily the person responsible for its final form. The beloved disciple is described as a 'witness' to the tradition about Jesus (John 21:24; *cf.* 20:8); and that is of primary significance.

So far then, and in spite of objections, none of which is insurmountable, we have seen that there is good reason to identify the beloved disciple with the apostle John. The facts in this case seem to fit well. Nevertheless, other candidates have been suggested, and we must look at these.

---

42. See further R.V.G. Tasker, *The Gospel According to St John*, TNTC (London: Tyndale Press, 1960), pp. 14–15 (= Tasker).

43. See P. Parker, 'John the Son of Zebedee and the Fourth Gospel', *JBL* 81 (1962), pp. 35–43, where the arguments against connecting John the apostle with John's Gospel are set out. See also Brown 1, p. xcviii.

44. So Barrett, p. 116.

45. See John 12:23, 27–28, *et al.*

John Mark

The possibility that Mark (note the first name) was the beloved disciple is not as wild a suggestion as may at first appear. Mark lived in Jerusalem, and his home was used as a central meeting place for the early church (*cf.* Acts 12:12). This may account for the emphasis on Jerusalem in the Fourth Gospel, and for John's topographical exactitude. Secondly, Mark and Peter are associated in Acts;[46] and this accords with the link between the beloved disciple and Peter in John. Thirdly, John Mark was related to Barnabas, who was a Levite;[47] and this would make it possible for the beloved disciple, if he is the unknown disciple of John 18:15, to be familiar to the high priest. Finally, there was a connection between Mark and Luke (see Philemon 24), which may account, if Mark is the beloved disciple and the fourth evangelist, for the often-noticed proximity between the Johannine and Lucan Traditions.[48]

However, there are objections to this theory.

(a)   If Mark is responsible for the Second Gospel, it is very difficult to see how he can also be the author of the Fourth. Moreover, John Mark and Mark the evangelist are not identified by those in the second century (such as Papias and Irenaeus) who refer to the Second Gospel; and Luke always uses the double name 'John Mark' for Mark in Acts. Evidently, therefore, there was no certainty in the early church that John Mark and the second evangelist were the same person.

(b)   The beloved disciple was apparently one of the Twelve, and according to John's Gospel an important figure in the ministry of Jesus. If so, it is odd, to say the least, that there is no explicit mention of Mark (should he be the beloved disciple) in the synoptic tradition, or indeed in any of the lists of the disciples of Jesus.[49]

Lazarus

The third possible figure who could be identified as the beloved disciple is Lazarus. He is the only male disciple in the Fourth Gospel who

46.   Acts 12:12; *cf.* 1 Peter 5:13.

47.   See Col. 4:10. Acts 4:36 describes Barnabas as a Levite.

48.   See above, pp. 10–11. *Cf.* J. Wellhausen, *Das Evangelium Johannis* (Berlin: G. Reimer, 1908), pp. 100–127, *et passim* (= Wellhausen). See further L. Johnson, 'Who was the Beloved Disciple?', *ExpT* 77 (1965–66), pp. 157–58, who points out that the links between Mark and the Fourth Gospel appear to be stronger than those between Mark and the Second Gospel. The identity of the beloved disciple as John Mark, who is *perhaps* also the fourth evangelist, is favoured by Marsh (pp. 24–25). For the view that Mark was the fourth evangelist, who was not the beloved disciple (= Lazarus), see J.N. Sanders, 'Who was the Disciple whom Jesus Loved?' in F.L. Cross (ed.), *Studies in the Fourth Gospel* (London: A.R. Mowbray, 1957), pp. 72–82; also J.N. Sanders, *A Commentary on the Gospel According to St John*, ed. B.A. Mastin, BNTC (London: A. and C. Black, 1968), pp. 24–52 (= Sanders).

49.   So Brown 1, p. xcvi.

is described as being loved by Jesus.[50] This fact, combined with early uncertainty about the authorship of the Fourth Gospel, and the appearance of the beloved disciple in John only after the raising of Lazarus in chapter 11, has led some scholars[51] to regard Lazarus as the disciple whom Jesus loved.

But, apart from the lack of support for this view in early Christian tradition, it is difficult to imagine that the final edition of John's Gospel could have referred to the same disciple by name in two chapters (11 and 12), and then anonymously in the remainder. No doubt a man in the position of Lazarus, who had been brought back to life, would feel a deep commitment to Jesus and to the tradition which he began; and doubtless after his resurrection Lazarus would have occupied a position of prominence among the disciples, and intimacy with the Lord's family. But in this case there is every reason why Lazarus should appear in his own right, as he does in John 11 and 12, and none at all why he should suddenly become otherwise named from John 13 onwards. Indeed, Lazarus and the beloved disciple appear on any showing to be two distinct figures in the Gospel of John.

The ideal disciple

A final attempt to identify the beloved disciple may be considered. This is the view that he is a non-historical symbol for the perfect Christian, close to Jesus in the important moments of his passion, and the first to believe in his resurrection.[52]

But even if the beloved disciple also represents (as Gregory the Great saw) aspects of the believing Christian community, whether Jewish or Greek,[53] he appears in John's Gospel as a real person. He

50. John 11:3, 5, 36; cf. 11:11. The verb is φιλεῖν (the noun φίλος, 'love', in John 11:11) in every case except 11:5, which uses ἀγαπᾶν. In the case of the beloved disciple, as we have noticed, ἀγαπᾶν is normative, and φιλεῖν is used only once. Cf. Mark 10:21, where the rich (young) man (ruler) is described as loved by Jesus (ἠγάπησεν αὐτόν, 'he loved him'). But there is no reason to identify that person as the beloved disciple.

51. E.g. F.V. Filson, 'Who was the Beloved Disciple?', JBL 68 (1949), pp. 83–88 (Lazarus was the beloved disciple, and in some sense the author of the Fourth Gospel); also Sanders, pp. 29–52, who argues that the Gospel of John was composed by John Mark (the Elder) on the basis of memoirs from Lazarus, the beloved disciple. M.W.G. Stibbe, John as Storyteller: Narrative Criticism and the Fourth Gospel, SNTSMS 73 (Cambridge: Cambridge University Press, 1992), pp. 77–82, 85–86, assumes that the beloved disciple was Lazarus, and that the fourth evangelist was John the Elder.

52. So Loisy, pp. 127–28. See also Corell, Consummatum, pp. 204–205; Kysar, Fourth Evangelist, pp. 169–70.

53. Bultmann (pp. 483–85) regards the beloved disciple, like the fourth evangelist himself, as symbolising Gentile Christianity, and Peter as the representative of Jewish Christianity. For Gregory, the symbolism was reversed.

is not mentioned very often, which is strange if he is supposed to be an ideal, all-inclusive character; but when he is, the circumstantial details connected with him point in the direction of history, rather than pure symbolism.

Other disciples

We have seen that there is good reason, if not final proof, for identifying the beloved disciple as John the apostle; and certainly his case appears to be stronger than that of any of his rivals.[54]

There are three other possible references to unnamed disciples in the Fourth Gospel, however; and we must examine these, to see if they throw any further light on our subject.

John 1:41

The call of the first disciples in this Gospel (John 1:35–42) includes the summoning of two followers of John the Baptist, one of whom was Andrew. Verse 41 tells us that 'he first found his brother Simon', and informed him that the Messiah had been discovered. The Greek at this point contains a variant. If we read πρῶτος (the adjective, 'the first'),[55] rather than the more likely πρῶτον (the adverb, 'firstly'),[56] it is possible that the sense is, 'the first (of the two disciples who had a brother) found Simon, while the other (James or John) found his brother'. But this stretches the text unnecessarily; and even if we discover a hidden allusion to the apostle John at this point, it helps us in no way to solve the authorship problem.

John 18:15–16

Reference has already been made to this passage, which describes 'another disciple known to the high priest' who accompanied Jesus into the priestly court for the Jewish trial, and also secured Peter's entry. While it is not impossible that this unknown disciple was the beloved disciple (and therefore John), especially if he purveyed fish to the high priest (!), and although he is associated here with Peter, this identification seems unlikely. In the first place, it would be strange for John to be as familiar with the high priest's family as this passage (only) suggests; and secondly, there seems to be no good reason why, if the beloved disciple were involved in this incident, he would not be designated as such. His presence at this moment would have suitably

---

54. E.L. Titus, 'The Identity of the Beloved Disciple', *JBL* 69 (1950), pp. 323–28, suggests Matthias as a further possible candidate.

55. So ℵ * W, *et al.*

56. So P66 A B Θ *et al.*

enhanced his role as a witness to Jesus. We conclude, therefore, that this disciple was another person altogether, who has no bearing on the authorship question.

John 19:35

The final reference to an unnamed disciple in the Fourth Gospel occurs at the time of the crucifixion of Jesus. In this case a bystander at the cross, who saw the spear-thrust (verse 34), is described as 'bearing witness': not only to the spear-thrust by a soldier, presumably, but also to the events of the passion as a whole. The truth of the testimony of this witness is emphasised twice, and the intention of his testimony is referred to as belief on the part of the readers of the Gospel. In view of the fact that the beloved disciple is mentioned only shortly beforehand, with Mary at the cross (19:25–26), it is reasonable to suppose that this anonymous witness is the beloved disciple himself. In this case it is significant that he is not described as the author of the Gospel, but as one to whom the writer can appeal in support of his tradition.

The disciple witness

We can now return to the crucial reference to the beloved disciple in John 21:24: 'This is the disciple who is bearing witness to these things, and has written them (ὁ γράψας ταῦτα); and we know that his testimony is true.' The chief role occupied by the beloved disciple here is that of a witness. We may notice that this is precisely the role, described in very similar terms, of the 'unknown' disciple at John 19:35, who in all probability is the beloved disciple. He is the only one of the three unknown disciples just considered who appears likely to help us with the problem of the authorship of John's Gospel.

But if the disciple of John 21:24 is a witness, to what exactly does he bear witness? What is the reference of the 'things' ([περὶ] τούτων), to which it is said he testifies? And what are the 'things' (ταῦτα) he has written? There are two major problems involved in the exegesis of this verse: the meaning given to ταῦτα and ὁ γράψας, and the relation of John 21 to the rest of John's Gospel.

John 21:24 should no doubt be taken with verse 23, which indicates that the 'things' of verse 24 refer in the first place to the corrected version of the report that the beloved disciple would not die. The disciple himself is testifying to the truth that Jesus merely said he would 'remain until I come'. But by implication the reference of verse 24 could be to the whole of John 21, which reads very much like an eyewitness account (notice verses 7–9 and 11 especially). Beyond that again, the reference could be to the whole Gospel. This depends, of course, on the relation of the epilogue to the rest of John. There are good grounds, however, for arguing that John 21 is closely related to John 1–20, even if it were added to the Gospel at a later date.[57]

The 'testimony' of John 21:24, then, could well relate to the tradition about Jesus preserved in the Fourth Gospel as a whole. If ὁ γράψας in that verse means 'the one who has written (these things)', the beloved disciple is claimed not only as a witness to the Jesus tradition but also as the evangelist himself or herself. However, ὁ γράψας may also be translated as 'the one who caused (these things) to be written'. In this case the verse maintains that the beloved disciple was responsible for the tradition behind John's Gospel. His witness is then authenticated: 'we know (οἴδαμεν) that his testimony is true.' The subject of οἴδαμεν need not be the church which finally published this Gospel; it could as well be the author(s) responsible for its final version. So that the whole verse may be paraphrased as follows: 'The beloved disciple is responsible for the tradition recorded in this Gospel; he caused the tradition to be written down, and the authors can vouch for its reliability.'[58]

Conclusion

None of this gives the final answer to the question, who was John? All we have suggested so far is that the beloved disciple was very probably John the apostle, and that he appears in the Fourth Gospel as an early eyewitness on whose testimony the Johannine tradition rests. But evidently he was not the final redactor of that tradition. Those who were responsible for the Gospel of John in its final form[59] appear in the closing two verses of the Gospel (John 21:24–25), as concerned to emphasise and safeguard the reliability of the source from which their tradition came. In verse 24 they write as the representatives of the Christian tradition being preserved (hence 'we know');[60] in verse 25 a personal opinion is being expressed (hence 'I suppose').[61] There are problems involved in the identification of the beloved disciple as John the apostle, just as there are in the thesis we have outlined concerning the relation between the beloved disciple and the transmission of the Johannine tradition. For example, why should John remain anonymous in the Fourth Gospel, and

57. Cf. S.S. Smalley, 'The Sign in John XXI', NTS 20 (1973–74), pp. 275–88, esp. 275–77.

58. Cf. Tasker, pp. 12–14.

59. Given the prominence of women and their ministry in John, it is not impossible that some female members of the Johannine community were involved in the composition of the Fourth Gospel: perhaps in its final redaction. For a discussion of the roles of women in John's Gospel see R.E. Brown, *The Community of the Beloved Disciple: The Life, Loves, and Hates of an Individual Church in New Testament Times* (New York: Paulist Press and London: Geoffrey Chapman, 1979), pp. 183–98.

60. Cf. 1 John 5:20 (οἴδαμεν δὲ ὅτι ὁ υἱὸς τοῦ θεοῦ ἥκει 'we can be sure that the Son of God has come').

61. See further below, pp. 155–56.

appear under a fairly laudatory title, if in fact he could be easily recognised? If the answer is that the Johannine community or church is responsible for this description, why does it continue in Christian tradition to be confined to Johannine circles alone?

Nevertheless, although we have yet to investigate the question of the Fourth Gospel's actual composition, the evidence so far surveyed yields, on one reading at least, the information that John the apostle, the beloved disciple and a witness in the Gospel, was responsible for preserving the tradition underlying John, but that he and the fourth evangelist(s) were not the same people. This solution makes sense of the external evidence for the authorship of the Fourth Gospel, which as we have seen associates John the apostle eventually with the Gospel, but hesitates over this link at first. It also provides us with an illuminating rationale for the presence and function of the beloved disciple in the Fourth Gospel.[62]

On the basis of our researches into the authorship of John's Gospel, we can now give some attention to a dependent question: when was this document written?

THE DATE OF THE GOSPEL

We are here investigating not the date of the Johannine sources, which we have seen good reason to regard as primitive and reliable,

---

62. The external and internal evidence for the authorship of the Fourth Gospel is clearly and usefully set out in Bernard 2, pp. xxxiv–lxxviii, and Barrett, pp. 100–123. See also Brown 1, pp. lxxxviii–xcviii, where the beloved disciple is identified with John, son of Zebedee (but not as the fourth evangelist). However, Professor Brown has now changed his mind, and disputes that identification; see Brown, *Community*, pp. 33–34. See further Beasley-Murray, pp. lxvi–lxxv (the beloved disciple is neither the apostle John nor the author of the Fourth Gospel); Carson, pp. 68–81 (John is both the beloved disciple and the fourth evangelist!). H.P.V. Nunn, *The Authorship of the Fourth Gospel* (Eton: Alder and Blackwell, 1952) argues without qualification for the apostolic origin of the Gospel. F.L. Cribbs, 'A Reassessment of the Date of Origin and Destination of the Gospel of John', *JBL* 89 (1970), pp. 38–55 (esp. 55), claims, on the basis of certain 'primitive' Johannine elements and concerns, that this composition was undertaken by a 'cultured Christian Jew' of Judea during the late 50s or early 60s of the first century AD. Apparently, however, the author was not, in the view of Cribbs, the apostle John. In his fascinating book *John, the Son of Zebedee*, Alan Culpepper offers us a wide-ranging survey of the 'legends' which have gathered around the apostle John. Among them, Culpepper shows, the claim that John the apostle (= the beloved disciple) was in some way responsible for the Fourth Gospel, while continuing to be challenged, shows no sign of disappearing completely. See Culpepper, *John*, pp. 313–32, esp. 321. Culpepper himself (pp. 72–85) argues against the direct claim. See also J.H. Charlesworth, *The Beloved Disciple: Whose Witness Validates the Gospel of John* (Philadelphia: Trinity Press International, 1996).

but the date of the Gospel of John in its completed form, however that came about.

An upper limit may be set of AD 150, or a little earlier. The theory that the Fourth Gospel belongs to a period later than the middle of the second century, because of its supposed Hellenistic associations and developed theology,[63] has been proved unacceptable, as we have seen,[64] by the discovery in Egypt of two papyri which cannot be dated later than AD 150: Rylands Papyrus 457 (P52), and Egerton Papyrus 2. The latter includes part of a Gospel probably, but not certainly, using John as well as the Synoptics. For this manuscript (like Tatian's *Diatessaron, c.* AD 175) to use the Fourth Gospel alongside the others clearly indicates that John had not just been written.

There are no other conclusive external grounds for placing the Fourth Gospel earlier.[65] We know that it was familiar to gnostics like Ptolemaeus, and used by him in the middle of the second century. It was also used by the writers of the apocryphal *Gospel of Peter* (*c.* AD 150), and of the Valentinian document *The Gospel of Truth* (AD 150?), which forms part of the Jung codex in the library of Chenoboskion. Thereafter the Fourth Gospel is known and ascribed without question to John the apostle. But earlier than *c.* AD 150 we have no evidence that second-century writers knew John; which is one reason for previous attempts to place the Gospel late in that century.

The *terminus a quo* of the Gospel is more difficult to fix. Three factors may be considered.

(a) The relation of John's Gospel to the synoptic Gospels is relevant. If, as we have argued, the Fourth Gospel was written independently of the others, its dating does not depend on theirs. This frees us in our search for a date, but does not really help us. The same is true of the relative dates of the Gospel and Letters of John, since the date of the epistles and indeed their authorship are debatable issues.[66]

(b) An important clue is provided by the reference in John 9:22 and 16:2 (*cf.* 12:42) to the possibility of Jews who confessed Christ being 'put out of the synagogue' (ἀποσυνάγωγος). If this is a redaction, and alludes to the Test Benediction introduced by Rabbi Gamaliel II *c.* AD 85–90, it could point to a lower limit for the date of one edition – at least – of the Gospel. The same is true of the contact which John seems to have with Jewish-Christian discussions generally, suggesting that the Gospel may

63. So Loisy, esp. pp. 68–70.

64. Above, pp. 32–33.

65. There are echoes of John in Ignatius (*Mag* 7.1; 8.2; *Philad* 7.1), whose letters may be dated *c.* AD 115. But the differences are more significant than the resemblances; and they make it unlikely that Ignatius, although close to John in many ways, depends on him.

66. *Cf.* S.S. Smalley, *1, 2, 3 John*, WBC 51 (Waco: Word Books, 1984), p. xxxii, for the suggestion that the Johannine Letters can be dated to the last decade of the first century AD.

have been started earlier than AD 85, before the break, even if it were finished later.[67]

However, as John Robinson points out, unless one *begins* with a 'late' date for John, there is no compelling reason to connect John 9:22 with the events of AD 85–90.[68] Robinson reminds us that excommunication is not specifically mentioned in the wording of the Benediction, which is in any case imprecise; that exclusion was already a regular discipline at Qumran;[69] and that 'being put out of the synagogue' could as well refer to the kind of treatment meted out to Paul in the middle of the first century, as to a formal eviction of believers from Judaism.[70] The use of ἀποσυνάγωγος in John, that is to say, need not preclude a date for the Gospel earlier than AD 85.

(c) Finally, it is probable that time is needed to allow for the development of John's distinctive and expanded theology, especially his christology.[71] Conclusions based on this argument, however, are notoriously subjective and unreliable (how long is 'long'?); and a linear development of New Testament theology is in any case impossible to trace. But if we accept that Luke was the third Gospel to be written, as seems likely, and John the fourth, and if we give a date of around AD 70 for Luke,[72] then a date of around AD 80 becomes possible for John's Gospel.[73]

The limits for the dating of the Fourth Gospel, then, appear to be AD 80–150. There is no reason to look for a period much after AD 100, since a fragmentary manuscript which existed any time from (say) AD 135 obviously depends on an original composition written considerably earlier. Equally, if we have respect for the counter arguments

67.   *Cf.* Lindars, p. 37. For a proposal about the editorial history of John's Gospel see below, pp. 155–57.

68.   Robinson, *Redating, p. 273.*

69.   See 1QS 5.18; 6.24–7.25; CD 9.23, *et al.*

70.   Acts 14:1–6; 17:5–9, 13, *et al.* See Robinson, *Redating*, pp. 272–74; similarly Witherington, III, pp. 27–29, 37–39, esp. 39. Note also the 'throwing out' (using ἐκβάλλειν) of Jesus himself (John 9:34; Luke 4:29), Stephen (Acts 7:58) and Paul with Barnabas (Acts 13:50). *Cf.* also Barrett, pp. 361–62.

71.   See below, pp. 238–48.

72.   So I.H. Marshall, *The Gospel of Luke*, NIGTC (Exeter: Paternoster Press, 1978), pp. 33–35; C.F. Evans, *Saint Luke*, TPINTC (London: SCM Press and Philadelphia: Trinity Press International, 1990), places Luke-Acts between AD 75 and 130 (see pp. 13–15, esp. 14).

73.   Against the argument that John's theology required a long period of time in which to develop fully, see Robinson, *Redating*, pp. 269–72, 283, 308–310. See further the whole section, pp. 254–311, on 'The Gospel and Epistles of John'.

in (b) and (c) above, we can now propose that the final edition of the Gospel of John was published around AD 80.[74]

There is one further problem however. Irenaeus, an important early witness to this Gospel, as we have seen, informs us that John, who was involved in the writing of the Fourth Gospel, lived at Ephesus until the reign of the Emperor Trajan (AD 98–117).[75] If Irenaeus is right about John's association with this Gospel, and if John died before its final edition was published (which may be the implication of John 21:20–24), we shall need to date the Fourth Gospel in its finished form c. AD 100. But if we are not tied to the single tradition of Irenaeus about the date of John's residence at Ephesus, an earlier date of c. AD 80 for the Fourth Gospel is both possible and reasonable.

The composition of the Gospel is related to its authorship. We can now proceed to examine how John wrote. In so doing, the significance of the testimony of Irenaeus to the authorship of John, which we discussed earlier in this chapter, will emerge; and we shall be able to determine the extent to which John's Gospel may be regarded as apostolic.

74. This represents a modification of the conclusion about the dating which I drew in the original edition of this book (on p. 84). But I see the new date as fitting comfortably into the progression which I now detect in the composition of the Johannine corpus as a whole, reflecting as this does the developing history of John's community itself. My scheme places Revelation first in order (AD 70), followed by the Gospel (c. AD 80) and then the Letters (c. AD 90) of John. See further Smalley, *Thunder and Love*, pp. 40–50, 68–69, 134–37.

75. *AH* 2.22.5; *cf. HE* 3.23.1–4.

5

JOHN'S SOURCES

The authorship and composition of the Fourth Gospel are intimately related questions. We have seen that tradition is in the first place a more vital issue in the study of John than authorship. But, as we have also seen, authorship is still an important matter, particularly when it comes to identifying the exact nature of the Johannine tradition. Taking these together, the manner in which John's tradition was transmitted is obviously a question that follows next; and it is to this area, in our study of the Fourth Gospel, that we must now address ourselves.

To consider how the Gospel of John was written involves us in two major methodological approaches. We need first to uncover, if we can, the nature of the fourth evangelist's sources. Given, as we have argued,[1] that there is a historical as well as theological undergirding to the basic tradition behind the Fourth Gospel, from whence did John's particular information about the Jesus story derive? How has his material been shaped? In what stages have the Johannine narratives and discourses been assembled, if that is what has happened, before the Gospel was finally published?

Questions such as these dominated the study of John's Gospel, as of scripture in general, from the rise of biblical criticism in Germany in the 1850s until the 70s of the twentieth century. This method of investigating the text is known as *diachronic*,[2] or historical. It is as if we are looking *through* (Greek, διά) a window, to see what has been going on behind the scenes. We are then in a position to dissect the underlying sources of the Gospel, and to identify the stages in which it has been written.

Secondly, once a diachronic study has been undertaken, it is then possible – and indeed necessary – to examine the document in question as a whole, in order to understand the writer's message, and to learn from its distinctive presentation. This is the *synchronic*,[3] or descriptive, approach: a method which gained popularity in the last quarter of the twentieth century. It is as if we are looking into a mirror, to see what

1. See above, chapter 2.
2. The term 'diachronic', lit. 'through time', from the Greek διαχρόνος, was originally applied to the study of language.
3. 'Synchronic' is also a linguistic term in its initial associations. The word means lit. (studying language) 'at one time', from the later Latin *synchronus*, 'contemporary'. As we shall see, the diachronic and synchronic approaches belong together.

story is reflected back to us from the work put *together*. To this way of discovering John's Gospel we shall return in the next two chapters.[4]

Meanwhile, we can begin our exploration of John's composition with a diachronic study of the sources he might have used.

JOHN'S SOURCES

If, as Christian tradition suggests, only one hand is responsible for the Fourth Gospel as it stands – that of John the apostle – there is, of course, no real problem. We can then say, with at least one modern commentator, that the apostle John was an eyewitness of the events he is recording, and that he himself put his Gospel together before AD 70.[5] However, the composition of the Fourth Gospel is a more complex issue than this view allows. For if we investigate the evangelist's material closely, certain facts emerge which suggest that the Gospel did not begin life as a literary unit, even if it became such in the end. Rather, it can be proposed that the Johannine Gospel was composed from information belonging to a number of different sources; that it came to birth in several, edited stages, rather than all at once; and that more than one writer was involved.

To the history of Johannine source criticism, and its results, we accordingly turn.

The problem

First, we may notice four characteristics of John's composition which do not appear to agree with any plea for consistency within the Fourth Gospel. Although it is possible to argue in general for a unity in John of style and vocabulary,[6] and – as we shall do – for a unity of structure and

4. See further (for the synchronic discipline) M. Powell, *What is Narrative Criticism? A New Approach to the Bible* (London: SPCK, 1993) esp. pp. 1–34, 85–101.

5. So Morris, pp. 4–25, esp. 5–6. *Cf.* Westcott, pp. v–xxxii, esp. xxxii; also, more tentatively, Carson, pp. 68–81, esp. 81.

6. E. Ruckstuhl, *Die literarische Einheit des Johannesevangeliums: Der gegenwärtige Stand der einschlägigen Forschungen* (Freiburg in der Schweiz: Paulusverlag, 1951), argues for the literary unity of John, and therefore its composition, by one hand without the use of sources, on the grounds of the Gospel's stylistic coherence (see esp. part 2). Ruckstuhl follows and advances on the position of E. Schweizer, *Ego Eimi: Die religionsgeschichtliche Herkunft und theologische Bedeutung der johanneischen Bildreden*, 2nd edn., FRLANT ns 38 (Göttingen: Vandenhoeck & Ruprecht, 1965). But see the critique of the approach adopted by both writers in H.M. Teeple, *The Literary Origin of the Gospel of John* (Evanston: Religion and Ethics Institute, 1974), pp. 19–22. Note also B. Noack, *Zur johanneischen Tradition: Beiträge zur Kritik an der literarkritischen Analyse des vierten Evangeliums* (Copenhagen: Rosenkilde og Bagger, 1954), pp. 9–42, who maintains that the Fourth Gospel depends upon oral traditions, rather than written sources.

thought in its final form,[7] the following features nevertheless belong to the Gospel.

(a) There are differences between some parts of the Fourth Gospel and others in the Greek style and language used. Although, for example, we shall insist[8] that John 1 and 21 are closely related to the Gospel as it now exists, it remains true that John 1:1–18 is distinctively poetic, indeed hymnic, in style. That passage also contains terms which do not appear again in the Gospel, such as Λόγος ('word'), χάρις ('grace') and πλήρωμα ('fulness'). There are also stylistic features in John 21 which are unusual for John, as well as those which are normatively Johannine.[9]

(b) The discourses in John at times contain overlapping material. For example, the words of Jesus in John 5:19–25, dealing with the relationship between the Father and the life-giving Son, seem to be repeated with very little variation in 5:26–30. The chief difference between the two passages is their eschatological perspective; in the first the judgment of the Son is present (cf. verse 24), and in the second it is future (cf. verses 28–29). Again, parts of the discourse in John 6 appear to overlap, so that the successive passages 6:35–50 and 6:51–58 not only treat the same subject (Jesus as the bread of life), but also do this in similar terms. The only change is in the more directly sacramental tone of the language used in the second of these two paragraphs (cf. verses 53–57). Similarly, the material in John 14, at the opening of the farewell discourse of Jesus, is virtually repeated in chapter 16. It is possible, of course, that this near duplication of discourse material reflects the teaching method of the evangelist, not to say that of Jesus himself, where the repetition of salient points has a place. Nevertheless, an examination of the synoptic record of the teaching of Jesus, at least, reveals generally the use of varied illustration without direct repetition.

(c) Occasionally in the Fourth Gospel, discourse material is not strictly related to its context. Thus in John 3, where a discussion is in progress between Jesus and Nicodemus, verses 16–21 may be either the words of Jesus or the comment of the evangelist. In the same chapter, verses 31–36 follow immediately upon some words of John the Baptist (verses 27–30); but it is not clear whether they are spoken by John or Jesus, or (once again) are a commentary provided by the evangelist. These uncertainties perhaps indicate that the original setting of this material has been lost.[10]

---

7. So also R.H. Strachan, *The Fourth Gospel: Its Significance and Environment*, 3rd edn. (London: SCM Press, 1941), pp. 81–82; Lightfoot, pp. 11–21. *Cf.* further *IFG* part 3, esp. pp. 289–91.

8. See below, pp. 135–40.

9. See pp. 139–40.

10. *Cf.* also John 12:44–50, where Jesus apparently speaks in public after going into hiding (verse 36).

(d) The Fourth Gospel is characterised by frequent 'aporias', or breaks in sequence. In view of the character which any Gospel possesses, and the fact that none of the evangelists is writing a biography as such of Jesus,[11] in which exact sequences of time and place could be vitally important,[12] we need not make too much of the 'jumps' which are to be discovered in John's Gospel. But it remains true (and odd, if we try to defend the unity of this work) that the ordering of John's material is not always logical or consequential.

For example, we read in John 1:29–34 of John the Baptist's witness to Jesus; and this takes place apparently in the presence of John's disciples (see verse 28). Yet John 3:25–30 suggests that these disciples had understood nothing about Jesus, and explanation follows.[13] Again, Jesus performs his 'first' sign at Cana in Galilee (John 2:11), and what is described as his 'second' sign (4:54, referring to the healing of the official's son) also takes place at Cana. Nevertheless, we are told that while he was in Jerusalem between those two occasions, Jesus performed signs which resulted in the faith of many (2:23). Similarly, John 3:22 records that Jesus and his disciples 'went into the land of Judea', although the setting of chapter 3 is already Judean ('he was in Jerusalem', 2:23).[14]

Further examples of such aporias are not hard to find. The geographical sequence of John 4–7 (where 6:1 mentions that Jesus 'went to the other side of the sea of Galilee', as if he were already in the north, rather than – as chapter 5 indicates – in Jerusalem) is awkward. In John 7:3–5 the brothers of Jesus imply that no signs have been witnessed in Judea, whereas 2:23 and 5:1–9 (the healing of the sick man at the pool of Bethesda) do not agree with this. Immediately after this occasion Jesus announces that he is not going up to Jerusalem for the feast (7:8); but two verses later we are told that he went up (verse 10).[15] During a discourse passage in John 8, Jesus addresses 'Jews who had believed in him' (verse 31); yet very shortly afterwards he appears to claim that this audience is seeking to kill him because his word finds no place in them (verse 37). Possibly John 10:40–42 and 12:37–43 are both descriptions of the way in which the public ministry of Jesus came to a close.[16] Peter's

11. However, see Burridge, *What are the Gospels?* esp. pp. 258–59.

12. See above, pp. 25–28; and below, pp. 125–26.

13. Nevertheless, this is a *further* explanation on the part of the Baptist; there is no reason to suppose that John's disciples were necessarily quicker on the uptake than the Twelve (see Mark 8:14–21, *et al.*).

14. Unless Ἰουδαίαν γῆν ('Judean land') means 'the *countryside*' of Judea, as opposed to the *city* (of Jerusalem). So NRSV.

15. This change of mind, however, may have been deliberate; and the addition of the phrase '(he went up) not publicly but [some MSS add *as it were*] in secret', is obviously significant.

16. See Brown 1, pp. xxiv–xxv.

question in John 13:36, 'Lord, where are you going?' (*cf.* 14:5), seems to contradict the later statement of Jesus, 'none of you asks me, where are you going?' (16:5). A famous break occurs at John 14:31, where Jesus says to his disciples, 'Rise, let us be going', in the middle of the extended farewell discourse: which then continues without a break for a further three chapters (15–17). Finally, there is the example of the structural and geographical interruption (to be discussed in detail) between John 20 and the epilogue of John 21.[17]

Conclusion

The problem posed by these four characteristics of John's writing is clear: they militate against the unity of the Fourth Gospel, a good case for which can be argued.[18] It is possible to explain away some of the difficulties which have been mentioned, but not all. We are forced to conclude, therefore, that John's Gospel shows evidence at one and the same time of careful composition and obvious rearrangement. The signs of this editorial activity (however it may have been carried out) are, moreover, such as to suggest to some scholars the use of *sources* in putting together the Gospel of John; and historically this has been one of the major ways of solving the problem we are discussing. We may now go on to consider this solution; although first we must mention two others which have been advanced, but which are less important.

The solutions

An investigation into the literary origins of John's Gospel, such as the one upon which we are now engaged, is able to draw upon all the major critical methods used to study the work of any evangelist. These are: source criticism (what were the immediate oral or written materials upon which the Gospel writer depended?); form (tradition) criticism (what was the contribution of the church to the tradition, as it was transmitted?); redaction criticism (what was the evangelist's own theological contribution?); and narrative (literary) criticism (what story is the author trying to tell us, from his account of the Jesus tradition?).

These methods inevitably overlap. They have done so wherever John's text has been analysed in the past, and this must always be the case. It will be useful to remember, therefore, as we examine the criticism of the Fourth Gospel, past and present, from the point of view of its literary make-up, that the scholars whose analyses we shall

17. See below, pp. 139–40.
18. See chapters 6 and 7.

be reviewing here have not confined themselves to the source-critical approach, in isolation from any other.[19]

The Author's Method

Some scholars, and for obvious reasons this is particularly true of those who believe that John's Gospel is inherently a unity, explain the apparent disunity of the work quite simply. The aporias in John, and the other problematic features in the composition of the Gospel to which we have drawn attention are, it is maintained, the result of the evangelist's own style and method of working on the basis of different (narrative and discourse) materials. In other words, there is really *no* problem at this point; the Fourth Gospel possesses the character it does because this was the writer's intention. Such is the view of R.H. Strachan, among others;[20] and the work of Eduard Schweizer and Eugen Ruckstuhl, mentioned earlier,[21] evidently points in a similar direction.[22] A variation of this position is held by Kingsley Barrett, who argues that the differences and breaks within John stem partly from the fact that the Gospel was composed over a considerable period of time, during which the author could alter his mind or change his course.[23]

The difficulty presented by this first main solution is that the 'variations' we have noticed within the Gospel of John cannot be regarded as merely the result of using different kinds of material. Definite aporias and other awkward features are involved in the composition of the work, such as one person who was responsible for the complete writing of the Gospel could scarcely have allowed to stand – even in old age! The farewell discourse, for example, contains obvious signs of editorial retouching, so that the command at John 14:31 ('Rise, let us be on our way') now stands in an odd place, and much of the material in chapters 14 and 16 overlaps.[24] There are

19. *Cf.* R. Kysar, 'The Source Analysis of the Fourth Gospel – A Growing Consensus?', *NovT* 15 (1973), pp. 134–52, esp. 138–39. See also J. Ashton, *Understanding the Fourth Gospel* (Oxford: Clarendon Press, 1991), pp. 27–35, 45–50, 76–90, who surveys approaches to the source criticism of John before, during and after Rudolf Bultmann.

20. Strachan, pp. 79–82. See further Teeple, *Literary Origin*, pp. 24–26.

21. See p. 95 n. 6. *Cf.* also the view of Morris noted on p. 95.

22. Schweizer believes that the fourth evangelist used sources, but argues that these cannot now be detected because of the unity of style which has been imposed on John's Gospel (Schweizer, *Ego Eimi*, pp. 82–112). In Ruckstuhl's view the variations of style in John result from the different kinds of material used by the writer: narratives, sayings and longer discourses (Ruckstuhl, *Einheit*, pp. 218–19).

23. Barrett, pp. 25–26; see also the authorship hypothesis on pp. 133–34. Barrett accepts, however, that John's material was drawn from a variety of sources.

24. The origin of the Johannine farewell discourse is a matter of continuing interest and debate. Against the view that the discourse reveals an editor's hand at work, however, it could be argued with some justification that any editor worth his salt would eliminate awkwardness from the ordering of his material, and not introduce it. For a discussion of this point, with reference to John's Gospel as a whole, see below, pp. 114–20, 273–74. *Cf.* also Beasley-Murray, pp. 222–27.

also signs of revision evident in such places as John 4:1–4 and 6:22–24, where apparently some attempt is made, not necessarily with great success, to clarify a narrative situation and give it coherence.[25]

Displacements

A second possible solution to the problem under consideration, and one which need not detain us long, is that somehow and at some stage the contents of the Fourth Gospel have become accidentally displaced. By rearranging some of the chapters in John, it is possible to achieve what might be regarded as a more logical geographical sequence in the events which are being narrated. For example, if John 5 and 6 are reversed, the awkwardness of the switch from Jerusalem (chapter 5) to Galilee (chapter 6) is removed. This has led some scholars – since the second century, indeed – to suggest the theory that the aporias in the Fourth Gospel derive from a dislocation of its original order. How this happened is never very clearly explained. It is difficult to know how it *could* happen, unless we suppose that sheets in an original codex became detached and were then carelessly replaced. By rearranging John's material, it is claimed therefore, any confusions can soon be eliminated. J.H. Bernard, for example, in his commentary on the Fourth Gospel published in 1928, proposed an extensive rearrangement of John which involved not only the transposition of chapters 5 and 6, but also material in other parts of the work including the farewell discourse.[26] An even more elaborate scheme of rearrangement characterises the work of R. Bultmann.[27]

This solution cannot be regarded, however, as either convincing or relevant. It presupposes that John's Gospel in its present form has no unified character, although a case for unity of some kind is possible. Secondly, it depends on a subjective view of the Gospel's arrangement, according to the differing opinions of the scholars who do the arranging. Thirdly, it does not take full account of the nature of John's material: we are dealing here with a Gospel, not a travelogue. Finally, and most damaging of all, the theory of accidental displacements fails to explain

25.   The so-called *pericope de adultera* (John 7:53 — 8:11) requires some mention here, although it is not in fact a real part of our problem. This passage does not appear in the earliest Greek manuscripts of John's Gospel, and was probably inserted eventually from another source. The *placing* of these verses in the Gospels, however, rather than the authenticity of the incident they contain, was likely to have been in question. Thus some witnesses place the story elsewhere in John, and one group of mss locates the pericope after Luke 21:38.

26.   Bernard, l, pp. xvi–xxx.

27.   For example, Bultmann (pp. 312–91, esp. 312–15) questions the present order of John 8–10. On the other side see E. Haenchen, *John 1*, ed. R.W. Funk, HS (Philadelphia: Fortress Press, 1984), pp. 44–51 (= Haenchen 1).

all the features of John's disunity which we have noticed. It may solve, for example, the geographical breaks, although usually only by introducing fresh ones;[28] but it has nothing to say about stylistic differences in the Gospel, the overlapping discourse material, and the sayings which are not strictly related to their context.

Sources

We come next to the most important solution which has been offered to explain the varied character of the Fourth Gospel, and the one which involves the greatest complexity. This is the theory that the composition of John involves the use of a number of different sources, which have been brought together at different stages and by different hands, and eventually fused into the present form of the Gospel. The precise shape of this theory depends on the view taken by the scholar who puts it forward.

Every writer on John, of course, accepts that sources were involved to some extent in the composition of the Fourth Gospel; for, as with any Gospel, the sayings and narrative material contained in its Jesus tradition must have come from somewhere! Thus commentators such as Kingsley Barrett who believe, for example, that the fourth evangelist knew and used the synoptic Gospels, are obviously committed to a basic source theory; and, as in Barrett's case, this can be extended to include other sources, even when it is assumed that in the end the Gospel has been written by one person.[29] The difference between Johannine source theories of this type, and the source criticism of the scholars whose work we are about to survey, lies in the number and variety of sources proposed and, more importantly, in the presupposition that the Gospel of John has been built up over a period of time by a number of editorial hands, rather than being the work of a single author, the fourth evangelist, from the beginning.

Rudolf Bultmann's theory

In the previous chapter we considered the contribution made by the important German scholar Rudolf Bultmann to the study of the background of the Fourth Gospel.[30] Bultmann's influence on Johannine research, however, as with the effect of his scholarship on the study of the New Testament in general, is many-sided; and in no area is this

28. If John 5 is placed next to John 7, for instance, by reversing chapters 5 and 6, a break between Jerusalem and Galilee still occurs (see 7:1).

29. See Barrett, pp. 15–21. Barrett believes that John used the synoptic Gospels, material akin to the synoptic tradition, a discourse source, a Judean or Jerusalem source and a passion narrative.

30. See above, pp. 56–61.

influence more clearly apparent than in his investigation of John's sources. We can examine Bultmann's theory in this respect as a significant and useful starting-point for our survey of a selection of recent work on the literary origins of the Fourth Gospel.

Bultmann, following a 'history of religions' approach, believes that three principal sources were involved in the composition of John.[31]

1. *A Signs Source.* According to Bultmann, the fourth evangelist used a signs source (designated SQ, or *Semeia-Quelle*), from which he selected or took over a series of miracles attributed in it to Jesus: notice the enumeration 'first' and 'second' in John 2:11; 4:54.[32] The source was written, Bultmann proposes, in a Greek which has been influenced by Semitic languages, especially Aramaic. This source, introduced by the call of the disciples in John 1:35–49, makes up (in Bultmann's view) the major narrative sections of John 1-12, the first division of the Gospel. Bultmann regards the increased emphasis on miracle in SQ as a later, non-synoptic development in the Christian tradition, and he is accordingly suspicious about the source's historical value.

2. *A Discourse Source.* Bultmann also discovers behind the Fourth Gospel a source from which John derived the discourses which he assigns to Jesus. This second source consisted of *Offenbarungsreden*, or 'revelation speeches' (also known as RQ, or *Reden-Quelle*). These were poetic speeches written in Aramaic, beginning (Bultmann believes) with what is now the Johannine prologue (John 1:1–16, apart from the prose insertions). The collection, it is alleged, belonged originally to a gnostic environment of the kind reflected in the background of the *Odes of Solomon* and later the Mandean writings;[33] possibly it also had links with John the Baptist's circle. The fourth evangelist, or another, translated these speeches into Greek, keeping some of their poetic form, with the direct intention of placing them in a Christian and historical setting. Jesus, we now learn, is the new and definitive Revealer of true knowledge.

31. See Bultmann, pp. 6–7, *et passim*; also R. Bultmann, art. 'Johannesevangelium' in *RGG3* (1959) cols. 840–50, esp. 841–43. The reader should be warned that it is not easy to describe the limits of Bultmann's proposed sources from a casual study of his commentary. But see the reconstruction of the Greek text of the sources, according to the form suggested by Bultmann, in D.M. Smith, *The Composition and Order of the Fourth Gospel: Bultmann's Literary Theory* (New Haven and London: Yale University Press, 1965), pp. 23–34, 38–44, 48–51, 54–56, and the consideration of Bultmann's proposals on pp. 57–115. See also the discussion of the source theories of Bultmann and others in D. M. Smith, 'The Sources of the Gospel of John', in *idem, Johannine Christianity*, pp. 39–61, esp. 40–53.

32. *Cf.* John 2:23; 12:37; 20:30.

33. See above, pp. 49–51, 57–58.

The additions John made to the material can be discovered by the evident changes from poetry to his own prose in the discourses.[34]

3. *A Passion Source.* Thirdly, Bultmann argues that the fourth evangelist drew on a narrative source which dealt with the death and resurrection of Jesus. This source, again written in a Semitic Greek, has points of contact with the synoptic tradition of the passion, but was (Bultmann suggests) independent of it. The fact that a source was used in the composition of this section of John is indicated by the presence of material which, while written in the evangelist's own style, does not echo his theological interests: for example, the factual details of the trial of Jesus before Pilate, at the opening of John 19.

The final stage in the origin of the Fourth Gospel, in Bultmann's view, was reached when an 'ecclesiastical redactor' appeared on the scene. He was anxious to make the Gospel more acceptable to the church by introducing doctrinal references, particularly of an eschatological and sacramental nature, which John because of his gnostic outlook had omitted. The redactor-editor thus added, for example, allusions to baptism at John 3:5, to the Lord's supper at 6:51–58, and to both at 19:34. He also included such a passage as John 5:28–29, which describes what will happen at the last judgment. At the same time the redactor (Bultmann supposes) made some literary changes, including the addition of John 21. Having discovered the text of the Gospel out of order, he also rearranged it into its present order; although his task was evidently not successfully completed, since Bultmann himself has carried it on!

There are several queries which must be placed against Bultmann's suggestions about the sources of the Fourth Gospel; and it remains true that, even among his pupils, some have followed him in his conclusions while others have not.[35] Bultmann's basic position, for example, rests on assumptions which cannot be accepted without question: notably, the gnostic character of John's Gospel. Furthermore, the suggestions which Bultmann makes about John's three alleged sources present difficulties, particularly because they require three unrelated points of origin for the fourth evangelist's material (in one case a non-Christian source), which have very little historical connection with Jesus himself. This goes against the view, for which (as we saw in chapter 2) there is an increasing respect,

34. See further Smith, *Composition*, pp. 15–23. Bultmann (p. 7) cites, as an example of this stylistic criterion for determining the limits of the speech source, such a change as that occurring between John 3:18 (poetry) and 3:19 (Johannine prose).

35. E. Käsemann's review, for example, 'Rudolf Bultmann: Das Evangelium des Johannes', *VF* 3 (1942–46), pp. 182–201, is critical. H. Becker, *Die Reden des Johannesevangeliums und der Stil der gnostischen Offenbarungsrede*, FRLANT 50 (Göttingen: Vandenhoeck & Ruprecht, 1956), follows and develops Bultmann's thesis of a 'speech source', although not on internal, stylistic grounds; *cf.* esp. pp. 11–13.

that behind John there lies a basically historical, reasonably independent tradition of the words and works of Jesus. In any case the narrative and discourse material of the Fourth Gospel, as the Lazarus incident in John 11 shows clearly, cannot always or easily be separated in the way demanded by Bultmann's theory of isolated sources. Too often the discourse material of the Fourth Gospel arises *from* the signs, and is intimately bound up with them. Again, there is no independent evidence for the existence of sources such as SQ and RQ contemporary with the New Testament period, or prior to it.[36] It would help Bultmann's position if something like the signs source he proposes for John's Gospel, for example, were to be discovered outside it. Finally, Bultmann's identification of these separable sources on linguistic and stylistic grounds is problematic, since the criteria of Johannine style are in fact debatable, and the fourth evangelist's style, so far as it can be determined, now appears in all strands of the Gospel.

The chief reason for drawing attention here to Bultmann's work on John's sources, however, is not to criticise it in detail. It is rather to show how his scheme has been developed in the recent history of Johannine source criticism. For in the case of all three sources isolated by Bultmann, the signs, discourse and passion sources, further research into Johannine origins has proceeded apace, sometimes building on work which appeared earlier than the publication of Bultmann's commentary on the Fourth Gospel. We can now turn to consider the first of these avenues of exploration.[37]

Signs sources

The attempt to discover behind John a source which contained information mostly about the miracles of Jesus, and provided a kernel from which the Gospel could grow, is no new exercise. At the beginning of this century Eduard Schwartz and Julius Wellhausen used the method of redaction criticism to isolate a suggested *Grundschrift* (or 'basic document') on which the fourth evangelist supposedly based his work. Schwartz developed the hypothesis that John's Gospel in its present form was based on an original 'proto-John', a poem about the divine Jesus performing miracles.[38] Wellhausen produced in 1908 a commentary on John which suggested that the Fourth Gospel was composed by interpolating discourse and related material into a previously existing collection of miracle stories about Jesus.[39]

36. Despite the attempt of (among others) Becker, *Reden*, to locate Bultmann's RQ in a pre-Christian, gnostic source.

37. The survey which follows is necessarily selective, and includes only leading examples of Johannine source criticism since Bultmann.

38. E. Schwartz, 'Aporien im vierten Evangelium' in *Nachrichten von der Königlichen Gesellschaft der Wissenschaften zu Göttingen: Philologisch – historische Klasse* (Berlin, 1907), pp. 342–72; (1908), pp. 115–88, 497–560, esp. 558–59.

39. Wellhausen, pp. 102–19.

Two studies of a possible signs source behind John may, because of their importance, be mentioned in more detail; for in many ways they hark back to the earlier proposals of Schwartz and Wellhausen, and follow in the train of Bultmann. The first is an article by Jürgen (not to be confused with Heinz) Becker, which appeared in 1970.[40] Becker concludes that beneath the Gospel of John lies a signs source which presented Jesus as the θεῖος ἀνήρ (the 'divine man') of Hellenism,[41] as well as the Christ of Judaism. He claims that this source was expanded by the fourth evangelist in a non-docetic direction (Jesus is human, as well as divine), to accord with an orthodox theological outlook. Thus the notion of revelation through miracle is played down, and the theme of the cross and resurrection is added. Becker argues that the original signs source began with the witness of John the Baptist (in this he does not follow Bultmann), and included the call of the first disciples (John 1).

The work of the American scholar Robert Fortna, in *The Gospel of Signs*,[42] comes to very similar conclusions about the origin of the Fourth Gospel. Fortna's work has by no means won universal acceptance, but it must be reckoned with in any future study of Johannine sources. Working from the presupposition that source analysis is of greater importance in the literary criticism of the Fourth Gospel than any other method,[43] Fortna studies the aporias in John and decides that they are indications of editorial 'seams'. By this he means that John's Gospel as we now have it is 'the product of a development involving *more than one literary stage*',[44] in the course of which two written strata have been brought together by one principal author. One stratum is a definite signs source (SG), which Fortna uncovers from the narrative material in John; the other is the editorial expansion of this source into the present Gospel. This hypothesis is supported in Fortna's view by the fact that John's style (as described, for example, by Schweizer and Ruckstuhl) is absent from his reconstructed SG source, but present elsewhere in the Fourth Gospel. Like Becker, Fortna believes further that SG began with information concerning John the Baptist and an account of the call of the first disciples. Fortna also maintains that seven miracle stories (including the catch of fish in John 21) belonged to this source, together with the narrative of the Samaritan woman (John 4) and – here he parts company with both Becker and Bultmann – a passion narrative. In other words,

40. J. Becker, 'Wunder und Christologie: Zum literarkritischen und christologischen Problem der Wunder im Johannesevangelium', *NTS* 16 (1969–70), pp. 130–48.

41. See above, pp. 48–61.

42. R.T. Fortna, *The Gospel of Signs: A Reconstruction of the Narrative Source Underlying the Fourth Gospel*, SNTSMS 11 (Cambridge: Cambridge University Press, 1970).

43. *Ibid.*, pp. 1–25.

44. *Ibid.*, p. 3 (italics his).

Fortna's reconstructed signs source is not just one source used by John; he regards it as a complete if abbreviated Gospel in its own right, a 'mini-John' (shades of Schwartz!). In this respect Fortna's work on John's sources is particularly significant.[45]

Robert Fortna subsequently developed his source-critical approach to the Fourth Gospel, in a book which draws directly on the redaction-critical method. *The Fourth Gospel and its Predecessor*[46] again concentrates on John's narrative material, including this time the signs of Jesus, and his death and resurrection. Fortna sets out, and seeks to justify, his hypothetical text of the pre-Johannine sources (somewhat updated from his earlier volume), and compares the result with the text of the present Gospel. This enables Fortna to uncover the 'Johannine redaction': the theological shift from the pre-Johannine to the Johannine (finished Gospel) stage. By bringing together the thematic threads which run through the movement, as Fortna detects it, from John's sources to his existing work, the conclusion is reached that a single-mindedly, christological document has been transformed into 'still more a Gospel of salvation'.[47]

Under this heading may be mentioned a further study which, like the others we have been describing, is ultimately indebted to the method of redaction criticism as well as source analysis. This is the book by W. Nicol, *The Sēmeia in the Fourth Gospel* (1972),[48] in which the writer follows Fortna by discovering behind John a (Jewish-Christian) signs source (S) which had the character of a Gospel, and which after AD 70 was incorporated into the present Gospel of John. The basic difference between the 'Gospel of signs', as detected by Fortna, and Nicol is that Nicol excludes from his proposed source any reference to the passion or to the events contained in John 21.[49]

45. See also two relevant studies by the same author, which appeared before his 1989 volume: R.T. Fortna, 'Source and Redaction in the Fourth Gospel's Portrayal of Jesus' Signs', *JBL* 89 (1970), pp. 151–66; and *idem*, 'Christology in the Fourth Gospel: Redaction-Critical Perspectives', *NTS* 21 (1974–75), pp. 489–504. For a description and critique of the views of both Becker and Fortna see further B. Lindars, *Behind the Fourth Gospel*, Studies in Creative Criticism 3 (London: SPCK, 1971), pp. 28–37.

46. R.T. Fortna, *The Fourth Gospel and its Predecessor: From Narrative Source to Present Gospel*, SNTW (Philadelphia: Fortress Press, 1988 and Edinburgh: T. and T. Clark, 1989).

47. *Ibid.*, p. 264.

48. W. Nicol, *The Sēmeia in the Fourth Gospel: Tradition and Redaction*, NovT Sup 32 (Leiden: E.J. Brill, 1972).

49. *Ibid.*, pp. 14–40. J.L. Martyn, *History and Theology in the Fourth Gospel*, 2nd edn. (Nashville: Abingdon Press, 1979), also and in general accepts Fortna's thesis of a 'Gospel of signs' source behind John as a working hypothesis; see p. 24 n. 8; pp. 164–66, esp. 166. *Cf.* in addition Schnackenburg 1, pp. 59–74, esp. 72, who follows Bultmann in finding a probable, written signs source behind the Fourth Gospel.

Critical archaeologists are still at work in the substructure of the Johannine text. The monograph by Urban von Wahlde, for example, which appeared in 1989,[50] is a further and slightly more elaborate variation on the proposals already reviewed in this section. Professor von Wahlde believes that at least two editions[51] were involved in the composition of John's Gospel, and that the 'original' document dealt chiefly with the signs which Jesus performed. The second edition of the Gospel, von Wahlde claims, can be distinguished from its earlier version by identifying the linguistic, formal and theological differences between them. For example in the revision (it is argued) the miracles are described as 'signs', rather than 'works'; dialogue and discourse replace narrative material; and the view of Christ adopted becomes more exalted.

It is not intended to offer here a detailed assessment of these examples of Johannine signs source research. But, before we move on, some general comments may be made about the suggestion of such scholars as Becker, Fortna, Nicol and von Wahlde, that the origin of John's Gospel may be traced to one unified, narrative source, which subsequently underwent editorial expansion and redaction.

First, the attempt to isolate with any certainty a *single* source containing information about the miracles of Jesus, and virtually no other part of the Christian tradition, is beset with difficulties. In any case, there is no firm evidence outside the SQ hypothesis, whatever form it has taken, that SQ (or SG or S) ever existed. Also, it is notoriously speculative to determine the limits of a source by means of stylistic criteria (so Fortna and Nicol, as well as von Wahlde). If one writer is responsible for the expansion of SG (according to Fortna's reconstruction) into the present Gospel of John, it is likely that the style of that author will become observable in all parts of his final work, and so blur the joins between the seams. Fortna argues, against this, that John's characteristic style does not appear in his source material. But the features of 'Johannine style' are open to discussion; and, in any case, approximately one half of Fortna's stylistic criteria, by the absence of which he determines the limits of his SG, do not appear in *any* Johannine narrative material; so that their absence from SG tells us nothing.[52]

Second, a degree of circularity creeps into the argumentation of these source critics. This is particularly evident in the method of von Wahlde, who leans heavily on supposed contextual aporias in order to set out

50. U.C. von Wahlde, *The Earliest Version of John's Gospel: Recovering the Gospel of Signs* (Wilmington: Michael Glazier, 1989).

51. The limits of these editions, von Wahlde maintains, are sometimes marked by the Johannine 'aporias', or disjunctures. See von Wahlde, *Earliest Version*, pp. 17–25.

52. Fortna, *Gospel of Signs*, pp. 203–218, esp. 205–207; *cf.* Nicol, *Sēmeia*, pp. 13–14.

what *he identifies* as the marks of John's second edition. On this basis, the signs and their original context can easily be recovered![53] One such formal mark is (in von Wahlde's view) the presence of discourse, rather than narrative, material in John's account. However, just as story and sermon belong inextricably together in the Gospel of John as it now exists, the attempt to separate them completely at any stage seems misguided.[54]

This leads us to a third comment. The thesis that the Fourth Gospel rests on a signs *Gospel*, as such (Fortna, Nicol and von Wahlde, but not Becker), presents complications. In the first place, it is unlikely that a Gospel – at least, as we understand that *genre* – ever existed in a form which contained narrative accounts, but little if any teaching of Jesus: and, according to Nicol's estimate, no reference to the passion.[55] Even if such were the case, it is difficult to imagine a creative writer and literary craftsman such as the fourth evangelist taking over a 'mini-Gospel', and simply editing it for the purposes of a new edition. This understanding characterises especially the stance of von Wahlde.[56] He sees John as rejecting material from the first edition, and replacing it with deliberately nuanced passages in order to make an entirely different theological point;[57] whereas the history of the composition of the Fourth Gospel is much more likely to have involved a process of filling out what was already present in seminal form. Our evangelist, that is to say, was a sensitive interpreter, rather than a fussy editor.[58]

Discourse sources

We noticed earlier that Bultmann's theory about the origin of John's Gospel suggested that it grew out of three distinct sources: a signs source, a discourse source and a passion source. We have taken some account of twentieth-century criticism by New Testament scholars who have been exploring (and in one case denying) that this Gospel developed primarily

---

53. See von Wahlde, *Earliest Version*, pp. 26–65, esp. 26.

54. See further below, pp. 129–35.

55. One of the reverse problems about the Q hypothesis is that this putative source apparently contained the teaching of Jesus, but almost no narratives about his ministry.

56. von Wahlde, *Earliest Version*, pp. 176–88.

57. *Ibid.*, p. 96, *et passim*.

58. *Cf.* B. Lindars, *Behind the Fourth Gospel*, pp. 31–34. See further, as a study in Johannine signs source research, T.L. Brodie, *The Quest for the Origin of John's Gospel: A Source-Oriented Approach* (New York and Oxford: Oxford University Press, 1993). Brodie's approach differs from that of the scholars reviewed here, in that he believes John's sources can be located in the other Gospels, the Pentateuch, Luke – Acts, and even in Ephesians (pp. 116–34). The painstaking review by G. Van Belle, *The Signs Source in the Fourth Gospel: Historical Survey and Critical Evaluation of the Semeia Hypothesis*, BETL 116 (Leuven: Leuven University Press and Peeters, 1994), ends by *rejecting* the signs source hypothesis as valid for the study of the Fourth Gospel. See esp. pp. 359–77.

from a *signs* source. It is in this area that research of such a kind seems to have been concentrated in the last thirty years or so. But trends in the other two avenues of Johannine source analysis have not been lacking; and, beginning with *discourse* research, we may now turn to these. Bultmann's consideration of the sayings material in the Fourth Gospel led him to the conclusion that the discourses attributed by the evangelist to Jesus began life in a pre-Christian collection of gnostic 'revelation speeches' which had been written originally in Aramaic. The theory that the Johannine discourses have much in common with religious speeches of (Hellenistic) gnostic origin, proclaiming salvation through a particular deity and even using such a formula as 'I am', did not in fact originate with Bultmann. The important work of Eduard Norden, *Agnostos Theos*, which first appeared in 1913, started from this supposition. Norden developed the idea that the discourses in the Gospels, including John, were an attempt to reproduce the words of Jesus in terms which would appeal to the exponents of contemporary Hellenistic religions of salvation, at the same time making clear the distance between Christianity and paganism.[59] The book by Eduard Schweizer already mentioned, *Ego Eimi* (1965), points in the same direction by drawing attention to the common ground between pagan Greek speeches (using the 'I am' formula), current during the New Testament period, and the phraseology of the Johannine discourses.[60] Siegfried Schulz, in a work which finds a number of 'theme traditions' in the Fourth Gospel, has also shown sympathy for the theory that Hellenistic speeches are the key to the origin and content of John's discourse material.[61] Schulz believes that these traditions derived from a Jewish sectarian background, and were brought into John's Gospel through primitive Christianity of a gnostic type. Among the Johannine theme traditions he discovers appear the 'I am' sayings of the discourses.[62]

59. E. Norden, *Agnostos Theos: Untersuchungen zur Formengeschichte religiöser Rede* (Leipzig and Berlin: Teubner, 1913; Stuttgart: Teubner, 1956); see *e.g.* pp. 298–301 (on John 8). Norden discovers the influence of classical speeches on other parts of the New Testament beyond John's Gospel; and in fact he makes the missionary preaching of Acts, in particular Paul's Areopagus speech (Acts 17), his starting-point.

60. Whereas Bultmann (p. 225 n. 3, *et al.*) suggests that John derived his use of the 'I am' style from Mandean sources, Schweizer (*Ego Eimi*, pp. 46–82, esp. 81–82) argues that the Fourth Gospel and the Mandean writings were dependent in this respect on a common source. But see G. MacRae, 'The *Ego*-Proclamation in Gnostic Sources' in E. Bammel (ed.), *The Trial of Jesus: Cambridge Studies in Honour of C.F.D. Moule*, SBT(2) 13 (London: SCM Press, 1970), pp. 122–34, who proposes that the gnostic sources from Nag Hammadi may offer an even clearer parallel to the Johannine use of ἐγώ εἰμι ('I am'); see esp. p. 133.

61. S. Schulz, *Komposition und Herkunft der johanneischen Reden*, BWANT 5 (Stuttgart: W. Kohlhammer, 1960).

62. *Ibid.*, esp. pp. 85–90. The other traditions are those concerning the Son of man, the Son, the Paraclete, the parousia and the theme of the prologue.

The research mentioned so far in this section, in particular the work of Norden, Schweizer and Schulz, is characterised by two particular features. First, these writers are indebted to a 'history of religions' approach to the study of the New Testament, popular at the turn of the twentieth century, in which serious attention is paid to the possible influence exercised on the writers of the New Testament by their immediate religious environment, whether Jewish or pagan. Second, and in line with such an approach, this group of theorists about the writing of John's discourses believes that the key to their origin lies somewhere in the *Greek* world. As a result, little support is given here to the idea that the speeches in John have any contact with words which Jesus actually spoke, or even with the historical setting in which he spoke them.

This approach to Johannine discourse research, with its Hellenistic orientation, is not the only one which has been followed recently. For it has also been suggested, by other scholars, that a *Jewish* and consequently more traditional background lies behind the discourses of Jesus in the Fourth Gospel. Some of the most significant investigation in this area has been undertaken by Peder Borgen, and published in works by him which have already been cited.

Professor Borgen's monograph, *Bread from Heaven* (1965), is an illuminating study of the concept of 'manna' in the Fourth Gospel and the writings of Philo. In the course of this investigation, Borgen considers how the Old Testament has been used in the bread of life discourse, John 6, and finds that this chapter contains an exposition of the manna text at Exod. 16:4 ('I will rain bread from heaven for you . . .'), in the midrashic style of Philo and the rabbis. That is to say, the discourse of John 6:31–58 is an extended commentary on an Old Testament text (important in its exodus context, on any showing, and obviously relevant in the setting of the Christian exodus which Jesus brings about), in which a typically Jewish homiletic pattern is used. This homily pattern, common to Philo, John 6:31–58 and the Palestinian *Midrashim*,[63] is standard in form. It begins with an Old Testament text, continues with an exposition of that text, and concludes with a recapitulation of the text, usually in a slightly different form. The expository section, again in a characteristically Jewish manner, brings together Old Testament and haggadic (interpretative) words, in this case on the subject of the manna in the wilderness, and links them to other ideas: Greek, in the case of Philo, and Jewish or Christian in the case of John. Thus in the discourse of John 6, the text (Exod. 16:4) appears at verse 31, the exposition extends from verses 32 to 57 (during which words about manna are combined with

---

63. The *Midrashim* were commentaries on the text of the Old Testament, made up of *halakah* (the regulative content of rabbinic literature) and *haggadah* (the illustrative content). 'Palestinian' midrash is the description of a Jewish literary tradition, not only of a geographical centre where midrashes were to be found.

Jewish ideas of law and divine agency, and the Christian tradition of the eucharist), and the homily ends with a restatement of the text at verse 58.[64]

Borgen has also suggested in an article[65] that Jewish sources lie behind the prologue to John's Gospel, and he argues that these verses (John 1:1–18) are an exposition of Genesis 1:1. In each case, John 1 and John 6, Borgen maintains that the *contents* of John's material as well as the method of its composition, both in structure and in exegetical technique, may well point to a profoundly Jewish background. We may add that such a background would be familiar to Jesus, and no doubt (if our conclusions about the basic setting of the Johannine tradition, discussed earlier, are correct) to John himself.[66]

A brief but pertinent article by C.H. Dodd may be mentioned, at this point, on the subject of the origin of the hostile dialogue in John 8:31–58 between Jesus and Jews who, according to verse 31, had believed in him.[67] Dodd's viewpoint differs from Borgen's, since he does not regard John's discourse material (in John 8, at least) as deriving in terms of content and literary method from Jewish sources. But his suggestion is relevant to our survey of the possibly Jewish and traditional background which has been proposed by some writers for John's discourse material. For Dodd argues, with particular reference to John 8:31–47, that in this dialogue Jesus is addressing *Judaising* believers (not simply Jewish Christians) on the subject of loyalty to his teaching, and questioning the spiritual descent of his interlocutors. Because the arguments used in this part of the debate – freedom against servitude, descent from Abraham, and sonship to God – were common also to the controversy over Judaising in the early church (Paul uses them all in Galatians), Dodd suggests that the dialogue in John 8 was linked to this kind of episode; and he goes on to propose that the discourse derived originally from a primitive testimony represented by sayings of John the Baptist and Jesus which are related to the topic being discussed.[68] In other words, the discourse in question rests, Dodd believes, on ideas which belong to the earliest stratum of the Gospel tradition; and this provides a 'solid basis' for John's theological interpretation.[69]

---

64. Borgen, *Bread from Heaven,* esp. pp. 147–92. See further, on the general standpoint of Borgen with reference to the Jewish background of John 6, Lindars, pp. 235–36.

65. Borgen, 'Observations'.

66. On the general subject of the New Testament and Jewish exegesis see B. Gerhardsson, *Memory and Manuscript: Oral Tradition and Written Transmission in Rabbinic Judaism and Early Christianity,* 2nd edn. (Uppsala and Lund: C.W.K. Gleerup, 1964).

67. C.H. Dodd, 'Behind a Johannine Dialogue', in idem, *More New Testament Studies,* pp. 41–57.

68. *E.g.* Matt. 3:7–10; Luke 3:7–9; Matt. 7:21.

69. Dodd, 'Johannine Dialogue', pp. 56–57. See further M. Black, *Aramaic Approach,* pp. 149–51. Black outlines his belief that the Johannine speeches may stem from words of Jesus which originally existed in Aramaic, and were committed early on to a Greek form before being 'targumised'.

Suggestions of a possible Jewish background to the Johannine discourse material do not by themselves establish the precise origin of the speeches in John. Nor, of course, do they guarantee the authenticity of those speeches as actual words of Jesus; especially if, with Borgen, we appeal to later rabbinic method as the inspiration for their composition. (However, C.H. Dodd, as we have just seen, finds a more traditional character for the setting and even contents of John 8.) Nevertheless, research into the initial stages of John's discourses which looks in a Jewish rather than a Greek direction is likely to be fruitful; for even if first-century Judaism was, as we know, influenced by Hellenism, it is very probable that Judaism itself was the primary background of the Gospel tradition, and indeed of John's Gospel.

Passion sources

The third and final source suggested by Bultmann as involved in the original composition of John's Gospel, we saw earlier, is a continuous account of the passion of Jesus. Bultmann thinks that this drew on a pre-Marcan tradition; although he also believes that the fourth evangelist was 'directly or indirectly' acquainted with the Gospel of Mark itself.[70]

The character of the sources which John used for his passion narrative has not often been on its own a subject for research; although as long ago as 1910 Maurice Goguel published just such a study.[71] Goguel regards the history of the Johannine passion narrative, and indeed of the Fourth Gospel itself, as extremely complex. The account of the passion in John, he maintains, combines a number of different fragments. Of these, some are primitive and independent of the synoptic Gospels, possibly in contact with Mark's passion source; some are synoptic in type, elaborated before they were brought into John's narrative; and some are fragments introduced by a redactor. However, Goguel claims, it is impossible now to determine the precise origin and extent of these passion fragments, in view of the negligence of the redactor, whose interests were dogmatic and not historical.[72]

An investigation of the Johannine passion story has subsequently been undertaken by Anton Dauer.[73] The first part of his monograph is a study of the traditional elements lying behind the passion material in John, from the arrest of Jesus to his crucifixion. The second part is a consideration of the passion of Jesus in the understanding of the fourth evangelist.

70. Bultmann, p. 6.

71. M. Goguel, *Les Sources du Récit Johannique de la Passion* (Paris: G. Fischbacher, 1910). This book includes an analysis of the farewell discourse.

72. *Ibid.*, pp. 103–109, esp. 104.

73. A. Dauer, *Die Passionsgeschichte im Johannesevangelium: Eine traditionsgeschichtliche und theologische Untersuchung zu Joh 18.1–19,30.* SANT 3 (München: Kösel, 1972).

Dauer believes that the tradition(s) of the passion used in the Fourth Gospel can be uncovered most easily by isolating first of all the fourth evangelist's distinctive contribution to his source(s). This contribution may be determined by examining John's language and style, his composition technique and his theological outlook. By 'peeling off' this Johannine layer, Dauer argues, and by examining the pre-Johannine passion tradition as this appears in the synoptic Gospels (whether John depended directly on the synoptists or not), the source of John's material in chapters 18 and 19 will emerge;[74] although we should not attempt to reconstruct the actual text of the source. Dauer concludes that this source, which John has worked over theologically, is neither synoptic in itself, nor merely parallel to the synoptic Gospels; rather, it may be described as a (possibly written) source in which fixed oral and written (= synoptic) traditional elements have been fused together.[75]

One of the sources available to the fourth evangelist would obviously contain an account of the passion. The tradition of the death and resurrection of Jesus was of such central importance to the first Christians that it was likely to have been preserved and transmitted in a reasonably fixed form (oral or written, or both) from a very early date. Such a narrative would have been available independently to the writer(s) of the Fourth Gospel, as to the synoptic evangelists; and we do not need to explain the common use of a passion tradition and its basic similarity by presupposing John's literary dependence on the synoptists. Equally, the diversity within the Johannine account of the passion need not stem from the fourth evangelist's use of fragmented sources, as Goguel maintains. Each evangelist, including John, presents an account of the passion in his own way; and a distinctive presentation could easily arise from the evangelist's redaction of a unified source, or from the use of a pre-Johannine tradition in which differing narrative elements have already been brought together (so Dauer). John's passion tradition, in any case, undoubtedly presents us with a combination of basic, reliable source material, and the fourth evangelist's own understanding of this.[76]

74. *Ibid.*, esp. pp. 15–17.
75. *Ibid.*, esp. pp. 226–27. Dauer is conscious of the 'hypothetical' (and, we may add, inconclusive) character of his account of the origin of John's passion source (p. 227).
76. Possibly, for example, John sees Jesus in some ways as an Isaac figure; since only in the Fourth Gospel do we read that Jesus went out to be crucified 'bearing his own cross' (John 19:17; *cf.* Gen. 22:6). The synoptists all record that Simon of Cyrene carried the cross for Jesus. See further, on the whole area of John's literary sources and the development of his tradition, Beasley-Murray, pp. xxxviii–liii. For a study relating to the Johannine farewell discourse see J.Ph. Kaefer, 'Les discours d'adieu en Jean 13:31–17:26: Rédaction et théologie', *NovT* 26 (1984), pp. 253–82.

Editions

We have been considering three possible solutions to the problem of the literary character of John, a Gospel which shows signs of apparent disunity as well as unity in its composition. These solutions concern the author's own method, the possibility of displacements in the text of John, and most importantly the use of sources in the writing of the Gospel.

Before we leave the question of the literary criticism of John's Gospel, we may give some attention briefly to one further explanation which has been advanced in order to account for its literary character. This is in fact an extension of the proposal that the fourth evangelist used sources to compose his Gospel, and it is a solution which is frequently suggested by critics: namely, that John's Gospel came to birth in several redacted stages, or editions.

The source theories we have already reviewed depend ultimately on the basic presupposition that the fourth evangelist, possibly in the company of others, brought together into one the various traditions to which he (or she or they) had access. Scholars who favour the theory that the Fourth Gospel developed from a 'signs source' tend, as we have seen, to regard that source as a *single* point of origin, rather than one of several traditions which were eventually combined. But since John's Gospel contains material dealing with the deeds, sayings, death and resurrection of Jesus, it is likely, given sources at all, that the work will have been built up by adding together *different* traditional strands, representing the different types of material belonging to the Jesus tradition.[77] So Bultmann himself, for example, maintains that the three fundamental sources he regards as involved in the composition of John's Gospel were in the end put together by one 'ecclesiastical' redactor.

If John's Gospel were thus written by combining a number of different sources, this was obviously the work of either one hand, that of the 'fourth evangelist', or several hands. In either case redaction is involved, since committing the Jesus tradition to writing, in the case of *any* Gospel, inevitably means that the evangelist will edit and interpret this from his own point of view. A logical development of this idea is the supposition that if the Fourth Gospel were the responsibility of more than one writer, it went through *several* redactions – not just one – before it reached its present form. In other words the basic Johannine tradition, however it originated and however many sources it drew upon, may have been rearranged and developed – for theological or literary reasons – by different hands (possibly with the aid of further source material) in one or more subsequent editions.

77. At the same time, there is of course no reason why one Gospel source should not itself have contained *varied* types of material. A not very successful attempt to suggest a 'core' to the Gospel of John, consisting of both narrative and discourse material, is to be found in S. Temple, *The Core of the Fourth Gospel* (London and Oxford: Mowbrays, 1975). For the text of the reconstruction see pp. 255–82.

The recent history of the interpretation of John shows how frequently it is suggested that the Gospel was composed in different stages, each one later than its predecessor. The number of these stages, and the extent of the redaction involved in each case, varies considerably in the opinion of the critics.[78]

Wilhelm Wilkens, for example, in a book published in 1958,[79] believes that John is essentially a Passion Gospel which has been constructed in three stages. According to Wilkens, an original *Grundevangelium* ('basic Gospel') lies behind John, consisting of an anti-docetic 'Gospel of signs' which included an account of the passion. This 'basic Gospel' was edited and expanded, Wilkens believes, in a complex process carried out by the fourth evangelist himself. First he added discourses; and later he incorporated further new material in a radical rearrangement of the whole work designed to emphasise the theological motif of the Passover. At the final stage, for example, the evangelist (it is alleged) shifted the account of the cleansing of the temple to the beginning of the Gospel, and placed the eucharist in John 6.[80]

Important as this study is, the thesis of Wilkens is open to question at several key points. Is it true, for example, that John is primarily a 'Passion Gospel'? Did a 'Gospel of signs' ever exist by itself, and if so could it be regarded as *anti-docetic* if, as Wilkens maintains, its purpose was to demonstrate the exalted status of Jesus? Is it certain that the fourth evangelist rearranged his traditional material (for instance, the account of the temple cleansing) for purely literary and theological reasons, without regard to historical considerations? Why did John's 'Passover theology' emerge only when this material had been rearranged, and not earlier? Above all, can we be sure that the fourth evangelist was, as Wilkens believes, his own redactor?

The views of Rudolf Schnackenburg and Raymond Brown on the composition and editing of John's Gospel are more plausible. Schnackenburg regards the Gospel as essentially the work of the evangelist, who relied on diverse traditions, and allowed his Gospel to emerge slowly without finishing it completely.[81] In other words, three stages (once again) were involved in the composition of John. At the first stage existed the materials on which the evangelist drew: the synoptic tradition (probably not, however, known to him in the form of the synoptic Gospels),

78. The signs-source theories already mentioned (above, pp. 104–108) of E. Schwartz, J. Wellhausen, R.T. Fortna and W. Nicol, for example, also depend on the notion that John's Gospel was composed in redacted stages.

79. W. Wilkens, *Die Entstehungsgeschichte des vierten Evangeliums* (Zollikon: Evangelischer Verlag, 1958). Wilkens (p.1) acknowledges his debt to the work of Wellhausen and Bultmann, and is himself followed in his basic thesis about the origin of the Fourth Gospel by Fortna.

80. *Ibid.*, pp. 9–31, 164–70, *et al.*

81. Schnackenburg 1, p. 72; also pp. 387–88.

a written 'signs source', and a 'basic gospel' consisting of independent, early traditions of the words and deeds of Jesus, mostly in oral form. At the second stage the evangelist brought these sources together, and incorporated liturgical or kerygmatic matter which was circulating in the Christian communities, such as the prologue and parts of John 6. Thirdly, a final redaction of the work took place to give the Gospel its present form. At this stage discourse material left in draft form by the evangelist, including John 15–17, was inserted, and the epilogue (John 21) was added. 'Tensions', both structural and theological, in the Gospel as it now stands may well, in Schnackenburg's view, be the responsibility of the redactors at this final stage.[82]

Raymond Brown adopts a more complex view of the history of John's origin; and, if he is right, we are provided with a further interesting solution to the problem of the apparent 'jumps' in the Fourth Gospel.[83] Brown argues that the Fourth Gospel was composed in *five* stages. The first stage presupposes the existence of traditional material concerning the words and works of Jesus: material which was associated with, but independent of, the tradition preserved in the synoptic Gospels. The second stage involved the development of this material in Johannine patterns over a long period, probably through oral preaching and teaching. In Brown's view this was a formative stage, during which a 'master preacher and theologian'[84] gave shape to the Johannine tradition in the context of a 'school' of thought. At this point the stories of the miracles of Jesus were developed into dramas, and his sayings were woven into discourses. Stage 3 saw the organisation of the material described in stage 2 into a consecutive Gospel; and this would be the first, selective, edition of our present Fourth Gospel. The fourth stage Brown sees as concerned with 'secondary edition by the evangelist'.[85] This was one basic revision, and it included adaptation of traditional material to the current situation (as in John 9:22–23). The fifth and final stage (which, Brown admits, cannot always be clearly distinguished from stage 4) was a final redaction by someone other than the evangelist. The redactor, it is suggested, included material from stage 2 which had not been used in previous editions of the Gospel; and this explains why some of the material in John (for example, John 3:31–36 and 6:51–58) appears intrusive or repetitive. So at this final stage, Brown maintains, variant discourses of Jesus to his disciples, extant at stage 2, were included; hence the duplication of material in John 14 and 16, after the break at John 14:31. Also at stage 5, probably, were added the Lazarus material in John 11 and 12, the prologue (John 1) and the epilogue (John 21).

82. *Cf. ibid.*, pp. 72–73.
83. Brown 1, pp. xxxiv–xxxix.
84. *Ibid.*, p. xxxv.
85. *Ibid.*, p. xxxvi.

The important feature belonging to the theories of both Schnacken-burg and Brown is their insistence that, even if John's Gospel passed through various editions before it reached its present form, and was finally put together by a redactor (or redactors) other than the fourth evangelist, the making and shaping of the Fourth Gospel and the crea-tion of its distinctive theology were fundamentally the work of one mind, rather than the haphazard assembly of disparate sources by successive and unrelated hands.

The latter view is characteristic of the study by Howard Teeple, *The Literary Origin of the Gospel of John* (1974). Teeple claims that the Gospel of John consists of four main literary strands, in addition to material from other sources now present in John 1 (the prologue), 20 and 21.[86] The main strands are two written sources: the work of an editor (E) who expanded the sources, and the writing of a redactor (R) other than the editor, who made insertions in the Gospel and added material at the end. One of the editor's sources, Teeple suggests, was a narrative docu-ment (S) showing an interest in Jesus as a signs-worker; the other major source was a semi-gnostic collection of documents (G) which expounded a Christian theology of Hellenistic mysticism. It is maintained that S extends into the passion story, and G excludes all narrative material; although it is doubtful whether John's discourse material can really be characterised as 'semi-gnostic'. The evidence which Teeple uses to deter-mine the exact limits of the four literary strands now making up the Fourth Gospel (S+G+E+R) consists chiefly of linguistic criteria. The resulting structural analysis of the Gospel appears at the end of the book.[87]

Although Teeple is well aware that excessive reliance on stylistic criteria in literary studies can be dangerous,[88] he does not hesitate to use linguistic evidence for his literary analysis of John's Gospel to the same unguarded extent. Almost anything can be proved in this way, however, as his version of the literary structure of John shows. The apparently continuous narrative of the arrest of Jesus in John 18:1–14, for example, is assigned by Teeple to three separate literary strands (S, E and R), and broken up into 22 distinct fragments. Furthermore, material which by its very nature looks as if it should come from the same source, notably such material as that containing the Johannine Son of man sayings, is sometimes placed by Teeple in different literary strands. The saying in John 1:51, for example, belongs on his reckoning to G; that in 6:53 to R or G; and that in 13:31 to E.

Teeple's insistence on solely linguistic criteria to determine the sources and the editorial hands concerned with the composition of

86. Teeple, *Literary Origin*, pp. 142–43. See the whole chapter for his description of the 'writers of the Gospel'.

87. *Ibid.*, pp. 164–248.

88. *Ibid.*, p. 22.

John, and the artificial fragmentation of the Johannine material which his thesis involves, seems to ignore the fact that John is a *Gospel*, with a life of its own. It is misleading to treat a work of history and theology, tradition and interpretation, purely as a literary document which may be taken to pieces by means of exclusively literary methods. More importantly, in the light of our present discussion about the possible editions involved in the composition of the Fourth Gospel, it is likely that the writing and editing of John took place in a Christian community of a particular character, rather than stemming from a literary vacuum. It is equally probable that John's distinctive thought and theology derived from the understanding and guidance of one mind, rather than being the arbitrary result of adding together a series of otherwise unacquainted literary strands. (What is the origin of Teeple's S and G, and what is the exact relationship between the anonymous E and R?) Teeple's proposals hardly take account of the immediate and living setting of the Fourth Gospel: a context which should never be ignored.

The study of John's Gospel from the point of view of redaction criticism (examining its history in terms of the possible editions through which it passed) is always likely to be a subjective process. There is *prima facie* no more reason (and no less!) to give credence to the views of Schnackenburg and Brown than to those of Wilkens and Teeple. We need to be guided by the extent to which proper account is taken of the nature of the document before us, of its background, and of the community in which it arose. We may also ask whether the solutions proposed about the origin of the Fourth Gospel make sense of both the early traditions about its birth, and its present form.

Nevertheless John's Gospel, as we have noticed, bears the marks of editorial activity as well as literary unity.[89] Theories of redaction by stages, such as those we have been considering, certainly help to explain both of these features. This is the case whether one hand was active at all stages of the Gospel's history (the hand of John the apostle, or – if that person is somebody else – the fourth evangelist), or whether several writers, with a common outlook, were at work. In both instances the variations in the Jesus tradition will have given rise to a diversity of source material, which the maker(s) of the Fourth Gospel received in one way and the synoptic authors in another. John's Gospel seems to reflect not only this diversity of sources, but also a plurality of editions, as the underlying Johannine tradition was understood and developed and applied at different stages of its transmission.

89. Even Teeple, *Literary Origin*, p. 142, concedes unity as well as diversity in John's Gospel. But he argues that this results from two factors: the work of all the four writers he detects is scattered throughout the book; and the editor and redactor both 'made modest attempts to unify the diverse material'.

The recognition that the composition of the Fourth Gospel involved editorial activity, however that took place, does not affect, we may conclude, the possibility which has already been argued:[90] that beneath John as it at present exists lies an independent and historically reliable tradition about Jesus. What we are now saying is that this tradition has been interpreted in John's own way, and in line with his particular interests and purposes. No balanced study of the Fourth Gospel can be undertaken, in other words, which does not pay serious attention to both of these elements: the tradition belonging to John's Gospel, and the redaction of that tradition (in stages, or otherwise).

Conclusion

Before we go any further, it may be useful by way of summary to draw together some conclusions about the solutions, which we have been reviewing, to the literary problems of John.

(i) The literary, and indeed theological, diversity of the Fourth Gospel makes it unlikely that the author's method by itself will explain the character of John's composition.

(ii) Equally, theories of 'displacement' are sufficiently individual, and unsupported by firm evidence, to be an adequate explanation of the 'jumps' in John's text.

(iii) Although sources obviously lie behind the Gospel of John, we do not know very much about their original form and content. We cannot be certain, for example, of the relation between oral and written material in the substructure of John; nor can we be sure, even by deduction from the text, that the sources which are at times proposed as the nucleus of the Fourth Gospel (Bultmann's three independent units, for example, or Fortna's 'Gospel of signs', or Teeple's S and G) ever existed in the ways that scholars suggest. Theories such as Bultmann's rest on the assumption that the fourth evangelist drew on sources of a specific character; but this is an insecure foundation on which to build.

In the Fourth Gospel, moreover, the signs material is inextricably linked to the speech material, in a way which suggests not only that they began life together, but also that John took elements from both kinds of material in order to develop them. To maintain therefore (with Wilkens, for example) that John's Gospel emerged from a *Grundevangelium* which was made up solely of signs and passion material is doubly questionable.

(iv) There is an assumption which features in Johannine discourse-source research, that John's speech material is so much his own creation, or influenced by Greek writers (so Schweizer, Schulz), that few if any of the original words of Jesus are preserved in the Fourth Gospel. Further research needs to be carried out on the Johannine discourses, however,

90. See above, chapter 2.

particularly following the lead from the direction of Jewish studies given to us by Borgen, before an authentic base to the speeches of Jesus in John can be dismissed completely.

* * * * *

We have yet to offer our own suggested outline of the way in which John's Gospel was built up, by editing a basic tradition. But first, in the next two chapters, we shall investigate the nature of John's composition, and the precise way in which he wrote his story of Jesus. We have been looking *through* the window diachronically, and trying to discover the sources lying behind the evangelist's tradition. Now we shall look *into* the mirror, and appreciate synchronically the image that is reflected back to us. But even before we embark on that voyage of discovery, we need to take account of the extent to which the synchronic approach to this Gospel has become predominant, not to say fashionable, in Johannine scholarship at the turn of the twenty-first century. To that exciting topic we now turn.

JOHN'S COMPOSITION

Literary criticism of the Bible is not a new discipline. Indeed, a literary approach to the text has formed one facet of biblical criticism almost since it began.[1] Nevertheless, at the close of the twentieth century a fresh literary dimension to the study of the Gospels and Acts (at least) emerged, known as narrative criticism.[2] Moreover, whereas biblical criticism itself developed in Germany, the architects of narrative criticism are primarily North American in origin.

NARRATIVE CRITICISM

Narrative criticism is marked by two characteristics. First, narrative theory is an interdisciplinary, 'secular' technique, belonging as much to English literature, linguistics and historiography, as to theology and biblical studies.[3] For that very reason, as we shall see, the methods of novel writing, for example, can be drawn in to illuminate the text of John's Gospel.[4] Second, narrative criticism adopts a synchronic stance, and treats the material concerned as a unified whole.

What, then, is narrative criticism? This approach needs to be distinguished from both redaction criticism and composition criticism. These are literary methods of studying the biblical text, which came into promi-

1. See Stephen D. Moore, *Literary Criticism and the Gospels: The Theoretical Challenge* (New Haven and London: Yale University Press, 1989), pp. xiii–xxii, esp. xv. M.W.G. Stibbe, *The Gospel of John as Literature: An Anthology of Twentieth-Century Perspectives*, NTTS 17 (Leiden: E.J. Brill, 1993), assembles thirteen essays on this topic, two of which are dated 1923!

2. The descriptions of this discipline vary; they include 'rhetorical criticism', and 'literary criticism' itself. *Cf.* Moore, *Literary Criticism*, p. xvi. Narrative criticism can be applied to the text of the Old Testament, as well as the New. For an examination of the rhetorical dimension to any literary analysis of the Fourth Gospel see C.C. Black, ' "The Words That You Gave to Me I Have Given to Them": The Grandeur of Johannine Rhetoric' in Culpepper and Black (ed.), *Exploring the Gospel of John*, pp. 220–39.

3. Moore, *Literary Criticism*, p. xviii.

4. See below, pp. 122–26. It is perhaps significant that the book by D. Rhoads and D. Michie, *Mark as Story: An Introduction to the Narrative of a Gospel* (Philadelphia: Fortress Press, 1982) is the joint work of a Professor of Bible, in the United States of America, and a teacher of English.

nence during the middle years of the twentieth century. Although 'redaction' and 'composition' criticism are close together, they are strictly speaking different disciplines.[5] Redaction criticism (of the Gospels) is the study
of the evident changes introduced by the evangelists into the traditional
material which they received and handled. Composition criticism, on the
other hand, builds on redaction criticism and examines the *arrangement* of
this material, and how that arrangement has been motivated by the
theological understanding and intention of the Gospel writers. Some
scholars also expand the term 'composition' here to include the construc-
tion by the evangelists of wholly new sayings which are attributed to Jesus.[6]

Both of these methods have in common a preoccupation with the
theological perspective of the writer, by means of which the meaning of a
saying, a pericope, or indeed the Gospel as a whole, can be better understood. That is where the more recent theory of narrative criticism parts
company from them.[7] So Stephen Moore argues that, for composition
critics, narrative is the vehicle of theology, which can be separated from the
narrative form and then interpreted; whereas narrative criticism is *formal-
ist*, insisting that 'the meaning of the biblical text is located in the details of
its structure'.[8] Moore also claims that the narrative method of criticising
the Gospels has two salient features: a preoccupation with *story*, the way
the plot being narrated unfolds; and a concentration on the *readers* of the
Gospel, and their response to the events which are being narrated.[9] Consideration of the reader's role in this exercise forms the basis for a further
theory by which to analyse the material of the Gospels; and this is known
as 'reader-response criticism'.[10]

LITERARY APPROACHES TO JOHN

R.A. Culpepper

A pioneering piece of research, which in the last part of the twentieth
century exercised a profound influence on the study of John's Gospel,

5. Against E. Haenchen, *Der Weg Jesu: Eine Erklärung des Markus-Evangeliums und
der kanonischen Parallelen*, 2nd edn. (Berlin: Walter de Grutyer, 1968), p. 24. *Cf.* S.S.
Smalley, 'Redaction Criticism' in Marshall (ed.), *Interpretation*, pp. 181–95, esp. 181.
6. So N. Perrin, *What is Redaction Criticism?* (London: SPCK, 1970), pp. 66–67, esp. 66.
7. The broad discipline of *structuralism* also forms part of the literary approach to
the study of the text of the Gospels, and of the New Testament generally. The structuralist
treatment of narrative works on the assumption that each narration consists of two parts: a
story (what happens, and who is involved), and a discourse (the means by which the content
of the story is communicated). See further Moore, *Literary Criticism*, pp. 41–55, esp. 44.
8. *Ibid.,* p. 10; see the whole chapter, 'Reading for the Story I', pp. 3–13.
9. Moore, *Literary Criticism*, pp. xxi–xxii.
10. *Ibid.*, p. xxii.

and provided an important impetus for the literary approach to its text, is the book by the American scholar Alan Culpepper, *Anatomy of the Fourth Gospel*.[11] Using techniques of narrative analysis which have their origin in secular scholarship, particularly in work on the novel, Culpepper gives us in this volume a most comprehensive account of what may be described as the 'narrative mechanics' of a Gospel.[12] He concentrates on the categories used by Stephen Moore: story and readers. Culpepper extends his investigation of *plot* to include real and implied author, the narrator, narrative time and characters; and his examination of *readership* relates as well to implicit commentary and implied readers. A simplified version of his diagram, describing the elements which make up the Gospel of John, looks like this:[13]

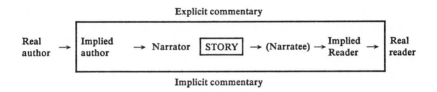

The movement is constantly, and evidently, from the author to the reader; and in this way the narrative critical method is based on communication models of speech-act theory, involving the interaction of author, text and reader.[14]

In Culpepper's scheme, as in any written document, the real author and the real reader, then and now, are clear people of history. But Culpepper believes that the text also embraces an *implied* author, who is to be distinguished from the real author and the narrator, as the literary artist or creative intellect at work in the narrative; this figure is the ideal version of the actual author. The narrator, on the other hand, appears as a rhetorical device: a voice, to tell the story and guide the reader through the plot. In John's Gospel, the narrator (= the evangelist) plays a part similar to that of the chorus in Greek drama: commenting on the action, and explaining its significance to the audience.

11. R.A. Culpepper, *Anatomy of the Fourth Gospel: A Study in Literary Design* (Philadelphia: Fortress Press, 1983). For a definitive study of the narrative critical approach to the biblical text see Powell, *What is Narrative Criticism?*, esp. pp. 85–101.

12. So Moore, *Literary Criticism*, p. 50.

13. See the full, slightly complicated, diagram in Culpepper, *Anatomy*, p. 6. See also Moore, *Literary Criticism*, p. 46.

14. So Powell, *What is Narrative Criticism?*, pp. 8–9.

Similarly, just as in the Fourth Gospel there is an implied author, so there also exist narratees and *implied readers*; although Culpepper does not really distinguish between the narratee and the implied reader.[15] This is the authorial audience: the community for which John wrote his Gospel in the first place. The nature of this circle, and the character of its members, may be deduced from the way John composed his story, the background it presupposes, and the information which the writer offers about the nature of Jesus.

Finally, the response of these readers to the story being unfolded is an important part of Culpepper's analysis. The story itself involves vivid characters and memorable events: what happened before, as well as during and after the ministry of Jesus. The reader is then invited to respond to the cast of characters directly, and to react with faith to the dramatic action of the plot.[16]

Culpepper also maintains that the reader's response to the story of Jesus in John is further shaped not only by the explicit commentary on the action which the narrator provides (as at John 3:31–36; 12:37–43, *et al.*), but also by an *implicit* commentary. This is primarily made up of misunderstandings (*e.g.* John 3:4), irony (5:39–40) and symbolism (1:4, light). In this way the implied author can communicate silently with the implied reader, just as the overt commentary allows the narrator to be in touch with the narratee.[17]

Other Johannine Literary Critics

We have taken some time to set out Alan Culpepper's theory, both because his book is a landmark in the literary approach to John, and also because it is a very useful handbook to the use of narrative criticism as a tool for understanding the Fourth Gospel. But Culpepper has not worked on his own. He has been joined by others in the literary quest for the meaning of John. For example, in 1993 Thomas Brodie published what is probably the first full-scale commentary on John's Gospel in English to adopt a literary handling of the text.[18]

Mark Stibbe's work on the Fourth Gospel has also contributed most usefully to this discussion. In *John as Storyteller*,[19] Stibbe sets out what he regards as the best method of narrative criticism with which to

15. Culpepper, *Anatomy*, p. 206.

16. See chapter 7, for a proposal that John's Gospel was written as a carefully constructed drama.

17. For this section see further Culpepper, *Anatomy*, pp. 6–8, *et passim*.

18. Brodie, *John* (1993). C.H. Talbert, *Reading John: A Literary and Theological Commentary on the Fourth Gospel and the Johannine Epistles*, RNT (New York: Crossroad Publishing and London: SPCK, 1992) is a work comparable to that of Brodie; but it is more popular, and much less detailed. See also Witherington, III, *John's Wisdom*.

19. Stibbe, *Storyteller* (1992).

research John's Gospel. This for Stibbe includes four multi-disciplinary components: a literary analysis of the text itself; a structuralist approach[20] to its plot and genre; a sociological analysis of the Johannine community; and an overview of John's redescription of his historical tradition in story form.[21] In the second part of this volume, those four narrative critical approaches are applied to the passion narrative in John 18 and 19.[22] Dr Stibbe claims that the result is the first scholarly, book-length study of these chapters to be written in English, and the first comprehensive narrative-critical treatment of the Johannine account of the passion of Jesus.[23]

Mark Stibbe has subsequently written two innovative works on the Fourth Gospel. *John*[24] is a passage by passage commentary on the Gospel, applying narrative critical methods to an examination of the complete text. Beginning always with the context (form) and structure within each section of John's material, Stibbe draws out its significance under relevant headings: for example, characterisation, themes, implicit commentary, narrative time (as the fourth evangelist slows down the action, or accelerates it) and intertextuality (transtextual references to Old Testament themes, stories and individual verses).[25] In a second monograph, *John's Gospel*,[26] Stibbe makes easily available to the general reader the fruits of his literary researches into the Fourth Gospel,[27] showing how the current plethora of narrative theories can be used to illuminate its text.[28]

An area of debate, which involves a literary approach to the study of the Gospels, concerns their genre. What *kind* of document is a New Testament Gospel? In answer to this question, it is interesting that some scholars, including Richard Burridge,[29] are currently returning to the view adopted in the nineteenth century that the Gospels are biographies.[30] Drawing on literary theory and the literature of the ancient, classical world, Burridge (for one) is driven to the conclusion that the literary species to which the Gospels belong is Graeco-Roman biography. For him, the writer of the Fourth Gospel 'also presents his theology

20. For structuralism see above, note 7.
21. Stibbe, *Storyteller*, pp. 5–92.
22. *Ibid.*, pp. 95–196.
23. *Ibid.*, p. 95.
24. M.W.G. Stibbe, *John*, Readings (Sheffield: JSOT Press, 1993). Note the introduction, pp. 9–19.
25. For a painstaking, intertextual study of the Fourth Gospel see A.T. Hanson, *The Prophetic Gospel: A Study of John and the Old Testament* (Edinburgh: T. and T. Clark, 1991), esp. pp. 21–253.
26. Stibbe, *John's Gospel* (1994).
27. As set out, for example, in Stibbe, *Storyteller*, esp. part 1.
28. Note esp. Stibbe, *John's Gospel*, pp. 1–4.
29. Burridge, *What are the Gospels?* (1992).
30. *Ibid.*, pp. 3–6; and note the literature, ancient and modern, cited on pp. 3–4.

in the form of a *life* of Jesus'.[31] As a result, Burridge argues, all four Gospels share the same *life* genre, and have in common features of Graeco-Roman *lives*: a formal opening; the dominance of the principal subject; the external size, structure and scale of the material; and the internal features of settings, topics and atmospheres.[32]

The position adopted by Richard Burridge was anticipated in the work of Charles Talbert,[33] who also believes that the Gospels belong to the category of ancient biography, which was narrated within the context of myth. The trouble with this basic understanding is that it forces the genre of the Gospels to conform to another existing literary form: in this case, classical *lives*. A Gospel, however, is a *unique* generic form, a distinctively kerygmatic and didactic composition, a story of Jesus which cannot be compared in form or content to any other literary genre. As James Dunn points out, for all its differences from the synoptic Gospels, John is far closer to them than to any other ancient writing![34]

CONCLUSIONS

The narrative critical approach to John's Gospel, with all its ramifications and associations, seems likely to be determinative as a way of analysing the Johannine text in future.[35] With that possibility in mind, we can now take some account of the strengths and weaknesses of using narrative critical tools, in order to analyse the material which belongs to the Fourth Gospel. As we do so, it is worth reminding ourselves that *the historical and literary methods of investigating John's composition belong together*. We shall see in a moment that to detach the synchronic stance from the diachronic, or the reverse, is likely to unbalance if not distort the resulting interpretation of the fourth evangelist's story.

31. *Ibid.*, p. 238.

32. *Ibid.*, pp. 220–39, esp. 238-39. See also R.A. Burridge, *Four Gospels, One Jesus? A Symbolic Reading* (London: SPCK, 1994).

33. C.H. Talbert, *What is a Gospel? The Genre of the Canonical Gospels* (Philadelphia: Fortress Press, 1977, and London: SPCK, 1978). See the critique of Talbert's arguments in E. Harris, *Prologue and Gospel: The Theology of the Fourth Evangelist*, JSNTS 107 (Sheffield: Sheffield Academic Press, 1994), pp. 10–11.

34. J.D.G. Dunn, 'Let John be John: A Gospel for Its Time' in P. Stuhlmacher (ed.), *Das Evangelium und die Evangelien: Vorträge vom Tübinger Symposium 1982*, WUNT 28 (Tübingen: Mohr- Siebeck, 1983), pp. 309–339, esp. 338–39.

35. See further the essay by D. Foster on the literary approach to John's Gospel in F. McConnell (ed.), *The Bible and the Narrative Tradition* (New York and Oxford: Oxford University Press, 1986), pp. 113–31; also S. van Tilborg, *Imaginative Love in John*, BI 2 (Leiden, New York and Köln: E.J. Brill, 1993). Note van Tilborg's narrative stance, set out on pp. 1–2. See further H. Servotte, *According to John: A Literary Reading of the Fourth Gospel* (London: Darton, Longman and Todd, 1994), esp. pp. 1–3, 97–104; also, on the challenge of narrative criticism, M.C. de Boer, *Johannine Perspectives on the Death of Jesus*, CBET 17 (Kampen: Kok Pharos, 1996), pp. 45–51.

Let us then consider first the main disadvantages, and then the advantages, of adopting narrative critical methods to study John's Gospel.

Disadvantages

(a) It has to be said that the literary approach to any text, biblical or otherwise, is open to the charge of being *subjective*. The results obtained will depend on the individual's reading of the material; and what is reflected back from the mirrored story in the judgment of one viewer, cannot be gainsaid by another. In the end, the parameters, rules and criteria of the narrative method of analysis are determined by ourselves.

(b) For all its illuminating results, narrative criticism is highly *complex!*[36] It draws on a number of disciplines and techniques, and offers a bewildering array of entries into the understanding of John's craftsmanship: implied, as well as actual. A literary model for exploring the Johannine presentation, as we shall see, can be much more straightforward.[37]

(c) This method is potentially *anti-historical*.[38] If the critic is not careful, the detection of literary devices can appear to be a more important way of gaining information about the biblical text, than the establishment of historical accuracy; and the one can take over from the other. For that very reason, as we have suggested, the literary and historical routes into John belong together, and need to be held – sometimes in tension – together.[39]

Advantages

(a) The narrative critical process takes the biblical text itself seriously, and treats it as a unity: whether we are speaking of the Old Testament, the New Testament, the four Gospels, or John's Gospel itself. The literary route drives any student of the Bible back to its contents, and to the world in which the text took shape.

36. So Culpepper, *Anatomy*, pp. 6, 15–49, *et passim*; Powell, *What is Narrative Criticism?*, pp. 19–21.
37. See chapter 7.
38. Against Powell, *What is Narrative Criticism?*, pp. 96–98.
39. J. Ashton, *Studying John: Approaches to the Fourth Gospel* (Oxford: Clarendon Press, 1994), pp. 141–208, wrestles with the possible advantages of using a story-line approach to John. But, in the end, he concludes that the contribution of this method to the interpretation of the Gospel has been small, and that the narrative discipline is 'unlikely to survive beyond the turn of the millennium' (p. 208)! Powell, *What is Narrative Criticism?*, pp. 91–93, addresses an additional objection to this method: namely, that it treats as coherent Gospel material which is in fact diverse in origin. But, as Powell points out, narrative unity does not depend on first establishing a consistency of content. The literary analysis of a document in its final form may be undertaken, that is to say, whatever its earlier genesis and history.

(b)   This method provides important insights into the meaning of the biblical material (in our case, Johannine), even when questions about its origin remain uncertain or unanswered. We do not have to be assured about the precise nature of John's tradition, for example, before we can appreciate his theological witness to the person and story of Jesus.[40]

(c)   Literary approaches to the text of the Gospel allow fresh interpretations of the material to occur. In any case, stories speak directly to people. But because narrative criticism can provide for the biblical material to be interpreted in a variety of ways, and at a number of levels, such a process of analysis releases the fourth evangelist (in this case) to transcend time and space, and address directly problems which may exist in today's church: for example, the nature of Christ's person. The synchronic stance needs to take account of the diachronic; but it will doubtless move beyond that analytical method when it comes to the application of John's testimony to our contemporary world and society.[41]

OUR OWN APPROACH

Given that the advantages of using a narrative method to study John outweigh the disadvantages, as seems to be the case, it is now time to set out our own way of analysing, and therefore interpreting, John's composition.

In the first edition of this book, an historical investigation into the tradition, background and authorship of the Fourth Gospel led into a consideration of the structure, sources and unity of John's work. This was followed later in the volume by an analysis of the Gospel as a carefully constructed drama. We have already considered, in the present edition, the nature of the sources which the fourth evangelist may have used in his composition, and the way in which these have been perceived by contemporary scholars. We may now move on, therefore, to determine the structure of John's Gospel, and then (in the next chapter) to describe its dramatic character. In so doing, we shall be arguing strongly for the unity of this Gospel as it now stands, and adopting once again a frankly literary approach to the interpretation of its contents.

John's Centre

There are many ways in which John's literary structure may be analysed. Barnabas Lindars, for example, sees the Gospel as made up of

40.   This conclusion is not intended to detract from the abiding importance (in my view) of establishing the basis, historical or otherwise, on which John's tradition rests (see chapter 2).

41.   See further, on this whole section, Powell, *What is Narrative Criticism?*, pp. 85–101; also Brodie, pp. 7–9.

fifteen sections. The first eight, ending at John 12:50, describe the effect
of divine glory being manifested in Jesus; the remaining seven sections,
including the 'appendix' of 21:1–25, narrate the sacrificial work of Jesus
in his death and resurrection.[42] Don Carson, on the other hand, divides
the Fourth Gospel into *five* sections: Prologue (1:1–18); Jesus' self-disclosure in word and deed (1:19–10:42); (Transition) Life and Death,
King and Suffering Servant (11:1–12:50); Jesus' self-disclosure in his
cross and exaltation (13:1–20:31); Epilogue (21:1–25).[43] Ben Witherington, III adopts a *sixfold* pattern in his presentation of John's material:
Beginnings (1:1–2:12); Public Ministry of Jesus, phases one and two
(2:13–12:11); Passion narrative, phases one and two (12:12–19:42); Resurrection narratives (20:1–21:25).[44]

None of these analyses, acceptable as they may be in themselves, takes
full account of one important aspect to the structure of John's Gospel:
that is, the marked presence in it of repeated signs, discourses and 'I am'
sayings.[45] Let us look more closely at the arrangement of these.

The Signs, Discourses and Sayings

The fourth evangelist selects[46] for the chief consideration of his readers a number of miracles performed by Jesus during his ministry. These
miracles are termed 'signs' by John,[47] because their spiritual significance
is drawn out in associated discourses which are sometimes pointed,
almost as a text points a sermon, by a connected saying introduced with
the formula ἐγώ εἰμι ('I am'). We must first decide how many signs are
present in John, and then see how the discourses and sayings, linked with
the signs, are arranged so as to form a carefully-constructed whole.

The signs

There are at least six miracles which belong to the main body of John's
Gospel, and which are included in what C.H. Dodd calls the 'book of
signs'.[48] These are: the changing of water into wine at Cana (John 2:1–11;
designated the 'first' – using ἀρχή – of the signs of Jesus, verse 11); the
healing of the official's son (4:46–54); the cure of the sick man (5:2–9);
the feeding of the crowd (6:1–14); the restoration of the blind man's sight
(9:1–7); and the raising of Lazarus (11:1–44). The incident following the

42. Lindars, pp. 70–73.
43. Carson, pp. 105–108.
44. Witherington, III, pp. v–vi, 43.
45. But see *idem*, pp. 156–58, on the close connection between the 'I am' sayings of
Jesus and the Johannine discourses; *cf.* also Morris, pp. vii–xi.
46. *Cf.* John 20:30.
47. *Cf.* John 2:11, *et al.*
48. *IFG*, pp. 297–389. Dodd finds *seven* signs in the book by including the so-called
'walking on the water' in John 6:16–21.

feeding of the crowd in John 6:16-21, when Jesus is described in verse 19 as walking ἐπὶ τῆς θαλάσσης (NRSV, walking 'on the sea'), cannot be regarded as a sign in the same sense as the others. Its meaning is obscure, and certainly not drawn out subsequently; the sign principle, which we are about to discover, is absent; and the ἐπί of verse 19 can just as well mean 'beside' (the water), as 'on' it.

The principle which makes these six signs what they are is announced in the introduction to the Fourth Gospel, John 1 (the whole chapter). There we learn of the Word of God becoming flesh (1:14). At that moment God took a fact of material existence (flesh), and expressed himself by means of it. From then on, the historical and the supra-historical merge in a particular manner. Jesus, who comes to do and to continue the Father's work (5:17), performs signs which express as well as symbolise their basic meaning: that there is new life in Jesus, who is the Christ.

The book of (six) signs, then, which stretches from John 2 to 11, is flanked by the record of the incarnation in John 1 on one side. On the other side we read of the passion followed by the resurrection of Jesus (John 13–21). The tabernacling of the Word forms the basis of all the signs; just as flesh has now become the carrier of spirit, so bread (for example) can convey life. The death and resurrection of Jesus, which John terms his 'glorification', provide at the close of the Gospel the fulfilment to which all the signs point. Because the Son has not only disclosed the glory of God, but has also been glorified (John 1:14; 13:31, et al.), any believer at any time can share in the life of glory (17:1–10). This glory the signs also reveal (cf. 2:11).

But there is a seventh sign, which completes John's collection; and this appears in the epilogue to the Gospel (John 21). The catch of 153 fish (verses 1–14) is both theologically and structurally related to the rest of the Gospel and to the main 'book of signs' in an important and illuminating manner.[49] The detailed reasons for saying this have been set out elsewhere;[50] at present we can only summarise the relevant conclusions.

Theologically the sign in John 21 makes the same point as the other six in the Fourth Gospel, and indeed the point made by the Gospel as a whole: that since the Word has become flesh, material facts of created existence can convey spiritual reality.[51] The catch of fish is made possible by the incarnate and now glorified Jesus. It looks back to the historical basis of eternal life in him, since the Johannine resurrection narrative, like the rest of John's Gospel, never allows us to forget that

---

49. Notice that 'Cana' is mentioned at the start of the narrative (John 21:2), thus picking up the setting of the first of John's recorded signs (2:1, 11), and spanning them all.

50. See Smalley, 'Sign', and the literature there cited.

51. Cf. Hoskyns, pp. 108–109.

the spirit and flesh of Christ, even of the risen Christ, are coherent. But the sign of the 153 fish also expresses the universal scope of the mission inaugurated and energised as a result of the life and death and exaltation of Jesus.

The structural placing of the sign in John 21 also has point. However it came to be part of the epilogue, and whatever the history of John 21 itself,[52] in its present position the miraculous catch of 153 fish harmonises with the other signs in John's Gospel, and caps them all. The only difference is that the exclusive character of the flesh and spirit of the incarnation (John 1) has given place to the inclusiveness inherent in the incarnate Word, and now revealed for all to see in the glorified Jesus. This difference is underlined by the variation in the audiences who witness all seven signs. Those involved in the first six are initially Jewish; although the implications of the signs are much wider, and the crowds of John 6 who were miraculously fed may have included non-Jews. But after the resurrection (John 20), the scope broadens considerably. The immediate audience of the sign in John 21 is no longer Jewish, but Christian; and the missionary dimensions implied by the sign itself are very far-reaching.

The catch of fish in its present setting of the Johannine epilogue, then, reminds us of the uniqueness of the event described at John 1:14. It recapitulates the six signs in the 'book of signs', where the true nature of the Word become flesh is expressed and illuminated; and on the basis of the glorification of the incarnated Word, the Saviour of the world (John 4:42), it typifies the future character of the church's evangelism.

We have yet to consider the over-all structure of the Fourth Gospel, with particular reference to the relation of the first and last chapters of John to the rest of the work. So far we have been examining the character of the seven signs in John's Gospel, in order to suggest that together they have a vital part to play in the plan of the whole Gospel. Not only do they provide it with a unifying framework; they also supply it with a centre by illustrating repeatedly its leading theme: life in Christ. As during the ministry of Jesus, moreover, the signs lead to belief, even if that belief is sometimes uninformed,[53] so from this side of the resurrection the fourth evangelist wishes his readers to 'see' and believe, in order that they may through Jesus the Christ receive eternal life.[54] Here, in the

---

52. There are good reasons for arguing that John 21:1–14 presents a primitive tradition which took shape in a post-resurrection (rather than pre-resurrection) context. See Smalley, 'Sign', pp. 284–88. For an alternative view of the original setting of this sign see Fortna, *Gospel of Signs*, pp. 87–98. Fortna regards the catch of fish in John 21 as the third of seven signs which formed John's basic source (108). We shall consider below the relationship of John 21 (the epilogue) to the remainder of John's Gospel; see pp. 139–40.

53. John 2:11; 4:53; 5:15; 6:14–15; 9:38; 11:27, 45; (*cf.* 21:7).

54. *Cf.* John 20:29–31.

Johannine signs, we thus discover a vitally important element in the structural and theological centre to the Fourth Gospel.

The discourses

The extent to which this is true is made even plainer when we examine the careful way in which John has put his Gospel together, so that each of the seven signs is associated with discourse material which explicates at leisure its real significance and spiritual implications.

The sign during the marriage at Cana (John 2) is followed by the cleansing of the temple (2:13–22). Together, these two actions (the second of which is not a sign in the sense defined here) point to the new era and new life brought in by Jesus. The discourse between Jesus and Nicodemus in John 3:1–21 explains this point in greater detail, and discusses the character of the spiritual regeneration which is made possible by the work of God in his Son and through his Spirit. The healing of the official's son (John 4) is introduced by a discourse (4:7–26), in which Jesus interviews a Samaritan woman. This discourse, concerning the water of life, looks backwards to the discussion with Nicodemus about new birth through water and Spirit (3:5), and forwards to the new life given at a distance to the official's son.[55] The two discourses so far mentioned, in John 3 and 4, are together proleptic of the universal scope of the gospel; for they involve first a Jew and then a Samaritan.

The cure of the sick man at the pool of Bethesda (John 5) is followed by a debate between Jesus and the Jews (verses 19–47), in which the authority and status of Jesus as Son of God and life-giver (5:26–29, 40) are defended. John 6 gives us the sign of the feeding of the crowd, followed by two discourses which are really one. The sermon (6:25–65), on the text 'I am the bread of life' (verse 35), draws out the inner meaning of the miraculous feeding of the five thousand. The debate-discourse in John 7:1–38 belongs with the sign and its subsequent sermon, in that the teaching of Jesus about himself as the bread of life is developed in terms of the definitive water of life which he makes available through the Spirit (verses 37–39). We notice here, as elsewhere, John's apparent preoccupation with the motif of water (present in John 7 in any case by its association with the feast of tabernacles, verse 2). Water is significantly present also in the signs of John 2, 5 and 21, and in the discourses of John 3 and 4.[56]

The restoration of the blind man's sight in John 9 is preceded by the second major conflict-discourse between Jesus and the Jews (John 8:12–59), which opens with the saying, 'I am the light of the world' (verse 12), and closes with the expression ἐγώ εἰμι used absolutely ('before Abraham was I am', verse 58).[57] This discourse expands the thought of Jesus

---

55. The connecting thought of 'water' is present even here; *cf.* John 4:46.

56. *Cf.* also John 6:16–21. See further L.P. Jones, *The Symbol of Water in the Gospel of John*, JSNTS 145 (Sheffield: Sheffield Academic Press, 1997), esp. 219–42.

57. John 9:5 ('I am the light of the world') does not use ἐγώ εἰμι ('I am') in the Greek.

as the light of life (cf. 1:4), the guarantee for which stems from his divine origin (8:23). The sixth sign, the raising of Lazarus (John 11), is a dramatic illustration of the saying of Jesus, 'I am the resurrection and the life' (verse 25), and a vivid anticipation of the resurrection of Jesus himself. It is introduced by the sixth major discourse (John 10:1–18), in which Jesus identifies himself as the true shepherd of Israel who both gives his life for others (verses 11, 15, 17–18), and as a result gives life to others (verse 10).

The final sign, of the catch of fish in John 21, is heralded by the farewell discourse in chapters 14-16. Here Jesus expounds further the meaning of the text, 'I am the (way, and the truth, and the) life' (14:6), and prepares his disciples for their subsequent Christian life and testimony. These thoughts are turned into petitions in the prayer of consecration in John 17.

The 'I am' sayings

The theme linking together the seven discourses, which we have just surveyed, is that of the *life* which Jesus makes available. As we have discovered, the same theme is present in each of the seven signs, and also links them together. If we examine the seven 'I am' sayings in the Fourth Gospel closely, we shall find that they exhibit a similar coherence, in that they are all variations on the same theme of 'life'.

The three 'I am' sayings which belong most closely with a sign and discourse for which they act as a focal point occur in association with the feeding of the crowd ('I am the bread of life'),[58] the restoration of the blind man's sight ('I am the light of the world')[59] and the raising of Lazarus ('I am the resurrection and the life').[60] All three sayings directly or indirectly associate Jesus with the thought and possibility of (eternal) life.

The other four sayings are not linked directly with the remaining signs and accompanying discourses; but in each case they provide a revealing commentary upon them. Thus the changing of water into wine may be linked with the saying, 'I am the true vine'.[61] Not only is there superficial contact in terms of wine and grapes; more importantly, the manifestation of the glory of Jesus in this first sign (John 2:11) makes clear that in him the life of the new Israel, the true vine, has come to birth.[62]

58. John 6:35 (41, 48, 51).
59. John 8:12; cf. 8:18 and 23, both using ἐγώ εἰμι ('I am'). Note also the conjunction of light and life in 1:4, *et al.*
60. John 11:25. For a possible Old Testament background to the 'I am' expression, and its (divine) significance, see below, pp. 225–26.
61. John 15:1(5).
62. The thought of Israel as the vine of God is characteristically Jewish. *Cf.* Psa. 80:8; Isa. 5:1–2.

The saying of Jesus, 'I am the way, and the truth, and the life',[63] is an all-embracing description which may be associated with any of the signs and discourses. But perhaps it may be drawn most readily into proximity with the healing of the official's son, and its preceding discourse in John 4. For there we learn of Jesus as Messiah, the way to God (verse 26), of the truth which characterises Jesus (verse 29) and should be typical of his followers (verses 23–24), and of the life which Jesus shares with the believer (verse 14).

The final two 'I am' sayings, both in John 10, involve shepherd imagery, which again we find anticipated in the Old Testament.[64] Jesus calls himself the 'gate for the sheep' (verses 7, 9), who comes to give life to the one who 'enters the sheepfold' by him (verse 10). There is a connection between this saying and the cure of the sick man at Bethesda. He is the only subject in any of the seven Johannine signs who is offered the choice of receiving the healing life of Jesus (John 5:6), and presumably accepts it (verse 7). The 'strangers', in the person of the Jews, criticise this sabbath healing, and thus make plain their real identity; whereas the sick man gladly hears and follows the voice of truth, and enters into life.[65]

The seventh saying, 'I am the good shepherd',[66] develops and caps the image of Jesus as the door of the sheep. It has obvious points of contact with the sign of the 153 fish. For Jesus the good shepherd, who gives life to others by giving up his life for them (John 10:14–15), is essentially concerned with the 'other sheep' who are to make up in the end the 'one flock'.[67] In the same way the implications of the sign in John 21, as we have seen, are missionary and inclusive; so that, on the basis of the realities to which the sign points, Peter is encouraged to feed the sheep in the flock of Christ,[68] and above all to follow him.[69]

The unity of thought and structure in John, evidenced by this survey of the signs, discourses and 'I am' sayings of the Gospel, has by now become clear. John's centre is to be found in seven signs, bound together with discourses and text-like sayings which expound various aspects of the theme of eternal life as that is to be found in and through Jesus the Christ. As a summary of our discussion so far in this chapter about the literary structure of John we may set out our findings in table form. From the viewpoint of John's centre, the Fourth Gospel looks like this:

63. John 14:6.
64. Psa. 80:1; Ezek. 34:12, *et al.*
65. John 5:10, 16, 37–38; *cf.* 10:5. Note the contrast in John 5:15; *cf.* 10:3–4. Schnackenburg 2, p. 292 associates John 10:9 with 14:6.
66. John 10:11 (14).
67. John 10:16; *cf.* 17:20–21.
68. John 21:16,17 (using πρόβατα, 'sheep'); *cf.* 21:15 (using ἀρνία, 'lambs').
69. John 21:19, 22.

Sign	Discourse	Saying
		'I am'
1. Water into wine (2)	New life (3)	the true vine (15:1)
2. The official's son (4)	Water of life (4)	the way, the truth, and the life (14:6)
3. The sick man (5)	Son, life-giver (5)	the door of the sheep (10:7)
4. The five thousand fed (6)	Bread of life (6) and Spirit of life (7)	the bread of life (6:35)
5. The blind man (9)	Light of life (8)	the light of the world (8:12)
6. Lazarus (11)	Shepherd, life-giver (10)	the resurrection and the life (11:25)
7. The catch of fish (21)	Disciple life (14–16)	the good shepherd (10:11)

Prologue and Epilogue

The structural and intellectual centre of John's Gospel, it may be claimed, is thus formed by seven signs and the discourse material which the fourth evangelist has associated with them. The careful arrangement of the Gospel, however, extends further than this, and includes the first and last chapters (John 1 and 21). We shall now examine the relation of these two chapters to the main body of the Fourth Gospel.

John 1

The so-called 'prologue' to John (usually regarded as John 1:1–18) appears to stand by itself, and to be detachable from the remainder of John 1, and indeed of the whole Gospel. The setting of these verses, for example, is pre-existence;[70] since the fourth evangelist takes us behind the start of the ministry of Jesus (Mark) and even of his life (Matthew, Luke), to the beginning of all things (John 1:1). The form of these verses, also, unusually consists of poetic parallelism, with only occasional prose interludes. Moreover, terms such as 'Word' (Λόγος, 1:1, 14), 'grace' (χάρις 1:14, 16) and 'fulness' (πλήρωμα, verse 16) do not occur elsewhere in John.

At the same time, there are links in terms of both language and ideas which tie the opening verses of the Fourth Gospel to the rest of the first chapter, and to the entire work. Thus, leading motifs which appear in John 1:1–18 are picked up in 1:19–51, and worked out in other parts of the Gospel. For example, 'life and light' is a theme which is announced in John's prologue (1:4–5), echoed in the later part of John 1 (verses

70. For a consideration of the immediate background to the Johannine prologue see Brown 1, pp.18–23, and the literature there cited; see also Schnackenburg 1, pp. 481–93.

33–34, 50–51) and developed, especially against a background of the contrast between light and darkness, in the debate of John 8 and the healing of the blind man and its sequel in John 9. Similarly, the constant Johannine idea of 'glory' appears in John 1:14, lies behind the saying of 1:51, and forms a vital point of contact between the seven signs of the Gospel (cf. 2:11).[71]

In addition to the theological themes which connect John 1:1–18 to the remainder of John's Gospel, there are titles of Jesus used in John 1 which create the same unifying effect. Six christological titles appear in the opening chapter of John, and each forms the starting-point of an associated theological theme which is then carried on and expanded throughout the Gospel. These are: (a) the 'Word' (John 1:1, 14), which is replaced by the title 'Son' in 1:14, 18;[72] (b) 'Christ' (1:17, 41);[73] (c) 'Lamb of God' (1:29, 36);[74] (d) 'Son of God' (1:34, 49);[75] (e) 'King of Israel' (1:49);[76] (f) 'Son of man' (1:51).[77]

The first chapter of John as a whole, then, appears to be a microcosm of the Fourth Gospel as a whole, and to summarise the entire sweep of salvation history with which it is concerned. This impression is strengthened when notice is taken of the universality of names, both personal and topographical, in John 1. For example, the representative figures (important in both Jewish and Christian history) of Moses, Elijah and John the Baptist are there; so are Joseph, Andrew and Peter, Philip, and the true Israelite Nathanael. Even more evocatively John 1, like the Gospel itself, is dominated by the eternal and historical presence of the Father, the Son and the Spirit. Similarly the place-names in John 1 indicate a setting which is broad, and indeed ultimately infinite. We read there of Palestine, both north (Galilee, Bethsaida and Nazareth) and south (Jerusalem and Bethany beyond Jordan); while heaven and earth together form the background to John's writing in this chapter and beyond it.

Already we can see that John's prologue extends in practice beyond John 1:18. The opening verses of the Gospel (1:1–18) certainly make up a unit, the source of which was probably a hymn composed in the Johannine church, either Jewish or Greek in background.[78] Neverthe-

---

71. Cf. John 7:39.

72. Cf. John 5:19–47.

73. Cf. John 20:31.

74. Cf. the Johannine passion narrative (18–19), which develops the sacrificial connotation (among others, no doubt) belonging to this title. See Schnackenburg 1, pp. 297–301; *IFG*, pp. 230–38.

75. Cf. John 20:31.

76. Cf. the idea of kingship especially present and commented upon in the Johannine passion narrative (see John 18:33–38; 19:12–22).

77. Cf. the twelve uses of the expression 'Son of man' in John (3:13, *et al.*), which follow and develop this seminal christological statement. See further M.D. Hooker, 'The Johannine Prologue and the Messianic Secret', *NTS* 21 (1974–75), pp. 40–58.

78. See further Brown, pp. 20–23.

less, the whole of John 1 forms an important introduction to the Fourth Gospel: an 'overture', as it were, in which the major themes and ideas of the work appear for the first time in brief and embryonic form. These are later taken up and developed in the rest of the Gospel.

At the conclusion of John 1, and forming a significant climax to the introduction we have been considering, stands the first of John's Son of man sayings (verse 51): 'Truly, truly, I say to you, you will see heaven split,[79] and the angels of God ascending and descending upon the Son of man.' The problems involved here are many. We need to investigate, for example, the relationship between this logion and the Son of man tradition in both Judaism and Christianity, as well as the authenticity of this verse as a word of Jesus.[80] At present, however, we are chiefly concerned with the theological meaning of John 1:51; although even at this level the complexity of the saying is almost baffling. Nevertheless, in the setting of the Johannine Son of man tradition as a whole, and in the light of the immediate context in which this logion appears, it is possible to suggest the main lines along which the saying may be interpreted.

The background to the Son of man tradition in the Fourth Gospel is probably to be located primarily in Daniel 7 (*cf.* especially verses 13–14) and Psalm 80 (*cf.* verse 17);[81] in both of these passages the figure of the Son of man represents the community of Israel, vindicated after suffering. The Son of man in John also appears to be both an individual and a corporate personality, and he is evidently identified with Jesus, honoured after humiliation.[82] If, as seems likely, the fourth evangelist uses the Son of man tradition christologically, and introduces his selection of sayings as a commentary on the identity of Jesus, which is without question his chief preoccupation in the Gospel,[83] then this first saying in 1:51 is crucial.

The context of John 1:47–51, a discussion between Jesus and Nathanael, has to do precisely with the revelation and recognition of the man from Nazareth (*cf.* verses 45–46). Already in John 1 we have heard

79. The typically Johannine reduplicated 'truly' (Gk ἀμήν, 'amen'), like the opening of heaven here and throughout scripture, signals the advent of an important divine disclosure. *Cf.* John 5:25; 8:58; 10:1, *et al.*

80. See Smalley, 'Son of Man Sayings', esp. pp. 287–89, and the literature cited generally in that article. See also C.F.D. Moule, ' "The Son of Man": Some of the Facts', *NTS* 41 (1995), pp. 277–79, who takes the expression 'Son of man' to be a description of Jesus himself (p. 278).

81. Smalley, 'Son of Man Sayings', esp. pp. 281–87. For the possible background in Psa. 80 see *IFG*, p. 245 and n. 1. The Johannine Son of man tradition should not be considered in isolation from the same tradition in the synoptic witness; but we cannot do more here than state that fact. See further Smalley, 'Son of Man Sayings', p. 281.

82. Against Higgins, *Son of Man*, pp. 153–56, 182–83.

83. *Cf.* John 5:27 (the Son of man as judge); 6:27 (the Son of man as saviour); 8:28 (the Son of man as exalted Lord), *et al.*

the nature of Jesus discussed in terms of the proximate titles 'Son' (1:14, 18) and 'Son of God' (verse 34); not to mention the other titles, 'Word', 'Christ' and 'Lamb of God'. Now our attention is turned finally to Jesus as the *true* Israel. Jesus recognises Nathanael, the true Israelite (verse 47); but Nathanael also identifies Jesus as Son of God and King of Israel (verse 49), both of which are titles of exaltation and vindication (*cf.* John 20:31; 19:19–22). In response, Jesus further reveals his identity to all true disciples, of whom Nathanael is typical, as the Son of man (verse 51), the embodiment of the true community made up by God's people. The Son of man is also Son of God, as Nathanael discerns (verse 49); and the reference to the opening of the heavens in verse 51 (ὄψεσθε τὸν οὐρανὸν ἀνεῳγότα 'you will see heaven split') points forward to the *dénouement* of the Gospel, when the Saviour of the world is glorified. But it may also include a significant allusion to the baptism of Jesus, when (so Mark 1:10–11 par.) the heavens were opened, the Spirit descended, and God declared Jesus to be his Son. As Son of man, moreover, Jesus establishes a decisive connection between heaven and earth, the eternal and the historical, in line with Jacob's vision at Genesis 28:12, a reference to which must be central in John 1:51. He also acts as judge[84] and saviour of the community of believers who, like Nathanael,[85] share the faith of Jacob.[86]

The Son of man saying in John 1:51, we may conclude, acts not only as an important climax to the opening chapter of John's Gospel, but also as a pertinent heading to the whole Gospel. It focuses the reader's attention on the person of Jesus, whom the evangelist wishes to identify as Son, Son of God and Son of man. In characteristically Johannine fashion, verbs of seeing occur in profusion around this saying.[87] John, in other words, invites his audience to 'see' that Jesus is Son of man, with all the meanings conveyed by that title, and therefore that he is the glorified as well as suffering Lord of Israel.

John 1 as a totality, it is being claimed, provides an important introduction to the Fourth Gospel; as a unity itself, this chapter is intimately related

84. *Cf.* the associations between this Son of man saying and the synoptic logion at Mark 14:62, which speaks of the parousia of the Son of man in glory for judgment.

85. The prototypical martyr Stephen, whose dying vision of the Son of man (Acts 7:56) included the sight of a split heaven (Ἰδοὺ θεωρῶ τοὺς οὐρανοὺς διηνοιγμένους, 'Look, I see the heavens opened'), is not far away from Nathanael as an exemplar of that faith which is rewarded by divine self-disclosure. See further C.K. Barrett, 'Stephen and the Son of Man' in W. Eltester (ed.), *Apophoreta: Festschrift für Ernst Haenchen* (Berlin: Alfred Töpelmann, 1964), pp. 32–38, suggesting that for Luke each Christian death after Acts 7:56 involves 'a private and personal *parousia* of the Son of man' (pp. 35–36).

86. *Cf.* R. Maddox, 'The Function of the Son of Man in the Gospel of John' in R.J. Banks (ed.), *Reconciliation and Hope: New Testament Essays on Atonement and Eschatology* (Exeter: Paternoster Press, 1974), pp. 186–204, esp. 190–191.

87. John 1:46,47,48, 50,51.

to the rest of John, and has a vital part to play in the Gospel's careful over-all structuring. It summarises and points forward to the theological material which will be treated in John 2–21: the revelation of the Word to the world (we notice the response foreshadowed in John 1:11), and the glorification of the Word for the world (see John 1:12).[88]

John 21

If the opening chapter of John is indeed linked to the Gospel so closely, what may be said about the closing chapter? We must now investigate the place of John 21 in the literary scheme.

At first sight, it appears difficult to maintain that chapter 21 belonged originally to John's Gospel. This is particularly evident when the close of John 20 and the opening of John 21 are examined together. John 20:29 is a word of blessing from Jesus on those who 'have not seen and yet believe'; but this reads oddly if further resurrection appearances of Jesus are to follow, as they do in chapter 21. Similarly, there is an apparent cadence at John 20:30–31, which sounds as if the writer were rounding off the work rather than intending to add another section. Again, there is a definite break between these two chapters. First, the scene shifts without warning from Jerusalem to Galilee; and second, John 21:1 (with a vague μετὰ ταῦτα, 'after this', at the outset) clearly implies a fresh start. Further, and more generally, the style and diction of John 21 differ from those in the body of the Gospel; and even if the new subject-matter of the chapter – the narratives of the catch of fish (verses 1–14) and the recalling of Peter (verses 15–19), followed by a coda describing the witness of the beloved disciple (verses 20–25) – may account for fresh vocabulary, the fact is that 28 words occur in John 21 which are not used elsewhere in the Fourth Gospel.

Nevertheless, there is no textual evidence to show that John's Gospel ever existed without John 21;[89] and, despite some admittedly untypical features in the chapter,[90] this section of John is markedly Johannine in many respects. Notice, for example, the distinctive use of 'Tiberias' for Galilee in verse 1; the occurrence in verse 2 of the characteristic names Simon Peter, Thomas the Twin and Nathanael of Cana; the appearance of the beloved disciple at verses 7 and 20–24;[91] and the double ἀμήν ('truly') in verse 18, to introduce a saying of Jesus.[92]

88. See further on this subject S.S. Smalley, 'Johannes 1,51 und die Einleitung zum vierten Evangelium' in R. Pesch and R. Schnackenburg (ed.), *Jesus und der Menschensohn: Für Anton Vögtle* (Freiburg im Breisgau: Herder, 1975), pp. 300–313. For the composition of the Johannine prologue *cf.* W. Schmithals, 'Der Prolog des Johannesevangeliums', *ZNW* 70 (1979), pp. 16–43. See also Brown 2, pp. 36–37.

89. Thus P66 Tert *et al.* include it.

90. *E.g.* the expression οἱ τοῦ Ζεβεδαίου (lit. 'those [the sons] of Zebedee') in John 21:2, and the use of the verb ἐπιστρέφειν ('to turn') in verse 20.

91. *Cf.* John 13:23, *et al.*

92. *Cf.* John 3:3, *et al.*

It is clear, then, that we cannot write off chapter 21 as a mere postscript to John's Gospel, and one which has no real connection with it. Even if John 21 appears to stand further away from the Gospel than John 1, which (as we have seen) is closely related to it, there is no real reason to regard John's epilogue in chapter 21 as non-Johannine or unconnected with the Fourth Gospel. Its general flavour is characteristically Johannine, as we have noticed; and in terms of the over-all literary structure of John the final chapter (as we saw earlier[93]), with its sign of the 153 fish, has an important part to play. However the Johannine epilogue came to birth (using, as it does, Galilean rather than Jerusalem traditions), and whenever it became part of the work as we now have it (a question which we shall consider later[94]), John 21 is very much involved in the composition and final arrangement of the Fourth Gospel.[95]

Conclusions

John 1 and 21, then, are chapters which both have a significant function within this Gospel, in terms of their placing as well as their theological content. John 1 introduces the fourth evangelist's presentation of the gospel in a seminally important manner; and John 21, the epilogue, points to the widening scope and broader implications of the gospel of the glorified Christ which has been unfolded. These two chapters support the Gospel's structure like matching buttresses; and they also balance each other in their varied but coherent treatment of John's central theme, the creative inter-relation of spirit and flesh in and through the Word incarnate.[96]

Our synchronic study of the literary structure of John's Gospel forms the basis for analysing it as a dramatic composition. To this topic we now turn.

93. See above, pp. 130–31.
94. See below, pp. 155–56.
95. See further, on the relation of John 21 to the Fourth Gospel, Hoskyns, pp. 561–62 (chapter 21 is not the work of a later editor); similarly Carson, pp. 665–68, esp. 667–68. On the other side see Barrett, pp. 576–78; also Schnackenburg 3, pp. 341–51. Beasley-Murray (pp. 395–98, esp. 396) is ambivalent.
96. For a study of the way in which both John 1 and John 21 are associated with the Fourth Gospel see in addition J.A.T Robinson, 'The Relation of the Prologue to the Gospel of St John', NTS 9 (1962–63), pp. 120–29.

7

JOHN'S GOSPEL DRAMA

In the last chapter we noticed that the Fourth Gospel is a work of superb literary craftsmanship. The careful arrangement of John's material, with its signs centre into which have been dovetailed discourses punctuated by 'I am' sayings, is evidence by itself that those who were responsible for the final and written form of this Gospel had a keen artistic sense.

We may now advance this discussion one stage further, and notice that John is an artist with a strong feeling for drama. This is not a fresh discovery, since many studies of the Fourth Gospel have drawn attention to its dramatic elements. Alan Culpepper, for example, analyses John's plot in terms of its literary design, and demonstrates the fourth evangelist's indebtedness to narrative art forms, including the fictional novel.[1] Even so, Culpepper is prepared to accept the dramatic character belonging to sections of the Fourth Gospel, including the introduction to Jesus and his work (John 1:19–2:11), and the passion narrative from the trial before Pilate to the burial of Jesus (18:28–19:42).[2] George Mlakuzhyil describes the Johannine Gospel in its totality as a 'five-act theological drama',[3] and identifies some of the dramatic techniques used in its composition: such as change of scenes, change of characters and double-stage action.[4] Similarly, Ben Witherington, III believes that John has drawn on the conventions of Graeco-Roman drama to present the story of Jesus 'in a dramatic mode'.[5]

1. Culpepper, *Anatomy*, pp. 79–98.
2. *Ibid.*, pp. 89–90; 95–96.
3. G. Mlakuzhyil, *The Christocentric Literary Structure of the Fourth Gospel*, AnBib 117 (Rome: Pontificio Instituto Biblico, 1987), p. 346; note 346–47.
4. *Ibid.*, pp. 112–21.
5. Witherington, III, p. 5. See also R.H. Strachan, *The Fourth Evangelist: Dramatist or Historian?* (London: Hodder and Stoughton, 1925), esp. pp. 11–40. The answer to the question, in the title of Strachan's book, is that John is both! The inspiration for John's dramatic instinct may have derived from the theatre at Ephesus. P.R. Trebilco, *Jewish Communities in Asia Minor*, SNTSMS 69 (Cambridge: Cambridge University Press, 1991), pp. 159–62, refers to excavations at Miletus – of the theatre, during the Roman period – which have uncovered named seats for Jewish civic dignitaries, who were presumably therefore familiar with the conventions of Greek drama. See further Witherington, III, pp. 4–5 and nn., for further discussion and literature on the affinities between the Fourth Gospel and ancient tragedy.

However, none of these writers – not even the latter two, who claim that the Fourth Gospel as a whole may be conceived in dramatic terms – follows through this perception, in order to analyse the Gospel of John as a structured play. The thesis to be defended here, by contrast, is that John is more than a Gospel with dramatic characteristics: rather, the work is presented as one continuous dramatic action. By considering the Fourth Gospel as a highly-wrought drama, moreover, we can determine John's distinctive presentation of the gospel tradition, centred in Jesus, and appreciate further the evangelist's theological understanding. We shall also discover that this literary-dramatic approach to the Gospel strengthens the case for its unity, already provided by its content and careful structuring.[6]

In this respect, John's interpretation moves beyond that of the synoptists. This is not to say, of course, that the synoptic evangelists have no dramatic instinct.[7] They are also theologians and artists, as well as historians, in their own right; and, because they are describing the drama of salvation, they are from time to time conscious of its dramatic possibilities.[8] But John's conception of the dramatic value of the material he is shaping and composing is altogether more heightened and consistent.

THE PLAY

We can now look at John's unfolding of the gospel drama. It consists of an introduction, two acts and an epilogue.

The Introduction (John 1)

Here the scene is set in heaven (verses 1–13), but moves swiftly to earth (verse 14): with heaven in mind. In this passage, as we saw earlier,[9] we encounter John's principal theological themes, and the chief characters in the drama: Jesus, John the Baptist and the disciples.

Act One (John 2–12)

The first Act deals with *the revelation of the Word to the world*, and consists of six signs with their associated discourses and 'I am' sayings (John 2–12).[10] Both the signs material and the discourse material in this section of John's Gospel are handled dramatically.

---

6. See above, pp. 128–40.
7. *E.g.* the scene in Luke 4:16–30, when Jesus preaches in the synagogue at Nazareth, is described with consummate dramatic skill (note verse 20); although Luke may well have derived this slant from his source(s).
8. I have argued elsewhere that John's Revelation is also dramatically structured. *Cf.* Smalley, *Thunder and Love*, pp. 103–110.
9. See above, pp. 135–39.
10. Note the summary scheme proposed at p.135, above.

The Signs

It is noteworthy, first, that the signs, and sometimes the discourses arising out of them, are presented in short scenes, each involving two active characters or groups of characters. J. Louis Martyn has analysed the 'drama of the blind man' in John 9 so as to make this clear.[11] Martyn believes that we have in this chapter an original healing story (verses 1–7), involving Jesus, his disciples and a blind man, which has been dramatically expanded for John's own purposes by the addition of six brief scenes, each with two main participants, or an individual with a group. These are as follows:

1. The man and the neighbours (verses 8–12)
2. The man and the Pharisees (13–17)
3. The Jews (Pharisees?) and the parents (18–23)
4. The Jews and the man (24–34)
5. Jesus and the man (35–38)
6. Jesus and the Pharisees (39–41).

Martyn's conclusion is that John has constructed a 'two-level drama' on the basis of tradition and in the light of actual contemporary events, even actual debates, in the Johannine church: the excommunication of Jews from the synagogue for confessing Christ, and hostility towards Christian preachers.[12]

The origins of the material in John 9 cannot now be determined exactly. But if we have here traditional material and John's own interpretation of it, this is precisely the combination we shall discover when we analyse the signs of 'water into wine' and the raising of Lazarus later.[13] However, *pace* Martyn, we need not make the mistake of assuming that John's traditional material is to be located only in the original miracle story. It is often difficult in any case to separate clearly sign material in John from discourse material, as the example from John 9 illustrates so well. Apart from this, it is possible to argue for a traditional base (at least) to the Johannine speeches of Jesus.[14] So, keeping Martyn's useful analysis in mind, but not necessarily committing ourselves to his conclusions, we may suggest that in the incident of the healing of the blind man John begins with an authentic story *and* its sequence,[15] presenting both as a dramatic whole.

11. Martyn, *History and Theology*, pp. 24–36.

12. *Ibid.*, pp. 68–81,82, 88–89. Martyn notes that the literary cycle John 9:1–10:42 echoes the 'two-level drama' in 5:1–7:52. For a similar view that John 9 is a fusion of tradition and debate material, which has been influenced by contemporary experience, see Hoskyns, pp. 350–62, esp. 362.

13. See below, pp. 212–23.

14. See esp. below, pp. 223–27.

15. The 'conflict' pattern in the debate which follows the sign is traditional; *cf.* Mark 3:1–6.

But the fourth evangelist has not stopped there. When his account of this episode was written up, it may well have been shaped by the character and needs of John's immediate audience. It will be proposed in due course that the intention of the Fourth Gospel is related to the needs of those in the Johannine church who came from a mixed background, both Jewish and Greek, in the sense of providing them with a diverse but necessarily balanced christology.[16] In that case, we should expect to find such a christology in John 9; for the miracle related in that chapter, with its dependent material, forms part of John's 'signs centre'.

As it happens, the portrait of Jesus in this episode is a fully-rounded one: he is both divine and human. He is the light of the world (verse 5) – a characteristically Johannine expression[17] – who is 'sent' by God, and opens the eyes of the blind (verse 7). He is not only a prophet (verse 17), but also Christ (verse 22) and Son of man (verse 35). Appropriately, therefore, the story ends with a confession of faith in the Lord who has brought life as well as judgment into the world (verses 38–39). At the same time, Jesus is described in this chapter in terms which remind us of his humanity. He is called a Rabbi (verse 2), and he uses his saliva for the act of healing itself (verse 6). Both of these details, which occur in the opening narrative, are presumably traditional.[18] But in the dramatically-fashioned debate which follows, the term 'man' ($\check{\alpha}\nu\theta\rho\omega\pi\sigma\varsigma$) is insistently applied to Jesus.[19] He is described by the healed person as 'the *man* called Jesus' (verse 11); the Pharisees claim that 'this *man* is not from God' (verse 16), and even – twice – that he is 'a *man* who is a sinner' (verses 16, 24). In reply to the Jewish taunt that the origin of 'this *man*' Jesus is unknown (verse 29), the formerly blind man says, 'if this *man* were not from God, he could do nothing' (verse 33). With that statement, John's christology achieves a perfect resolution. Jesus *is* 'a man',[20] but he is also a man 'from God'.[21]

Precisely how much 'shaping' in this direction has been undertaken by John it is difficult to tell. But the portrait of Jesus as we now have it in John 9 is significant, and suited to John's purposes as we shall analyse them.

We may sum up so far. Our brief study of John 9 has shown us that the fourth evangelist writes with dramatic sensitivity. John takes traditional narrative material (the miracle of a blind man healed), and by fusing it with discourse material which is partly traditional and partly influenced by the Johannine situation, he presents this material as a single dramatic unit.

16. See below, pp. 181–85.

17. *Cf.* John 8:12 (11:9–10; 12:35–36, 46).

18. *Cf.* esp. Mark 8:23.

19. E.M. Sidebottom, *The Christ of the Fourth Gospel: In the Light of First-Century Thought* (London: SPCK, 1961), p. 96, points out the potential significance of this language as used of Jesus. Sidebottom adds that 'the $\grave{\epsilon}\gamma\acute{\omega}$ $\epsilon\grave{\iota}\mu\iota$ ("*I am*") utterances are not less compelling because the blind man says $\grave{\epsilon}\gamma\acute{\omega}$ $\epsilon\grave{\iota}\mu\iota$ (John 9:9) of himself' (*ibid.*).

20. *Cf.* John 8:40; 19:5.

21. John 13:3; 17:8.

Does the pattern which we have thus uncovered in one section of the Fourth Gospel exist elsewhere in John? It can easily be shown that, in fact, there is a remarkable similarity in the way the signs are presented in this Gospel. Always we begin with a description of the miracle itself. Usually the narrative is terse, dramatic and memorable, retaining the structure whereby two characters, or one character and a group of people, are the active participants in the brief scenes involved. This can be illustrated from the first sign, the marriage at Cana (John 2).[22] There we are introduced at the outset to the main characters: Jesus, his mother and his disciples (verses 1–2); and the following scenes show us Mary with Jesus (verses 3–4), Mary and the servants (verse 5), Jesus and the servants (verses 6–8), and the steward with the bridegroom (verse 9).

Similarly, Brown claims that in John 4 the fourth evangelist has taken a substratum of traditional material and, with a 'masterful sense of drama', formed it into a 'superb theological scenario'. John does this, according to Brown, by using various techniques of stage setting, such as misunderstanding (John 4:11), irony (verse 12), the use of front and back stage (29), and the Greek chorus effect of the villagers (39–42).[23] Alan Culpepper has reminded us in addition that John's use of the historic present in the Cana passage of John 2 (the use of 'says', instead of 'said'), is a literary device which helps to switch the audience into the scene which is being played out.[24]

Once the sign itself has been narrated John links directly, or associates indirectly, with it his discourse material. On four occasions the debates or sermons arise immediately from a situation precipitated by the sign: the healing of the sick man[25] leads into a dialogue with the Jews, in this case linked dramatically to the preceding narrative by a reference to the sabbath;[26] the feeding of the five thousand[27] is followed by the 'bread of life' sermon, with its dramatic exchanges between Jesus and the crowds, the Jews and the disciples; the healing of the blind man[28] prompts a further disputation with the Jews; and the raising of Lazarus[29] includes dialogue as part of its dramatic narration.

22. See also B. Olsson, *Structure and Meaning in the Fourth Gospel: A Text-Linguistic Analysis of John 2:1–11 and 4:1–42*, ConBNT 6 (Lund: C.W.K.Gleerup, 1974), pp. 79–88, *et al.* This 'two-character' pattern may well be traditional, especially as it belongs also, but in a slightly blurred form, to the synoptic account of the miracles of Jesus. *Cf.* Mark 5:21–43.

23. Brown 1, pp. 175–76, esp. 176.

24. Culpepper, *Anatomy*, pp. 30–31.

25. John 5.2–9b. On this section see further pp. 38–39.

26. John 5.9c. Equally, in terms of dramatic structure, John 5:9–10 and 9:8. The debate in John 5 continues until John 8.

27. John 6:1–14.

28. John 9:1–7.

29. John 11:1–44.

But even where the Johannine signs are not linked so closely to the discourses, part of the fourth evangelist's dramatic technique in this first Act (John 2–12) is constantly to throw the interest of his readers forward by means of recapitulation. That is to say, John extends each sign in some way: either he refers to it again by name, or he allows a dramatically conceived situation to depend upon it, or he alludes to it by means of deliberate echoes. Thus, the changing of water into wine at Cana (John 2) is referred to again in John 4:46; the healing of the sick man (John 5) and the feeding of the multitude (John 6) are, as we have seen, springboards for ensuing dialogues; the healing of the blind man (John 9) is both extended by a debate situation and alluded to, probably for editorial reasons, in John 11:37; and the raising of Lazarus (John 11) is mirrored in the resurrection of Jesus (John 20).[30] The one exception to John's 'signs-projection' is the healing of the official's son (John 4); but this is followed immediately, with only a geographical break, by the sign in John 5.[31]

In this way we are not allowed to forget the signs structure of John's first Act. As a dramatic craftsman the fourth evangelist provides his material with coherence, and prepares the way for what is to come.

The discourses

If we allow that John handles his signs with dramatic instinct, can the same be said of his discourses? We have already noticed that John often treats his speech material dramatically in association with his signs material, perhaps by expanding an episode, containing both kinds of material, which he discovered in his source. But there is more that can be learned about the way the fourth evangelist uses the discourses in his Gospel.

First, we may notice that John's characterisation is not strong.[32] He tends to introduce individuals or (anonymous) groups for the purpose of a dialogue, and then to forget them. Nevertheless, the individuals are real people; and this is particularly true in those discourses of John which are straightforward sermons (John 3,4 and 6). For example, Nicodemus – who reappears in the Gospel[33] – and the woman of Samaria are not without characteristics which show them to be human: bombast in the case of the Jewish ruler, and moral laxity in the case of the Samaritan woman.

Second, John uses in his speeches two dramatic techniques.[34] One is dramatic irony, which occurs in paradoxical statements. Famous exam-

---

30. See further below, pp. 217–23, esp. 221–22.

31. The persistent reference to 'Galilee' as the location of this sign (John 4:43, 45,46,47, 54) may imply dependence on a self-contained, northern source.

32. So Lindars, pp. 53–54.

33. John 7:50; 19:39.

34. *Cf.* Lindars, p. 53.

ples may be found in the saying of Jesus about the temple of his body, and in the claim by the Jews that they were stoning Jesus because he – a man – was 'making himself God'.[35] The other technique is one whereby a character in a dialogue will misunderstand a meaning. The result is that Jesus can continue the discussion, and explore the subject further. Examples of this abound; but we may instance the bewildered questioning of Nicodemus, and of the Jews in the 'bread of life' discourse.[36]

Third, and most importantly, John – as Lindars has suggested[37] – structures his discourse material so as to advance his subject, almost in spiral fashion, through a series of dramatic disclosures towards a climax. Thus: at the close of the conversation with Nicodemus, Jesus declares that there is eternal life available for the person who believes in him, the Son of man;[38] after speaking to the woman of Samaria, Jesus reveals his messianic identity;[39] the dispute with the Jews following the Bethesda sign concludes with a challenge to have faith in Jesus, the new Moses;[40] the 'bread of life' discourse culminates in a confession by Peter that Jesus has 'the words of eternal life';[41] the disputations with the Jews in John 7 and 8 reach their climax with the claim of Jesus: 'before Abraham was, I am';[42] at the conclusion of the debate arising from the healing of the blind man, Jesus acknowledges himself to be Son of man, and claims to be bringing judgment and salvation to the world;[43] the 'shepherd' discourse finishes with a further challenge to accept Jesus on the basis of his person and work;[44] and at the end of his public ministry, Jesus – the resurrection and the life – identifies himself with God (verse 44, 'whoever believes in me, believes in the one who sent me').[45]

Involved in this 'spiralling' technique is John's habit of recapitulating the subject or leading statement of a discourse at the beginning of each section. For example, at the outset of the discourse in John 6 we hear –

35. John 2:19–21; 10:33. See also generally on this subject P.D. Duke, *Irony in the Fourth Gospel* (Atlanta: John Knox Press, 1985) esp. pp. 117–26 (a case study of the man born blind in John 9). Note also R.A. Culpepper, 'Reading Johannine Irony' in Culpepper and Black (ed.), *Exploring the Gospel of John*, pp. 193–207.

36. John 3:3–5; 6:41–59. *Cf.* (on Nicodemus) Haenchen 1, pp. 199–207; (on the Jews in John 6) Beasley-Murray, pp. 91–97.

37. Lindars, p. 53, *et passim*.

38. John 3:15; unless the discourse ends at 3:21, in which case there is an equally climactic saying about 'coming to the light'.

39. John 4:26.

40. John 5:46–47.

41. John 6:68 (*cf.* verse 58).

42. John 8:58.

43. John 9:35–41.

44. John 10:37–38.

45. John 12:50 (see verses 44–50); *cf.* 11:25.

almost as a text is announced before a sermon – the words, 'he gave them bread from heaven to eat' (verse 31). Shortly afterwards, Jesus identifies himself as this heavenly bread: the 'bread of life' (verses 33 and 35). In the continuation of the discourse, the Jews murmur at Jesus because he said, 'I am the bread which came down from heaven' (verse 41). In this way the earlier verses are recalled, the text is restated and the exposition can continue.[46]

To say that John structures his discourses carefully, and is aware of their dramatic possibilities in the first Act of the Fourth Gospel which we are considering, is not to say that they are simply Johannine compositions. A familiar view of John's speech material, in any part of the Gospel, suggests that it was adapted from homilies which were delivered – possibly at the eucharist – in the Johannine assembly.[47] However, we are dealing here with different kinds of material (teaching, preaching and debate), delivered to different audiences (friendly and hostile, Jewish and non-Jewish); and it will not suffice to treat John's discourse material as if it consisted merely of a series of homilies.[48] Even if the Johannine speeches have been shaped in a setting which is liturgical, and owe their origin in part to a homiletic background, there is probably insufficient reason for excluding from them altogether a nucleus of traditional material. In any case, as Brown says, 'the relation of the Johannine dialogues to the primitive tradition about Jesus of Nazareth and his sayings is not a question open to facile solution'.[49]

We have been considering John's feeling for drama in the presentation of the discourses which occur in the first part of his Gospel. As with the signs in Act 1, to which they are so closely related, these discourses illuminate dramatically the nature of Jesus the Word, as he in turn reveals the nature of God. The centre of the discourses is a christological one.

By the end of this first Act, therefore, a truly dramatic climax has been reached. Together, the signs and the discourses have shown us that Jesus is everything he was announced to be in the introduction (John 1): the Word made flesh, the Messiah, the Son of God, the King of Israel and the Son of man. By handling his material with a truly dramatic sensitiv-

46. Cf. further, for an analysis of John's discourse technique, Lindars, *Behind the Fourth Gospel*, pp. 43–60.

47. So Lindars, pp. 51–52. Lindars cites in support of the 'homiletic view' of the making of the Fourth Gospel, the names of Barrett, Braun, Brown, Sanders and Schnackenburg (p. 52). See also Lagrange, pp. 72–99 (esp. 72), on the discourse in John 3.

48. Lindars himself admits, however, that the Fourth Gospel does not consist *only* of homilies strung together (p. 51). Some pieces, he adds, are more likely to have been 'composed specially for the Gospel', and to have incorporated homiletic 'fragments' (*ibid.*).

49. Brown 1, p. 136. Brown notes the 'quasi-poetic' form belonging to the prose of the discourses as we now have them (pp. cxxxii–cxxxv, esp. cxxxv). But, according to the synoptic writers, this was the style that Jesus himself used.

ity, John has uncovered its full meaning. He has also captivated the reader's attention by continually throwing the interest forward. For this purpose, John adopts the broad chronological pattern of feast followed by sign followed by discourse.[50] Each scene within this structure is capped by a reference to the *effect* of the signs and discourses. In line with the principle of John 1:12, 'all who believe can become children of God', we find individuals and sometimes large groups believing in Jesus the Revealer and life-giver, in whom God's glory is clearly to be seen.[51] By projecting forward both the signs and the discourses, in the way we have seen, the fourth evangelist also leads us from one dramatic peak to another. To mark the progress of this action we hear, almost like the tolling of a bell, five of the 'I am' sayings of Jesus, which are by themselves highly dramatic expressions.[52] Then at last we reach the great 'curtain speech' of John 12:44–50 when, according to John, Jesus *cried out* and said, 'the Father who sent me has told me what to say' (verse 50). The Word of God speaks the very words of God!

Act Two (John 13–20)

The second Act of the drama (John 13–20) concerns *the glorification of the Word for the world*, and concentrates on those who acknowledged the claims for Jesus, the Word, already set out in Act 1. This is John's passion narrative for which, in characteristic fashion, he has prepared the way in Act 1. The sign of the death and raising of Lazarus (John 11) has deliberately foreshadowed the death and resurrection of Jesus; the final plans to arrest Jesus have already been made (11:57); and the preliminary scenes of the passion – the anointing at Bethany, and the entry into Jerusalem[53] – have already taken place. With a great sense of occasion, moreover, John has not only anticipated the start of the passion narrative proper; he has also delayed its actual beginning. First, he has inserted the Lazarus narrative; then he has followed the triumphal entry with a section of teaching which – as the scope of the drama widens – is addressed to Greeks as well as Jews.[54]

But now, after the interval, Act 2 opens, with the Johannine version of the episode in the upper room.[55] The setting is markedly different. At

50. *Cf.* John 2:13; 4:45; 5:1; 6:4; 7:2; 11:55.

51. *Cf.* John (1:14); 2:11; 4:53; 5:8–9, 24; 6:68–69; 9:38; 11:27, 45.

52. *Cf.* E.K. Lee, 'The Drama of the Fourth Gospel', *ExpT* 65 (1953–54), pp. 173–76, who notices in addition that John's dramatic action as a whole is carried forward with reference to certain critical 'hours', which mark the stages in the battle between faith and doubt on the part of those who react to the self-revelation of Jesus (note John 2:4; 7:30; 8:20; 12:23, 27; 17:1, *et al.*).

53. John 12:1–19.

54. John 12:20–50 (note verse 20). These are, at least, representatives of the Hellenistic world.

55. John 13:1–38.

the close of Act 1 the audience had been outside, in the noisy market place and among the predominantly hostile crowds, where Jesus had to shout to be heard. Here the atmosphere is friendly, intimate and quiet, as Jesus shares a meal with his closest followers. When the curtain rises, the spotlight falls on the central character in the drama, Jesus himself; and John tells us that he was aware 'that his hour had come' (John 13:1). The next person to be identified is not, as might be expected, the beloved disciple (who appears for the first time in John's Gospel during this supper scene), nor Peter. It is rather Judas, whose evil nature is under-lined much more by the fourth evangelist than by the synoptic writers. John alone tells us that Judas was a thief (12:6), that he was prompted and indeed taken over by the devil (13:2, 27), and that Jesus referred to him as 'a devil' (6:70) and as the 'son of destruction' (17:12).[56] In a highly dramatic fashion, John at the very outset of the passion narrative presents us with a vivid and visual contrast between light and darkness: Jesus, the incarnation of God, and Judas, the embodiment of Satan. Good and evil are locked in conflict. John's readers know the outcome; but, at the time, the battle is real.

The Footwashing in John 13 is itself a highly dramatised action. It is not a detached incident, reinforcing the ethic of humility by a memorable example;[57] this is an acted parable, which teaches that forgiveness and mutual love are grounded in the historical fact of the obedience of Jesus to his Father's will, and of his humiliation in death.[58] As such, the opening dramatic scene of this Act both introduces and interprets the Lord's passion. The subsequent prediction of the betrayal in John 13 is dramatically heightened, especially when compared with the synoptic account of the supper, by the mention of the positions occupied by the disciples at table (verses 23–26), the giving of the morsel to Judas as a last gesture of appeal (verse 26), the entry of Satan into the betrayer (verse 27), and the double-edged stage direction at the exit of Judas: 'and it was night' (verse 30). The figure of darkness disappears into the dark!

There follows the farewell or supper discourse (John 13:31–17:26),[59] which seems to hold up the action but once more prepares the way for it. Jesus instructs his disciples here about the future: the fact of his 'departure' and 'return', and the subsequent mission of the church. The events concerning the departure and return of Jesus will be narrated in

56. Significantly, in 2 Thess. 2:3 Paul uses the phrase ὁ υἱὸς τῆς ἀπωλείας ('the son of destruction, or doom') to refer to the Antichrist.

57. So Lagrange, pp. 348–49.

58. Cf. Hoskyns, pp. 436–37, esp. 437. See further *IFG*, pp. 401–403; also J.C.T. Thomas, *Footwashing in John 13 and the Johannine Community*, JSNTS 61 (Sheffield: JSOT Press, 1991), esp. the literary and exegetical analysis at pp. 61–125 (note the conclusions, pp. 115–16).

59. For justification of these limits to the farewell discourse, and a note on its composition, see Beasley-Murray, pp. 222–27.

chapters 18–20; and the future witness of the disciples will be heralded and signified in the final miracle of the catch of fish (John 21:1–14). Again, sign and discourse are closely related. But, in this instance, so are discourse and subsequent action. The passion events are still in the future; but in the supper discourse Jesus speaks of them either as already in process, or as already completed.[60] He 'is leaving' the world, and he 'is going' to the Father; he 'has overcome' the world, and he 'has accomplished' the work God gave him to do.[61]

The trial narratives which follow (John 18:19–19:16) provide the dramatic movement in this second Act with an obvious focus. Here, for a start, is a famous example of John's dramatic irony; not only in terms of paradoxical statement, as we have noticed before, but also in terms of paradoxical situation. In both the (briefly-related) Jewish trial, and in the Roman trial,[62] Jesus – the judge of all the world – is judged.[63]

Two points are worth noticing in connection with John's dramatic presentation of the trial of Jesus before Pilate. The first is that a discussion takes place between the two main characters, not reported by the synoptists, on the theme of kingship.[64] This is conducted on two levels: Pilate, at least to begin with, thinks in political terms when he says to Jesus, 'you are the King of the Jews' (18:33);[65] but Jesus interprets his kingship spiritually, as 'not of this world' (verse 36). In the end Pilate takes refuge, perhaps, in the ambiguity; and even if he has begun to suspect the real origin of Jesus – notice the worried question, 'where are you from?' (19:9)[66] – he hands Jesus over to be crucified for treason

60. *Cf.* Lightfoot, p. 266.

61. John 16:28,5; 16:33; 17:4.

62. For a discussion of the relationship between the synoptic and Johannine accounts of the trial narratives see S.S. Smalley, 'Jesus Christ, Arrest and Trial of', in G.W. Bromiley (ed.), *The International Standard Bible Encyclopedia*, 2nd edn., vol. 2 (Grand Rapids: Eerdmans, 1982), pp. 1049–55.

63. For a study of the Roman trial of Jesus in John's Gospel, from the viewpoint of its dramatic irony, see Duke, *Irony*, pp. 126–37. Brown 2, p. 809, thinks that at John 18:3, recounting the arrest of Jesus, the fourth evangelist's singular reference to the lanterns and torches carried by the captors may have been included to emphasise the theological theme of night (darkness), over against day (light). Brown acknowledges that the detail may also have been factual. But there is also irony present: the arrest takes place under a nearly full, paschal moon; and the artificial light, needlessly created, therefore underscores the fact that the soldiers and police could not 'see' Jesus, the Light of the World, himself (*cf.* John 8:12).

64. John 18:33–38; 19:1–16.

65. Almost certainly, as the Greek allows, this should be punctuated as a statement, not as a question. In this case Pilate's further statement, 'so you *are* a king!' (verse 37), gains force and point.

66. Notice also the discussion, about the title on the cross of Jesus, between Pilate and the Jews (John 19:19–22). *Cf.* also the double meaning of Pilate's announcements, 'Here is the man!' (19:5) and 'Here is your King!' (verse 14).

against Caesar (verses 12–16). The irony is complete, and the King dies.

Secondly, as Dodd has shown, John presents the Roman trial in pure dramatic form. Not only are the proceedings in Pilate's court 'depicted on a larger canvas, with an elaboration of detail, and a dramatic power and psychological subtlety', far beyond anything in the other Gospels,[67] but also John uses the dramatic technique of two 'theatres' – an inner, 'back' stage (private) and an outer, 'front' stage (public). Within the praetorium the dialogues between Pilate and Jesus are conducted in private; while outside there are public scenes of tension and tumult.[68] Meanwhile, the constant interventions from the Jews keep before the reader the relentless pressure exerted by the priests upon a weak imperial official.[69]

John's second Act reaches its culmination with the report of the crucifixion, to which we shall return, and the resurrection (John 19:17–20:29). The 'glorification' of Jesus is completed and pointed by the triumphant cry, 'it is finished' (19:30). The King after all does not die, but is vindicated; he is 'ascending' (even during the resurrection appearances!) to the Father (20:17). John's passion narrative, although close in outline to the synoptic, shows evidence here of his own sustained dramatic interest. For the account is presented as a series of brief scenes, usually involving (once again) two active participants: the incidents by the cross, including Mary and the beloved disciple; the burial of Jesus by Joseph and Nicodemus; the discovery of the empty tomb by (Mary Magdalene) Peter and the beloved disciple;[70] the meeting in the garden between the risen Jesus and Mary Magdalene; and the encounter in the upper room between first Jesus and the disciples, and then Jesus and Thomas.[71]

The Epilogue (John 21)

The epilogue is an important part of John's over-all dramatic structure in this Gospel. It contains an important sign – the catch of fish

67. HTFG, p. 96.

68. Ibid., pp. 96–97. There are seven scenes in John's account of the trial of Jesus before Pilate: John 18:29–32 (outer stage); 18:33–38a (inner stage); 18:38b–40 (outer); 19:1–3 (inner); 19:4–7 (outer); 19:8–12 (inner); 19:13–16 (outer). See further Brown 2, pp. 857–59; Schnackenburg 3, pp. 241–42, esp. 242.

69. Cf. John 18:30–31; 18:39–40; 19:6–7; 19:12,15. Dodd (HTFG, pp. 96–97) points out that, in the sequence of dialogues at the Feast of Tabernacles (John 7–8), John uses the same dramatic techniques of two stages, and repeated references to attempted violence against Jesus; and the evangelist reminds us continually of the hostile atmosphere in which the debates were conducted. Cf. also IFG, pp. 315, 347–48.

70. In the other Gospels, various disciples begin to run as soon as the empty tomb is discovered (Mark 16:8; Matt. 28:8; Luke 24:12). In John, Peter and the beloved disciple race to the sepulchre (20:4).

71. John 19:23–37; 19:38–42; 20:1–10; 20:11–18; 20:19–29.

(verses 1–14)[72] – which theologically recapitulates some of the primary Johannine themes (once again this is an 'epiphany' miracle),[73] and throws the interest forward to the mission of the Christian community in the future. The subsequent scenes between the risen Jesus and Peter, or Jesus and the beloved disciple (verses 15–23), bring the drama to a full close. The Word who became flesh, and brought heaven to earth, ascends to heaven; but not before the disciples receive the assurance of his continued presence on earth in the Spirit, and are sent out to follow and serve the risen Christ in his church.[74]

Conclusion

Before we leave our study of John as a drama, we must take note of three literary characteristics which generally help to create and sustain its dramatic quality.

(a)   The first is that John's thought always operates on two levels at once. Indeed, such is John's deliberate ambivalence that we are never quite sure at any one moment on which level he is to be understood: the earthly or the heavenly, in time or in eternity. For John, as we have already seen, moves easily between both. He is aware of history; but he is also aware of the supra-historical to which history itself points.

It is for this reason, for example, that John can use the verb ὑψοῦν ('to lift up') in John 12:32 (and elsewhere) with two different but related meanings. Jesus says, 'I, when I am lifted up (ὑψωθῶ) from the earth, will draw all people to myself'; and in these words he refers to his lifting up both on the cross and in exaltation. This Johannine ambivalence accounts for all the 'ups and downs' and 'comings and goings' in the Gospel. John has two theatres in mind at once. The Son of man has descended from heaven and will ascend into heaven; Jesus has come from God and will go to God; he goes away from his disciples in order to return to them.[75] It also accounts for the double meaning which charac-terises apparently innocent questions in John about location. When the first disciples ask Jesus where he is staying,[76] and when Pilate asks where he is from,[77] it is clear that the scene is set and the drama is being played out on the material and spiritual levels together.

---

72.   See further above, pp. 130–31.

73.   *Cf.* John 21:1 (*bis*), 14 (using the verb φανερόω, 'reveal').

74.   C.H. Dodd (*IFG*, pp. 400–423, *et al.*) suggests that the dramatic structuring of John's Gospel often follows the pattern: action — dialogue — monologue (as in John 5, 6, 9 and 10; and in the farewell discourse, John 13–17).

75.   John 3:13 (*cf.* 6:62); 13:3 (*cf.* 16:28); 14:28 (*cf.* 14:3).

76.   John 1:38–39; *cf.* 3:22, *et al.* The verb μένειν ('to stay') is used in John 15 (see verses 4–11) of Jesus abiding in the community of the faithful, in the Spirit, after the resurrection.

77.   John 19:9.

(b)   Secondly, John's dramatic description of the story of Jesus, as Mark Stibbe has shown us, involves narrative progression.[78] The Fourth Gospel as a whole shows a pattern of developing conflict and tension, deriving from hostility to Jesus. There is no significant conflict until chapter 5, when – after the healing at the pool of Bethesda – the situation changes dramatically, and the first mention of the wish by the Jews to kill Jesus is introduced (John 5:18). But then, and thereafter, Jesus becomes the 'elusive Christ';[79] and he escapes every attempt on his life,[80] until he chooses to be caught.[81] These themes of growing conflict and escape (hiding), we may add, contribute to the unity, tension and pace of the dramatic narrative.[82]

(c)   The final characteristic which helps to impart dramatic quality to the Fourth Gospel is the 'trial' motif which dominates John's presentation. As Théo. Preiss has argued, throughout this Gospel the setting is forensic.[83] Jesus – ironically, since he himself is judge – is on trial.[84] Once more, the court meets both in heaven and on earth; and, as the trial proceeds, witnesses from both courts are called. The Father and the Spirit bear testimony; so do the signs, the scriptures, and other people, including the crowds and the disciples.[85] Since their witness is unimpeachable, John can invite his readers to affirm with John the Baptist, Nathanael, Martha and Thomas[86] that Jesus is 'from the Father', the vindicated Son of God.[87]

78. Stibbe, *Storyteller*, pp. 89–92.
79. *Ibid.*, pp. 21, 89–90.
80. John 7:30; 8:20, *et al.* (the hour of Jesus 'had not yet arrived').
81. John 18:1–12.
82. *Cf.* also Stibbe, *John's Gospel*, pp. 5–31.
83. T. Preiss, *Life in Christ*, SBT (London: SCM Press, 1954), pp. 9–31. See also S. Pancaro, *The Law in the Fourth Gospel: The Torah and the Gospel, Moses and Jesus, Judaism and Christianity According to John*, NovT Sup 42 (Leiden: E.J. Brill, 1975). Dr Pancaro interprets the total confrontation between Jesus and the Jews in the Fourth Gospel in terms of a trial. Importantly, and in addition, he sees the Law as the hermeneutical key to much that John has to say about the person and work of Jesus, as well as noting in this Gospel the programmatic significance of John 1:17 ('the law was given through Moses; grace and truth came through Jesus Christ'). See *ibid.*, esp. pp. 534–46. For another treatment of the forensic character of John's material see A.E. Harvey, *Jesus on Trial: A Study in the Fourth Gospel* (London: SPCK, 1976); also A.A. Trites, *The New Testament Concept of Witness*, SNTSMS 31 (Cambridge and New York: Cambridge University Press, 1977), pp. 78–127.
84. John 5:22, 27, *et al.*
85. John 5:37; 15:26; 10:25; 5:39; 1:15; 12:17; 15:27. Equally, the Son bears witness to the Father (1:18).
86. John 1:34; 1:49; 11:27; 20:28.
87. John 6:28; 20:31. A focal expression of this motif in John is obviously provided by the Jewish and Roman trials themselves (John 18–19). For a further study, which draws attention to the importance of the witness theme in John, and maintains that for John 'witness' is a term of revelation, see J.M. Boice, *Witness and Revelation in the Gospel of John* (Exeter: Paternoster Press and Grand Rapids: Zondervan, 1970).

THE ORIGIN OF JOHN'S GOSPEL

Now that we have surveyed the narrative-critical approach to the fourth evangelist's work, argued for the fundamental unity of his Gospel as it now stands, and explored its composition as a carefully structured drama, we are in a position to complete this section of our study by offering some proposals about the genesis of John.

Given the tradition, background, sources and composition of John's Gospel drama, how exactly did it come to birth? We have discovered that there is reason to assume that this document was written in edited stages, rather than at one sitting. In that case, what kind of literary process was involved? Our suggestion is that *three* main stages may be detected in the production of the Fourth Gospel.

First, John the apostle, who was the beloved disciple, moved from Jerusalem[88] to Ephesus, where he handed on orally to his followers – much as, by tradition, Peter did to Mark[89] – accounts of the deeds (mostly the miracles) and sayings of Jesus, and of his death and resurrection.[90] These accounts preserved information about the ministry of Jesus in both Judea and Galilee.[91]

Second, the disciples of John – the nucleus of the Johannine church, which may have included women[92] – committed to writing the traditions presented by the beloved disciple. This was a 'first draft' of the Gospel, and consisted of a centre which narrated six miracles of Jesus, now treated as signs.[93] Other 'signs' may have been remembered by the

---

88. Note the existence of the house church of the beloved disciple and Mary, in Jerusalem, suggested by John 19:27; Acts 1:13–14.

89. It is possible that John's Gospel also preserves early traditions connected with Peter, which are associated substructurally with independent Petrine material behind (Mark and) Matthew. *Cf.* John 1:40–42; 18:10 (*cf.* Mark 14:47); 21:15–22.

90. There is no reason, however, to exclude entirely the possibility that the first stage was completed *before* the move to Ephesus. See Robinson, *Redating*, p. 296, and the literature there cited (although Robinson is dealing with the first *draft* of the Gospel). Perhaps John had in any case visited Asia Minor, and Ephesus, for missionary purposes as early as the middle of the first century AD. See Gal. 2:9, which may imply a visit by John to the Jews of the diaspora; and notice also (as a preparation for this?) John's positive role in the Hellenist mission to Samaria (Acts 8:14–15).

91. Against P. Parker, 'Two Editions of John', *JBL* 75 (1956), pp. 303–314, who maintains that the first edition of John was a Judean Gospel, to which traditions concerned with Jesus in Samaria and Galilee (John 2, 4, 6, 21) were added later. For the Ephesian provenance of this Gospel see below, p. 186.

92. The important place accorded to the ministry of women in John's Gospel suggests that some female followers of the beloved disciple may have had a hand in its composition. See further Brown, *Community*, pp. 183–98, esp. 189-90 (on Mary Magdalene as a member of the apostolate).

93. Water into wine; the official's son; the sick man; the feeding of the five thousand; the blind man; the raising of Lazarus.

community, and even recorded in writing. With this centre were inter-
woven explanatory discourses, including the farewell discourse in its
basic form, organised in a cyclic feast-sign-discourse pattern. At this
stage what we now recognise as 'Johannine' thought emerges, by the
development of the seminal theological ideas handed on by the apostle
himself. The material thus arranged by the writer(s), whom we may
conveniently call the fourth evangelist(s), led into a passion narrative
(excluding John 21). In addition an introduction to the work was composed, consisting of the present section John 1:19–51. This included
traditions about John the Baptist, which may have derived from the
Baptist himself, possibly through John the apostle.

Third, the Johannine church at Ephesus, after the death of the beloved
disciple, published a finally edited version of the Gospel. This included
a summary prologue (John 1:1–18), written last, based on a community
hymn and now tied securely to the rest of the introductory first chapter;
some editing of the discourses (especially marked in John 6 and 14–17;
possibly the prayer of John 17, liturgically developed on the basis of an
actual prayer of Jesus,[94] was added at this stage); and an epilogue (John
21, incorporating for special reasons one additional sign from the collection preserved at the second stage). The whole Gospel thus assembled
then carried an authenticating postscript (John 21:24–25), which may be
roughly translated as follows. 'The beloved disciple is the witness to the
basic tradition preserved here, and he was responsible for its composition. Those who undertook the writing of this Gospel can vouch for the
truth of his testimony. The material we have included, however, is
deliberately selected from a much larger corpus, available within and
beyond the Johannine church.'[95]

If some such process as this were involved in the making of the Gospel
of John, it would explain various features in its history and composition
of which we have already taken note. For example, it would account for
the likelihood that more than one author was responsible for the Gospel's writing; for the fact that at first the Fourth Gospel was not ascribed
to John, the son of Zebedee; and finally for the reality that the church
eventually accepted the Gospel as apostolic, so that in time it became
more and more firmly known and acknowledged as such. If the beloved
disciple's witness lies behind the Gospel's production, and others were
responsible for its actual writing, the work retains its apostolic character,
and the particular features of its composition and history are explained.

The writing and editing of the Fourth Gospel, which we have been
discussing in these chapters, would scarcely have been undertaken for its
own sake. The redaction of the Johannine tradition has an obvious
bearing on its intention. What led the Johannine church to compose the

94. See Smalley, 'Testament'; also below, pp. 227–29.
95. For the exegesis of this passage see further above, pp. 88–89.

Gospel of Christ in the way its members did? Definite theological, community and situational interests must have been in view, directly related to the purpose of the whole work. It is to that purpose, the intention behind the composition of John's Gospel, that we shall turn in the next chapter.

8

JOHN'S PURPOSE

So far in this book we have been investigating the nature of the Johannine tradition, the background and authorship of the Fourth Gospel, and the dramatic way in which John used his sources in order to unfold his story of Jesus. It is now time to consider the *intention* of John's Gospel. Given the material at his disposal, and the way in which he presented it, why did the fourth evangelist write a Gospel in the first place, and who were his initial readers? Our answers to those questions will raise the further issues of the nature of the community in which the Fourth Gospel arose, and the Gospel's provenance: where it was published when completed. The former of those two problems, the precise character of the Johannine church, is an important matter which is at present arousing considerable scholarly interest and excitement.

We shall begin our discussion of the purpose behind John's Gospel by suggesting four possible reasons for its composition which have been put forward in the past.

EARLIER SUGGESTIONS

(a) To replace, interpret or supplement the synoptic Gospels

A familiar view of the fourth evangelist's intention is that he wrote his Gospel in order to go beyond the existing synoptic Gospels. This assumes that John knew the other three Gospels, and that he wished to present his own version of the tradition preserved by them. In that case he wrote either to replace the Synoptics completely, or to ·complement them in some way.

The thesis that John's Gospel was intended to supersede, rather than to supplement, the synoptic Gospels was propounded, for example, by Hans Windisch in 1926.[1] He believed that the Fourth Gospel incorporated Palestinian traditions connected with John the apostle, and that the document finally arose around AD 100 in Syria or Asia Minor; it was the work of a single author, who clothed the Gospel in the form of an

---

1. Windisch, *Johannes und die Synoptiker; cf.* above, pp. 3–5. See also W.F. Howard, *The Fourth Gospel in Recent Criticism and Interpretation*, 4th edn. (London: Epworth Press, 1955), pp. 72–74, 135 (on Windisch); Smith, *John Among the Gospels*, pp. 19–31.

oriental-Hellenistic message of redemption. According to Windisch, the fourth evangelist knew the Gospel of Mark and other synoptic material. But his use of the Synoptics shows that John is an 'autonomous and sufficient' Gospel;[2] it was not completely independent of the other Gospels, nor was it written to supplement or interpret them. Windisch concludes rather that John wrote to *replace* all the Gospels current in his day, and in doing so chiefly made use of a non-synoptic source (oral or written) which contained a 'signs' collection.

R.H. Lightfoot also believes that John knew the synoptic tradition in its written form; indeed, Lightfoot's commentary is written in the firm belief that the fourth evangelist knew and used all three synoptic Gospels.[3] However, John's purpose in writing another Gospel, according to Lightfoot, was not to supersede the other Gospels, nor even to supplement them. In any case, it is argued, the synoptic Gospels probably held too strong a position in the church when John wrote for this to have been possible. Rather, John sought to *interpret* the other Gospels, and 'to draw out the significance of the original events' concerning Jesus.[4] John's Gospel, on this showing, is not to be regarded as theological interpretation *rather than* history. The fourth evangelist himself is well aware of the historical truth which lies at the heart of the Christian good news; and even if he can sit lightly to 'subordinate aspects' of his main historical subject, he may also on occasions give us historically better guidance than the synoptic writers.[5] But John's chief role, Lightfoot maintains, is as an interpreter of the synoptic tradition. He writes in the light of the origins of the Jesus tradition, and of two generations of Christian experience, to provide his readers with 'a searching and profound interpretation of the Christian mystery of the Lord's Person and of His life-giving death and resurrection'.[6]

The view of John's intention represented by Windisch and Lightfoot, that the Fourth Gospel was written as an addition to the (known) synoptic Gospels, whether to replace or interpret them, is by no means a modern one. When, according to Eusebius,[7] the theologian Clement of Alexandria (*c.* AD 150–215) tells us that John composed a 'spiritual Gospel', knowing that the 'outward' (literally, 'bodily') facts had already been set forth in the other three Gospels, he is obviously regarding the Fourth Gospel as in some sense a *supplement* to the first three Gospels.

Nevertheless, this understanding of the fourth evangelist's purpose, in whatever form it appears (to replace, interpret or supplement the Synop-

---

2. Windisch, *Johannes und die Synoptiker*, p. 88.
3. Lightfoot, p. 29.
4. *Ibid.*, p. 33.
5. *Ibid.*, pp. 34–36.
6. *Ibid.*, p. 42; see the whole section on the relation between St John and the synoptic Gospels, pp. 26–42.
7. *HE* 6.14.7.

tics), needs to be questioned seriously. The theory of Windisch that John wrote to replace the other Gospels is artificial, since manifestly the Fourth Gospel does not stand alone, in the face of the synoptic tradition, as a complete account of the ministry of Jesus. In any case this approach, like that which sees the Gospel of John as in one way or another the 'crown and completion' of our Gospel records,[8] cannot be maintained if doubt is cast to any extent on the likelihood that John knew the synoptics. In the second chapter of this book it was argued that there are strong reasons for believing that, while John was familiar with the common Christian tradition underlying the synoptic Gospels, he did not know or use the written form of this as it appears in the first three Gospels themselves. If this suggestion carries any weight at all, then clearly John cannot have been produced to correct or modify the synoptic Gospels.

(b)   To restate the Christian gospel in Hellenised terms

A second reason, which has been suggested for the composition of John, regards the Fourth Gospel as written to present the Christian good news to the Gentile world in a version which would be intelligible to the Greek mind. Such a view of the fourth evangelist's intention is taken, for example, by Ernest Scott.[9] The Gospel of John, Scott maintains, is a work of transition. The fourth evangelist addresses a new *age*, and he reinterprets the story of Christ's coming accordingly, appealing to both outward, historical fact and inward experience as vital to Christian discipleship. But John also addresses a different *culture* from the one in which the gospel came to birth. To communicate with the wider, Hellenistic audience now involved, he is not content merely to use 'a Greek idea here and there'; rather, he 'attempts an entire restatement of the Christian message in terms of the current philosophy'.[10] In this radical restatement, where 'Logos' replaces 'Messiah', 'eternal life' translates 'kingdom', and so on, the fourth evangelist (according to Scott) at times breaks with the 'literal tradition', and 'substitutes the language of Greek reflection for the actual words employed by Jesus'. In so doing, elements of the gospel message are given 'truer expression' than in the synoptic Gospels, which John used, and 'come to their own'.[11]

Working from this starting-point, Scott sees other purposes, both polemical and ecclesiastical, as involved in the writing of the Fourth Gospel; and we shall return before long to his view that John contains

---

8. Lightfoot, p. 32; against Beasley-Murray, p. lxxxviii.

9. E.F. Scott, *The Fourth Gospel: Its Purpose and Theology*, 2nd edn. (Edinburgh: T. and T. Clark, 1923), pp. 1–28, esp. 4–9.

10. *Ibid.*, p. 6.

11. *Ibid.*, pp. 6–7. *Cf.* W.L. Knox, *Some Hellenistic Elements in Primitive Christianity* (London: Oxford University Press, 1944), pp. 55–90, who sees Hellenism as one of the major elements involved in the composition of the Fourth Gospel.

anti-gnostic polemic.[12] But an integral part of Scott's basic position is that John's Gospel is a reinterpretation of the Christian tradition for a new age, and a new, Hellenic culture. Adopting a similar approach, stemming from the 'history of religions' school, C.H. Dodd's work on this Gospel evinces his belief that John was addressing the contemporary Greek, pagan world in order to persuade its members to embrace Christianity.[13] However, while it is true that Dodd regards the non-Christian society of his day as an important background for interpreting the Fourth Gospel,[14] he is at the same time well aware of the distance between the world of Hellenistic paganism and Johannine Christianity, and also of the likelihood that there is an inter-active *Jewish*-Hellenistic setting for the Gospel.[15]

In the third chapter of this book we examined the background to the Gospel of John, and came to the conclusion that it is best understood, in line with the basic view of C.H. Dodd himself, as essentially Jewish-Christian in character; even if, for the sake of the Gospel's final audience, some Hellenistic tinting is also to be found. If the Johannine ethos is indeed primarily Palestinian Jewish-Christian and not pagan Greek in its nature, it becomes impossible to sustain the thesis that John wrote his Gospel to restate the Christian gospel in Hellenised terms.[16] In any case, such a thesis presupposes that John's purpose was evangelism in the sense of a mission to outsiders; and, as we shall see, this is by no means certain.

(c)   As polemic or apology

The theory that the Gospel of John was written for polemical reasons, and therefore (in terms of the positive result of this intention) as apologetic, has been advanced often and in varied forms. We shall for the moment look at four versions of this theory.

Polemic against the Baptist Sect

The light in which the fourth evangelist presents his account of John the Baptist, as we saw earlier,[17] seems at first glance intended to demon-

12. See below, pp. 169–72.

13. So *IFG*, part 1.

14. *Ibid.*, pp. 7–9.

15. *Cf. HTFG*, pp. 424–29, where Dodd summarises his argument that the pre-canonical tradition behind John's Gospel was originally shaped in a Palestinian, Jewish-Christian environment (p. 426). Palestine was in any case cosmopolitan at this time.

16. Scott, *Fourth Gospel* (pp. 32–45) maintains that John drew upon the synoptic Gospels for this restatement (p. 32). Such an argument, which we have found it impossible to support, is not (as it happens) essential to the thesis that John is presenting his readers with a Hellenised version of the gospel. The fourth evangelist, if he wrote for this purpose, may still have been indebted to an independent Jesus tradition.

17. See above, pp. 24–25.

strate the inferiority of John to Jesus. In the synoptic Gospels John points to Jesus as the coming one who is greater (Mark 1:7 par.), while in the Fourth Gospel John the Baptist is described simply as 'a man sent from God' (John 1:6). By comparison with the synoptic account in general, where the people wonder whether John is the Christ (Luke 3:15), and he is plainly identified with the Elijah figure of the new age (Matt. 11:14;[18] Luke 1:17), the Johannine record, to say the least, seems restrained. There the role of John is to all intents and purposes played down. Jesus, not John, is the light (John 1:8); the Baptist is neither the Christ nor Elijah, but merely a crying voice (1:19–23; cf. 3:28–30); Jesus existed before John, and is greater (1:30); Jesus performed many signs, but John never worked a miracle (10:41).

The particular view of John the Baptist presented by the fourth evangelist has given rise to the suggestion that John's Gospel was written primarily or in part to refute the claims of a 'Baptist group'. This group, it is supposed by some scholars, continued to venerate John the Baptist after his death, and to make claims for their leader which became a threat to the Christian church. From these excesses, the argument runs, the need arose to clarify the Baptist's real status.

Wilhelm Baldensperger, for example, in a monograph published in 1898,[19] maintained that this was one of the chief purposes for writing the Fourth Gospel. Dr Baldensperger found the key to John's composition in the contrast between the Baptist and Jesus, which (he claimed) appears in the prologue and features directly or indirectly throughout the Gospel.[20] This opinion has been surprisingly influential; and while few commentators would go so far as Baldensperger and regard the *main* intention behind the Fourth Gospel as polemic against the sect which exalted John the Baptist at the expense of Jesus,[21] many have subscribed to the view that this was one of John's subordinate aims. Such is the position, for instance, of R.H. Strachan.[22] Rudolf Bultmann also follows Baldensperger in detecting anti-Baptist polemic behind the prologue (at least) of John's Gospel; although he suggests that the Johannine

18. Cf. also Matt. 11:11.

19. W. Baldensperger, *Der Prolog des vierten Evangeliums: Sein polemisch – apologetischer Zweck* (Freiburg im Breisgau: J.C.B. Mohr, 1898).

20. *Ibid.* esp. pp. 58–92.

21. Howard (*Fourth Gospel*, pp. 57–58) points out that by pressing his theory too far, Baldensperger caused an important suggestion about the nature of John's tradition, made in the course of his book, to be overlooked. For Baldensperger believed that an apologist who wished to win converts from a rival sect might handle his material freely; but that he would not *create* material, the historicity of which could be immediately challenged. See Baldensperger, *Prolog*, pp. 93–152.

22. Strachan, pp. 45, 109–12. The original edition of Strachan (1917), however, did not mention anti-Baptist polemic as even a subordinate aim of the Fourth Gospel (see pp. 13–21).

prologue originated as a hymn in the Baptist community.[23] Bultmann goes further when he also maintains that the fourth evangelist himself was probably a former, gnostic follower of John the Baptist.[24]

However, the assumption that the Fourth Gospel was intended in any way to counter exaggerated claims which were being made at the time by followers of John the Baptist, and that this lent a distinctive colouring to the Johannine portrait of the Baptist, is open to serious question. For a start, such an idea depends on the view that in the first century AD there actually existed a sectarian Baptist group which could and did become a serious rival to Christianity. The evidence beyond John's Gospel for the existence of such a group at the time of the early church is slight; but appeal can be made to two further witnesses, and these we shall examine.

First, Acts 19:1–7 records a meeting between Paul and some 'disciples' at Ephesus (where, by tradition, John's Gospel was published). Possibly these people belonged to a Baptist group, such as the one suggested. Certainly they appear to have been committed to John the Baptist, rather than Jesus: they had been baptised 'into John's baptism' (19:3); they needed instruction about Jesus (verse 4), as well as the Holy Spirit (verse 2); and they were eventually baptised 'in the name of the Lord Jesus' (verse 5). However, it is by no means certain what kind of disciples these were, or whether they were exclusively John's supporters. 'More than Jewish, less than Christian' might be one description; and it is perhaps not without significance that they accepted Christian baptism so readily (19:5). Furthermore, since Paul met only 'about twelve of them in all' (verse 7), presumably they did not constitute a large group, even if some members were missing.[25] The incident in Acts 19, then, cannot be used as evidence for the existence during the first century AD of a Baptist sect, the claims of which needed to be countered.

A second, more important piece of evidence, to which reference is made in this connection, is provided by the Pseudo-Clementine *Recognitions*. This work was written in the third century AD, and made use of earlier – no doubt second-century – sources. At the time of its writing, the unknown author of the *Recognitions* realised that followers of John the Baptist were claiming *their* leader, and not Jesus, as the Messiah.[26] Here indeed is evidence that Baptist sectarians survived as opponents of Christianity into the third century. But we cannot use the *Recognitions* to suggest that they posed a threat to the church, or even existed as a

23.   *Cf.* Bultmann, pp. 17–18; see also above, p. 102.

24.   *Ibid.*, p. 108.

25.   The reference to Paul finding 'some disciples' at Ephesus (Acts 19:1) seems in any case to imply the whole group.

26.   *Recognitions* 1.54.8, which speaks of the Baptist's disciples as separating John from the people, and preaching about him 'as if he were the Christ' (*velut Christum praedicarunt*); *cf.* also 1.60, esp. 1–3.

large group, at the time when the Fourth Gospel was being composed. In any case, we have almost no information – even from the *Recognitions* – about the theology of this group, or the way in which its members really thought about John the Baptist.[27]

Nothing so far compels us, therefore, to regard anti-Baptist polemic as part of John's intention, even subordinately. The alleged need to withstand the claims of a Baptist group disappears if it cannot be established that such a group created any real problem for the early Christian church.

There are two further reasons for dismissing anti-Baptist polemic as a motive for the writing of John's Gospel. One is the fact, which we noticed earlier,[28] that the tradition about John the Baptist in the Fourth Gospel probably has the appearance it does because it is primitive, and to that extent more reliable even than the synoptic account. So, far from deliberately playing down the role of the Baptist, the fourth evangelist is more likely to be reflecting accurately the Baptist's self-estimate, rather than the subsequent opinion of the early church. The other reason for questioning whether John wrote his Gospel with an eye, or even half an eye, to the Baptist sectarians, is quite simply the fact that this is a Gospel about Jesus, and not about John the Baptist.[29]

Polemic concerning the Sacramental Teaching of the Church

Another polemical-apologetic motive, primary or subordinate, found by some scholars behind the composition of the Fourth Gospel, concerns the sacramental teaching ascribed to John the evangelist. Here there are two main views. One is that John's Gospel reflects a growing need in the early church to give *more emphasis* to teaching about the sacraments of baptism and the Lord's Supper. This is the position, for example, of Oscar Cullmann, in his book *Early Christian Worship*.[30]

The fourth evangelist writes, Cullmann claims, so that his readers should 'see', in the sense of 'believe', that the Jesus of history – as the Christ – is the mediator of God's entire plan of salvation, including its outworking in the present. The 'aim of this whole literary undertaking', Cullmann therefore maintains, is that his audience 'should have faith now in this *post-paschal present*'.[31] To achieve this, it is argued, John

27. Bultmann's suggestion (pp. 13–108) that the followers of John the Baptist (including the fourth evangelist?) were gnostic in outlook, is similarly unsupported by the Pseudo-Clementines (*Homilies* and *Recognitions*). There is just possibly a link between the followers of John the Baptist and gnosticism through the patristic tradition which traces gnostic origins to Samaria (where the Baptist may have worked; *cf.* John 3:23) and Simon Magus (*cf.* Acts 8:9–13).

28. See above, pp. 24–25.

29. *Cf.* further Schnackenburg 1, pp. 167–69.

30. Cullmann, *Early Christian Worship*, esp. pp. 38–59.

31. *Ibid.*, p. 39, italics his. *Cf.* John 20:31.

offers his readers a selection of narratives illustrating the theological principle on which his Gospel is based. Cullmann interprets these narrative events, and in particular the Johannine signs, in line with the *liturgical* interest which he discovers as the key to the Fourth Gospel, and claims that they are to be associated directly with one or other of the two sacraments of baptism and the Lord's Supper.[32] Thus the changing of water into wine at Cana in John 2 and the feeding of the five thousand in John 6 are connected by him with the eucharist; the healing of the lame man in John 5 and of the blind man in John 9 are linked to baptism; and the Footwashing in John 13 and the spear-thrust in John 19 are associated with both.[33] This proves, to Cullmann's mind, that according to John 'the sacraments mean the same for the Church as the miracles of the historical Jesus for his contemporaries', and it substantiates his thesis that one of John's 'chief concerns' is to 'set forth the connection between the contemporary Christian worship and the historical life of Jesus'.[34]

Cullmann, then, regards the Fourth Gospel as written to oppose Christian teachers who, as the history of early Christianity progressed, gave too little place to the sacraments in the life of the church. The other, more common, view among those who believe that the intention of the Fourth Gospel is in some way related to the place of the sacraments in the early church, is that John reflects a growing need to give the *right emphasis* to sacramental teaching. The work of Wilbert Howard, in his *Christianity According to St John*, is a representative example of this outlook on John's Gospel.[35]

Dr Howard begins by noticing the 'strongly sacramental tone' of the Fourth Gospel. He claims, for example, that the baptismal reference of the discourse in John 3 and the eucharistic reference of the discourse in John 6 are both 'generally recognised'.[36] If the sacramental interpretation of this Gospel is *not* universally accepted, Howard suggests, this is either because the discourses of John are regarded as authentic, in which case the sacramental reference would be anachronistic; or because Johannine theology is thought of as being too 'spiritual' to require attention to a material medium, in which case

32. *Ibid.*, pp. 59–116.

33. *Ibid.*, pp. 105–110. See further Thomas, *Footwashing*, pp. 11–18, esp. 13–14, where the author seems to believe that Cullmann associates the Footwashing with the eucharist alone. Thomas himself argues that footwashing was a sacrament practised in the Johannine community in connection with the eucharist (see pp. 184–89, esp. 184–85).

34. Cullmann, *Early Christian Worship*, pp. 70, 37. But see Cullmann, *Johannine Circle*, pp. 17 and 104 n.16. Cullmann now refutes the idea that 'the sacraments play the dominant role in the Fourth Gospel' (p. 104 n.16).

35. W.F. Howard, *Christianity According to St John* (London: Duckworth, 1943), pp. 143–50.

36. *Ibid.*, pp. 143–44.

the sacramental reference would be superfluous.[37] John's interest in the sacraments, Howard argues, is consonant with the 'deeply sacramental' character of the church at his time, and resembles a similar interest in the writings of Ignatius and Justin Martyr. But 'the perils of such an attitude to sacramental grace were clear to this practical mystic';[38] and the fourth evangelist therefore aims to put the sacraments in their proper place. For him, 'the symbolism of externals was but the fitting raiment of the interior meaning'.[39] Thus, teaching about baptism (in John 3) is given without specific reference to the rite of Christian baptism, and instruction about the Lord's Supper (in John 6) is removed from the sacred context of its institution. In this way the true, and important, sacramental testimony of the church could emerge, and stand in opposition to those who were giving the wrong meaning to the sacraments either by denying their genuinely historical basis in the person and work of Jesus, or by reading into them magical ideas derived from setting of pagan mysteries.[40]

However, as we shall see in due course,[41] it may be argued against both Cullmann and Howard that the fourth evangelist is not preoccupied with the sacraments of either baptism or the eucharist as such. While there is no need to exclude entirely references to these rites in such places as John 3 and 6, there is no need either to regard them as central to John's theological concern. The evangelist is more interested in what we shall be calling the 'sacramental dimension' of Christian experience than in the ritual expression of that dimension. If so, polemic concerning the current sacramental teaching of the church, either for it or against it, cannot be accepted as exerting to any extent an influence on John's purpose in writing his Gospel.

Polemic concerning the Eschatological Teaching of the Church

It is frequently suggested that John wrote his Gospel, at least in part, to correct mistaken ideas about the return of Christ at the end of time. Such a view is adopted in Kingsley Barrett's commentary on the Fourth Gospel.[42] Barrett finds in John the answer to a 'twofold crisis' in Christian thought at the end of the first century AD, in which the church was

---

37. *Ibid.*, p. 144. Howard cites Bultmann's commentary on John as a 'conspicuous instance' of the refusal to acknowledge any sacramental allusions in the Fourth Gospel, and of the consequent need to remove all such passages with 'the critical knife'.
38. *Ibid.*, p. 145.
39. *Ibid.*
40. *Cf.* also, on similar lines, Bauer, pp. 95–103; Scott, *Fourth Gospel*, pp. 122–32. See further E.C. Colwell and E.L. Titus, *The Gospel of the Spirit: A Study in the Fourth Gospel* (New York: Harper and Row, 1953), pp. 50–52.
41. See below, pp. 232–38.
42. Barrett, pp. 139–40.

required to give an authoritative response to the two 'urgent problems' of eschatology and gnosticism.[43]

We shall refer again, in the next section, to Barrett's opinion that anti-gnostic polemic formed a part of John's purpose in writing. At present we may notice his argument that the Fourth Gospel contains polemic against erroneous eschatological teaching.

Early Christian expectations about the parousia (the appearing of Christ in glory at the end), Barrett maintains, were apocalyptic in character.[44] As the synoptic Gospels show, the primitive church antici-pated the climactic and triumphant appearing of Christ soon after the resurrection, and while some first generation Christians were still alive.[45] However, the expected parousia did not take place; and when it was not precipitated even by the fall of Jerusalem, the process of expecting the end of the world, which had been going on for some fifty years, could no longer be indefinitely prolonged. What had previously been an interim period to be patiently endured, now required 'a positive meaning in the purpose of God'; eschatology could no longer have a merely 'crisis' character. Barrett concludes that even if John would not have spoken of this requirement as an 'eschatological problem', he wrote his Gospel partly to give the 'present tense' of salvation its proper significance, and to counter the wrongheadedness of those whose hopes of Christ's immi-nent return persisted. 'That Christianity was in the end able to survive', he claims, 'and to maintain its unique and authentic tension of realisation and hope, was due in no small measure to John's contribution to eschatological thought.'[46]

This understanding of John's intention, as in part the interpretation of early Christian eschatological expectations in a more 'realised' direc-tion because the parousia was delayed, cannot be lightly dismissed. Clearly first-century attitudes about the future changed as time went on; so much so that, because the parousia did not appear to be happening, scoffers were heard to say in due course, 'Where is the promise of his coming?'[47] Moreover, John's eschatology certainly has a distinctive appearance, with its emphasis on eternal life in the present. But, although it is an assumption regularly made in New Testament scholarship, we need to question whether the so-called 'delay of the parousia' created such real problems for the early Christians that they were forced to rethink their eschatology entirely, and change from an apocalyptic to a realised view-point.

For early Christianity, as for Judaism, the 'day of the Lord' was always 'at hand'; and the crisis of God's kingly rule, making its claims

43. *Ibid.*, p. 139.
44. *Cf.* Mark 13:26; 14:61–62.
45. *Cf.* Mark 9:1; Matt. 10:23; note also 1 Cor. 15:51; 1 Thess. 4:15–17.
46. Barrett, p. 140; see also below, pp. 265–70.
47. 2 Peter 3:4.

upon people's hearts, was perpetually breaking into history by stages: all of which pointed to the end. With the coming of Jesus, a decisive stage in the arrival of the kingdom of God was reached. From the time of Christ's exaltation, the Christian church looked forward to the consummation in a mood of confidence that the winding-up of history could be left to God, whose control over it had been finally demonstrated, and whose saving purposes had been made clear in the Christ-event. Poised between these two moments of the 'beginning time' (*Urzeit*) and the 'end time' (*Endzeit*) – marking the first and the final appearances of the Messiah – the primitive Christians sometimes expected the parousia to be near at hand, and at other times further off.[48] But if the return of Christ did not take place immediately (as it did not), there was need for another eschatological emphasis rather than for another eschatology.

So, for example, the earlier letters of Paul contain an emphasis on the imminent return of Jesus in glory, without ignoring the experience of salvation in the present; while his later letters concentrate on the blessings of Christ available here and now, without forgetting the final 'day of the Lord'.[49] The fact that the New Testament as a whole seems to contain one basic eschatology, and not different eschatologies replacing each other in a one-to-one relation, reflects the teaching of Jesus himself. There we discover a similar ambivalence, so that at one moment he expects his parousia to take place within the lifetime of his hearers, and at another moment he anticipates a settled interval before the arrival of the end.[50]

In the light of considerations such as these, that the 'delay of the parousia' was not a real problem for the early Christians, and that it is in any case difficult to separate so-called 'realised' and 'futurist' eschatologies from each other, since they are but two aspects of one understanding, it is difficult to claim that John was writing his Gospel to correct mistaken eschatological beliefs. This becomes all the more apparent when we take note of the fact that although the Fourth Gospel is 'realised' in its general eschatological outlook, it contains – as do the synoptic Gospels – both present and future strands of eschatology.[51] Indeed, a characteristic Johannine formula ('the hour is coming, and now is')[52] places both strands in careful juxtaposition.[53]

48. *Cf.* the variation in Paul's outlook suggested in 1 Thess. 4:13–18 and 2 Thess. 2:1–12 (two of his earlier letters, written within months of each other); and even within 2 Thess. itself (with 2 Thess. 2:1–12, *cf.* 1:5–10).

49. *Cf.* 1 Thess. 4:16–5:3; 4:1–12; also (assuming it to be Pauline) Eph. 1:3–2:10; 4:30.

50. *Cf.* Matt. 16:28; 28:19–20. In the ministry of Jesus itself there were several 'parousias' (for example, at his baptism and transfiguration), each of which foreshadowed his final appearing and shared in its character.

51. Note the apocalyptic tone of John 5:25–29; *cf.* also 14:3; 21:22.

52. John 4:23 (and note verse 21); 5:25, *et al.*

53. See further, on this general point of the nature of New Testament eschatology, Smalley, 'Delay of the Parousia', pp. 41–54.

Polemic against Heresy

A final polemical intention attributed to John suggests that he was writing his Gospel to defend orthodox Christianity against the inroads of heresy. The heresy in question, it is claimed, was gnosticism, and in particular that form of gnostic thought against which the writer of 1 John also warns his readers: namely, docetism (belief in a 'phantom' Jesus).[54] As we saw in chapter 3,[55] influences from gnostic – or at least 'pre-gnostic' – ideas, including those ideas of salvation which were docetic in character, were inevitably brought to bear on the Christian gospel once it was carried from a Palestinian to a Graeco-Roman environment. We also know from gnostic redeemer myths, in which deliverance from the 'lower world' of matter is effected by a non-earthly, ideal saviour figure and appropriated by 'knowledge', that such ideas – when taken over by Christian thinkers – naturally involved a denial of the physical reality of the person of Jesus in his life and death.

The belief that the Fourth Gospel was written to combat heretical views of this kind is held, among others, by Ernest Scott in a work cited earlier.[56] Dr Scott regards the Gospel of John as basically a restatement of the Christian good news in Hellenistic terms. But within that general purpose he also finds evidence that the fourth evangelist, like the writer of 1 John, wrote to counteract heretical, gnostic teaching. Thus John insists – against the docetists – on the reality of Christ's life, denies the gnostic hierarchy of intermediate spiritual agencies, opposes the gnostic idea that divine sonship is possible apart from Christ, avoids gnostic watchwords, and so on. At the same time, however, Scott discovers features in John's Gospel which lead him to conclude that the evangelist was sympathetic towards the gnostic position, and indeed was himself 'semi-docetic' in outlook.[57] John does not condemn gnostic heresy directly, he is aware of the ideal value as well as the earthly reality of the life of Jesus, he accepts a dualist framework for his theology of salvation, and he is sensitive to the importance of 'knowledge'. Scott reconciles this antinomy in the Fourth Gospel, that there is both antagonism and approximation to a gnostic way of thinking on the part of the evangelist, by deciding that even if he seems sympathetic towards the gnostic movement, John himself was in no true sense a gnostic. The fourth

54. *Cf.* 1 John 4:1–3, *et al.* On the opposition to gnosticism, as reflected generally in the New Testament, see N. Perrin, *The New Testament: An Introduction* (New York: Harcourt Brace Jovanovich, 1974), pp. 124–25, 315–17. An early tradition claimed that the Fourth Gospel was written to refute the views of the gnostically-inclined heretic Cerinthus, whose outlook was semi-docetic; see Irenaeus, *AH* 3.11.1. Note also Smalley, *1, 2, 3 John*, pp. xxvi–xxxii.

55. See above, esp. pp. 160–61.

56. Scott, *Fourth Gospel*, esp. pp. 86–103.

57. *Ibid.*, p. 95.

evangelist's views appear similar to those of the gnostics in some ways; but this is because he adopted ideas which formed part of his cultural background, and only later became identified with one prominent and heretical school. In the end John's 'conscious attitude' towards gnosticism may be described as antagonistic; he 'stands for the historical tradition as against the attempts to dissolve it in a vague idealism'.[58]

The view that polemic against a docetic form of gnosticism formed one of the main purposes of the Fourth Gospel is also held by Robert Strachan,[59] who regards the Johannine emphasis on the real humanity of Jesus (he was weary, he wept, he thirsted on the cross) as evidence that the evangelist wished to refute the heretical opinion that the faith and message of the Christian church can be separated from 'the historic person and teaching of Jesus of Nazareth'.[60] Similarly, Kingsley Barrett maintains that anti-gnostic (including anti-docetic) polemic was one of the two motives behind the composition of John's Gospel.[61] To answer the urgent problem facing the church of John's day, whereby a heretical religious system close to Christianity was being passed off in some quarters as Christianity itself, the fourth evangelist (Barrett claims) wrote a Gospel which reaffirms the historical basis of Christian faith in the person of Jesus, as well as revealing the interpretation of that history for the present.[62]

Several variations on this theme, that John wrote his Gospel as an answer to heresy, are evident in the work of Johannine scholars. We have already seen, for example, that Bultmann's commentary is committed to the view that the fourth evangelist was himself a former gnostic, who was attempting to restate the kerygma in gnostic categories which had been Christianised.[63] In this attempt, John's relationship to the gnostic view of the world (Bultmann argues) is seen to be one of *difference* as well as affinity.[64] By every means, however, John tries to convince 'adherents of gnostic circles as to the truth of the gospel'.[65]

Those scholars mentioned in chapter 5, who believe that the Fourth Gospel was composed by expanding a 'signs source' (at least), must also be brought into the present discussion. For on this showing, the reason that John wished to edit such a source – whatever its original form – is

58. *Ibid.*, pp. 101–102.
59. Strachan, pp. 41–45.
60. *Ibid.*, pp. 44–45.
61. For the other motive suggested by Barrett see above, pp. 166–68.
62. Barrett, pp. 140–42.
63. See above, pp. 56–61, esp. 57.
64. Bultmann, pp. 7–9, *et passim*.
65. *Ibid.*, p. 9. Similarly Grant, *Gospels*, pp. 159–72. Grant argues that the Fourth Gospel is best understood in a 'gnostic Christian' light. He sees the fourth evangelist as a converted gnostic, who addressed himself to the threat of gnostic, and especially docetic, heresy (see esp. pp. 160–64).

usually described as the need to correct some kind of heresy, and particularly heresy concerning the person of Christ. Thus Jürgen Becker claims that the Fourth Gospel defends a fully catholic christology by enlarging a signs source in terms opposed to docetic heresy.[66] Robert Fortna sees John as the revision of a 'Gospel of signs', intended perhaps for Jewish-Christians (not, however, gnostic in outlook), who regarded Jesus as simply a miracle-worker and over-valued the 'signs tradition' of the church.[67] W. Nicol believes that the fourth evangelist edited and interpreted a signs source in order to draw out the real significance of 'miracle-faith' – as faith in the earthly as well as exalted glory of the miracle-working Jesus – for the benefit of Jewish-Christians, and Jews who were still members of the synagogue, but interested in Jesus.[68] On the other hand, Luise Schottroff accepts the existence of a signs source behind the Fourth Gospel, and goes on to argue that the Gospel corrects the source by *devaluing* the miraculous; but (she says) this was conducted from a fundamentally *gnostic* view-point![69]

It is true, as we shall see, that christology is an important preoccupation of the fourth evangelist, and one which has helped to determine his reason for writing a Gospel. But to say that he was answering heresy in being thus preoccupied is probably going too far. Although, as we have noticed, it is possible to produce material from the Fourth Gospel which favours the conclusion that John was opposed to gnosticising (docetic) tendencies, there is insufficient evidence to prove that he was clearly arguing against gnostic heretics. Equally, despite the views of Käsemann and Schottroff, it is impossible to read off from the Fourth Gospel a thoroughgoing gnosticism, and claim that the evangelist supported it. The worlds of John and the true gnostics are in the end too far apart for that.[70]

However, the fact to which both Scott and Bultmann draw attention, that John seems on occasions to approximate to a gnosticising way of thought while at other times appearing antagonistic to it, points to a further important consideration. At the time when John was writing, the interaction between Christianity and gnosticism was still at an early,

66. Becker, 'Wunder', pp. 130–48.
67. Fortna, *Gospel of Signs*, esp. p. 224.
68. Nicol, *Sēmeia*, pp. 142–49.
69. L. Schottroff, *Der Glaubende und die feindliche Welt: Beobachtungen zum gnostischen Dualismus und seiner Bedeutung für Paulus und das Johannesevangelium*, WMANT 37 (Neukirchen-Vluyn: Neukirchener Verlag, 1970), esp. pp. 228–96. We are reminded of Käsemann's view, in *Testament of Jesus*, that the present form of John's Gospel is entirely dependent on a docetic christology. Teeple, *Literary Origin*, also accepts a signs source as the basis of the Fourth Gospel; but he thinks that an editor has simply combined with this source (showing Christ as a Hellenistic miracle-worker) another source containing a semi-gnostic Son-Father theology, and produced a syncretistic Gospel for a syncretistic environment: probably Alexandria (p. 160).
70. See above, pp. 54–61.

developing stage. As a result, it was difficult to decide – even then – what was overtly 'gnostic' and what was not. It follows that it was equally difficult to determine what was 'orthodox' at this stage, and what was 'heretical'. In fact, John's Gospel is a classic example of the theological diversity which was entirely characteristic of the first Christian century. Moreover, in no area is Johannine diversity more evident than in the christological. At one moment Jesus can be reported by St John as saying 'I and the Father are one' (John 10:30), and at another, 'the Father is greater than I' (14:28). Again, Jesus in this Gospel is both one with God and distinct from him; he is 'from the Father', but he has also come 'into the world' (16:28). So far as the relation between Jesus and God or Jesus and humanity is concerned, John's christology swings quite happily between the extremes of what were later defined as doceticism and adoptionism.[71]

John's Gospel is not, then, concerned with orthodoxy as such or heresy as such. If it were, presumably the evangelist would not have been so unguarded in his theological statements that these could have been used, as they were used, by orthodox and heretic alike in due course in support of their respective positions. It therefore becomes difficult, if not impossible, to sustain the opinion that the purpose of the Fourth Gospel was polemic against (gnostic) heresy.

(d)   For liturgical use

We have considered six suggestions which have been made about the intention of John's Gospel, and we have found that there are difficulties in the way of accepting any of these as an accurate description of the fourth evangelist's aims – primary or secondary – in writing. There is one further proposal about the purpose of the Fourth Gospel which must be mentioned briefly; although it is not an explanation which has won much acceptance among scholars. This is the view that the immediate background to the Gospel is liturgical.[72]

An example of this way of accounting for the composition of John is to be found in the work of W.H. Raney, who believes that the Fourth Gospel contains prose-hymns which originally formed part of the worship of the early church, and were written by the evangelist to be sung or chanted by a cantor or choir. Examples of these 'hymns', most of which occur in Johannine speech material, are to be found (Raney argues) in the prologue to the Fourth Gospel, in parts of chapters 3 and

---

71. See further Smalley, 'Diversity and Development', pp. 279–81.

72. The attempt to explain the documents of the New Testament in terms of early Christian liturgical worship is a fashionable exercise in some scholarly circles. This has been done for Matthew's Gospel, for example, by M.D. Goulder, *Midrash and Lection in Matthew* (London: SPCK, 1974).

10, and in the farewell discourse (John 14–17).[73] However, even if this speculative thesis helps to account for the existence and shape of some Johannine discourse material, it does not explain the composition of John's Gospel as a whole. Furthermore, Raney's theory by itself does not explain the very arbitrary placing and sequence – on his view – of the 'liturgical' material in John. To solve this problem, Raney resorts unconvincingly to the theory of 'accidental displacement'. In his opinion the hymns in question were written on detachable sheets, which became displaced as the manuscript of John's Gospel passed from one chorister or church to another.[74]

A more recent liturgical view of John's aim, and one which deserves more serious attention, is presented by Aileen Guilding, in her book *The Fourth Gospel and Jewish Worship*.[75] Dr Guilding finds the starting point for the interpretation of the Fourth Gospel in synagogue worship during the first Christian century. The Gospel, she suggests, is a Christian commentary on Old Testament lectionary readings, as these were arranged in a triennial cycle such as could be found in Palestine even before the first century AD. Only thus, according to Guilding, can the order of John's material (following the pattern: feast–miracle–discourse) be understood; since the evangelist correlated his material with the pentateuchal and prophetic lessons read in Jewish worship at the feast in question. An obvious example of this 'correlation' is to be found (according to Guilding) in John 6, where the material – the feeding of the multitude, the walking on the water and the bread of life sermon – reveals intimate connections in thought and language with the Jewish synagogue readings for Passover time,[76] and seems to have been determined by them.[77]

On the assumption that the background to the Fourth Gospel is essentially liturgical, Guilding is able to guess at John's purpose in writing. She argues that the evangelist was above all concerned to present Jesus as the fulfilment of Judaism (so that, for example, all the Jewish feasts are fulfilled in the passover-eucharist), and to show that compromise with Judaism itself is impossible: hence the opposition to 'the Jews' in the Gospel. In Guilding's view, John may also have wished to preserve a tradition of dominical sermons, not found in the synoptic Gospels,

73. W.H. Raney, *The Relation of the Fourth Gospel to the Christian Cultus* (Giessen: A. Töpelmann, 1933). Raney believes that Babylonian, Egyptian and Hebrew hymnody provided the fourth evangelist with models for his composition (see pp. 18–19).

74. *Ibid.*, pp. 75–79.

75. Guilding, *Jewish Worship*. See also below, p. 71 n. 131.

76. The appropriate readings for Nisan dealt with the gift of manna in the wilderness (*e.g.* Exod. 16 and Num. 11), the overthrow of the Pharaoh at the Sea of Reeds (Exod. 15), and prophetic utterances which provided a comment on those events (*e.g.* Isa. 54–55).

77. See Guilding, *Jewish Worship*, pp. 58–68.

which he arranged according to the Jewish liturgical year and possibly intended as readings during worship at the major Christian festivals. In its present form, Guilding concludes, the Gospel provided the necessary help and encouragement for Jewish-Christians who had been excommunicated from the synagogue.[78]

This thesis is put forward with much scholarship and not a little ingenuity.[79] However, at several points it is open to serious question. First, we cannot be certain about the use and limits of the triennial lectionary (and in fact Dr Guilding suggests that there was a *double* cycle of readings shaping the contents and chronology of John's Gospel), which is fundamental to the structure of the argument; nor can we be sure that this lectionary was 'well-established in Palestine by the first century and that it can be adequately reconstructed'.[80] Secondly, we know very little about the nature of Christian worship – apart from the eucharist – during the first century AD, or whether John's alleged liturgical purposes in writing the Fourth Gospel would have been welcomed and understood by his congregation. Thirdly, we have no knowledge of the liturgical use of Greek among Jewish-Christians in Palestine – or even beyond – at this time; although Guilding assumes that Septuagintal echoes are integral to the relationship between John's work and the Old Testament lections to which he is indebted. Finally, the entire argument of this book stands or falls by the accuracy of Dr Guilding's assumption that the Fourth Gospel was written for a Jewish (or at least, Jewish-Christian) audience. This may very well have been the case in part, as we shall see; but if John's readers were drawn from a wider circle, Dr Guilding's explanation of John's intention runs into grave difficulties.

No one doubts that early Christian worship exercised some influence on the composition of the documents in the New Testament. But the attempt to explain the Fourth Gospel entirely in liturgical and lectionary terms is altogether too strained, and fails to take proper account of the fact that John was writing a *Gospel* as such. It seems clear, therefore, that we must look elsewhere for an answer to the question of John's purpose.

THE AIM OF THE GOSPEL

Why, then, did John write his Gospel? It so happens that John himself tells us. These (signs) are written, he says, 'that you may believe that Jesus is the Christ, the Son of God, and that believing you may have life in his name' (John 20:31). Obviously we must take such a statement of the writer's intention seriously. His aim, it appears, is to invite his readers

78. *Ibid.*, pp. 54–57; 229–33.

79. Significantly, Aileen Guilding (like Michael Goulder; see n.72) was a pupil of Austin Farrer, himself a notable devotee of lectionary theories.

80. Guilding, *Jewish Worship*, p. 6.

to believe and live. That is to say, John's Gospel seems to have a primarily evangelistic purpose. To this end a selection of the signs of Jesus has been made (20:30), which will enable the reader to understand the real identity of the Gospel's central figure, and by faith in him to receive the eternal life of which he is the carrier.

This reading of John's purpose agrees with the nature of a Gospel. By definition, a Christian Gospel is a written statement of the 'good news' (εὐαγγέλιον) proclaimed about Jesus as the Christ. A Gospel is thus a unique literary *genre*, concerned in some way with the preaching of the evangel.[81] Need we go further, then, in order to discover John's intention? If he wrote *a* Gospel, was he not above all preaching *the* gospel?

Unfortunately, the problem and its solution cannot be dismissed so easily. To begin with, John's statement is a very general one, and by itself tells us nothing about the *readers* he had in mind. Furthermore, there is a textual variant in the Greek of John 20:31, which gives two different senses to the evangelist's statement of purpose. The better manuscripts[82] read ἵνα πιστεύητε (present subjunctive), meaning '(these are written) that you may go on believing'; while the remaining witnesses have ἵνα πιστεύσητε (aorist subjunctive), meaning 'that you may believe for the first time'. In the first case the Gospel was written, it would appear, for Christians; in the second case it was written for unbelievers.

Nevertheless, John's description of his intention in writing this Gospel provides us with some important clues which will help us, and lead us into a fuller discussion of the present issue.

'Seeing and believing'

The summary which the fourth evangelist gives of his intention (John 20:30-31) occurs in the context of a discussion between Jesus and Thomas after the resurrection, on the subject of sight and faith. Thomas, the doubting disciple, is finally brought to a confession of faith in Jesus as Lord and God (verse 28) by his encounter with the risen Christ (verses 26–27). In response to the acknowledgement of Thomas, Jesus asks whether the former doubter has believed merely because he has been granted physical sight of his glorified Lord. Happy are those, Jesus goes on, who have not seen physically, and yet believe – that is, 'see' or understand – spiritually (verse 29). In other words, with or without sight of the figure of Jesus on earth, faith is supremely a matter of spiritual perception. Furthermore, the fourth evangelist comments, the present Gospel is written with precisely such an aim in mind: that, on the basis of the evidence marshalled, his readers may have eyes to see that Jesus is the life-giving Messiah and Son of God (verse 31).

81. *Cf.* Moule, 'Intention', esp. pp. 175–76; against Burridge, *What are the Gospels?*
82. א* B Θ.

Verbs of seeing are very important in the Fourth Gospel, and they are regularly used in association with the idea of faith.[83] The Samaritan woman, for example, invited people to 'come to see' the man who had told her all that she had ever done (John 4:29); and eventually many Samaritans believed in Jesus as Saviour (verses 39–42), Again, the sight of the blind man was restored by Jesus, so that he *saw* physically (9:7), and also *believed* in Jesus as Son of man (verses 35–38). Moreover, when the beloved disciple went into the tomb of Jesus, and discovered incontrovertible evidence of the resurrection, we are told that 'he saw and believed' (20:8).

It is no accident, therefore, that the ideas of sight and faith are from time to time linked together in the words of Jesus himself in John's Gospel,[84] reaching a climax with the saying to Thomas about 'seeing and believing' in the passage already mentioned (20:29). The importance of 'seeing faith' in the Fourth Gospel is underlined throughout by the characteristic contrast between 'light' and 'darkness' which John uses. This motif, with its Jewish as much as Hellenistic background,[85] is introduced at the opening of the Gospel as a description of the Word of God. In him, whom we know eventually as Jesus, are to be found light and life; whereas in the world opposed to God exist only darkness and death (John 1:4–5).

The contrast between Jesus as light and his enemies – who are also the enemies of God – as darkness, is sustained throughout the Fourth Gospel, particularly in the debates between Jesus and 'the Jews'. Here the conflict between light and darkness, good and evil, life and death, is presented almost antiphonally; and it becomes abundantly clear that those who refuse to see and accept the real identity of Jesus bring judgment upon themselves. For example, the discussion about the true origin of Jesus in John 8 is introduced by his claim to be the 'light of the world' (verse 12); and it ends with Jesus 'hiding' himself – symbolically, as well as literally, no doubt – from his opponents when they attempt to stone him (verse 59). In John 9, the healing of the blind man paves the way for an inevitable contrast between 'sight' and 'blindness' (verses 39–41). In the classic treatment of this theme at John 12, where John's own comments are supported by the quotation from Isaiah 6 about sight and faith, 'believing in the light' and 'walking in the darkness' are set in stark opposition to each other (verses 35–46). 'I have come as light into the world', Jesus concludes, 'so that everyone who trusts me may not stay in the dark' (verse 46).

---

83. *Cf.* G.L. Phillips, 'Faith and Vision in the Fourth Gospel' in Cross (ed.), *Studies in the Fourth Gospel*, pp. 83–96. Verbs of 'hearing', often in association with the concepts of 'believing' and 'living', are also important in this Gospel (*cf.* John 5:24–25; 10:27–28; 14:24; 18:37, *et al.*)

84. John 6:36; 12:44–46; 14:9–10, *et al.*

85. Note its occurrence in the Qumran literature; see above, pp. 33–36, esp. 34; 72–73.

JOHN'S AUDIENCE

Evidently, then, John's Gospel is designed to invite 'sight' and 'faith' (whether for the first time, or constantly) from its readers. The evangelist wants his audience – like some of the characters in the Gospel, but unlike the majority of the Jews who are mentioned – to 'see' and believe and live. However, given that this was John's aim, we still need to sift the evidence of the Gospel itself, and try to discover which particular readers he had in mind. Assuming that he did not write a Gospel merely for its own sake, and launch it into the blue without an audience in mind,[86] can we discover for whom John wrote? Earlier in this chapter we found reasons for rejecting the view that John was addressing the *Greek* world exclusively, even if he may have had Gentiles in mind. Four other groups of readers may therefore be suggested; and by considering these we shall be able to focus the 'evangelistic' purpose of the Fourth Gospel more clearly.

(a)   Unbelieving Jews

If John wrote an evangelistic document with the intention that his readers should 'see' the true identity of the life-giving Jesus-Messiah, it could be argued that he was writing for unbelievers, to bring them to faith. In this case, however, who were the unbelievers?

One answer to this question was provided in 1928 by Karl Bornhaüser of Marburg, who propounded the theory that John's Gospel was written as a straightforward missionary tract for unbelieving *Jews*.[87] Only members of Israel, Bornhaüser argues, would have fully understood this document, which is not only preoccupied with Judaism and 'the Jews' but also omits any reference to the institution of the Christian (believers') rites of baptism and the Lord's Supper.[88] On this showing, then, John's Gospel was addressed to Jewry in general, as a means of justifying the Christian claim that Jesus is Messiah, and winning its members to faith.[89]

A variation of this view claims that John's evangelism was directed towards unconverted Jews who were in the *diaspora*, beyond Palestine.

86. Against Barrett (pp. 134–41), who claims that even if the Fourth Gospel and its author are related to a particular world of thought, it is easy to believe that John wrote primarily to satisfy himself. His Gospel must be written; 'it was no concern of his whether it was also read' (p. 135). Similarly Bultmann, pp. 698–99: 'a precise circle of readers is obviously not in view' (p. 698 n.6). The specific character of John's Gospel appears to militate against this opinion; see below pp. 181–85.

87. K. Bornhaüser, *Das Johannesevangelium: eine Missionsschrift für Israel* (Gütersloh: Bertelsmann, 1928).

88. *Ibid.*, esp. pp. 158–63; see also, on 'the Jews' in the Fourth Gospel, pp. 19–23.

89. *Cf.* Bultmann (p. 698) who maintains that it is irrevelant to the fourth evangelist whether his potential readership is Christian, or not yet such.

That Hellenistic as opposed to Palestinian Jews were being addressed, is perhaps suggested by the fact that the Gospel (in its final edition) was written in Greek, and that terms such as 'Messiah' and 'Rabbi' are carefully translated.[90] An entirely Palestinian audience, presumably, would not require these concessions. Thus W.C. van Unnik, for example, believes that the fourth evangelist wrote to a synagogue in the dispersion – consisting of both Jews and Godfearers – in order to show them that Jesus was the true Messiah of Israel.[91] John Robinson has similarly argued that the Gospel of John is an attempt to bring the good news of Jesus the Messiah to Greek-speaking diaspora Judaism.[92]

However, there are two main difficulties in the way of regarding the Fourth Gospel as evangelistic in the sense of being a missionary document designed to convert Jews – whether in Palestine or in the dispersion – to Christianity. First, by the time this Gospel was written the Christian mission to Israel was largely over. 'The Jews' who feature so frequently in John are the *enemies* of Jesus, not potential Christians; and they consequently appear in a polemical light. The controversies in the Gospel take place in a Jewish setting; and even if some Jews believe in Jesus (12:11),· the majority are responsible for his death. This exactly reflects the situation after the destruction of the temple in AD 70, when the parties and groups within Judaism – so evident in the synoptic Gospels – had disappeared, and only Pharisaism remained (hence, simply, 'the Jews'); and when 'Jews' were those who had rejected Jesus.[93] John's attitude towards Judaism was likely therefore to have been polemical, rather than missionary.[94]

Second, and more crucially, is it likely that unbelieving Jews would be converted simply by reading this Gospel? It is possible that they might be made to think, and even to re-examine their own faith so as to take it more seriously. But if John were primarily concerned to make evangelistic inroads into Judaism, it is doubtful if he would have succeeded in this task (or has succeeded!) by casting the Jews in the role of the chief opponents of the gospel – enemies of God himself – and treating them with undisguised hostility.

90. John 1:41, 38; 20:16; *cf.* 4:9; 7:35; 11:51–52.
91. W.C. van Unnik, 'The Purpose of St John's Gospel', *SE* 1 (1959), pp. 382–411.
92. Robinson, 'Destination'.
93. *Cf.* Matt. 28:15.
94. *Cf.* Brown 1, pp. lxx–lxxv. Brown makes the point that John is not being deliberately anachronistic in his use of the term 'the Jews', since he indicates by it his belief that the Jews of his own day are the 'spiritual descendants of the Jewish authorities who were hostile to Jesus during the ministry' (p. lxxii). On 'the Jews' in John see Brodie, pp. 240, 254–55 (as representative of negative reaction to Jesus); 328–29 (as representative of all superficial belief).

For these reasons we cannot accept the view that John was written as an evangelistic document for unbelieving Jews.[95] In any case, as we shall see in a moment, the character and contents of the Fourth Gospel suggest that its audience was chiefly *inside* the Christian church, rather than outside.

(b) Diaspora Jewish-Christians

It has been suggested that, even if the fourth evangelist were not writing for Hellenistic Jews in the dispersion, he was (in part, at least) addressing diaspora Jewish-*Christians*. This is the tentative proposal of Raymond Brown,[96] who draws attention to the crisis through which Jewish-Christians passed during the last part of the first century AD. By this time the attitude of orthodox Jewry towards Christianity had become more rigid than before, and Jews who confessed Jesus but had not yet broken with the synagogue were regarded with suspicion as potential subverters of the law: which, after the destruction of the temple, was the mainstay of Judaism. During the 80s, for example, a systematic attempt was made to exclude Christian Jews from the synagogues. We know this from the eighteen Benedictions (*Shemoneh Esreh*) which were recited in the synagogue at this period. The twelfth of these (c. AD 85) was a curse on heretics, particularly those of the Jewish-Christian variety. Moreover, under Rabbi Gamaliel II, the Jewish assembly at Jamnia in about AD 90 introduced formal excommunication to exclude dissent from the faith of Judaism.

There are indications, Brown argues, that the Fourth Gospel is an appeal to Jewish-Christians who are in precisely this situation, torn between their faith in Jesus and their loyalty to Judaism. The Johannine polemic against 'the Jews' would not apply to them; and, positively, the fourth evangelist's emphasis on Jesus as Messiah and as the fulfilment of all Jewish feasts and institutions would be a strength to their faith if

95. *Pace* Schnackenburg 1, pp. 165–67, who does not exclude from John's Gospel a missionary intention with regard to diaspora Jews, even if this were not one of the Gospel's principal aims. *Cf.* also Meeks, *Prophet-King*, p. 294, who thinks that substantial parts of the Johannine tradition were 'shaped by a fluid situation of missionary and polemical interaction with a strong Jewish community'; and S. Pancaro, 'The Relationship of the Church to Israel in the Gospel of St John', *NTS* 21 (1974–75), pp. 396–405, who claims that John is 'a Jew writing for a Jewish audience' (p. 396). See further Martyn, *History and Theology*, pp.37–62; also W.A. Meeks, ' "Am I a Jew?": Johannine Christianity and Judaism', in J. Neusner (ed.), *Christianity, Judaism, and Other Greco-Roman Cults*, vol. 1: *New Testament*, SJLA 12 (Leiden: E.J. Brill, 1975), pp. 163–86. The suggestion that John wrote his Gospel to win (or instruct) *Samaritan* converts is entirely speculative; see above, p. 73 n. 146. C.H. Dodd believes that the Fourth Gospel was written to win converts from *paganism* (*IFG*, pp. 6–9). For a defence of John's evangelistic aim see Carson, p. 91.

96. Brown 1, pp. lxxiii–v. *Cf.* also W. Wilkens, *Zeichen und Werke: Ein Beitrag zur Theologie des 4 Evangeliums in Erzählungs – und Redestoff* (Zürich: Zwingli Verlag, 1969).

they were allowed to remain in the synagogue, and an encouragement to them if they were forced to withdraw. Furthermore, there are three possible references to excommunication and 'being put out of the synagogue', in John's Gospel;[97] and twice the fourth evangelist gives instances of those who overcame their fear of the Jews and, even at the risk of expulsion from the synagogue, publicly acknowledged Jesus: the blind man who was healed, and Joseph of Arimathea.[98] Brown concludes that John is inviting Jewish-Christians in the synagogues of the diaspora to follow the example of such people.[99]

This suggestion is attractive, and there is some evidence to support it from the Fourth Gospel itself. However, although it is true that the fourth evangelist is particularly concerned to demonstrate the messianic identity of Jesus, the nature of his christology, as we shall see, suggests that his real audience was not confined to diaspora Jewish-Christianity alone. The possibility that the Fourth Gospel was intended for a wider readership leads us to consider a third group which John may have been addressing.

(c)   Christians

A Gospel can be evangelistic in the sense of being a missionary tract for unbelievers. If John wrote such a tract, it is unlikely that he would have done so without some particular readers in mind; and the same may be said for Mark, Matthew and Luke. However, we have not yet found a suitable readership for John answering to such a purpose.

But a Gospel can also be evangelistic (or kerygmatic) in the sense of being a document written to encourage believers, to challenge their faith and help them to grow in the Christian life. If John wrote such a document, we have seen that he need not have been addressing – at least, with any sense of exclusive concern – diaspora Christian Jews. It is possible that John's Gospel was written for Christian believers *anywhere*, to prompt them in the face of all difficulties to go on 'seeing' who Jesus is, and to believe in him. If so, the better-attested reading at John 20:31 (ἵνα πιστεύητε, 'that you may continue to believe [that Jesus is the Christ, the Son of God])', which is likely to be original, agrees with this purpose.

Certainly the Fourth Gospel is a Gospel for Christian disciples. The Christ of St John invites people not only to live, but also to go on living in him. The profound teaching of the Gospel, notably in the discourses of Jesus, is not so much an explanation of the fundamentals of belief as

---

97.   John 9:22; 12:42; 16:2. However, these texts could as well allude to unofficial exclusion from the synagogue in the light of Jewish-Christian missionary activity. See above, p.92.

98.   John 9, esp. verses 34–38; 19:38 (*cf.* also Nicodemus, verse 39).

99.   Brown 1, p. lxxv.

an exhortation to understand and apply that belief. Furthermore, while any Jewish believers are obviously included in this exhortation, John writes for Gentile Christians as well. There is nothing exclusive about this Gospel; on the contrary, its perspective is infinitely wide. Apart from the (secondary) Hellenistic features of the work, which undoubtedly owe their origin to its ultimate audience rather than its basic tradition, there are many pointers to the Johannine belief that the church is inclusive in character. Jesus is the Saviour of the world, who draws 'all people' to himself.[100] He has 'other sheep' to bring into the fold, and prays for the world to believe in him.[101] The Gentiles, who are included in such references, also appear in the Gospel at a crucial moment, on the eve of Christ's glorification, and ask to 'see Jesus'.[102]

As John opens out the Jesus-event to eternity, then, without confining it to one moment in time, so he also opens it out to more than one ethnic group, without limiting it to Israel. It may be that in the end John's Gospel has in mind a very wide audience indeed; and, while nothing would prevent any reader from learning about Jesus for the first time, the likelihood remains that John is writing for the benefit of readers from *any* background – although possibly they would need to be fairly intelligent readers! – who desired help towards Christian growth and maturity.[103]

Even so, we have not yet taken full account of the contents of John's Gospel, and particularly of the distinctive nature of its christology. While it may be true that the evangelist addresses all Christians anywhere, it is most probable, as we have already hinted, that he has a particular group – in this case, a particular group of Christians – in mind. Where, if anywhere, are they to be found? To answer this, we turn to a fourth group of John's possible readers.

(d) The Johannine church

It cannot be over-stressed that the Fourth Gospel was originally anchored in a real life-situation, which helped to shape its basic tradition,

100. John 12:32. *Cf.* 1:29; 3:17; 4:42, all referring to salvation through Jesus as intended for the κόσμος ('world').

101. John 10:16; 17:20–21.

102. John 12:20–21, assuming that Ἕλληνες here means Gentiles, rather than proselytes or Hellenistic Jews. So Barrett, *Gospel of John and Judaism*, p. 18.

103. *Cf.* further G. MacRae, 'The Fourth Gospel and *Religionsgeschichte*', *CBQ* 32 (1970), pp. 13–24, esp. 23–24. 'John attempts to assert both the universality and the transcendence of the divine Son Jesus'; although in the end his message is that Jesus 'can only be understood on Christian terms' (p. 24). Possibly John 20:31 has an inclusive audience in mind, since belief in Jesus as 'Messiah' may have had particular appeal for the Jewish section of John's readership, and belief in Jesus as 'Son of God' may have contained special attraction for those from a Gentile religious background, where 'sons of gods' were common.

and caused its eventual publication. It is most improbable that in the first place John wrote without being sensitive to some particular group around him. In that case, what more natural group is there than the Johannine church or community itself?[104]

Research into the nature of the church, which gave rise to what is now recognised as a distinctively Johannine form of Christianity, is still in progress.[105] Several factors in this investigation need to be taken into account: for example, the origin of the Johannine tradition as such, the part (if any) played by the beloved disciple in its transmission, and the inter-relation of the different parts of the total corpus of Johannine literature. But the existence cannot be doubted of a group of Christians who were not only committed to Jesus, but also followers of John as a leading exponent of Christian discipleship and living. The way in which John's Gospel itself was composed, described in previous chapters, suggests a community of this kind, in which the Jesus tradition was handed on and developed in a characteristic way. So does the closing section of the Fourth Gospel (John 21:20–25), in which the importance of the beloved disciple's witness is attested, and authentication is given to the Gospel's testimony – for which the beloved disciple is ultimately responsible – by the church-group surrounding him (verse 24).

It is here, in the Johannine church, that the key to the purpose of the Fourth Gospel is to be found. Inevitably, John describes the origin of the Jesus tradition, and reflects the earliest stages of the Christian mission to Palestine and even beyond. But the immediate cause of the Gospel's final form, and the reason for its launching on the Mediterranean world, seems to have been directly related to the needs of the local church in which it came to birth. The particular contents of John's Gospel will help to throw light on those needs.

The structural centre of the Fourth Gospel, as we argued in chapter 6, is to be found in John's selection of seven signs. But the theological

104. The terms 'church' or 'community', as a description of the setting in which the Fourth Gospel arose, are preferred to the expression '(Johannine) school', since the latter contains technical overtones which may or may not be appropriate to the real situation. But see Culpepper, *Johannine School*. By investigating the nature of ancient academic schools, Dr Culpepper evaluates the suggestion that the Gospel of John was composed by one or more members of a similar *milieu*. He concludes that the Johannine fellowship, founded by the beloved disciple and gathered around him for purposes of teaching, learning and worship, was indeed a 'school' as such (see esp. pp. 261–90). Cullmann, *Johannine Circle*, p. 86, *et passim* admits the terms 'church' and 'community' in this connection; but he seems to prefer the description '(Johannine) circle', in view of his belief that the Fourth Gospel grew out of a situation in which different groups within what he terms 'marginal Judaism', impressed by the mind of the beloved disciple (who is the fourth evangelist, but not the apostle John, p. 84), were brought into one orbit.

105. See D.M. Smith, 'Johannine Christianity' in *idem, Johannine Christianity*, pp. 1–36. For the nature of the Johannine community see further Smalley, *Thunder and Love*, pp. 17–19.

centre to which those signs eventually point is without question a christological one. The signs clarify the real identity of the person whose
life-giving ministry and glorification are being described. This again is
in line with John's declared purpose in writing his Gospel: 'These (signs)
are written that you may believe that Jesus is the Christ, the Son of God'
(John 20:31).

What does John have to say specifically about Jesus as Christ and Son
of God? There is a marked diversity in his christology, of which we have
already taken note. Jesus in St John is one with God, but also distinct
from him; he is the Messiah from God (John 4:25–26), and yet he does
nothing on his own authority (8:28). This ambivalent view could – and
did – cause John to be accused of heresy, as well as provoking the
heretical (gnostic) use of the Fourth Gospel in the second century.[106]
Equally, it meant that second-century writers such as Irenaeus and
Tertullian were able to come to the successful defence of John's orthodoxy without appearing to waste their time.[107]

John is not concerned about 'orthodoxy or 'heresy' as such; his
christology is too diverse for such lines to be drawn: at least, by him. But
he *is* concerned to provide his readers with a fully-rounded christology;
to remind those who found it difficult to accept that Jesus was 'from
God' of his true origin, and to persuade those who were reluctant to see
that Jesus was the Word made flesh that he had really come 'into the
world'.

Who were these readers, and why was John addressing them in this
way? We have already suggested that John's Gospel was written for a
mixed audience of believers, including those from a Gentile as well as a
Jewish background. It is reasonable to suppose that these two groups of
believers belonged to the Johannine church itself, in which certain problems had arisen. Let us consider a possible situation in that church which
could have resulted in the writing of the Fourth Gospel.

The Christian church as a whole in the first century AD had a difficult
time. Outside, persecution from the Roman state became more intense,
and more systematic. Inside, there were problems of belief and behaviour, especially caused by those with sectarian or heterodox attitudes and
ideas. In the Johannine community, perhaps, internal troubles were also
making their presence felt. These were no longer problems such as those
caused by the Judaisers in Paul's Galatian churches, when Christians

106. See above, pp. 77, 91. *Cf.* also W. Bauer, *Orthodoxy and Heresy in Earliest
Christianity* (Philadelphia: Fortress Press, 1971 and London: SCM Press, 1972), pp. 187,
206–212. On the use of the Fourth Gospel by the Alexandrian gnostics see Sanders, *Fourth
Gospel in the Early Church*, pp. 47–66.

107. *Cf. ibid.*, pp. 66–84; also Smalley, 'Diversity and Development', p. 281. Note
further the account by T.E. Pollard, *Johannine Christology and the Early Church*, SNTSMS
13 (Cambridge: Cambridge University Press, 1970); see esp., on the nature of John's
christology, pp. 18–19.

from an orthodox Jewish background, who were over-reliant on the law, insisted on exclusive regulations for admittance to church membership or table-fellowship. Nor, as we have argued, was John's church beset by definable heresy, of the kind that eventually flourished when Christianity and paganism interacted. In our view the most compelling explanation of the actual content of the Fourth Gospel is rather that the community of Christians, gathered – in some sense – around John the beloved disciple, included Jews and Christians who in a unique situation were discovering their apparent mutual incompatibility. This incompatibility was manifested and experienced above all in the realm of christology.

Here were two groups of believers from very different backgrounds, worshipping together in one church and encountering difficulties in their understanding of the person of Christ. On the one hand there were Jewish-Christians who had come out of the synagogue and professed commitment to Jesus, but who still felt a loyalty to their Jewish heritage. As a result, these Christians may have thought that Jesus was less than fully divine. This would be all the more likely if, after AD 70, they were under pressure from unbelieving fellow-Jews in the dispersion, and were tempted to slip back into Judaism by denying – as do 'the Jews' throughout John's Gospel – the messiahship of Jesus. Such a group might have something in common with the Ebionites, a primitive sect of Jews who, according to some scholars, believed in Jesus but seem to have regarded him simply as 'a man chosen by God', and who were faithful observers of the law.[108]

On the other hand there were Hellenistic-Christians, including possibly some Hellenistic *Jewish*-Christians, who were still influenced by their pagan religious background and inclined towards beliefs which were later to be defined as heretical. As a result, these Christians may have thought that Jesus was less than fully human. This would be all the more likely if the 'divine man' tradition of their Gentile religious environment – the 'redeemer figure' mythology, of which mention has already been made – exercised any influence on the Johannine community.[109]

Both groups in John's church, it may be presumed, had begun to comprehend the real identity of Jesus; but neither had fully 'seen' the mystery of the Word made flesh. Possibly friction resulted, with each group taking its particular theological stance; in which case the Johannine emphasis on mutual love (John 15:12), and unity within the church (17:11, 21–23), would have been entirely relevant. No longer, as in Paul's day, were the issues concerned with the place of the law and the scope of

---

108. The evidence on the Ebionites is confusing; but see further J. Daniélou, *A History of Early Christian Doctrine before the Council of Nicea*, vol. 1: *The Theology of Jewish Christianity* (London: Darton, Longman and Todd, 1964), pp. 55–64.

109. This is possible, but by no means yet established. See Nicol, *Sēmeia*, pp. 48–52. Some of the churches in Asia Minor addressed by Paul, as at Colossae, may also have been troubled by Greek, gnosticising influence.

the church's mission. Now the question was simple, but crucial: it was the nature of the person of Jesus.

Two extreme interpretations of the nature of Christ may thus have characterised Johannine Christianity: one which did not accept Jesus as God, and the other which did not acknowledge him as man.[110] It is quite likely that the history of John's church, and the developing nature of its problems, can be traced back to Revelation: which, we would claim, may be dated to AD 70.[111] We can then plot a theological, and especially christological, trajectory from the Apocalypse through the Gospel to the Letters of John, where we discover the outcome of the doctrinal polarisation which characterised the Johannine community.[112]

For by the time 1 John was written, the two christological extremes of which we have spoken seem to have emerged as heterodox beliefs which could be defined: Christ is *either* divine *or* human. The writer of 1 John feels obliged, therefore, to restate the fundamentals of the Christian faith; and, by recalling his community to accept a balanced view of Christ's person, he provides its members with an orthodox refutation of both extremes. But, from 1 John 2:18–19, we discover that secession has already begun. It is the last hour; and some adherents – from both Jewish *and* Hellenistic backgrounds, no doubt – are leaving the circle, finding it spiritually uncomfortable to remain within it.

At 2 John 7 we learn that 'many deceivers' – again, we believe, on both sides of the divide – have 'gone out' into the world, not acknowledging Jesus Christ incarnate. When we reach 3 John (see verses 9–10), the final doctrinal and political schism has taken place, brought to a head by Diotrephes; so that heresy is being regarded as orthodoxy, and *vice versa*.[113]

Evidently, therefore, the writing of the Fourth Gospel, with its particular christological approach, did little to lessen the tensions which – we have suggested – troubled the Johannine church; even if it provided the church in general and for all time with important guide-lines for understanding the nature of the person of Christ. But, even if they found it difficult to accept, for the two sides in this debate (Jewish-Christian and Gentile-Christian) the balanced christology of John's Gospel was at the time exactly what they needed.[114]

110. This thesis does not exclude the possible existence of a *third* group of believers in the Johannine circle: those whose understanding of the nature of Christ, and therefore of the life which is to be found in him, was entirely balanced, and to that extent 'orthodox'.

111. So Smalley, *Thunder and Love*, pp. 40–50.

112. *Cf. ibid.*, pp. 134–37.

113. For this section see Smalley, *1, 2, 3 John*, pp. xxiii–xxxii; see also S.S. Smalley, 'What about 1 John?', in *Studia Biblica 1978*, III (Sheffield: JSOT Press, 1980), pp. 337–43. For the slippery terms 'orthodoxy' and 'heresy' see Smalley, *1, 2, 3 John*, p. xxv; also above, pp. 169–72.

114. For further consideration of John's christology see below, pp. 238–48. On the nature of John's church see also Brown, *Community*; and on the disciples as friends of Jesus, to whom the love command was first addressed, see van Tilborg, *Imaginative Love*, pp. 111–68.

PROVENANCE

Where precisely was this Johannine community to be found? And where, consequently, was the Fourth Gospel published?

The connections between John's tradition and *Palestine* cannot do more than suggest that the Johannine tradition took root (rather than being finally written) there, since other influences were clearly involved in due course. *Syria* (Antioch) has been suggested as a place of origin,[115] because of the gnostic associations in John, and its alleged affinity with the *Odes of Solomon* and the letters of Ignatius. But all these links are superficial; and even if Syrian influence on the Gospel of John can be established, it is probably secondary. Because of the fact that John's Gospel in its final form was from an early date known and used in *Egypt*, it is arguable that the work has an Alexandrian provenance.[116] However, even if the finished work was known in Egypt early on, the recognised tendency associated with Alexandria to allegorise and gnosticise any Gospel suggests that the Egyptian church was unlikely to have had a hand in *constructing* the essentially historical and traditional Johannine Gospel for which we have argued.

In the end, there seems to be no reason for disputing the tradition, associated with Irenaeus,[117] that John's Gospel was finally produced at *Ephesus*.[118] Although there is no demonstrable proof that Asia Minor is the correct setting, it is an eminently suitable one. Apart from the traditional links, such an environment is favoured by the controversy with contemporary Judaism and Hellenism reflected in the Gospel, both of which may well have taken root in Phrygian soil; by the fact that the religious syncretism of Asia Minor would readily have nurtured the heretical tendencies which, using John's Gospel as a springboard, came to the surface in John's Letters; and by the links between Asia Minor and the Apocalypse of John.[119]

115. So Bauer, pp. 241–44; Bultmann, p. 12.

116. W.H. Brownlee, 'Whence the Gospel According to John?', in Charlesworth (ed.), *John and Qumran*, pp. 166–94, esp. 187–91, opts for this provenance. Brownlee also believes, however, that 'the work of translating (from Aramaic into Greek the apostolic sources used in) John's Gospel may have begun in Palestine' (pp. 187–88). Sanders, *Fourth Gospel in the Early Church*, esp. pp. 85–87, also suggests the 'possibility' (p. 85) that John's Gospel originated in Alexandria, and was then introduced into Asia Minor. But see the modification in Sanders' later book, *The Foundations of the Christian Faith: A Study of the Teaching of the New Testament in the Light of Historical Criticism* (London: A. and C. Black, 1950), pp. 161–62.

117. See above, pp. 76–79.

118. For the provenance of the Fourth Gospel beyond Ephesus see further Schnackenburg I, pp. 151–52.

119. This assumes a definite association within the Johannine corpus between the Revelation, Gospel and Letters of John; but this appears to us to be a reasonable supposition.

JOHN: EVANGELIST

We saw in the last chapter that John's Gospel was written to meet the needs of a church congregation. John – or the writer(s) responsible for the Fourth Gospel in its final shape – began in the appropriate place, with the Christian good news itself. The Fourth Gospel is above all a presentation of the Jesus tradition, on the basis of which any reader could be invited to 'see' the real identity of Jesus and live. But we have also argued that John the Evangelist was specially alive to the particular problems which existed in his own community, and that he was writing to point the way forward in this situation. It has been suggested in this connection that John was concerned to provide his believing but uninstructed audience with a relevant christology, mediating between the extreme theological positions which denied either the human or the divine nature of Christ. The result is a Gospel which didactically as well as kerygmatically centres in Jesus himself.

John the evangelist, therefore, must also be described as John the interpreter; he is not just one or the other. As evangelist, he is passionately involved with the gospel from which his appeal ultimately stems. He must remind his readers of the historical and traditional basis on which all Christian faith rests. Moreover, his approach is kerygmatic in the broad sense: he desires his audience to respond to the implications of his subject matter. As interpreter, on the other hand, John presents and explains that gospel more fully for his congregation, relating it directly to their particular situation. The formulation of John's preaching and the precise content of his teaching arise from the life-setting of his own church, and are shaped by its demands.

Because of this, the writer of the Fourth Gospel was essentially a pastor. It is sometimes alleged that the Gospel of John is evangelistic in character, whereas the Johannine Letters are pastoral. That is to say, John's Gospel is regarded as an invitation to *live* (addressed to those outside the church), while John's epistles are characterised as an encouragement to *grow* (written for those inside the church family).[1] But if our

1. *Cf.* B.F. Westcott, *The Epistles of St John*, 4th edn. (London: Macmillan, 1902), pp. xxxvi–xxxix; Stott, *Epistles,* pp. 22–24, 41–50, esp. 41. Both commentators, however, acknowledge the obviously polemical intention of the Johannine Letters, as well as their pastoral approach. We do not accept their description of the Fourth Gospel's purpose as evangelistic.

own view of John's purpose in composing his Gospel be allowed, then its character is just as pastoral as that of the Letters.

Moreover, the story of John's community is continued from the Gospel into the Johannine Letters; by which time the threat of secession had become a reality (1 John 2:19; 2 John 7).[2] The elder therefore recalls his readers to the essentials of the Christian scheme, as an evangelist, and demonstrates the care which he has for his followers, as their shepherd. It may be concluded that *both* writers, evangelist and elder, are pastors who are concerned to proclaim as well as to explain the message of Christ.[3]

In his Gospel, then, John is both evangelist *and* interpreter, preacher and teacher. As with any Gospel writer, these roles belong together and need to be held together; although for convenience we shall treat them separately. In this chapter we shall concentrate on John as an evangelist among other evangelists. In our final chapter we shall need to explore more fully the nature of John's interpretation of the Jesus tradition, and try to discover the special ways in which, as an interpreter, the fourth evangelist stands apart from the synoptic writers.

JOHN AS EVANGELIST

John need not and should not be regarded as an eccentric writer, simply because his Gospel has a distinctive appearance about it, and because his interpretation of the Jesus tradition is his own. On the contrary, to the extent that John is an evangelist, his writing – like that of the other canonical evangelists – is in line with the preaching content of the New Testament as a whole. As the author of a Gospel – and 'Gospels' are those particular documents which put into writing the spoken proclamation of the early church about Jesus – the fourth evangelist was indebted to a common Christian tradition. His interpretation of the evangel, therefore, like that of the synoptists, was based on a foundation of *kerygma* ('preaching') about Jesus which was shared by the whole primitive church. We may now investigate a little further what is meant by New Testament *kerygma* in this context.

C.H. Dodd, following Alfred Seeberg and Martin Dibelius, has argued persuasively that the writers of the New Testament drew upon a basic tradition of apostolic preaching to which they all had access.[4] As

2. See above, pp. 181–85, esp. 185; also Smalley, *1, 2, 3 John*, pp. 101–104; 327–30. Note further S.S. Smalley, 'The Johannine Community and the Letters of John' in M. Bockmuehl and M.B. Thompson (ed.), *A Vision for the Church: Essays in Honour of J.P.M. Sweet* (Edinburgh: T. and T. Clark, 1997), pp. 95–104.

3. *Cf.* further Smalley, *1, 2, 3 John*, pp. xxiii–xxv; Smalley, *Thunder and Love*, pp. 134–36.

4. C.H. Dodd, *The Apostolic Preaching and its Developments*, 3rd edn. (London: Hodder and Stoughton, 1963); A. Seeberg, *Die Didache des Judentums und der Urchristenheit* (Leipzig: A. Deichert/Georg Böhme, 1908), esp. pp. 83–100; M. Dibelius, *From Tradition to Gospel* (London: Nicholson and Watson, 1934), esp. pp. 9–36.

we know from the speeches of Acts, when the first apostles proclaimed the good news of Jesus they tended to do so in similar ways.[5] Using the speeches of Peter recorded in Acts 2–4 as a model which may be said to represent in summary form the kerygma of the primitive Jerusalem church,[6] Dodd finds that these six points recur: (i) Old Testament prophecy has been fulfilled, and the messianic age has dawned (Acts 2:16–21); (ii) this fulfilment has taken place in the ministry, death and resurrection of Jesus, who was descended from David (2:22–32; 3:15); (iii) Jesus has been exalted as Lord and Christ, and as messianic head of the new Israel (2:33–36; 4:11); (iv) this fact has been confirmed by the gift of the Spirit to the church (2:33, 38; cf. 2:17–21, where Peter sees Pentecost as a fulfilment of Joel 2); (v) Jesus will return, to bring God's purposes to their consummation (3:20–21; cf. 10:42); (vi) meanwhile people are to repent, so that they can receive forgiveness of sin and the gift of the Holy Spirit (2:38–40; 3:19–20).[7]

Dodd's suggestion is that a tradition of early apostolic preaching, such as we find in Acts, underlies the New Testament generally at the substructural level. Thus not only Peter but also Paul, for example, acknowledge a debt to the kerygma we have just outlined. When Paul summarises the message about Jesus which he inherited when he became a Christian (in 1 Cor. 15:3–5), it is found to be similar in basic content to the kerygma of the church in Jerusalem at an early period. Like Peter in Acts, Paul also proclaims the fulfilment of scriptural prophecy in the life, death and resurrection of Jesus the Messiah; although it is true that the Pauline version of the kerygma seems to go beyond the Jerusalem version by interpreting the death of Jesus explicitly as being 'for our sins'.[8]

The thesis of Professor Dodd about a possible kerygmatic tradition beneath the New Testament writings has been questioned at several

5. For an extensive bibliography, relevant to the complex issue of the nature – in particular, the historical nature – of the speeches in Acts, see S.S. Smalley, 'The Christology of Acts Again' in Lindars and Smalley (ed.), *Christ and Spirit*, p. 79 n. 3; also F.F. Bruce, 'The Speeches in Acts – Thirty Years After' in Banks (ed.), *Reconciliation and Hope*, pp. 53–68.

6. Dodd, *Apostolic Preaching*, pp. 17–21.

7. *Cf.* further *ibid.*, pp. 21–24.

8. 1 Cor. 15:3. However, note the offer of forgiveness after mention of the death of Christ in the Jerusalem preaching (Acts 2:38; 3:18–19, *et al.*), and also the vicarious, piacular implications of the 'Servant' christology which appear in the apostolic kerygma (Acts 3:13, 26; 4:25). *Cf.* further Dodd, *Apostolic Preaching*, pp. 24–31. For a claim that Paul's interpretation of the death of Christ differs completely from that of the Jerusalem church see S.G.F. Brandon, *The Fall of Jerusalem and the Christian Church*, 2nd edn. (London: SPCK, 1957), pp. 77–78; against W.D. Davies, *Paul and Rabbinic Judaism: Some Rabbinic Elements in Pauline Theology*, 3rd edn. (London: SPCK, 1970), pp. 227–30. For Paul's debt to the existing Christian tradition into which he entered see A.M. Hunter, *Paul and His Predecessors*, 2nd edn. (London: Nicholson and Watson, 1961), esp. pp. 15–23.

points. It is not certain, for example, that a sharp distinction between 'preaching' and 'teaching' material in the New Testament can be consistently maintained, since these inevitably overlap. More seriously, it is by no means clear that a single fixed tradition of apostolic preaching, on which all Christians could draw, ever existed in the early church. As now, so then, preaching involves 'activity' as well as 'content'. Even if the gospel preached remains in essence the same, therefore, its presentation and to some extent its material will be adapted to the situation of the preacher and the audience. As a result, we cannot be over-confident about the exact nature of the first Christian sermons.[9]

Nevertheless, it may be assumed that a 'hard core' of kerygma formed the basis of any primitive proclamation about the person and work of Jesus: the fact that prophecy had been fulfilled, the announcement that the Messiah who had ushered in the new age was Jesus, and the declaration that as a part of God's salvific purposes this Jesus had been crucified, raised and exalted.[10] The central point of such a proclamation, as we know from Acts, was the activity of God in Christ. God has spoken decisively in and through Jesus the Messiah (Acts 10:36); the death of his Son took place with God's foreknowledge (2:23); and God raised Jesus from the dead (3:15). Indeed, God has visited the nations in a new way (15:14).

Can it be shown that John was in touch with this fundamental, Christian preaching tradition? To this question we must now turn.

JOHN'S KERYGMA

In the second chapter of this volume it was argued that there are good reasons for describing the tradition behind the Fourth Gospel as 'independent'.[11] It is important to understand exactly what this means.

9.   Note the important critique of the position which defines kerygma solely in terms of 'content' by C.F. Evans, 'The Kerygma', *JTS* ns 7 (1956), pp. 25–41; also J.P.M. Sweet, 'Second Thoughts: VIII. The Kerygma', *ExpT* 76 (1964–65), pp. 143–47. If the work of C.H. Dodd represents the understanding of kerygma as 'content', Rudolf Bultmann's writing suggests the opposite extreme, that kerygma is merely 'activity'. See the sections on 'the kerygma' in R. Bultmann, *Theology of the New Testament*, vol. 1 (London: SCM Press, 1952), pp. 33–182; also the collection of essays by Bultmann and others in H.-W. Bartsch (ed.), *Kerygma and Myth: A Theological Debate*, 2 vols (London: SPCK, 1953 and 1962). Bultmann and his school consistently use the term 'kerygma' without defining its content in any way. See also J.I.H. McDonald, *Kerygma and Didache: The Articulation and Structure of the Earliest Christian Message* (Cambridge: Cambridge University Press, 1980), esp. pp. 1–11, 126–27.

10.   *Cf.* D.E.H. Whiteley, *The Theology of St Paul*, 2nd edn. (Oxford: Blackwell, 1974), pp. 9–10.

11.   The view of Johannine independence adopted originally in this book has been slightly modified in the present edition. See above, p. 13; and chapter 2, esp. p. 43.

To say that John was independent of the first three evangelists implies that he wrote without direct reference to them. It cannot imply, obviously, that he was out of touch with the basic Christian tradition which all the Gospels ultimately share. To write a 'Gospel' in the first place, John must have known about Jesus. That is why his Gospel is broadly similar to the synoptic Gospels; and that is why it is also possible to argue, although we do not accept this argument, that John knew and used Mark and perhaps Luke as his starting-point.

Undoubtedly, the fourth evangelist handled and interpreted in his own way the Jesus tradition he received. But if his *basic* tradition is indeed common to all the Gospel writers, we should be able to find in the Fourth Gospel a 'hard core' of kerygma similar to that which, as we were suggesting earlier, formed the centre of any early proclamation about Jesus, and which – in Dodd's view, at least – underlies the New Testament generally. Let us test this claim at various points.

At the heart of the apostolic preaching, according to Acts, lies the conviction that in Jesus a decisive intervention from God has taken place. Eternity has broken into history in an entirely new way, and God has finally visited his people.[12] In the Fourth Gospel we have an expansion of this same kerygmatic formula. John does not use the verb 'to visit' (ἐπισκέπτομαι) at all; but the thought of visitation is strongly present in his Gospel. From the introduction onwards it is made very clear that in the incarnate Word we have come face to face with God's visitation once and for all.[13] Accordingly, even before the resurrection, it is possible to point to Jesus and say, 'This is (the Christ) the Son of God.';[14] here is a teacher 'come from God';[15] in this man can be discovered 'the Holy One of God'.[16] In a unique way, the Son makes the Father known.[17] This is equally the testimony of Jesus about himself in John's Gospel. He is continuing God's work in time and space;[18] he claims equality with the Father, and identifies himself openly as God's Son;[19] he has come from God and is going to God;[20] he who has seen Jesus has seen the Father.[21]

John as much as the writer of Acts, then, is vividly aware that God has visited his people in terms which are inescapably historical. But he also knows that Israel has neither understood nor accepted this visita-

12. *Cf.* Luke 1:68; 7:16.
13. John 1:14.
14. John 1:34; 11:27.
15. John 3:2; *cf.* 9:33.
16. John 6:69.
17. John 1:18, following the reading ὁ μονογενὴς υἱός ('the only Son'), as in A W Θ, *et al.*
18. John 5:17.
19. John 5:18; 10:36.
20. John 6:62; *cf.* 13:3.
21. John 14:9.

tion. The Jews have not 'seen' the real nature of Jesus; so that, as with the reception given to the Word of God before the incarnation, 'his own people did not receive him'.[22] The climax of this rejection occurs when the self-disclosure of Jesus is given its most challenging expression, and he uses the divine title 'I am' without qualification: 'Before Abraham was, I am.'[23] At these words, not surprisingly, the Jews attempt (unsuccessfully) to stone Jesus.

This Johannine pattern of rejection in the face of visitation provides a constant background to the special appeal of the Fourth Gospel, and causes that appeal to be widened considerably. For while in John 'the Jews' do not receive their Messiah, 'the Greeks' actually ask to see him.[24] The progression 'from Israel to the nations' was an evangelistic strategy familiar to the first apostles. In Acts, for example, Paul's mission was directed through the Jews to the Gentiles.[25] Similarly, the scope of John's gospel message is ultimately unrestricted. The fourth evangelist, as we suggested in the last chapter, may have been writing for those in his church who came from two different backgrounds: *Greek* as well as Hebrew.

We may go even further in our attempt to define the kerygmatic character of the Fourth Gospel. For as well as enshrining the essence of the Christian proclamation about Jesus, presented in a characteristically Johannine manner, the Gospel of John also includes and expands the six major themes of the primitive apostolic preaching as C.H. Dodd has identified these for us. First, Old Testament prophecy has been fulfilled and the new age has arrived; the glory of God has been decisively manifested.[26] Second, this fulfilment has occurred in the incarnation, ministry and glorification of the Word of God. John's Gospel refers emphatically to the humanity of Jesus, and even to his Davidic descent;[27] it also places the description of his death and resurrection firmly in the context of scriptural fulfilment.[28] Third, by the exaltation – in Johannine terms, the glorification – of Jesus, the new and true Israel, of which he is the messianic head, has been established.[29] Fourth, this fact has been confirmed by the gift of the

22.   John 1:11; 5:43; *cf.* Acts 13:26–27.

23.   John 8:58. Significantly, the divine title 'I am' in the Old Testament is associated with one period when, through Moses, God visited his people Israel (Exod. 3:14–15; and note esp. 4:31).

24.   John 12:21.

25.   Acts 13:46; and note an allusion to the 'visitation' of the Gentiles at 15:14. According to the synoptic writers, the evangelistic strategy 'through the Jews to the Gentiles' was practised and enjoined by Jesus himself. *Cf.* Matt. 15:24, 28; 10:5–6, 18.

26.   John 1:1–2, 14, interpreting profoundly (for example) Isa. 60 (*cf.* esp. verses 1–3, 19–20).

27.   John 1:14; 7:42, *et al.*

28.   John 19:24, 28 (*cf.* 11:49–52); 20:8–9, *et al.*

29.   John 17:20–22; *cf.* 15:1–6.

Spirit to the community of believers.[30] Fifth, a consummation at the 'last day', accompanied by the return of Christ, is expected;[31] and sixth, on the basis of all that has been proclaimed and narrated an evangelistic appeal is made by the writer.[32]

JOHN AND PAUL

Connections between the Gospel of John and the primitive kerygma, however, do not stop here. We have found that the Fourth Gospel is in touch with the basic shape of the apostolic preaching as this is recorded in Acts. But there are observable and significant parallels, in terms of kerygmatic material, between John and other parts of the New Testament as well.

Common ground exists in this respect, for example, between John and Paul.[33] These two writers, it has often been noticed, are theologically similar in many ways. We need not overestimate the extent of Paulinism in John.[34] To go no further, there are real differences in the areas of soteriology (Paul's view of salvation history as the work of the second Adam is not John's) and ecclesiology (John does not speak of the church as the body of Christ).[35] Moreover, leading terms and categories in Paul – such as 'justification', 'righteousness' and 'law' – are either absent from John altogether, or used by him differently.[36]

Nevertheless, there are striking agreements in general theological outlook between the Fourth Gospel and the Pauline writings. Both contain, for instance, a high estimate of the person and work of Christ;[37] and this estimate is pointed in both by emphasising the intimate way in which Jesus is related both to the Father and to the Spirit.[38] Moreover, there are far-reaching parallels between John and Paul in their presentation of the fellowship uniting the church and the Christian with the living Christ.[39]

30. John 7:39; 16:7; 20:21–22, et al.

31. John 6:39–40, 44; 14:3, et al. Admittedly, the apocalyptic element in the fourth evangelist's eschatology is not strong.

32. John 20:31.

33. See Dodd, *Apostolic Preaching*, pp. 57–78.

34. Cf. Fuller, *The New Testament in Current Study*, pp. 128–30.

35. But notice the probable preparation for this in John 2:19–22; and the 'vine' imagery in John 15:1–8 contains ideas which approximate to Paul's notion of the church as Christ's body.

36. Cf. the varied use of νόμος ('law') in John 1:17 and Eph. 2:15.

37. Cf. John 1:1, 14 and Phil. 2:6–7; John 1:18 and 2 Cor. 4:4–6; John 10:10–11 and Gal. 2:20.

38. Cf. John 10:30 and Col. 1:15–17; John 15:26 and Rom. 8:10–11.

39. Cf. John 17:20–24 and Col. 1:18; John 15:4–5 and Phil. 3:8–9. In all these instances the individual and corporate dimensions overlap. See further S.S. Smalley, 'The Christ–Christian Relationship in Paul and John' in D.A. Hagner and M.J. Harris (ed.), *Pauline Studies: Essays Presented to F.F. Bruce* (Exeter: Paternoster Press, 1980), pp. 95–105.

Of even more force for our present purposes are the correspondences between Paul and John in the formulation of their kerygmatic themes. Paul's own summary of the gospel he had received, and was transmitting, contains the essence of the kerygma as this has already been identified in both Acts and John. We noticed earlier that the heart of Paul's preaching (reported in 1 Cor. 15:1–3) also refers to God's special activity for salvation, 'in accordance with the scriptures', which is located in the death and resurrection of Christ Jesus.[40] Furthermore, in Paul as in Acts and the Fourth Gospel it is possible to discover the six points of the apostolic preaching which Dodd has isolated. The fact that Paul has a gospel to preach means that prophecy has been fulfilled.[41] This fulfilment has occurred in the life, death and resurrection of Jesus Christ.[42] Through him the true Israel has been established, and the Holy Spirit given to the church.[43] At present the return of Christ is anticipated, and meanwhile an appeal is issued to respond to the preaching about him.[44]

However, Paul obviously does more than merely repeat the kerygma to which he was in the first place indebted. He is alive to the implications of the elements which made up the preaching; and he restates, for example, the fact that the Spirit has been given to the church after the exaltation of Christ as meaning that the Spirit, who is also the Spirit of Jesus, indwells both the Christian church and the Christian believer.[45] John is to take this kerygmatic point further. For while both John and Paul insist that Christian experience in the present is based on historical fact (and in this instance, of course, they share further common ground), for Paul it is the death of Jesus which is crucial,[46] whereas for John the *life* of Jesus is also important in the salvation event. We shall return to this vital point in a moment.

Meanwhile, we may ask, what is suggested by these impressive links – both theological and kerygmatic – between Paul and the writer of the Fourth Gospel? They do not, of course, imply that John depended directly on Paul. Rather, they indicate that both writers rested their work on a common Christian tradition. But this is in itself a significant conclusion, which was reached as long ago as 1905 by William Sanday.[47] Unlike his contemporary Benjamin Bacon, who regarded John's teaching as 'a more developed Paulinism', out of touch with either historical

40. See above, p. 189.
41. Rom. 1:2.
42. Rom. 1:3; 1 Cor. 15:3–4.
43. Gal. 6:16; Eph. 2:21.
44. 1 Thess. 4:15–17; 1 Cor. 15:1–2.
45. Rom. 8:9–17, *et al.*
46. *Cf.* 1 Cor. 1:23; 2:2, *et al.*
47. Sanday, *Criticism.*

tradition or apostolic witness,[48] Sanday believed that the 'two great apostolic cycles' – Johannine and Pauline – stood apart, but were connected in what may be termed the 'main underground'.[49] If we accept this proposal – and there now seems more reason than ever to do so – it means that neither Paul nor John can be written off as theological innovators and no more. On the contrary, the theological contribution of both, which cannot be doubted, is now seen to stem from a single primitive and historical preaching tradition.[50]

JOHN AND MARK

We may pursue further the parallels between John and other New Testament writings by considering the common ground between the Fourth Gospel and the other Gospels. In this connection we shall concentrate on Mark's Gospel, believing that this is the earliest Gospel and therefore the most primitive evangelical witness to the Christian tradition about Jesus.

For obvious reasons John is closer to Mark, and the other evangelists, than to Paul in kerygmatic points of contact. To begin with, John and Mark are both Gospels. All the themes characteristic of the early apostolic preaching, we therefore find, appear in the Second Gospel as in the Fourth;[51] and this need not surprise us. For what the evangelists are doing is – like the apostles themselves – to *witness to Jesus*. In their own way they all testify to the real identity of the man from Nazareth, and to the good news of the eternal life that is available in and through him.[52]

Let us consider in more detail the extent to which John and Mark are kerygmatically related. Mark's particular witness to Jesus is summarised in the opening verse of his Gospel, where it is declared that what follows is 'the beginning (ἀρχή) of the gospel of Jesus Christ'.[53] There has been much discussion about the precise meaning of this verse, and especially about Mark's use here of the term ἀρχή.[54] It may well be that the writer is merely introducing the contents of the first section (Mark 1:2–13) of

48. B.W. Bacon, *The Fourth Gospel in Research and Debate*, 2nd edn. (London: T. Fisher Union and New Haven: Yale University Press, 1918), pp. 295, 438–39; *cf.* Scott, *Fourth Gospel*, pp. 46–53.

49. Sanday, *Criticism*, pp. 231–32.

50. See further Dodd, *Apostolic Preaching*, esp. pp. 62–65; also Smalley, 'New Light', pp. 50–55.

51. Mark 1:2; 11:10; 14:49; 16:7; 12:1–11; 1:8; 13:26–27; 1:15.

52. *Cf.* Mark 1:1; Matt. 1:1; Luke 1:4; John 20:31.

53. Mark 1:1. The words '(Jesus Christ), the Son of God' are omitted by ℵ* Θ, *et al.*, but included by B D W, *et al.*

54. See *e.g.* C.E.B. Cranfield, *The Gospel According to Saint Mark: An Introduction and Commentary* (Cambridge: Cambridge University Press, 1959), pp. 34–35.

his Gospel, starting with the ministry of John the Baptist. With these preliminary events, Mark could be saying in effect, the gospel period began.[55] But it is just as likely that Mark is providing a title for his whole Gospel in this verse; in which case the words may be paraphrased as follows: 'I am about to relate the gospel facts concerning Jesus the Messiah; and my starting-point is the traditional one of John the Baptist's ministry.'[56]

Once Mark's theme has been announced, he unfolds his account of the Jesus tradition according to the outline of the kerygma which we have been considering. The age of fulfilment, heralded by John the Baptist and inaugurated by Jesus, has dawned. The Lord of that age is Christ himself, whose ministry, death and resurrection Mark goes on to describe. The tragic character of the Marcan passion narrative, which occupies such an extensive place in the Gospel, is offset not only by the transfiguration, forming its introduction, the predictions of vindication, and the triumphal entry into Jerusalem,[57] but also by the eschatological discourse of Mark 13 which speaks so eloquently of the return of Jesus in glory.

Mark's Gospel, then, like John's, is another form of the kerygma. This does not mean that Mark – any more than the fourth evangelist – introduces the themes of the apostolic preaching into his work in a random and unrelated fashion. Rather, the whole Gospel is itself a sermon based on traditional, kerygmatic foundations. Mark is not simply describing a series of isolated events which happened to culminate in the crucifixion of Jesus. His unifying theme is that of the kerygma itself: the new age of fulfilment has been brought in by Jesus the Christ, the King of the kingdom.[58]

The traditional and kerygmatic character of Mark's Gospel receives support from one other direction, moreover, if we follow C.H. Dodd's suggestion about the framework of the Gospel narrative.[59] Dodd finds in Mark an interest in the chronology of the ministry of Jesus, and believes that this can be traced to a kerygmatic source. He notices in particular that when Mark's own 'generalising summaries' (*Sammel-*

55.   For the idea that John the Baptist's ministry formed the 'beginning of the gospel' see Acts 1:21–22; 10:37; note also a similar use of the term ἀρχή ('beginning') in John 15:27; 16:4.

56.   *Cf.* H.B. Swete, *The Gospel According to St Mark: The Greek Text, with Introduction, Notes and Indices*, 3rd edn. (London: Macmillan, 1909), p. 1.

57.   Mark 9:1–8; 10:33–34, *et al.*, 11:1–10.

58.   Interestingly enough, the idea of God's kingdom – which, according to the synoptic evangelists, was a central category in the teaching of Jesus – does not often receive expression in Luke's account of the preaching of the apostles in Acts. But *cf.* Acts 8:12; 20:25, *et al.*

59.   C.H. Dodd, 'The Framework of the Gospel Narrative' in *idem, New Testament Studies* (Manchester: Manchester University Press, 1953), pp. 1–11.

berichte) of the ministry are put together, they form a continuous narrative which virtually outlines the activity of Jesus in Galilee. Dodd therefore concludes that the order of Mark's Gospel was largely determined by a chronological outline of the ministry of Jesus which was preserved and transmitted by the primitive church, and to which the second evangelist had access.[60] If so, it is not impossible that, to some extent at least, the order of the Fourth Gospel was similarly determined.

We have seen that Mark and John are close together in the kerygmatic background they share. Both are indebted – although independently – to some form of the early apostolic preaching about Jesus. For this reason the basic 'gospel' content of their writings, and even their shape, are related. Both Gospels, we may conclude, are literary versions of the preaching activity recorded in Acts.

There is one further point to be made in this connection; and by treating it we shall return directly to the subject of John's evangel. For to say that the Gospel writers are all in touch with some form of the kerygma does not by itself take sufficient account of the actual material which the evangelists used. Whatever sources were involved, the Gospels provided (at least) a record of the life and death of their central character, Jesus. In so doing, they filled an obvious gap left by the first preachers. There are very few references in the Jerusalem kerygma, and even fewer in Paul,[61] to the actual life and ministry of Jesus. This need not suggest a lack of interest in such historical data; it is simply that in the early preaching attention is directed chiefly towards a recital of the main points in the history of salvation, and their immediate theological import. The life of Jesus is *mentioned*,[62] but little more.

It is left to the writers of the Gospels to develop the historical section of the kerygma. In so doing, they draw on all the facts at their disposal, and interpret those facts in accordance with their particular theological understanding and for their special purposes. Ralph Martin has made an interesting suggestion, in the light of our present discussion, about Mark's purpose in expanding the historical section of the kerygma.[63] It is that Mark was *supplementing Paul's kerygma*. After Paul's death,

60. But on the other side see K.L. Schmidt, *Der Rahmen der Geschichte Jesu* (Berlin: Trowitzch & Sohn, 1919), the study of which stimulated Dodd's examination of the Marcan *Sammelberichte*; also J.M. Robinson, *A New Quest of the Historical Jesus*, SBT 4 (London: SCM Press, 1959), pp. 56–58. See further the critique of Dodd's argument by D.E. Nineham, 'The Order of Events in St Mark's Gospel – An Examination of Dr Dodd's Hypothesis', in *idem* (ed.), *Studies in the Gospels: Essays in Memory of R.H. Lightfoot* (Oxford: Blackwell, 1955), pp. 223–39.

61. Unless Paul's speech at Pisidian Antioch (Acts 13:16–41) is regarded as representing an interest in the historical Jesus; so Dodd, *Apostolic Preaching*, pp. 28–31. See further F.F. Bruce, 'Paul and the Historical Jesus', *BJRL* 56 (1973–74), pp. 317–35.

62. As in Acts 2:22; 10:39, *et al.*

63. Martin, *Mark*, pp. 140–62, esp. 156–62; and *cf.* the literature there cited.

Martin argues, a situation arose in the churches founded by the apostle whereby the historical basis of the Pauline preaching became diluted. Mark therefore wrote for those areas a Gospel which would echo Paul's own christology, and yet emphasise the 'mundane existence' of Jesus, as the spring-board for that christology, by using material to which Paul had no access (the Jesus tradition). The result was a document which made an appeal for discipleship; and Mark was well aware that Christian discipleship could in practice involve the same paradox of glory through suffering which characterised the ministry of Jesus himself.[64]

Whether or not this was really Mark's intention, it is a reasonable hypothesis, and one which does justice to Mark's practical concern in his Gospel for history as well as theology. He does not speculate or philosophise about the existence, or pre-existence, of Jesus. He begins with the historical person of the Christ as he is, and proceeds from there.

John's starting-point, on the other hand, lies further back than that of Mark or any of the other evangelists. His Gospel begins with the pre-existent Word of God. Nevertheless the historical *life* of Jesus is essentially important to the fourth evangelist; for without the life of Jesus, his 'glorification' has no possibility or meaning. Indeed it is the life, the flesh itself, of Jesus that in the fullest sense reveals his glory. When the Word tabernacled among us, only then did we behold in reality the glory of the Father.

John (like Mark) is concerned about history, and takes it seriously. The Fourth Gospel is therefore to be considered, much as in the case of any other Gospel, as an expansion of the 'life of Jesus' section of the kerygma. For this reason, if for no other, we find in John an almost brutal emphasis on the humanity of Jesus, and on the sober history of what he was doing.[65] The Gospel of John is concerned with the Jesus of history, as well as the Christ of faith.

In the last chapter we discussed the reasons for rejecting the view that John's Gospel was written to supplement the work of the other evangelists.[66] But perhaps Eusebius had a point when he said that one of John's objects in writing was to provide his readers with a fully-rounded account of the ministry of Jesus; for example, John wanted to tell them 'the things which Christ did before the Baptist was cast into prison'.[67] It was not so much, however, that the fourth evangelist was filling gaps left by the other Gospels, which (we have been maintaining) he did not know. Rather, starting from the Christian kerygma – which he obviously *did* know – he added to its basic framework information about the historical Jesus derived from the various traditional sources which we have already

64. *Ibid.*, pp. 161–62.
65. John 1:14; 6:56; 11:54, *et al.* See also M.M. Thompson, *The Humanity of Jesus in the Fourth Gospel* (Philadelphia: Fortress Press, 1988), esp. pp. 117–28.
66. See above, pp. 158–60.
67. *HE* 3.24.12.

considered.[68] As we shall see, John was in the end doing more than this; but certainly he was doing no less.

CONCLUSIONS

We may sum up so far. It has been suggested that fundamental to John's Gospel is a preaching tradition about Jesus to which the New Testament writers as a whole seem to have been indebted. John himself is first and foremost an evangelist, whose point of departure is a shared gospel, a common evangel.

But, as with the synoptic evangelists, secondly, John elaborates the kerygmatic structure upon which his Gospel depends, in that he expands the 'historical' section of the apostolic preaching. He knows about the historical Jesus event, and to some extent he presupposes a knowledge of it. John is especially concerned about the flesh as well as the glory of Jesus, and their inter-relation. For this reason he selects from his own sources material dealing with the life of Jesus as such, and uses this to assist his main purposes in writing.

In line with this principle, thirdly, John adds to the kerygma, and to the Jesus tradition[69] which he uses in order to expand it, his own understanding of the person of Jesus. John is an interpreter as well as an evangelist. His interpretation, indeed, controls his work as an evangelist; because he selects and uses his kerygmatic and traditional material (in particular, information about the *signs* which Jesus performed) in order to make his chief theological points.

By saying that John is both an evangelist and an interpreter, we come back to the key question which has already been raised in this book: what exactly is the relation between history and theology in the Fourth Gospel? To answer this further we must stay a little longer with the important issue of John's work as an evangelist.[70]

JOHN AND HISTORY

We have been suggesting that the kerygmatic background to John's Gospel, and the fourth evangelist's interest in the historical life of Jesus, indicate that there is a traditional character to this Gospel. The writer,

68.   See above, chapter 2, esp. pp. 41–43.

69.   By 'the Jesus tradition' as against 'the kerygma', in this context, is meant information about Jesus, originating from him and his disciples, which circulated in the early church in oral or written form, including sermons, apart from the activity and content of the apostolic preaching as this is recorded in Acts.

70.   For this section as a whole see further N.T. Wright, *Christian Origins and the Question of God*, vol. 1: *The New Testament and the People of God* (London: SPCK, 1992), pp. 341–58.

it is inferred, stands firmly within the mainstream of Christian tradition and experience, without cutting loose from its primitive and historical roots. As an evangelist, and indeed as a theologian, John treats with great seriousness the historical basis of salvation.

However, this inference – that as a Gospel writer the fourth evangelist was also a genuine historian – needs to be examined carefully, particularly in the light of our present discussion about the kerygmatic content of the Johannine Gospel. For the statement that John is an evangelist, whose work shows affinity with a traditional scheme of preaching about Jesus, cannot be used as proof that there is an historical basis to the material being transmitted. To speak of a 'Jesus tradition' in any form, indeed, begs the historical question.

Some would argue that in the early days of the church, a tradition about the founder of Christianity existed which was primitive in character without being 'historical' in the sense that it consistently reported what actually happened.[71] That is to say, the first apostles may have preached about Jesus (it is argued) merely on the basis of their own understanding of what he said and did. Equally, in the general information about the life of Christ used by preachers and teachers and writers alike, discourses and narratives may have gathered round the figure of Jesus which were attributed to him, even if they did not stem from him originally.

Such a point of view as this distinguishes between 'history' as fact (what happened) and 'tradition' as the *record* of fact (what was said to have happened). The question of John and history, then, is beset by this problem: can we be sure that John's traditional material, variously derived and shaped, takes us back to the real origins of Christianity? We have spoken regularly in this book of John's tradition as independent, to some extent, of the other Gospels, and suggested on this basis that it is likely to be historical and therefore reliable. But what about the very history of that historical tradition? We must now investigate Johannine 'history', in this sense, and try to discover how far we can probe behind the fourth evangelist's (kerygmatic) tradition. Does John's Gospel, as we now have it, provide us with dependable facts about the historical life of Jesus, in addition to an interpretation of those facts?

Such an investigation is complicated by two further critical issues which have already been mentioned briefly, and which must now receive some further attention. The first of these includes the nature of the account in Acts of the apostolic preaching, and the second concerns the nature of the Gospels themselves.

---

71. See, in the school of Bultmann, *e.g.* N. Perrin, *Rediscovering the Teaching of Jesus* (London: SCM Press, 1967), esp. pp. 15–53; 207–248. Perrin deals chiefly in this book with what he regards as the 'reconstruction' of the Jesus tradition reflected in the synoptic Gospels.

(a)   History and Tradition in Acts

John speaks of Jesus in terms of the kerygma. He builds up his Gospel on the basis of a preaching tradition. All the evangelists, presumably, were influenced by the ongoing life of the churches in which they lived and worked. They received their information about Jesus in the living context of preaching, teaching and worship. We have been suggesting that the fourth evangelist was also indebted to this kind of religious background. Probably at an early stage in the composition of his Gospel – perhaps the second stage of the three we have proposed[72] – John drew in part upon a Christian tradition which had been shaped in one direction by the preaching of the first apostles. Acts gives us the clearest account of that preaching, and it is the real nature of this account which we must consider for a moment.

As we have seen, 'preaching' in the present context is an elusive term. What is 'the kerygma', and what does 'kerygmatic' mean? Certainly we ought not to think of 'kerygma' as one stereotyped sermon. It is always necessary to remember that preaching is an *activity*; and while the early Christian apostles proclaimed a message at the heart of which certain leading themes were constantly to be found, their sermons were never contained within a rigid structure.

But there is a further problem about the nature of the kerygma in Acts, and this is the one which concerns us at present. Granted that there must be an element of flexibility in deciding what in either Acts or John may be described as 'kerygmatic', can we be sure that the apostles really spoke about Jesus in the way that the author of Acts (whom we will assume for the moment to be Luke) says that they did? How do we know that the sermons in Acts are an historically reliable account of the primitive apostolic witness to Jesus?

Some scholars find no problem here at all, because they regard the speech material in Acts, which is chiefly assigned to Peter, Stephen and Paul, as completely unhistorical. Martin Dibelius, for example, represents a typical view.[73] Dibelius believes that Luke was himself a preacher rather than a writer of history, and that the speeches in Acts are theological constructions rather than accurate reports. In his composition of the preaching material, Dibelius believes, Luke has followed the pattern set by Thucydides (the Athenian historian who flourished in the fifth century BC), who on his own admission used to

72. See above pp. 155–56.
73. M.F. Dibelius, 'The Speeches in Acts and Ancient Historiography' in *idem*, *Studies in the Acts of the Apostles*, ed. H. Greeven (London: SCM Press, 1956), pp. 138–85. See also the comments on the speeches in Acts made by J.M. Robinson, *New Quest*, p. 58 n.1 (where further relevant literature is also cited).

record what his various speakers *might have said,* when he could not remember the exact words they spoke.[74]

The trustworthiness of Acts, particularly with respect to its account of the early apostolic preaching, is a delicate and complicated matter which cannot be discussed in detail here.[75] It should be noticed, however, that a scholarly case can be made out on both sides of the debate. Against Dibelius, for example, Professor F.F. Bruce opts for the view that the speeches in Acts are summaries (but no more!), which give an accurate report of the essence of what was said at any one time by the apostles.[76] Bruce argues his case on five main grounds. (a) The style of these sermons is not Luke's own style, but suggests rather that he is either recording the language of those whose Greek was impure, or translating from an Aramaic source. (b) When he was writing his *Gospel,* Luke (as we can tell by comparing the synoptists with each other) was basically faithful to his sources, even if he has reproduced these in his own way.[77] We need not therefore assume that he was less faithful to his sources when writing Acts, although in this case we have no means of checking his fidelity. (c) The Old Testament quotations in the speeches seem to be derived from an early Christian collection of *testimonia,* or proof-texts.[78] (d) The outline of the kerygma in Peter's speeches corresponds to the scope of Mark's Gospel, which was probably constructed on the framework of a similar outline, and traditionally rests on the authority of Peter. (e) The christology of Acts is primitive, although none the less real because of that.[79]

Considered separately, perhaps, these arguments might not be judged as equally weighty and convincing. But together they provide a very reasonable case for concluding with Bruce that the speeches in Acts are 'valuable and independent sources for the life and thought of the primitive Church'.[80] Not everyone will accept such a conclusion. But if we allow that it is possible to determine the real nature of the apostolic

74. Thucydides, *History of the Peloponnesian War* 1.22. However, Thucydides claimed also to adhere 'as closely as possible to the general purport of what was actually spoken' (*ibid.*). For a reappraisal of the historical value of the speeches in Acts, with reference to Thucydidean literary method, see T.F. Glasson, 'The Speeches in Acts and Thucydides', *ExpT* 76 (1964–65), p. 165.

75.   *Cf.* further the literature cited in n.5 on p. 189 above.

76.   F.F. Bruce, *The Acts of the Apostles: The Greek Text with Introduction and Commentary,* 2nd edn. (London: Tyndale Press, 1952; reprinted Grand Rapids: Eerdmans, 1984), pp. 18–21. See also the same scholar's treatment of this topic in greater detail: F.F. Bruce, *The Speeches in the Acts of the Apostles* (London: Tyndale Press, 1944).

77.   *Cf.* Luke 21 and Mark 13.

78.   Note the similarity of exegesis in Acts 2:25–28 (Peter) and 13:55 (Paul), where both speakers interpret Psa. 16 in terms of the resurrection of Jesus.

79.   See further on this point S.S. Smalley, 'The Christology of Acts', *ExpT* 73 (1961–62), pp. 358–62.

80.   Bruce, *Acts,* p. 21.

kerygma with some confidence by studying Acts and other 'kerygmatic' parts of the New Testament, then we can say more about John's work as an evangelist. We have claimed that the Fourth Gospel has a kerygmatic background. So now we may go on to claim that if John depends at all on the kerygma, he is reliant upon an historical activity, the basic content of which has been reliably reported by Luke.

One more point may be made in this connection; and it relates to the criticism of the New Testament in general, as well as to the study of John and Acts in particular. There is a tendency on the part of some critics of the New Testament documents to assume automatically that what is 'traditional', in the sense of 'kerygmatic', cannot be authentic. If the early church *could* have attributed a saying or deed to Jesus (the argument seems to run), then the church *did* so.[81] But the formula 'kerygmatic, therefore inauthentic' needs to be challenged strongly, even if this formula is now a part of critical orthodoxy. It is no less possible that what became traditional in Christianity did so precisely because its background was historical. Thus the formula 'authentic *because* kerygmatic' has an equally serious claim to be considered in any critical study of the New Testament.[82]

The relevance of this point to our present discussion is obvious. To say that the Fourth Gospel has an early, 'traditional' background in the apostolic preaching – as reflected in Acts and elsewhere in the New Testament – does not prove that this background is historical. But neither does the kerygmatic character of John's Gospel make it impossible for the writer(s) to have been in touch with the very origins of Christianity – the person of Jesus, what he said and what he did – through the preaching of the first apostles themselves. On the contrary, the likelihood that John was thus linked to the source of Christianity is to my mind very strong indeed.

81. *E.g.* Perrin, *Rediscovering*, pp. 39–43. One of Perrin's main principles for establishing the authenticity of the teaching of Jesus is what he calls the 'criterion of dissimilarity', which he formulates as follows: 'The earliest form of a saying we can reach may be regarded as authentic if it can be shown to be dissimilar to characteristic emphases both of ancient Judaism and of the early Church' (p. 39). This implies that what was 'kerygmatic' in early Christianity may not necessarily have derived from Jesus himself, and therefore could have been (and probably was) attributed to him. For a critique of Perrin's general approach to the Gospel records see M.D. Hooker, 'Christology and Methodology', *NTS* 17 (1970–71), pp. 480–87. *Cf.* also two further related studies by M.D. Hooker: 'On Using the Wrong Tool', *Theology* 75 (1972), pp. 570–81, esp. 574–77; and *idem*, 'In his own Image?' in M.D. Hooker and C.J.A. Hickling (ed.), *What about the New Testament? Essays in honour of Christopher Evans* (London: SCM Press, 1975), pp. 28–44. Note in addition Smalley, 'Redaction Criticism', in Marshall (ed.), *New Testament Interpretation*, pp. 181–95, esp. 187.

82. See further, for the continuity between the Jesus of history and of tradition, Moule, *Phenomenon*, pp. 43–81; also G.N. Stanton, *Jesus of Nazareth in New Testament Preaching*, SNTSMS 27 (Cambridge: Cambridge University Press, 1974), esp. pp. 137–71.

(b)   History and Tradition in the Gospels

We are exploring the nature of 'history' in the Fourth Gospel. As an evangelist, we have suggested, John – much as any other Gospel writer – was indebted to the kerygma, and therefore to the historical tradition about Jesus on which the apostolic preaching was ultimately based. But our feet have not yet reached firm ground. Before we can really make up our minds about the historical value of John's witness, and decide that we have come upon a bedrock of genuine history, we must consider one further matter: the nature of the Gospels themselves.

We have argued that John is not simply a 'theological' Gospel. The writer is interested in history, as the medium in which the events of salvation have taken place. He expands the 'historical' section of the kerygma, to show what happened when the Word became flesh. And the Fourth Gospel, as the work of C.H. Dodd[83] and others has shown, is becoming increasingly respected for the independent and historical tradition upon which it may well rest.

However, statements such as this, about the historical character of John's Gospel, still raise their own questions. Is John's *interest* in history the same as *preserving* history? How do we know that the fourth evangelist's expanded version of the kerygma – particularly since the expansion is so much his own – can be regarded as historically accurate? And can we be sure that the search for an independent and primitive tradition behind the Fourth Gospel will guarantee that we are in touch with a truly *historical* tradition? For 'early' and 'historical' in the context of this discussion are not necessarily synonymous.

These are questions which relate, of course, to the study of *all* the Gospels, and indeed to the study of the New Testament itself in its entirety. In particular, they bear directly on an issue which is fundamental to our present discussion: the so-called 'Jesus of history' quest. And that issue is sharpened by the one already raised: the precise nature of the Gospels, as documents which embody the Jesus tradition. We shall now look at these two matters together, since they are obviously related, in a final attempt to assess the relation between history and tradition in John. In such a discussion, where the complexity of the subject and the extent of the relevant literature[84] are both immense, justice cannot be done within the present limits to every aspect of the question. But a start – at least – can be made, in order to focus the scope and meaning of John's 'real history'.

---

83.   Esp. in *HTFG*; see above, chapter 2; also pp. 7–8.

84.   There is a useful, annotated bibliography on the general question of 'the historical Jesus' in Perrin, *Rediscovering*, pp. 262–66.

What are the Gospels?

The four Gospels, as we have pointed out already, belong to a literary type of their own.[85] They are *written* proclamations of what was in the first place *spoken*, the 'gospel' of Jesus Christ as Lord. But clearly these documents were not committed to writing by their authors at one sitting. They are composite, and consist of different layers of tradition. Oral and written material concerning the life of Jesus has been collected over a period of time, and put together in a finished, literary form by the evangelists themselves. The task of every serious student of the New Testament, therefore, is to probe behind the Gospels in their present shape, in order to discover everything possible about the origins of Christianity. Who was Jesus? How did it all begin?

To assist in this task, there are available the well-known disciplines of source criticism, form criticism, redaction criticism, and narrative criticism. The first enables us to analyse the immediate sources from which the evangelists drew their material; the second seeks to determine the origin of those sources and the church's influence on the material they contain; the third examines the contribution made to the continuing Jesus tradition by the evangelists themselves; and the fourth views the documents as literary unities, and helps the reader to interpret the story they have to tell.

These critical methods must be used in any analysis of the Gospels, and they must be undertaken together. But when they are used, one feature of the Gospel records becomes plain. In the course of its transmission, the material now embodied in our present Gospels has been subject to a number of varied influences, each of which has contributed to its understanding and interpretation. The chief and obvious influences stem from Jesus himself, from the growing Christian community during the first century AD, and from the writers who were eventually responsible for the composition of the Gospels.

This means that – as we have already noticed in the case of John – the Gospels contain not just facts about Jesus, but facts about him which have been interpreted. So we have to ask in the case of any Gospel, as we are doing with John, whether the gap can be bridged between the Jesus-event and the written version of that event in the Gospels. If a Gospel contains kerygma as well as history, what about that history?

One answer to that question is contained in the 'life of Jesus research' (*Leben-Jesu-Forschung*) which has been in progress since the eighteenth century, and is associated with the names of H.S. Reimarus, D.F.

---

85. See further, on the nature of the Gospels, R.P. Martin, *New Testament Foundations: A Guide for Christian Students*, vol. 1: *The Four Gospels* (Exeter: Paternoster Press and Grand Rapids: Eerdmans, 1975), esp. pp. 15–29. But *cf.* also, for the 'biographical' character of these writings, Stanton, *Jesus of Nazareth*, pp. 137–91, esp. 170; and Burridge, *What are the Gospels?*

Strauss, E. Renan and of course A. Schweitzer.[86] These scholars, and others like them, distinguished in the Gospel material between historical accounts and later interpretations of them. But in their attempt to recover the historical Jesus who lay hidden behind his interpreters, the liberal writers of the nineteenth and early twentieth centuries forgot that in Gospel research history and theology, fact and interpretation, cannot be separated. They therefore produced from the pages of the Gospels a sentimental or anonymous Jesus who was largely made in their own image, and certainly far removed from the New Testament portrait of the Christ as we know it.

With the work of Schweitzer, a theological era came to an end. The quest for the historical Jesus seemed to have produced very negative results, and for the moment it was overshadowed by other concerns in the biblical field, and particularly – in the early years of the twentieth century – by the rise of form criticism in Germany. But although Schweitzer's own conclusions about the founder of christianity were odd, to say the least – he saw Jesus as a deluded eschatological storm-trooper, who struggled vainly to bring about the arrival of God's kingdom – this writer has left us with an invaluable scholarly legacy, bearing on the nature of the Gospels themselves. Just as the teaching of Jesus cannot be separated from his person, so the Gospels contain an inseparable and interactive mixture of history and theology.

Does this mean, then, that our search for history in the Gospels must be finally abandoned? More recently, the 'Jesus of history' quest has been taken up again, but in a new form. In the wake of the pioneering work of Rudolf Bultmann, a 'new quest' – associated with such names as E. Käsemann, G. Bornkamm and J.M. Robinson has been in progress.[87] The character of this renewed search for the historical Jesus behind the Christ of faith (and perhaps it is not so different from the 'old' quest, after all) owes – naturally – a great deal to the position of Bultmann himself; in particular to Bultmann's programme of 'demythologising' (the attempt to 'unpack' the essential content of the New Testament from the language of myth in which it is presented),[88] and to his insistence that

---

86. The story of the 'quest' for the historical Jesus is well told in Neill and Wright, *Interpretation*, pp. 205–215. A leading document, deserving careful study, is A. Schweitzer, *The Quest of the Historical Jesus: A Critical Study of Its Progress from Reimarus to Wrede*, 3rd edn. (London: A. and C. Black, 1954).

87. *Cf.* E. Käsemann, 'The Problem of the Historical Jesus' in *idem, Essays on New Testament Themes*, SBT (London: SCM Press, 1964), pp. 15–47; G. Bornkamm, *Jesus of Nazareth*, 2nd edn. (London: Hodder and Stoughton, 1963), esp. pp. 13–26; Robinson, *New Quest.* See also the comprehensive bibliography on the 'new quest' movement in J. Reumann, *Jesus in the Church's Gospels: Modern Scholarship and the Earliest Sources* (London: SPCK, 1970), pp. 500–505.

88. Bultmann's first major work on the subject of demythologising was his monograph, *The New Testament and Mythology*, published in German in 1941, and now in Bartsch (ed.), *Kerygma and Myth*, vol. 1, pp. 1–44. See further the survey by J. Macquarrie, *The Scope of Demythologizing: Bultmann and his Critics*, LPT (London: SCM Press, 1960).

it is the existential, personal encounter – especially through the word of preaching – with the risen Christ which is ultimately significant for the believer, rather than the historical Jesus-event by itself.[89]

Thus James Robinson describes the 'new quest' as involving a 'radically different understanding of history and of human existence'.[90] Through it, he says, we are not committed to 'getting back to Jesus', or verifying the truth of the kerygma: by which he seems to mean 'preaching' about Jesus in a general sense. Rather, by means of this new approach we can encounter Jesus by reading the Gospels existentially, and then see if our understanding of his life corresponds to the one suggested by the evangelists.[91] This approach implies, as Bultmann himself seems to suggest, that although the kerygma is in one sense 'centrally concerned with a Jesus "in the flesh" ',[92] its underlying historicity is 'irrelevant'. Since we can meet Jesus in the kerygma, that is sufficient.[93]

Such a view, however, leads to the inevitable conclusion that, for the 'new questers' as for the old, history in the Gospels is important, yet not important; indispensable and yet dispensable.[94] But will this conclusion suffice for John, or indeed for any of the Gospels? How vital *is* history for the evangelists?

Did it happen?

In the case of John, perhaps more than in the case of the other three Gospels, the question of history is a very urgent one. Did John regard history – in the sense of that which actually happened – as important, or not? The Jesus of St John seems in many ways so different from the prophetic figure who in the synoptic Gospels announces the arrival of the coming kingdom of God. He performs different acts in other ways, and speaks different words in other forms. Who is right? Did it all really happen as John tells us?

One answer to that question, as we know, is to discount the historical value of the Fourth Gospel more or less completely. Rudolf Bultmann,

89 See his important, early work, relevant to this point: R. Bultmann, *Jesus and the Word* (New York: Scribner's, 1934, 1958, and London: Nicholson and Watson, 1935).

90. Robinson, *New Quest*, p. 66.

91. *Ibid.*, pp. 93–95.

92. Robinson believes that the kerygma is not concerned with a Jesus 'according to the flesh', in the sense of an historically proven Lord, but in the sense that the heavenly Lord was a historical person; *ibid.*, pp. 87–88.

93. *Cf. ibid.*, pp. 85–92.

94. See further the critique of the 'new quest' position by R.P. Martin, 'The New Quest of the Historical Jesus' in C.F.H. Henry (ed.), *Jesus of Nazareth, Saviour and Lord* (London: Tyndale Press, 1966), pp. 25–45. *Cf.* also Wright, *New Testament and People*, pp. 468–69.

for example, once committed himself to the view that 'the Gospel of John cannot be taken into account at all as a source for the teaching of Jesus'.[95] Such a commentator as Edwyn Hoskyns, while not dismissing completely the problem of John's historicity, writes in the belief that the author of the Fourth Gospel 'presses upon his readers the far more important, far more disturbing, problem of history itself and of its meaning'.[96] On this showing the real concerns of John are seen as theological, rather than historical. Nevertheless the question 'did it happen?' must still be asked so far as the Johannine tradition is concerned; and, as we are discovering, it cannot be easily dismissed.

We are well aware by now that we cannot look for history apart from faith in either John or the Synoptics. Because these are Gospels, they contain both faith *and* history. But as we have found, the implication of one current approach to the study of the Gospels is – while finding a theoretical place for history in them – to elevate faith (the personal encounter with Jesus through the kerygma) *above* history, and therefore to raise interpretation above fact. Can we still find a place in the Fourth Gospel, then, for history *as well as* faith?

The following comments are a brief attempt to enquire into, if not to solve, the question of 'happenedness' as a basis for John's material.

(i)   The 'new quest' of the historical Jesus, like its forerunner, starts from philosophical rather than historical presuppositions. Bultmann himself, to whom this movement – both in Germany and beyond – owes so much, is above all an existentialist. His chief attachment is to the 'Christ-kerygma' (Christ truly proclaimed today), which in his view confronts people with the all-important challenge to decide for 'authentic existence'. This does not mean that Bultmann is entirely sceptical about the historical existence and activity of Jesus; although scepticism has in fact been a frequent mark of German New Testament scholarship! On the contrary, Bultmann is genuinely interested in Jesus of Nazareth, as the one to whom the church's kerygma is tied in history. But the problem, he claims, is how far the church has preserved an objectively true picture of the person and message of Jesus in the Gospels; and Bultmann admits that in the end this problem has 'no particular significance' for him.[97] So he acknowledges that he has no interest in the life or personality as such of Jesus; his concern is more with his teaching and message, inasfar as these can be recovered.[98]

However, philosophical presuppositions such as these, which lead to a detachment from the life-history of Jesus even if there is an interest in personal encounter with him, are not the only ones which can be made when studying the Gospels. Here are documents which, in the words of

95.   Bultmann, *Jesus and the Word*, p. 17.
96.   Hoskyns, p. 58; see also pp. 58–85.
97.   Bultmann, *Jesus and the Word*, p. 18. For this whole section see *ibid.*, pp. 11–19.
98.   *Ibid.*, pp. 16–17.

C.F.D. Moule, 'steadily refuse to be settled' in the direction of *either* history *or* a 'transcendental call to decision'.[99] So there is every reason to approach them from the stand-point of serious enquiry into their historical and traditional content, carefully using all the objective critical methods at our disposal, and not only from the stance of their existential challenge in the present.[100]

(ii) Our second comment follows from the first. The critical judgments which stem from the 'existentialist' approach we have been describing are all too often subjective, and the principles on which they are based are largely determined by the critics themselves. The attitude adopted towards the Gospel of John in particular, by scholars who espouse the existentialist cause, is a relevant case in point. Bultmann, as we have seen, dismisses John completely as a possible source for the history of the teaching of Jesus.[101] Similarly, Norman Perrin can write a full study of the teaching of Jesus which deals exclusively with the material in the synoptic Gospels, and makes no reference to the Fourth Gospel at all in this connection.[102]

However, assumptions about the historical nature of either the synoptic or the Johannine traditions which are purely subjective in character need to be questioned closely. Certainly we are not entitled to begin by assuming without argument that John's Gospel is historical at every point in its witness to the work and words of Jesus. But equally, no serious student of the New Testament should be allowed to begin by assuming that the Johannine witness is *un*historical at every point. Still less should this be permitted in the face of recent research on John, which is at least reopening the question of the possibly real historical value of the tradition behind John's testimony. Yet it remains true that the 'new questers' pay little if any attention to the new light which has been shed on the character of the Fourth Gospel.[103]

(iii) John is interested in history, and takes it seriously. To say this, as we have agreed already, is not the same as saying that John's witness to Jesus is unswervingly historical. Nevertheless, history is vitally important to John's thinking and purposes, because he believes that history is the arena in which God's lifegiving activity has always – and now decisively – taken place. For the purposes of creation and recreation, as

99. Moule, *Phenomenon*, p. 80.

100. *Cf.* further O. Betz, *What do we know about Jesus?* (London: SCM Press, 1968), pp. 9–27, for a useful and hard-hitting defence of the importance of historical facts as the basis of the Jesus tradition.

101. Bultmann, *Jesus and the Word*, p. 17.

102. Perrin, *Rediscovering*; note the assumption contained in the opening paragraph (p. 15), that only the synoptic witness to the teaching of Jesus needs to be considered.

103. *Cf.* Perrin, *New Testament*, pp. 221–51, esp. 222–31 (on the 'historical questions' concerning the Gospel and Letters of John), where virtually no reference is made to what was then the 'new look' on John.

we shall see in the next chapter, God has been at work in time and space: in the world, and in the world of humanity. So at last the Word became *flesh*, nothing less than that; and as a result Jesus the Word could be heard and seen and touched.

Even Hoskyns, who takes a manifestly 'theological' view of John's Gospel, insists on the importance of history to the fourth evangelist. In John, he says, we are taken through history to eternity, and through flesh to spirit. Even if we are not to stay with the flesh and blood of the incarnation we, like the evangelist himself, must begin there. God has been specially active for the purpose of salvation through a particular person, in a particular place and at a particular moment. John's starting-point is therefore Jesus, the Son of man, whose words must be remembered and whose flesh and blood are needful for spiritual nourishment.[104]

In this case it is unlikely that John the evangelist would have cut loose altogether from the historical roots of his tradition. Indeed, if he did, his message – of the life that has become possible because the Word has tabernacled in the world – would have no real meaning. Furthermore, John's christology would immediately become a docetic one, for he would be speaking of a tabernacling which was incomplete, and of a God who appeared among us in the costume of humanity without becoming fully human. Precisely such a claim for John's christology has been made, as we noticed earlier, by Ernst Käsemann;[105] but we also noticed the grounds on which such a claim must be rejected: in particular, John's serious attention, which we are now discussing, to the historical basis of his message.

The Christ of St John, then, is Jesus of Nazareth, who is at once historical as well as beyond history, human as well as divine. It fits the general purpose of the Gospel, which we considered in the last chapter, and it fits what we know of the fourth evangelist and his tradition, to say on this basis that John is likely to be a genuine historian as well as an evangelist. Since history is indispensable to his witness, John would be less ready to corrupt than to preserve its historical basis. He would more probably transmit and interpret his tradition with an eye to the historical facts which took place when Christianity began, than interpret the Jesus story with no historical sense or concern at all.

(iv)   How did such a phenomenon as Johannine faith arise in the first place? The theological interpretation of the Jesus tradition given by the fourth evangelist must have had some factual background; for if there were initially no historical facts in the Jesus story to which a meaning

---

104. *Cf.* Hoskyns, pp. 58, 85.

105. Käsemann, *Testament*: see above, pp. 60–61. For the Johannine theme of divinity revealed in the humanity of Jesus, and for an additional critique of Käsemann's view of John's christology, note further A.T. Hanson, *Grace and Truth: A Study in the Doctrine of the Incarnation* (London: SPCK, 1975), pp. 26–36.

could be given, there would be no meaning! That is true of any Gospel. As Hoskyns and Davey saw long ago, all four Gospels challenge us to account for the origin of the Christian church, and for an historical basis to the kerygma which that church preached. Where else is that origin to be found, but in the life and death of Jesus?[106]

Admittedly this does not solve the obvious problem, to which (as we saw earlier) Bultmann himself points.[107] How can we be sure that the historical facts which must belong to the origins of the Jesus tradition have been accurately transmitted, by John or any other writer? And in this case, how do we know that John's own theological interpretation of those facts is a correct one?

Because of the very nature of the documents with which we are dealing, the Gospels will never provide us with positive proof of their historical basis and reliability; nor, perhaps, should we look for this. But elsewhere in this book, we have sought to demonstrate that John is in touch with the same basic Christian tradition as the one which was shared by all the Gospel writers, and that a case can be made for the primitive character and indeed historical nature of that tradition. Similarly, we have tried to show earlier in this chapter that inasfar as John connects with the *kerygmatic* tradition of the early church, as reflected generally in the New Testament, he also locks into a tradition which is historical in origin and background. Even if the guarantees of authenticity for which we may be looking finally elude us, then, at least on grounds such as these we can put forward two associated claims for further consideration:

(a)   John begins in the same place as the other evangelists, although he moves beyond them in the end.

(b)   By tapping the same original, varied sources as the other evangelists, those who were responsible for the birth and eventual publication of John's Gospel knew, like the beloved disciple himself, a good deal about what happened during the ministry of Jesus; and when they interpreted these facts, they did not necessarily distort them.

We shall now test this second claim, by looking at some examples of Johannine narrative and discourse material in the light of our present question, 'did it happen?'.

History behind the signs

Did the Johannine signs really happen? If John has a serious concern for history, as we have been maintaining, can we conclude that Jesus performed all the miracles that John tells us he did, and in the way they are described? No doubt, since in John they become 'signs' as such, the

106.   E.C. Hoskyns and F.N. Davey, *The Riddle of the New Testament*, 3rd edn. (London: Faber and Faber, 1947), p. 170; see also, on 'history in the New Testament', pp. 51–59.

107.   *Cf.* above, p. 208.

fourth evangelist has interpreted these miraculous acts of power; and in any case he attaches discourses to them as a means of explaining their significance. But did Jesus perform the seven signs in the first place?

Here is a crucial problem, and a good point at which to begin our brief testing of John's historical accuracy. We shall not attempt to consider *all* the Johannine signs from this point of view, since this would require a monograph on its own. Instead we shall take, as examples, two of John's signs which are most 'difficult': in the sense that only John records them, and that both involve a heightened degree of miraculous power. These are the changing of water into wine at Cana, and the raising of Lazarus.

1. *The Marriage at Cana.* The changing of water into wine (John 2:1–11) is one of the most problematic actions of Jesus described in the Fourth Gospel. It contains a host of difficulties: strictly speaking, the miracle was unnecessary; Jesus addresses his mother beforehand in what appears to be a peremptory manner (verse 4); Mary (verse 5) and Jesus (verse 7) give orders, although they are guests in an unfamiliar household;[108] Jesus initially refuses to act (verse 4), and Mary persists in the face of this refusal (verse 5);[109] there is an almost 'magical' appearance to the circumstances of the miracle (verses 8–9.); the amount of wine produced (up to 700 litres) seems excessive (verse 6);[110] no saying or discourse of Jesus is directly attached to this sign, as often with the Johannine miracles, in order to point its spiritual meaning – on the contrary, the last word is left with the steward, or toastmaster, who does not expound the meaning of what has happened in his brief comment (verse 10); and there is a great deal of possible symbolism in the narrative, which seems to place its historical value at a discount.

On the other hand, John obviously believed that a miracle took place on this occasion, and he reports what he knew, or what his traditional sources told him, about the events at Cana for the purpose of including in his Gospel the effect of the miracle mentioned in verse 11: through this act the glory of God was manifested in Jesus, and his disciples' faith was

---

108.   Although John 2:1, which says that the mother of Jesus was (ἦν) in Cana at the time of the marriage, compared with verse 2, which says that Jesus and his disciples were called (ἐκλήθη) to the marriage, may imply that Mary was in fact already in residence in the household.

109.   But *cf.* Matt. 15:23.

110.   This is particularly true if, as may be implied, the party was a small one, and therefore the arrival of the disciples caused the wine to run out. However, (a) we are not told that *all* the disciples were present (*cf.* the vague οἱ μαθηταὶ αὐτοῦ ['his disciples'] in verse 2); (b) if the disciples had been invited in advance, as verse 2 suggests most naturally, presumably they would have been catered for in advance; (c) we are not in fact told that *all* the water became wine (*cf.* verse 9) – it may have been only the water 'drawn' (from the well) which was found to have been changed.

increased. How then, are we to interpret this sign, and how historical is it?

It will not do to dismiss the Cana sign as unhistorical, unless good reason for this can be shown. Bultmann, however, assumes that the story has been 'taken over from heathen legend and ascribed to Jesus', because the motif of changing water into wine is a typical part of the Dionysus cult.[111] Nevertheless, although there *are* Hellenistic parallels of this kind, they are by no means exact.[112] Similarly, we are not compelled to regard this narrative as the transformation of a saying – whether it originated from Jesus *or* John – into a miracle. H.H. Wendt, for example, thinks that a figurative saying of the apostle about 'turning the water of legal purification into the wine of marriage joy' (*cf.* Mark 2:18–20) in due course became the Cana miracle.[113] Still less need we accept without argument the view that the Cana story was an allegorical reconstruction from synoptic material[114] (especially if John did not know the other Gospels), or even grew out of a rumour started by chance at the marriage feast itself.[115] Although such an approach does not necessarily preclude the historicity of the Cana narrative, the attempt to interpret John 2:1–11 in strongly liturgical, sacramental terms is also unwarranted.[116] But while the historical value of the 'water into wine' account cannot be set aside without question on grounds such as these, equally the episode cannot be accepted uncritically as factual simply because John here records a miracle, which had a profound effect on those who had begun to follow Jesus.[117]

Before we offer our own view on the Cana story, it is worthy noticing that various features belonging to this material point in the direction of an authentic background to it. (a) Although the Cana miracle has no

111. Bultmann, pp. 118–19. Similarly M. Smith, 'On the Wine God in Palestine (Gen. 18, Jn. 2, and Achilles Tatius)' in *S.W. Barron Jubilee Volume* (Jerusalem: American Academy for Jewish Research, 1975), pp. 815–29, esp. 816-18. For an alternative view see M. Hengel, 'The Interpretation of the Wine Miracle at Cana: John 2:11' in L.D. Hurst and N.T. Wright (ed.), *The Glory of Christ in the New Testament: Studies in Christology, In Memory of George Bradford Caird* (Oxford: Clarendon Press, 1987), pp. 83–112. Hengel argues that a Jewish, as well as a pagan, background is needed to interpret this sign.

112. *Cf.* further Hoskyns, pp. 190–92.

113. H.H. Wendt, *The Gospel According to St John: An Inquiry into its Genesis and Historical Value* (Edinburgh: T. and T. Clark, 1902), pp. 240–41. However, it is possible that such a process was at work in the pericopes at Mark 11:12–14, 20–21 (the cursing of the fig tree) and Matt. 17:24–27 (the coin in the fish's mouth). In both cases, parabolic sayings of Jesus may have been transmitted and developed as miracles.

114. *Cf.* Loisy, pp. 138–46, esp. 146. The synoptic sayings about new and old wine (Mark 2:22 par.) would in this case be regarded as furnishing the fourth evangelist with the literary material for his allegory.

115. See Carson, pp. 166–67, for a critical account of these theories.

116. *Cf.* Cullmann, *Early Christian Worship*, pp. 66–71; note also *HTFG*, pp. 227–28.

117. *Cf.* Carson, p. 175.

parallel in the synoptic tradition, while the other signs in John do have parallels of some kind,[118] it should not for this reason be treated in isolation as 'unlikely'. If we accept that Jesus was able to exercise miraculous power at all, changing water into wine is just as 'likely' as multiplying loaves.[119] Furthermore, since John seems to be working within a traditional framework (his 'signs source'?) for all his other miracle-narratives, there is no reason why in the case of the Cana story he should be inventing, or otherwise using untraditional sources.[120] This point gains strength, of course, if we take seriously the implications of recent research on the nature of John's tradition. (b) While the Cana story is obviously symbolic, in that it points to a spiritual meaning beyond itself, it is not necessarily *more* symbolic than the other Johannine signs. In this case, as always, the temptation to read off a symbolic or allegorical meaning which is not allowed by the context should be resisted.[121] (c) Because no 'I am' saying or discourse of Jesus is directly attached to John 2:1–11, it could be argued that John is reporting authentic signs material rather than constructing an incident which is tailored to his theological purposes. However, the 'new life' discourse of John 3 is not far away, and the saying 'I am the vine' may be associated with the Cana episode.[122] At the same time, it need not be assumed that the signs which *are* linked directly to sayings and discourses of Jesus must be judged automatically as *in*authentic! (d) The Cana narrative contains sober, circumstantial details (including the 'awkward' saying of Jesus to his mother in verse 4) which suggest the report of an actual incident. In this connection there is no real warrant for distinguishing artificially between the 'history' of the basic action at Cana and the 'theology' (only)

118.   For the healing of the official's son (John 4), see Matt. 8:5–13 par.; for the restoration of the sick man (John 5), see Mark 2:1–12 par.; for the feeding of the five thousand (John 6), see Mark 6:34–45 par.; for the gift of sight to the blind man (John 9), see Mark 8:22–26 (10:46–52) par.; for the raising of Lazarus (John 11), see Mark 5:22–24, 35–43 par. and Luke 7:11–16; and for the catch of fish (John 21), see Luke 5:1–11.

119.   Brown 1, p. 101, points to the echoes of the Elijah-Elisha tradition behind the miracles in John 2 (water into wine) and John 6 (the five thousand fed). This cycle of Old Testament stories, he reminds us, narrates miracles performed on behalf of individuals in unexpected physical need.

120.   *Ibid. Cf.* also the similarity between the comments 'they have no wine' (John 2:3), and 'they have nothing to eat' (Mark 6:36).

121.   The mention of 'the third day' in John 2:1 for example, is much more likely to be a part of John's chronology – theologically significant as that is – than a forward reference to the blessings of the resurrection. See Bernard 1, p. 72; against Lindars (hesitantly), pp. 124–125. *Cf.* further Olsson, *Structure and Meaning*, pp. 18–114. Olsson interprets the Cana incident as 'symbolic-narrative text with many allusive elements' (p. 14), which was written up by the fourth evangelist against the particular 'screen' of the events at Sinai.

122.   See above, pp. 133–35.

of the conversation which Jesus has with his mother.[123] (e) In the ancient near east, the supply of wine at weddings depended in part on the gifts of the guests who attended. Possibly the poverty of Jesus and his disciples meant that they could not contribute as much as was required, and this was one of the reasons for the shortage of wine.[124] If so, the miracle gains credence, and a factual detail in its account (verse 3) receives support from another source: that of oriental law. (f) It is just conceivable that the allusive reference in verse 9 to the 'water now become wine', without further recitation of the manner in which this happened, suggests that this story was already traditional and in circulation.

What, then, do we make of the historical nature of the 'water into wine' account? Barnabas Lindars has an interesting version of the theory that this story stems from an authentic saying of Jesus. Lindars thinks that the Cana narrative is a legend which has been created by John from a 'submerged parable' of Jesus, the climax of which is now in verse 10 without its former (parabolic) setting. The saying is, 'you have kept the good wine until now'; and it referred in the original parable to the superiority of Jesus over the old law.[125]

There is indeed a parabolic or proverbial saying in verse 10, but it is doubtful whether it should receive the place in this narrative which Lindars wishes to give it. For the main point of the Cana story has to do with the contrast between the water and the wine (verse 9); that is, even if the new element (Christianity) is in continuity with the old (Judaism),[126] it has finally replaced it. But the meaning of the parable in verse 10 according to Lindars – and it is there that he finds the point of departure for this narrative – is in line with the synoptic sayings of Jesus about old and new wine, particularly Luke 5:39: 'no one after drinking old wine desires new; but says, the old is good.'[127] However, that saying, like the Matthean (and Lucan in some MSS) redaction of the logion about new wine being put in fresh skins,[128] refers to the place of Judaism in Christianity (the old *vis à vis* the new), rather than, as in John 2, to the basic *quality* of Christianity (the new ultimately going *beyond* the old). This is the heart of the matter in the Cana incident, in the cleansing of

123. So M. Bourke, reviewing Brown, in *CBQ* 24 (1962), pp. 212–13; *cf.* also R.J. Dillon, 'Wisdom Tradition and Sacramental Retrospect in the Cana Account', *ibid.*, pp. 268–96, esp. 288–90.

124. So J.D.M. Derrett, 'Water into Wine', *BZ* NF 7 (1963), pp. 80–97; note also the conclusions about the nature and purpose of the Cana miracle (which Derrett regards as genuine) on pp. 96–97.

125. Lindars, pp. 123–28, esp. 126–27.

126. It is no accident that the wine is made from water placed in jars which were associated with *Jewish* ceremonial laws of cleansing.

127. Lindars, p. 126.

128. Matt. 9:17 = Luke 5:38 (*cf.* Mark 2:22).

the temple, and indeed in the whole of the Fourth Gospel: the new age of fulfilment is here, and Judaism has been replaced by Christianity.

My own suggestion is therefore somewhat different. It is not impossible that the Cana story has an authentically historical base: there was a feast at Cana, and at it Jesus unexpectedly supplied the needs of a wedding party.[129] John found this story in his source; and attached to it he also found an incidental family story which involved the mother of Jesus, whom curiously enough John does not name. He kept this addition, possible because of the link between Mary and the beloved disciple to which the Fourth Gospel witnesses,[130] although it does not contribute to the main interest of the sign as it now stands. He was able to use this material as the introduction to his book of signs, where it now acts as a decisive comment on all that is to follow: as an epiphany miracle, a leading demonstration of the glory of God revealed in Jesus Christ. As so often in John, however, we do not see Jesus actually performing the miracle itself; God's grace and truth are revealed here, but only to those who appreciate the fact by faith.[131]

Many theological themes cluster round the Cana sign;[132] but uppermost is this thought of the activity of revelation which was initiated by the Word of God incarnate. The moment of 'fulness' (John 1:16) has arrived, and a new centre to Judaism has been given by Jesus. To make this point even clearer, John now attached to his narrative the saying in verse 10, which may have been no more than a 'secular' proverb in circulation at the time; and he introduced it with the link in verse 9b: 'the steward called the bridegroom and said, ". . . you have kept the good wine until now." ' Such a comment was not necessary as proof that the water had been changed into wine, although it has the effect of heightening the miraculous element in the Cana story even further. But it *was* necessary for John's purposes as a means of underlining the quality of the new age which has begun, and is here being symbolised. This is not only a new age, but the best of new ages!

John finally worked over this material in his own way, and with his own style (notice the appearance of the typically Johannine motifs of 'hour' in verse 4, and 'glory' in verse 11), and placed it deliberately next to his account of the cleansing of the temple (John 2:13–22). Together, these two incidents illustrate the same truth of fulfilment. At Cana it is given in terms of a determinative sign, and in Jerusalem it is given in terms of a prophetic action which dramatises and further illustrates the meaning of that sign. In the Cana story, then, John has not created a miracle out of a parable; he has *created a parable out of a miracle*.

129. *Cf.* Bernard 1, p. clxxxii.
130. John 19:25–27.
131. *Cf.* Hanson, *Grace and Truth*, pp. 28–31.
132. See further Brown 1, pp. 103–110; Beasley-Murray, pp. 35–36 (on the *glory* and *power* of the Word made flesh).

Such a suggestion as this about the genesis of the Cana miracle does not solve all the problems. But it shows that John's narrative may be interpreted at an historical, as well as theological, level. We have already seen that this is characteristic of John's work as an evangelist.[133]

2. *The Raising of Lazarus.* This sign (John 11:1–44 or 46) is an important one, both in the setting of the Fourth Gospel as a whole and as an example of the nature of John's history. The narrative will provide us, therefore, with a useful test case.

Once more we find that the account of this sign bristles with potential difficulties. These are the obvious problems: a dead man is said to have been restored to life (unless the references to the 'sleep' of Lazarus are pressed);[134] this narrative occurs only in John, and it contains evident Johannine characteristics;[135] the Lazarus episode interrupts John's recitation of the passion events, and in John alone it is the short-term cause of those events; Lazarus himself is a silent figure, who is unknown outside the Fourth Gospel, and scarcely appears there beyond John 11;[136] and what is the point of a miracle which merely protracts physical life, if, as we shall see, it is intended to be instructive about life in the spirit?[137]

What are we to make of this incident, then? As usual, opinions differ. Some critics appear to find no difficulty in believing that John is narrating what really happened.[138] Others are doubtful, and argue that the Lazarus story is fictional, and composed by John on the basis of synoptic material: in particular, the parable of Dives and Lazarus (Luke 16:19–31, with its closing reference to resurrection from the dead).[139] In answer to

133. For a possible balance, between the theological and historical aspects in John's narration of this incident, see Brodie, pp. 171–76.

134. John 11:11–13; *cf.* also verse 4, 'this sickness is not to end in death'. But it is impossible to argue that, as a part of this incident, Lazarus did not really die, in the face of the comment by Jesus himself in verse 14, 'Lazarus is dead', and in view of the care taken to emphasise that Lazarus had been dead 'four days' (verses 17, 39), and was therefore in human terms irretrievably dead. Without question we are meant by John to understand that a miracle took place, and that it was momentous.

135. *E.g.* the use of the terms 'glory' (John 11:4, *et al.*) and 'light' (verse 9, *et al.*); the 'I am' saying in verse 25; the confession of Martha in verse 27 ('you are the Christ, the Son of God'); the reference to the sign of John 9 (the healing of the blind man) in verse 37; and possibly the prayer of Jesus in verses 41–42.

136. Unless Lazarus is to be identified with the beloved disciple! So Sanders, pp. 29–32, esp. 31–32. Sanders believes that, because of this, the material in the Fourth Gospel concerning Martha, Mary and Lazarus was of particular historical value; see pp. 11–12, 276–77.

137. See further C.F.D. Moule, 'The Meaning of "Life" in the Gospel and Epistles of St John', *Theology* 78 (1975), pp. 114–25.

138. *Cf.* Bernard 1, pp. clxxxii–clxxxvi; Beasley-Murray, pp. 199–201, esp. 199; Carson, pp. 403–404.

139. So Richardson, pp. 137–39; *cf.* Loisy, p. 355.

the sceptics it may be said first that John himself evidently believed a miraculous event to have taken place; second, that there is no real parallel in the synoptic Gospels – not even the parable of Luke 16 – which could have given rise to this narrative; and third that anyway John, we suggest, did not know the synoptic Gospels.

Is it possible, therefore, to defend the historicity of John's account? Did the raising of Lazarus really take place? First, we may draw attention to the features in the Lazarus incident which support the possibility that its background was traditional, and that its origin was historical. (a) The other healing miracles in John (the official's son, the sick man and the blind man) stem from a traditional basis, with synoptic associations; so there is no reason why the Lazarus account should not be traditional, even if there is no synoptic parallel. (b) In view of the increased respect which is being shown towards the historical value of John's Gospel, we no longer have to begin by regarding the Lazarus tradition automatically as unhistorical. (c) The basic language of the Lazarus narrative is described by Bultmann as 'semitising'; but this could suggest an early source, rather than John's own work.[140] (d) The account is full of vivid and circumstantial details, suggesting the presence of eye-witnesses.[141] (e) The geographical setting (Bethany, verses 1, 18) and the family names Mary and Martha, already known to us from the synoptic Gospels, suggest a traditional basis for this narrative.[142] (f) The naming of the principal character in a healing/resurrection story is equally unusual in John and the Synoptics; but in both traditions it occurs once. As we have Lazarus, so we have Bartimaeus.[143] (g) The 'fading out' of the principal character in a healing/resurrection miracle is typical of the Gospels generally; so that the virtual non-appearance of Lazarus after his raising need not be regarded as unlikely or untraditional (especially if, having been raised, he were still alive when John wrote).[144] (h) The editorial comment in verse 2, identifying two of the participants in this drama, includes the use of the title 'the Lord' for Jesus. This is non-Johannine, and suggests a traditional source, possibly with Lucan associations: since this is one of Luke's favourite christological titles in his Gospel. (i) The inclusion of an 'I am' saying at verse 25 ('I am the resurrection and the life') looks Johannine and untraditional; and it may well be. But it has yet to be shown

140. Bultmann, p. 395 n. 2. He points to such features as placing the verb at the beginning of a sentence, the primitive linking of sentences, and the use of ἴδε ('see'; John 11:3, 36, et al.).

141. Note, e.g. John 11:20, 28, 33, 35, 44, et al.

142. Cf. Luke 10:38–42. However, it is John who (from his own source?) names the woman who anoints Jesus at Bethany as the Mary of the Lazarus episode (John 12:3; cf. Mark 14:3 par., where she is anonymous); and it may be John himself who locates the sign of John 11 at Bethany as a result.

143. Mark 10:46 (cf. 5:22–23).

144. With John 12:2 (a silent Lazarus at table), cf. Mark 5:42–43; Luke 7:15, et al. The 'silence' of Lazarus may also result from John's desire to make him a universal (resurrection) figure, rather than to individualise him.

conclusively that John could not have drawn on some kind of traditional, even dominical, source for his 'I am' sayings.[145]

Considerations such as these suggest that in the Lazarus narrative we may be in touch with a groundwork which has its roots in history. On this basis we may continue our historical investigation by making the following comments.

(i) The fact that the raising of Lazarus is unknown beyond the Fourth Gospel, and that the figure of Lazarus himself in any form (other than parabolic) is not known to the synoptic writers, need not constitute a real problem. First, what is historical in the Gospels is no longer determined by what is synoptic. Second, lack of knowledge about Lazarus in Mark is just conceivably explained by the absence of Peter from the scene. It could be argued that Peter was not in Jerusalem at the time of the raising of Lazarus, because his name does not appear in this section of John's Gospel.[146] If Peter did not know about the Lazarus incident first-hand, he might well have refrained from mentioning it to Mark, whose informant – by tradition – he became. In this case we may say, although this is problematic, that the omission of Lazarus from Matthew and Luke was due to Mark, whom they followed, and that there was no reference to him in any of the sources used by the first and third evangelists.[147] Third, if it be claimed that stories about those who had been brought back to life must have been, like the characters themselves, in general circulation and widely-known, it may be answered that Mark and Matthew do not know about the raising of the widow of Nain's son;[148] and indeed John (we would argue) knows neither about that episode, nor about the raising of Jairus' daughter.[149]

(ii) The *placing* of the Lazarus story in John is interesting, and crucial. As it stands, it seems to interrupt the beginning of the Johannine passion narrative. By the time we reach the end of John 10,[150] all seems

145. See below, pp. 225–26.

146. Peter is not mentioned by name between John 6:68 and 13:6. There are similar gaps in the synoptic Gospels, which may indicate that Peter joined the other disciples after they had arrived in Jerusalem, and just in time for Passover. Note also that in John 11:16 Thomas, and not Peter, is the spokesman.

147. *Cf.* Sanders, pp. 276–77; see also W. Temple, *Readings in St John's Gospel*, 2nd edn. (London: Macmillan, 1945), pp. 175–77. Temple further notes that, unlike John, Mark does not refer to events in Jerusalem immediately before the passion week (p. 176). In answer to the general point that the omission of Lazarus in Mark may be accounted for by the absence of Peter from the raising incident itself, it may be said: (a) that if Mark's Gospel were written by John Mark, whose home was in Jerusalem, he is likely to have known about Lazarus for himself; (b) that even granted the historicity of the Lazarus story, we cannot be sure of its exact placing in the ministry of Jesus if, as we shall see, it owes its present placing to John.

148. Luke 7:11–18.

149. Mark 5:22–24, 35–43 par.

150. Although Bultmann (pp. 392–94) sees John 10:40–42 as the introduction to the Lazarus narrative.

set for the passion of Jesus. The confrontation with the Jews is at an end; and now that the identity which Jesus is claiming for himself has been made clear, his arrest is only a matter of time (John 10:39). But, as Lindars has shown, John holds up the announcement of the passion, which begins in chapter 12, with the anointing and triumphal entry, by inserting the Lazarus story.[151] To do this, the fourth evangelist probably engaged in a certain amount of editorial work. For example, chapter 11 is now linked with chapter 9 by means of a reference to the healing of the blind man, and by the use of 'light' imagery.[152] John 11 is also tied to chapter 10 by means of the theme of 'life', which is strong in both the Lazarus episode and the shepherd discourse. Similarly, John 12 (the opening of the passion narrative) is reshaped so as to tie it in with the Lazarus material. The motif of 'light and life', for example, is continued.[153] Also, and more importantly, the effect of the triumphal entry as a factor in the arrest of Jesus is played down. In the other Gospels the triumphal entry and the cleansing of the temple (and for his own reasons John has placed the latter event much earlier) are the immediate causes of the arrest.[154] In John, however, the Lazarus incident has already provoked the final attempt of the Jews to take Jesus.[155] As a result, the entry into Jerusalem brings forth little more than an aside from the Parisees (John 12:19).

But interestingly enough it is not *only* the 'political' activities of the triumphal entry and temple cleansing which, according to the synoptic tradition, set in motion the events leading to the crucifixion. Luke tells us that when Jesus entered Jerusalem the whole crowd of disciples praised him for all the mighty *works* which they had seen; and this caused particular annoyance to the Pharisees.[156] If this were indeed an important element in the tradition of the arrest, which John knew, we can now see why the Lazarus event should occupy the place it does in the Fourth Gospel. John has chosen from his source one highly significant miracle, and used it representatively both to introduce his account of the passion and to comment upon it.[157] The death and resurrection of Lazarus point forward to the death and resurrection of Jesus. Whether or not John is

151. Lindars, pp. 378–82. Brown 1, pp. 427–30, argues that the material in *both* chapters, John 11 and 12, comes from Johannine circles and formed a later addition to the plan of John's Gospel.

152. John 11:37 (*cf.* 9:1–38); 11:9-10.

153. John 12:35–50.

154. Mark 11:1–18 par.

155. John 11:47–57; *cf.* 12:9–11.

156. Luke 19:37, using δύναμις ('work', or 'deed' of power); *cf.* verse 39.

157. Note John 12:18–19, where the Lazarus sign is presented as a leading motive for the arrest of Jesus. If John is drawing on historical tradition for the Lazarus episode, however, we need not assume that his chronology at this point is completely inaccurate. *Cf.* further Brown 1, p. 429; Beasley-Murray, pp. 184–87 ('we must be content to acknowledge a certain indefiniteness as to the time when the rising of Lazarus took place'; p. 187).

right about his placing of the cleansing of the temple, moreover, we find that he is not so far after all from the synoptic history of the passion. Like the other evangelists, he knows that the hostile reaction to Jesus was brought about by actions as well as teaching; and the climax came at the moment of triumphant arrival of the Messiah in Jerusalem. John follows tradition by reporting that moment. For historical reasons, also, he prefaces it with a sign of great proportions which will represent all that has been going on: miraculous activity which, like the teaching of Jesus, gave rise to increasing hostility. Theologically, however, once the Lazarus episode is in place, John (as we shall see) can use it for his own purposes.

We conclude by suggesting, in the light of these observations, how the narrative of the raising of Lazarus may have reached its present form. First, John found a sign in his source which would gather up the other signs so far recorded, and provide a bridge to his passion narrative. The basic story he chose concerned the raising of a man called Lazarus from the dead. Given the miraculous power of Jesus, such a miracle is not impossible, and indeed the synoptic tradition also records incidents of Jesus raising people from the dead.[158] To that factual account John gave a setting, both a place and a family,[159] which it may not have possessed originally, but which suited his chronology: Jesus was about to enter Jerusalem for the last time, and Mary of Bethany (John says) was about to anoint him. At the same time the fourth evangelist added for theological reasons certain narrative and discourse elements to his basic structure, as a way of drawing out further the spiritual meaning of this sign. In the first place, he included touches which emphasise the parallels between the raising of Lazarus and the resurrection of Jesus, events which both speak in some way of life beyond the grave. Thus we hear not only that Lazarus was buried in a tomb covered by a stone (verses 38–39), but also that when he came out of the tomb he did so in grave-clothes similar to those of Jesus: even to the specially noted cloth in which the face had been wrapped (verse 44).[160]

Secondly, John drew in sections of dialogue. (a) Possibly he added the saying of Jesus about the reason for Lazarus' illness (verse 4), with its Johannine-sounding reference to 'glory'; and almost certainly he included the conversation with the disciples about walking in the light (verses 7–10), particularly if he were using this to link chapter 11 with chapter 9. The fact that Jesus delayed his performance of the miracle (verse 6) is likely to be an authentic part of the original narrative because of its very difficulty. But if we say that John himself added the material

158. Mark 5:22–24, 35–43 par. (Jairus' daughter); Luke 7:11–16 (the widow of Nain's son).

159. On the reliability of John's tradition concerning the Bethany family see J.N. Sanders, ' "Those whom Jesus loved" (John xi.5)', *NTS* 1 (1954–55), pp. 29–41.

160. John 20:1, 7.

around it (an editorial comment in verse 2, as well as verses 4 and 7–10), this means that the original opening of the story (verses 1, 3, 5–6, 11–16) was considerably tightened up.[161] (b) John may also have added the saying about Jesus as the life-giver (verses 25–26), which underlines the theological significance of the whole episode, together with the subsequent doctrinal confession of Martha in verse 27.[162] (c) The prayer of Jesus in verses 41–42, with its Johannine ring ('that they may believe that you have sent me'), could also have been attached by John.[163] In each of these three groups of sayings, which John may have incorporated into his narrative, the possibility that he was still drawing on traditional sources should not be overlooked.

Finally, John inserted his Lazarus material between chapters 10 and 12, making (as we have seen) the editorial adjustments which were necessary. As it now stands, we have in the raising of Lazarus – even if he is physically to die again – a decisive sign of Jesus as life-giver. Like the Cana episode, the story of Lazarus is an epiphany miracle, which reveals the glory of God in Christ (verses 4, 40); and, like the earlier sign, the raising of Lazarus evokes faith on the part of the witnesses: there, the disciples; here, some of the Jews (verse 45). The basic difference is that whereas in Cana the 'hour' of Jesus had not yet arrived (2:4), in Bethany it has struck (verse 9).

Thus in John 11, it may be argued, we begin with material which has its basis in the historical account of an actual miracle. So far from the miraculous raising of Lazarus being derived from the parable about Lazarus in Luke 16, it is even possible that the Lucan parable is indebted (at least for the name Lazarus) to the miracle![164] For as we know, the Lucan and Johannine traditions, while independent, are close together

161. *Cf.* W. Wilkens, 'Die Erweckung des Lazarus', *TZ* 15 (1959), pp. 22–39, who goes much further, and argues that the original form of the miracle story omitted virtually the whole of the present opening section (John 11:1–16); see esp. pp. 23–28. Wilkens believes that the Lazarus story is an authentic narrative, written up by John. But because he assumes without warrant that no theology belonged to the earliest forms of the narrative, which he attempts to uncover by removing all the Johannine elements, Wilkens is left with a mere 10 verses from which, he supposes, John worked.

162. *Cf.* John 10:10. Bultmann (p. 402 n. 3.) suggests that John 11:25–26 was originally part of the (revelation-) discourse used at 5:19–29 (with its mention of both resurrection and life).

163. *Cf.* Loisy, p. 353, 'le Christ johannique prie pour exposer les thèses de l'évangéliste', ('the Johannine Christ prays in order to set out the propositions of the evangelist'). But, against this, note the primitive sound of Πάτερ ('Father') in verse 41.

164. Brown 1, p. 429; *cf.* Hoskyns, pp. 396–97; *HTFG*, p. 229. Note the word about Lazarus rising from the dead at Luke 16:31. It may be significant that the Lucan parable and the Johannine miracle are both introduced by the typically Semitic prose idiom, 'a certain man (τις). . . '. This is especially characteristic of Luke, both in reporting parables (*e.g.* 15:11) and miracles (*e.g.* 14:2).

in several ways.[165] Once again, we have found reason to believe that John's work as an evangelist involves factual history, as well as theology.

History behind the discourses

We turn finally, in our attempt to explore the historical content of John's Gospel, to the subject of the Johannine discourse material. This is a much more delicate and complex issue, and one that requires further research – especially in the case of the farewell discourse – before we can achieve assured results. Obviously we cannot undertake here a complete examination of John's speech material from the point of view of its origin. The most we can do is to offer a number of considerations which need to be borne in mind during any investigation of this kind.

(i)   As with the signs material, we no longer need to begin by assuming that the Johannine discourses are the product of John's own imagination, composed on the basis of his knowledge of synoptic sayings but moving far beyond this. While John has indirect points of contact with the synoptic tradition, we saw earlier that he probably had access to an independent tradition of his own for the words as well as the works of Jesus. There is no necessary reason, therefore, why John's discourses, and even the theology they contain, should not rest upon traditional sources, and run back in many cases to actual sayings of Jesus himself.

(ii)   This is not to conclude, of course, that we must now rush to the other side of the boat, and assume that the Johannine discourses are entirely dominical.[166] Clearly the influence of the beloved disciple, the fourth evangelist and the Johannine church itself can all be detected in the transmission of the basic words of Jesus and in the composition of the speeches which derive (it may be suggested) from those words. But to say that an evangelist has imposed his own style and outlook on discourse material, which he has received from different sources, is not the same as saying that he has departed entirely from historical tradition. Presumably we should not wish to argue for such a conclusion in the case of Matthew's composition of the Sermon on the Mount; and there is no intrinsic reason why we should do so when we come to John's speech compositions: even if we do not have the check on sources which is available in the case of Matthew 5–7.

(iii)   It is true that the formal and stylistic differences between the sayings of Jesus in John and the Synoptics are apparently and obviously great. In the Fourth Gospel the terse saying gives place to the lengthy debate or sermon, and the synoptic parables of the kingdom disappear. Nevertheless: (a) The synoptic Gospels also contain long

---

165.   We have noted this earlier, when discussing the nature of the Johannine tradition; see above, pp. 10–11.

166.   Except in the sense that the risen Christ speaks through the tradition of Christian prophecy which has been inherited by the New Testament writers.

discourses,[167] and John also contains pithy, memorable sayings.[168] (b) John has his own parables, and (although separately) a theology of the kingdom.[169] (c) A difference of audience will have caused differences in the form of address used by Jesus. Even in the synoptic Gospels he does not speak to the disciples in the same way that he speaks to the crowds. But as in the Synoptics, so in John, Jesus (according to the evangelists concerned) can use, for example, the form of a lengthy speech when dealing with crowds, including opponents, and a longer or shorter explanation in private for the disciples.[170]

(iv) A common teaching method used by Jesus with enquirers, as we have already noticed, involved repetition. Thus: Jesus makes an important statement; it is misunderstood; and then it is repeated and expanded in order to bring out its meaning.[171] A good example is to be found at the outset of the Gospel, in John 3. Jesus says, 'truly, truly, I tell you, no one can see the kingdom of God without being born anew' (verse 3). Nicodemus misunderstands this (verse 4), and the saying is repeated and further explicated (verses 5–8). The continued bafflement of Nicodemus in this instance (verse 9) provides the signal for further explanation (verses 10–15).[172] Now this is a characteristically Johannine technique, appearing even in the farewell discourse,[173] and might therefore suggest that the form, if not the content of the addresses which include it, stems from the evangelist himself.[174] It so happens, however, that the same pattern is typical also of the teaching of Jesus for enquirers in the synoptic Gospels. There also Jesus will make an arresting statement, often in the form of a parable; it will not be understood; and an explanation will follow.[175] Thus in Mark 7:15 Jesus gives his disciples a 'parable' (verse 17) about the clean and the unclean. They do not understand this, and ask Jesus about it (verse 17). Jesus then repeats and explains his initial statement (verses 18–23). Since this was evidently a teaching method traditionally associated with Jesus, we need not conclude that when John uses it he is being completely unhistorical.

167. E.g. Mark 13 par.; Matt. 5–7. Robinson, Redating, p. 277, interestingly notices that many features of the synoptic apocalypses appear in the Johannine farewell discourse: injunctions against alarm, forewarnings against apostasy, predictions of persecution, the need for witness, the promise of the Spirit's help, and references to 'that (eschatological) day'.

168. E.g. John 4:34; 6:27a; 12:24; 15:13.

169. Cf. John 5:19–20; 3:3, et al. See above, pp. 29–30.

170. Cf. Matt. 23 (addressed to both 'the crowds and the disciples', verse 1) with John 5:17–47; Mark 13 (also 4:10–20) with John 14–16 (also 6:60–65).

171. See further Bernard 1, pp. cxi–cxiii; Brodie, pp. 16–19, 184–87.

172. Note also the discourses in John 4 and 6.

173. See e.g. John 14:4–5,6–14; 16:16,17–18,19–24.

174. Particularly if John is indebted at this point to the rabbinic technique of midrash; see above, pp. 70–71, 110–111.

175. Although in the synoptic witness Jesus initiates dialogues less frequently, and interlocutors are involved more fully, than in John. Cf. HTFG, pp. 317–18.

(v) When we discussed the Johannine discourses earlier in this book in terms of the composition of John as a whole, we noticed that current research is suggesting Jewish rather than Greek influence as the basic background to the Johannine discourses;[176] and this is confirmed by what we now know about the character of John's Gospel. If so, an early and traditional basis for the speeches in John is no longer out of the question.

(vi) The 'I am' (ἐγώ εἰμι) sayings in the Gospel of John constitute a special problem. They look theological, they have Hellenistic associations,[177] and they are distinctively Johannine. If Jesus had really made these large claims in this way, would not this have been apparent to the other evangelists? Here are real problems; and instinctively, perhaps, we are tempted to regard these sayings as John's own creation, and as a clarification of his particular understanding of Christ's person. However, it is worth noticing two points in this connection.

First, there is a possible Old Testament background to the 'I am' formula, which may be located in the phrase especially associated with Second Isaiah: 'I am God, and there is no other'.[178] Admittedly, the Isaianic 'I am God' formula chiefly reflects an awareness of the supremacy of monotheism over against polytheism; and it is only used absolutely, rather than (as in all but one of the Johannine 'I am' expressions) with predicates. Nevertheless, the 'I am' expression appears in the setting of the Old Testament as above all a divine self-proclamation; and this is precisely the way in which ἐγώ εἰμι is used in the Fourth Gospel: supremely in its one absolute occurrence (John 8:58; but see the use of ἐγώ εἰμι, meaning 'I am he', at 8:24, 28; 9:9 and 13:19). The second point concerns the saying just mentioned, 'before Abraham was, I am'. On at least one occasion in the *synoptic* tradition it is recorded that Jesus used the expression ἐγώ εἰμι absolutely: when he warned his disciples that deceivers would come in his name, saying 'I am (Christ)'.[179] Mark and Luke use the phrase ἐγώ εἰμι without adding ὁ Χριστός, while Matthew includes the title in order to clarify the obvious meaning. It is possible that this indicates a typical way in which Jesus was known to have spoken; and it certainly makes the use of the ἐγώ εἰμι expression at John 8:58 look less uniquely Johannine.[180]

Naturally factors such as these do not by themselves begin to account for the Johannine 'I am' sayings, or to establish their authenticity; but

176. See above, pp. 108–112.

177. See above, p. 109–110.

178. *E.g.* (LXX) Isa. 45:5–6, 18; 46:9; 47:10, *et al.*; but also Exod. 3:13–14; 20:2–3; Deut. 32:39; Ezek. 6:7; Joel 2:27, *et al.*

179. Mark 13:6 = Luke 21:8 (*cf.* Matt. 24:5). Mark 6:50 par. is probably not significant in this discussion; nor is Mark 14:62 (= Matt. 26:64 = Luke 22:67, 70) a real parallel; against E. Stauffer, *Jesus and His Story* (London: SCM Press, 1960), pp. 149–50.

180. *Cf.* also John 4:26; 6:20; 13:19. On the 'I am' formula, as a characteristic, divine self-affirmation in the teaching of Jesus, see Stauffer, *Jesus*, pp. 142–59, esp. 149-59.

these are two considerations, at least, which may need to be reckoned with in any further research on this subject.[181]

(vii)   The distinctive and frequently-used 'Amen, amen' formula in the Johannine discourses of Jesus ('very truly, I say to you . . .'), which appears 25 times in the Fourth Gospel,[182] probably harks back to the single 'amen' expression in the synoptic Gospels; and this was no doubt a sayings pattern created by Jesus himself. It may be, therefore, that on these occasions (at least) the fourth evangelist is preserving traditional and indeed primitive material in his speeches.[183]

None of these points, of course, can be regarded as conclusive evidence that the discourses in John's Gospel are historically based. There are in any case special difficulties involved in trying to probe the origin of the Johannine speeches. Their character and length seem at first sight to set them far apart from the speech material in the synoptic Gospels;[184] and they also appear to be the product of profound spiritual reflection and theological meditation, so that (as in John 3, for example) it is not always certain where the words of Jesus end and the comment of the evangelist begins. Nevertheless, even if it is not easy to recover genuine sayings of Jesus from John's redaction, we do not have to presuppose that the attempt is unreasonable. On the contrary, the points we have just considered suggest cumulatively that a traditional element may well lie behind the Johannine discourses, and that the important task of any student of St John is to determine the nature and extent of that element. Early tradition, as we have said before, is not necessarily the same as genuine history. But the indications are that there may be a larger measure of historical tradition behind the discourse material in John than was previously regarded as possible, and that this subject is worth pursuing.[185]

We shall now look briefly at one example of Johannine discourse material from the stand-point of its possibly historical background. As in the case of the signs, we shall choose an example which is 'difficult', in that it comes from the farewell discourse (John 13–17). This section of John's Gospel stands notoriously by itself, and seems most obviously Johannine in its theological flavour. The prayer of Jesus in chapter 17 appears from this point of view to be insuperably difficult (who heard

181.   On 'I am' in John see further Brown 1, pp. 533–38; also D.M. Ball, '*I AM*' in *John's Gospel: Literary Function, Background and Theological Implications*, JSNTS 124 (Sheffield: Sheffield Academic Press, 1996).

182.   John 1:51; 3:11; 8:51, 58; 14:12, *et al.*

183.   *cf.* J. Jeremias, *The Prayers of Jesus*, SBT (2) 6 (London: SCM Press, 1967), pp. 112–15; *idem*, *New Testament Theology*, vol. 1: *The Proclamation of Jesus*, NTL (London: SCM Press, 1971), pp. 35–36.

184.   It should be remembered, however, that the problem of tradition and interpretation belongs to the study of synoptic, as much as Johannine, speech material.

185.   See also *HTFG*, part 2.

it?) and infinitely far removed from an early and authentic sayings tradition. It is to an examination of this material, therefore, that we shall now turn our attention.

John 17. Is it possible that behind the prayer of consecration in John 17 there lies a genuinely primitive tradition? In support of this possibility, three lines of enquiry may be suggested.[186]

(i) John 17 contains several phrases and ideas which have parallels in the synoptic tradition, but are obviously independent of it. Echoes can be found, for example, of the Sermon on the Mount/Plain, and of the Lord's Prayer.[187]

(ii) Some of the categories in this prayer which appear to be adamantly Johannine (for example, 'hour', 'knowledge', 'glory' and 'truth') may well have their own early background.[188]

(iii) The uses of the address 'Father' (Πάτερ, Πατήρ) by Jesus in John 17 suggests an underlying, early tradition. This statement may be supported by three further considerations. (a) The Gospel tradition in every part reveals that Jesus normally addressed God as 'Father' in his prayers, even if it is also true that the use of the term 'Father' is ascribed more frequently to Jesus – in general usage – as that tradition advanced.[189] In the words of Jeremias, 'this constancy of the tradition shows how firmly the address "Father" was rooted in the tradition of Jesus'.[190] (b) The Aramaic word *Abba* seems to underlie the use of Πάτερ in John 17, and there is little doubt that *Abba* as an address to God formed a characteristic part of the *ipsissima verba* ('actual words') of Jesus.[191] Such an intimate form of address to the Father, indeed, is unlikely to have been put into the mouth of Jesus at a secondary stage of literary composition.[192] (c) Jesus himself already belonged to a strong,

186. For further details, including biblical and bibliographical references, see Smalley, 'Testament', pp. 498–501.
187. *E.g.* John 17:2, 7 = Matt. 11:27 (28:18) = Luke 10:22; John 17:11 = Matt. 6:9 (5:48; 6:14) = Luke 11:2, *et al. Cf.* further Bernard 2, p. 559.
188. Similarly, there are parallels in the synoptic tradition to the Johannine use of ὥρα ('hour'), as in Mark 14:41 = Matt. 26:45; *cf.* Luke 22:53. See *HTFG*, p. 371, and n. 2. For a possible background in Qumran to the Johannine concepts of 'knowledge' and 'truth' see Brown, 'Qumran Scrolls', pp. 107–108, 121–23; *cf.* also Schnackenburg 1, p. 108. For the proposal that there is a non-Hellenistic background to the theme of 'glory' in the Fourth Gospel see D. Hill, 'The Request of Zebedee's Sons and the Johannine δόξα-theme', *NTS* 13 (1966–67), pp. 281–85; also Smalley, 'Johannine Son of Man Sayings', pp. 296–97.
189. See Jeremias, *Prayers*, pp. 29–35.
190. *Ibid.*, p. 55.
191. *Cf.* Mark 14:36; and, for the liturgical use of this term in the early church, see Rom. 8:15; Gal. 4:6. See further Jeremias, *Prayers*, pp. 55–57, 108–112; *idem, Proclamation*, pp. 36–37, 61–68; also Black, *Aramaic Approach*, pp. 149–51.
192. Even the extended form, 'Holy Father' (John 17:11; *cf.* verse 25), might be authentic, if it were a dominical variant of the address in the Lord's Prayer, 'Father, hallowed be your name' (Luke 11:2 = Matt. 6:9).

Jewish liturgical tradition. The content of his prayers is reported by the synoptic writers less often than the fact that he prayed. But the existence of the brief and vivid Gethsemane petition, in Mark 14:36 par.,[193] indicates that manifestly primitive material of this kind was capable of being preserved and handed on.[194]

Doubtless the prayer of Jesus in John 17 as we now have it is a literary composition, which owes its character to the Johannine church. But there is no reason at all why the origin of the prayer should not be located in the historical situation of the upper room, which is the setting for the discourse in John 13–17.[195] In that case, where might the core of original words be found? If we allow the presence of traditional material in John 17, my suggestion (on the basis of the points we have just considered) is that it is to be found in the three petitions which are introduced by Πάτερ: verses 1, 11 and 24. These are in fact the only straightforward petitions in the whole chapter,[196] and one occurs in each of its three natural divisions (verses 1–5, 6–19, 20–26).[197] If these three petitions originally formed the heart of the prayer, they would have summarised its present content: Jesus prays first for himself, then for his disciples, then for the universal church in all ages ('glorify your Son'; 'protect them in your name'; 'that they [all] may be with me'). Thus, in the light of his coming death and exaltation, Jesus commends to his Father the faith and life of his disciples and their successors. An early oral report of this prayer from the beloved disciple, who was near Jesus at the time, might then have been handed on, shaped in a Johannine setting,[198] and eventually written up by the fourth evangelist.[199]

193.   Mark uses Αββα (ὁ πατήρ); Matthew and Luke use Πάτερ (cf. Matt. 26:39, 42 = Luke 22:42).

194.   Notice also the 'traditional' character of John 17 at verse 12, where an earlier prophecy of Jesus about the betrayal by Judas is regarded as having been scripturally fulfilled (cf. John 13:21). See also HTFG, pp. 69–71, where Dodd aligns the synoptic tradition of a Gethsemane prayer with the prayer of Jesus in John 12:27–28 (also using Πάτερ). In both cases, Dodd argues for authenticity.

195.   cf. John 13:2; and see Hoskyns, p. 495.

196.   John 17:5 is an extension of verse 1; verses 21 and 25 are more in the nature of 'addresses', than petitions.

197.   So, for the divisions, Marsh, p. 553.

198.   An obvious context would have been the eucharist itself. But cf. Loisy (p. 441) who sees in John 17 as a whole 'a type of eucharistic prayer', created by a Christian prophet and attributed to Jesus.

199.   On the prayer of consecration (John 17) as a whole see Schnackenburg 3, pp. 167–202, esp. (for its origin) 201–202: the prayer 'clearly breathes the spirit of the Johannine community' (p. 202), rather than reflecting directly the words of Jesus. On the other side note O. Cullmann, Prayer in the New Testament (London: SCM Press and Minneapolis: Fortress Press, 1995), pp. 106–110, who sees the prayer in John 17 as 'a further development of the preaching of the incarnate Jesus' (p. 107).

In both the narrative and discourse material of the Fourth Gospel, then, we have found evidence which – while not offering us conclusive proof of historicity – suggests that John's witness rests on a traditional foundation, the historical value of which is potentially important and demands serious consideration.

CONCLUSION

In this chapter we have seen that John is an evangelist among the evangelists. His is a shared gospel, to which all the New Testament writers owe allegiance; and to this basic kerygmatic tradition John adds from his own sources information about the life of Jesus. We have then asked to what extent the Fourth Gospel may really be described as historical, if in fact it is kerygmatic and if in due course John's material has been interpreted by those who handed it on and committed it to writing. In answer, we have found reasons for believing not only that *tradition* lay behind the Gospel of John, but also the real possibility of genuine *history*.

Thus we may conclude that John is an evangelist whose Gospel concerns salvation history. As such it contains both history – which the fourth evangelist takes seriously – *and* theology; not one, without the other. As we saw in the previous chapter, John is not an evangelist in the sense of writing a mission tract for unbelievers; but he *is* an evangelist in the sense that for the sake of believers in his own church he makes the Christian good news his point of departure and the heart of his message. As such, he writes with an inescapable sense of history.

But John is also an interpreter. He takes over a developing, kerygmatic tradition about Jesus, and for his own purposes develops it further. It is to John's special contribution to the Gospel tradition, as one of its leading interpreters, that we shall turn in our final chapter.

10

JOHN: INTERPRETER

In this chapter we shall be considering the special contribution which John makes to the Gospel tradition as one of its interpreters. For John, like all the Gospel writers, is an interpreter as well as an evangelist. He understands the Jesus story in his own way. John has his own theology; and he adds his own slant to our knowledge of Christian beginnings. We need therefore to study John the interpreter very carefully, and to learn from him.

We can best approach our consideration of John's interpretation by discovering how he has redacted the Jesus tradition. Even if, as we have argued earlier, the fourth evangelist did not know and use the synoptic Gospels as such, he knew and used the ongoing Christian tradition to which all the evangelists were indebted. What has John done with that tradition? To what extent has he developed it in his own way, and even gone beyond it? What, in the end, makes Johannine theology 'Johannine'?

We shall now address ourselves to these questions. As we do so, it will be worth bearing in mind two points. First, we shall inevitably be forced occasionally in the present chapter to summarise theological ground which we have covered earlier in this book. Second, we shall be examining here the Gospel of John in its finished form. But it is possible, of course, for a Johannine interpretation or theological theme to have emerged at any stage in the evolution of the Fourth Gospel. If, as we have suggested, the basic tradition behind the Gospel of John stems from the beloved disciple, there is no reason to exclude from that earliest stage an understanding of the gospel message which we should now describe as 'Johannine'. Similarly, at the second stage of the Gospel's composition – according to our analysis – the fourth evangelist might well have given written expression, at least in seminal form, to distinctively Johannine theological characteristics. And the final edition would have imparted to the Gospel a literary and theological shape which was a community product, but which arose out of a Johannine method of interpretation already in existence.

With these considerations in mind, we can now proceed to our study of John as a Christian interpreter, beginning with his understanding of salvation.

SALVATION IN THE FOURTH GOSPEL

All that John says about the gospel of Jesus the Christ is ultimately concerned with salvation. John's distinctive description of salvation is 'eternal life' (ζωὴ αἰώνιος); and, despite some variations,[1] this is a regular Johannine term for the wholeness which humanity needs and can obtain. In this respect, again, John is set apart from the synoptic Gospels.

According to the Fourth Gospel, eternal life is a gift of God.[2] This life, this salvation, is mediated to the believer through Christ: in his incarnation, death, resurrection and exaltation.[3] The life-giving activity of Christ with which, as we have seen, the symbol of 'light' is regularly linked,[4] thus involves both the person and work of Jesus, the Word who revealed God's nature and was glorified by him.[5] It is no accident that the titles used by Jesus of himself in John, therefore, always contain or imply the thought of life and light.[6]

Here is the basis of salvation in Johannine terms: eternal life is only possible inasfar as it derives from God through Christ by the Spirit.[7] Thus people can be rescued from darkness, judgment and wrath; and thus can they pass from death to life.[8] This concept of salvation in John, moreover, has a continuing reference: past, present and future are involved in it. The believing Christian, who has passed from darkness to life and light, is called to abide in Christ, and to practise a love and service reflecting those of the earthly Jesus himself.[9] For this purpose the spiritual life of the believer is sustained by the risen Christ on the basis of his historical ministry and glorification.[10] But there is a future tense as well. The person who honours the Son of God now is promised the 'resurrection of life' in the age to come.[11]

John's theology of salvation is thus a theology of revelation as well as glorification. Jesus, in Johannine terms, has made God known, as

---

1. Note John 4:42 (using Σωτήρ); 4:22 (using σωτηρία); and 3:17 (using σώζω).

2. John 3:16; 17:2.

3. John 5:24; 1:4, 14; 10:10-11; 11:25–26; 3:14–15.

4. John 1:4–9; 8:12, *et al.*

5. John 5:21; 10:10–11.

6. John 6:35; 14:6, *et al.* The 'I am' sayings in John almost always contrast the 'life' available in Jesus with the 'lifelessness' of Judaism.

7. The Spirit's agency in salvation receives expression during the discussion between Jesus and Nicodemus on the subject of salvation as regeneration (John 3:5, 8, *et al.*). *Cf.* also John 17:3.

8. John 12:46; 3:18–19; 3:36; 5:24.

9. John 15:4–10; 13:1, 14–15, *et al.*

10. John 6:47–51.

11. John 5:25–29.

well as making it possible for human beings to approach him.[12] It is important to grasp, nevertheless, how John views the *context* in which the revelation and glorification have taken place; for in one sense his total theological outlook derives from this. We now turn, therefore, to consider what may be termed the 'sacramental dimension' of the Fourth Gospel, from which John's special theological understanding takes its character.

THE SACRAMENTAL DIMENSION OF THE FOURTH GOSPEL

It cannot be denied that the Gospel of John contains 'sacramental' overtones which are absent from the synoptic Gospels. John 6, for example, in the 'bread of life' discourse following the feeding of the five thousand, has a decidedly eucharistic flavour.[13] It was interpreted in this light by the fathers of the early church, notably Clement of Alexandria, Origen and especially Cyprian.[14] Similarly, some modern commentators regard the discourse in John 6:25–71 as making explicit a connection, already present implicitly in the synoptic Gospels, between the feeding of the multitude and the events of the last supper;[15] and one writer claims that in Christ's vision of the great multitude needing to eat bread (John 6:5), 'every future eucharistic gathering could be seen'.[16]

If we allow that John introduces a 'sacramental dimension' into his Gospel, we must ask what accounts for this, and – more fundamentally – how John himself understands this dimension.

One explanation for the presence of 'sacramental' references in the Fourth Gospel is that John was writing his version of the Jesus tradition against a liturgical background. We noticed in the previous chapter that the influence of early church worship may be detected, for example, in the shaping of the Johannine supper discourse.[17] Even earlier, we found that such a scholar as Oscar Cullmann[18] has carried the 'liturgical-

12.   *Cf.* further, on the concept of 'eternal life' in the Fourth Gospel, *IFG*, pp. 144–50. On salvation as revelation in John see also J.T. Forestell, *The Word of the Cross: Salvation as Revelation in the Fourth Gospel*, AnBib 57 (Rome: Biblical Institute Press, 1974), esp. pp. 103–146. On 'glorification' in John see further below, pp. 248–56.

13.   Note esp. John 6:51–58.

14.   See Wiles, *Spiritual Gospel*, pp. 52–54. Wiles points out, however, that the eucharistic interpretation of John 6 takes a 'comparatively subordinate place' in the earliest exegesis of John, especially in that deriving from Alexandria (p. 52).

15.   So Lightfoot, pp. 155–56.

16.   Phillips, 'Faith and Vision', p. 90.

17.   See above, pp. 227–28; also Strachan, pp. 271–305, esp. 274–77, who believes that a 'Christian prophet', perhaps the fourth evangelist himself, presiding at the Lord's table, expanded and interpreted the words of Jesus in the upper room to give us the present supper discourse (p. 277).

18.   See Cullmann, *Early Christian Worship*, part 2.

sacramental' view of John to an extreme position,[19] in line with his conclusion that one of the chief purposes of this Gospel is to set forth the connection between the historical life of Jesus and the worship of the Johannine church. The result is that Cullmann interprets the narrative events of the Fourth Gospel, and especially the signs, in explicitly sacramental terms; and, as we saw, he associates most of John's signs directly with either baptism or the eucharist. According to Cullmann, this was John's own understanding; the evangelist believed that the sacraments are to the contemporary Christian church what the miracles of the historical Jesus were to his contemporaries.[20]

Such a view as Cullmann's represents one extreme of Johannine interpretation. The other extreme is illustrated in the work of Rudolf Bultmann, who (among others) regards the absence of overt references in the Fourth Gospel to baptism and the eucharist – notably the omission of the institution of the Lord's Supper – as evidence that John was a (gnostic) 'anti-sacramentalist'. Such precise sacramental reference as we now have in John, Bultmann argues, is the later work of an ecclesiastical redactor, who wished to make the Gospel more acceptable to the church at large.[21]

A more balanced opinion is provided by Raymond Brown, who nevertheless admits the validity of some of the points made on both sides of this debate.[22] Brown maintains that the fourth evangelist may well have been concerned to show how the institutions of the Christian life are 'rooted in what Jesus said and did in his life'.[23] But Brown hesitates to introduce a sacramental reference into John's 'symbolism' when none is positively demanded by the text itself, or derived from it by the early church.[24] He also suggests that some of the more explicit sacramental references in this Gospel may have belonged to later stages of its composition: but in terms of developing latent ideas, rather than introducing new ones.[25]

We may enquire, however, whether at any stage in the composition of the Fourth Gospel John is *primarily* concerned about the Sacraments of baptism and the eucharist as such – from the viewpoint of either a 'pro-sacramentalist' or an 'anti-sacramentalist'. To go no further, it *is* true – in favour of the 'anti-sacramental' view of John – that there is no direct narrative of the baptism of Jesus in the Fourth Gospel,[26] and no

19. See above, pp. 164–66.

20. Cullmann, *Early Christian Worship*, p. 70.

21. *E.g.* John 3:5; 6:51–58; 19:34–35. *Cf.* Bultmann, pp. 11, 138 n. 3, 234–37, 677–79.

22. See the useful section on 'sacramentalism' in Brown 1, pp. cxi–cxiv.

23. *Ibid.*, p. cxiv.

24. *Ibid.*, pp. cxii–cxiii.

25. *Ibid.*, p. xxxviii. *Cf.* the balanced view of the sacraments in John's teaching presented by Smith, *Theology of John*, pp. 155–60.

26. The baptism of Jesus is reported by John the Baptist, indirectly, in terms of the descent of the Spirit (John 1:32–34).

parallel to the baptismal charge of Matthew 28:19.[27] Furthermore, John omits any account of the institution of the eucharist, and replaces it with the narrative of the feetwashing (John 13). At the same time it is also true – in favour of the 'pro-sacramental' view – that allusions to one or other of the rites of baptism and the Lord's Supper cannot be excluded altogether from the natural exegesis of John's material in every part. Given this characteristic Johannine diversity, then, how are we to understand best the nature and quality of the 'sacramentalism' in the Fourth Gospel?

Symbolism and sacrament

It may help to clarify our thinking about this matter of the 'sacramental' in John, if we approach it by considering John's use of symbols.

The Fourth Gospel is full of symbols. Because John, as we have seen, thinks and moves so easily on two levels at once, the material and the spiritual, he is quick to evoke a spiritual truth by condensing it into the intelligible form of symbolic language. The motif of 'ascent and descent' in John – the 'ups and downs' of the Gospel – may be said to form a part of John's symbolism; so also may his theological contrast between light (representing goodness and life) and darkness (representing evil and death). Similarly the idea of 'witness' in this Gospel, which belongs centrally to John's theological conception of the ministry of Jesus as a 'trial', in which the defendant is also the judge, includes an obvious and important quality of symbolism.[28]

Even more obviously symbolic, it would seem, are the images which are used to describe Jesus in the Johannine 'I am' sayings. In a truly Hebraic fashion the spiritual qualities of Jesus, and thus the real nature of his person, here receive concrete expression. Symbolically, he is presented as the bread of life and the light of the world; the door of the sheep and the good shepherd; the resurrection and the life; the way, and the truth, and the life; and as the true vine.[29]

Possibly the 'geography' of John's Gospel is also symbolic in some respects. Wayne Meeks has suggested,[30] for example, that there is a 'geographical symbolism' in John, which is not – as in Luke, we may add – dominated by Jerusalem. Instead, John's symbolism in this respect is 'shaped by the apparently deliberate dialectic between Jerusalem, the place of judgment and rejection, and Galilee and Samaria, the places of acceptance and discipleship'.[31] Meeks further argues that this 'symbolism of places' reflects the experience of the Johannine

27. But cf. John 20:21–23.
28. For this section see above, pp. 153–54.
29. John 6:35; 8:12; 10:7, 11; 11:25; 14:6; 15:1.
30. W.A. Meeks, 'Galilee and Judea in the Fourth Gospel', *JBL* 85 (1966), pp. 159–69.
31. *Ibid.*, p. 169 (*cf.* John 11:7–8; 4:39–40, 45).

circle of Christianity. As Jesus 'stayed' in Samaria and Galilee because he was 'received' there,[32] but met with opposition in Jerusalem, so perhaps the Christians of John's church encountered polemic in the south but missionary success in the north – where possibly communities existed which gave rise to some of the Johannine traditions. If Meeks is right, of course, his thesis calls into question the claim – for which C.H. Dodd has argued so strongly[33] – that John's geographical framework and precise topography derive from an historical, southern Palestinian, tradition behind the Fourth Gospel.

In any case, the importance of symbolism to John cannot be doubted. He uses his own symbols in his own way; and he uses them to express and illuminate his particular theological understanding.[34] But John does not stop with the symbolic; he also thinks in terms of the 'sacramental'. The difference between these two concepts is important.[35] A symbol, within the Christian context, evokes and represents that which is spiritual and divine; whereas a sacrament actually *conveys*, through the material elements involved, what is spiritual and divine. For example, when Jesus says, 'those who drink from the water that I will give, will never be thirsty' (John 4:14), this may be described as a symbol of the life-giving power available to the believer through the living Christ. But when Jesus says, 'I am the resurrection' (John 11:25), and demonstrates this both by raising Lazarus from the dead, and by being himself raised from the tomb, this may be described as a part of the sacramental dimension to John's Gospel.

This brings us back to the seven signs, which form the structural and theological centre of the Fourth Gospel; for these will give us the clue to the real nature of John's sacramentalism. The principle underlying all the signs, as we have already discovered,[36] is announced in the introduction to this Gospel (John 1). There we are told of the Word made flesh (1:14). The flesh of Jesus is a fact of created existence, which for John not only symbolises the presence of God but also mediates it. The 'tabernacling' in Palestine was not a *picture* of God dwelling among his people.

---

32. Meeks (*ibid.*, pp. 167–68) notices that in the Fourth Gospel Jesus is frequently said to have 'stayed' (using μένειν) in the north, whereas μένειν ('to stay') is never used of his visits to Judea and Jerusalem. *Cf.* John 2:12; 4:40, *et al.*; see also 7:1–2. The theological theme of Jesus 'staying' or 'remaining' with his disciples is obviously related to this kind of language, and indeed derived from it; *cf.* also John 8:35; 12:34 (14:17); 15:4.

33. *Cf.* esp. *IFG*, pp. 452–53; *HTFG*, pp. 233–47, esp. 244–45.

34. For a useful and in-depth treatment of Johannine symbolism see C.R. Koester, *Symbolism in the Fourth Gospel: Meaning, Mystery, Community* (Minneapolis: Fortress Press, 1995). Koester shows how John's symbolic figures, actions and ideas can be interpreted at different levels, but find their centre and meaning in the person and work of Christ; *cf.* pp. 1–31, esp. 31.

35. When dealing with John's 'sacramental symbolism', Koester (*Symbolism*, pp. 257–62) does not appear to observe this distinction.

36. See above, pp. 129–31, esp. 130.

It was a real event, in which God was really and decisively present. From that moment of 'glory' onwards, history must be viewed in a new light; for now the material must always be regarded as the potential carrier of the spiritual, and the temporal as the possible medium of the eternal. Jesus has made God known in a new way; and now in a new way believers can know him, and live for him.[37]

This principle controls John's thinking throughout his Gospel. He sees very clearly that the incarnation is a climactic moment, the highest expression of the truth that God gives himself to humanity through material things. In and with the tabernacling of the Word of God among his creatures, a final intersection of spirit and matter has occurred. The signs in John's Gospel then demonstrate this truth effectively. In each case, John's readers are encouraged to look beyond the surface meaning of the signs to their real content. For John takes a number of ordinary facts, with which (like flesh, indeed) we are very familiar: water, wine, health, bread, sight, fish and even physical life itself. He thinks these through with what Hoskyns has called 'a truly biblical realism',[38] until the facts *become* what they represent. Jesus not only changes water into wine, for example; he is also responsible for the fresh centre to Judaism which that change signifies. He not only multiplies loaves, he also provides spiritual sustenance in the Christian life.

Together, the signs which Jesus performs in John's Gospel express as well as symbolise their basic meaning: that eternal life is given by God, to the believer, through Jesus the Messiah. The first six signify this meaning for the time of Jesus, and the seventh (the catch of fish) indicates the scope of the church's mission beyond that time. All seven signs find their fulfilment in the glorification of Jesus, who having revealed the glory, the true nature, of God was 'lifted up' in glory; and this is the basis of the Christ-Christian relationship for all time.

We can now begin to see the distinctive character of John's sacramentalism, and how it moves on from his symbolism. If we say, as we are doing, that John is a sacramentalist, this does not mean that he is concerned only about the two Sacraments of baptism and the eucharist. Rather, he is concerned more generally about 'the sacramental': the fact that since the incarnation there can be a new dimension to life, and that as in the time of Jesus, so now, the spiritual can give life to the material in a qualitatively new way. John focuses this understanding in the miracles of Jesus which he selects for our consideration, and which he treats sacramentally in association with the discourses. Symbolism is still involved, of course, in John's over-all sacramental thought; so that when Jesus speaks of 'eating the flesh of the Son of man and drinking his blood',[39] for example, we must assume (unless an exegesis is followed in

37. John 1:18; 17:3; 14:12–13 (*cf.* 6:63).
38. Hoskyns, p. 108.
39. John 6:53.

this passage which interprets these words in terms of eucharistic transubstantiation) that he is using a symbol. However, the symbolic and the sacramental are obviously inter-related. But whereas the sacramental in John is always symbolic, not every symbol is sacramental.

A vital part of John's sacramental thinking, arising from his distinctive view of history (which we discussed earlier),[40] is that he takes creation seriously. John sees that the material can mediate the spiritual;[41] and the focus of this understanding appears in his presentation of the signs, where the 'first level' (matter) points to and conveys the second (spirit). Therefore the world in all its aspects is important to John. His special sacramental outlook emphasises that the basis of salvation – the eternal life which God gives through Jesus – is historical. Even if the events which he describes in the life of Jesus have a symbolic and sacramental value, they begin as facts: as real events in time and space. Creation is significant for John, as well as recreation.[42]

This does not mean that John was a pantheist, who blurred the distinction between God and his creation by seeing everything through 'sacramental' eyes. Instead, he believed that for the purpose of salvation God worked *through* creation. For this reason Oscar Cullmann may well be right when he argues that in the Fourth Gospel as a whole John, through the incarnate life of Jesus, throws light backwards and forwards on the entire history of salvation in such a way as to reflect deliberately the Old Testament pattern of creation followed by the history of Israel.[43]

It was not only creation in general which concerned John. His sacramental treatment of the signs in this Gospel shows that life in all its aspects – physical, as well as spiritual – engaged his attention. As C.F.D. Moule has shown,[44] God through Jesus is responsible – according to John – for *all* life. As a result, in the Johannine signs Jesus constantly restores the *physical* norm (the sight of a man blind from birth, for example, or the life of a man who had been dead four days – and would die again); and only when this has taken place is physical renewal fitted to point to spiritual regeneration.

40. See above, pp. 209–210.

41. *Cf.* John 1:51; and above, pp. 137–39.

42. It is interesting that Evelyn Underhill, who regards the Fourth Gospel as 'in no sense a historical, but poetic and devotional book', should nevertheless insist that the events described by John were not merely symbols. For him, she claims, 'they were doubtless facts *and* symbols'. See E. Underhill, 'The Johannine Mystic' in *The Mystic Way: A Psychological Study in Christian Origins* (London and Toronto: J.M. Dent, 1913), pp. 211–57, esp. 216–17, 224–25.

43. O. Cullmann, 'L'Évangile Johannique et L'Histoire du Salut', *NTS* 11 (1964–65), pp. 111–22, esp. 120. Note the 'creation' allusions in the opening of John provided by the echo of Gen. 1:1 in John 1:1, and the possible (creation) 'week' of six days covered in John 1:29–2:1. But see Olsson, *Structure and Meaning*, pp. 23–25, 102–104, who finds in John 1:19–2:11 an 'introductory week' of six days, related to the week of preparation at *Sinai*.

44. Moule, 'Meaning of "Life" '.

Thus, in John's particular sacramental theology, much as in his theology generally, the 'glory' and 'flesh' of Jesus cohere. The Jesus who raises Lazarus also weeps at his tomb. Similarly, the life which Jesus makes available to the believer in every age is both symbolised and signified in the miraculous actions which he performs by using ordinary elements. Throughout the Fourth Gospel those actions are emphatically great: the amount of water changed into wine is vast, Jesus is far from the official's son when he heals him, the crowds needing food number thousands, and before Lazarus was raised to life he had been dead four days. The reason for this emphasis is not that the miracles are intended to be understood as acts of power which herald the arrival of God's kingdom. Such was perhaps the synoptists' view. Rather, John wants his readers to see that both levels of existence (the human and natural, as well as the divine and supernatural) are important, and that one level points to the other. At the same time, just as the Johannine miracles (unlike the synoptic) consistently provoke reaction – whether faith or unbelief – so John wishes the signs which he records to evoke from his audience a free decision of faith.[45]

We have seen that in one sense everything for John is potentially sacramental. Even if, for this very reason, he omits such an overt reference to the Sacraments themselves as the institution of the eucharist, we need not conclude that he wishes to exclude all mention of baptism and the Lord's Supper. If these should occur to the reader, as surely they must when parts of John are read, the fourth evangelist would not perhaps complain. But our suggestion is that he would be happier if the whole of the Gospel were read, and all Christian experience viewed, with the sacramental dimension in mind.[46]

THE CHRISTOLOGY OF THE FOURTH GOSPEL

It is a marked feature of John's Gospel that its presentation of the person of Christ in many respects goes beyond the christology of the synoptic Gospels. No doubt this is the result of the further reflection which was undertaken within the Johannine church, when on the basis of authentic Christian tradition a more profound interpretation was given to the nature of Jesus. In John's christology, moreover, we now have the key to his theology.[47]

45. *Cf.* John 7:40–41; 9:16 (20:31). See further, on this section, E. Lohse, 'Miracles in the Fourth Gospel' in Hooker and Hickling (ed.), *What about the New Testament?*, pp. 64–75, esp. 72–73.

46. See further, on the Johannine sacramentary, Smalley, 'Liturgy and Sacrament': esp. for a critique of Cullmann's view of John's sacramentalism in his *Early Christian Worship*.

47. Note Mlakuzhyil, *Christocentric Structure*; also Smith, *Theology of John*, esp. pp. 80–135.

The special contribution which John makes to the understanding of Christ's person concerns the relation between Jesus and God on the one hand, and between Jesus and believers on the other. First, John sees Jesus – in true synoptic fashion – as God's functionary, his agent on earth, who was sent to accomplish the Father's work.[48] But also, and in this respect there is an advance upon the synoptic view of Christ, John perceives that there is a complete unity at the level of being, which also existed before time, between Jesus (as the Word) and God.[49] Moreover Jesus, in St John's Gospel, is aware of this special relationship between himself and God. He knows, for example, about the glory which he shared with the Father before the world was made.[50] Above all, in the words of Anthony Hanson, he does not seem to live on earth by faith; 'he gives the impression of omniscience'.[51] Thus, by his very presence in the world, the Word, who was with God in the beginning, is able to reveal the glory of God; and by performing the tasks which God has given him to do, he continues the work of God himself among his people.[52] Both functionally and ontologically, then, Jesus (according to John) is one with God. Therefore the Johannine Christ who says, 'my Father is greater than I', also claims that 'I and the Father are one'; therefore the judgment and life of God himself are not only present in the ministry of Jesus, but also mediated by him.[53] For John, the Father is 'in' Jesus, and Jesus is 'in' the Father.[54]

Secondly, John also sees Jesus as one with us. The stress on the humanity of Jesus in the Fourth Gospel is well known, and we have discussed it earlier.[55] In this respect John's christology coincides with that of the synoptic writers. They also insist that Jesus shared with God's creatures a fully human existence. John's christology develops beyond this understanding, however. He is not only aware of the genuine humanity of Jesus, as well as the Son's unity of being with God the Father; he is also aware that the divine nature of God is communicated *through* the human nature of Jesus. In the flesh of Jesus, the grace and truth of God are to be found.

48. *Cf.* John 4:34; 5:36; 17:4.

49. Notice the high christological implications in the designation θεός ('God'), as used of Jesus in John's Gospel (John 1:18, *s.v.l.*; 20:28; *cf.* John 1:1; 1 John 5:20). See further B.A. Mastin, 'A Neglected Feature of the Christology of the Fourth Gospel', *NTS* 22 (1975–76), pp. 32–51.

50. John 17:5.

51. Hanson, *Grace and Truth*, p. 73.

52. *Cf.* John 1:1; 1:14 (2:11); 5:17. Note the hostile reaction of the Jews in 5:18 to the claim of Jesus, 'My Father still works, and I am working', because they interpreted those words as a bid from the Son for equality with God.

53. John 14:28; 10:30; 3:35; 5:26–27.

54. John 10:38.

55. See above, pp. 56–61. *Cf.* John 1:14, *et al.*

By saying this, we have been brought back to the characteristic diversity of John's christology, which perhaps, as we suggested earlier,[56] arose from the aim of his Gospel: to provide a balanced view of the person of Christ for the sake of those with an unbalanced christological outlook. We have also returned to the theme of our previous section in this chapter, where we noticed that the essence of John's sacramentalism is to be discovered in his opinion that with the incarnation, and since that moment, the spiritual is decisively given and received through the material.

John's distinctive presentation of the person of Jesus in terms of both pre-existent divinity and real humanity is noteworthy for two further reasons. One is that this christological approach is the basis of John's total theology of salvation. As always in the new Testament, soteriology and christology are inextricably related. Because Jesus participated fully in the two natures, human and divine, he was able to make God fully known and also to be perfectly the way to him. Furthermore, the unity of the incarnate Son with the Father is the ground, in Johannine terms, of unity between the believer and the Godhead, as well as of unity between the believer and other Christians.[57]

The other noteworthy fact about John's christology is that it seems to stand alone in the New Testament. Here was a courageous theological development in primitive Christianity: for John did not merely state the fact that Jesus shared fully in two natures; he also pointed the way towards a resolution of the tension which such a christology involves. It was from John, in fact, that the early fathers took their cue when they eventually formulated their own 'two natures' christology at the Council of Chalcedon in AD 451.[58]

We may now test and expand the description of John's christology just offered, by looking briefly at four richly descriptive titles for Jesus which are freely used by the writer(s) of the Fourth Gospel.[59] Only one, the title 'Son of man', is used openly of Jesus in the synoptic Gospels; and John's Son of man sayings are all unique to him. So again we are dealing here with what may be regarded as distinctively Johannine theological interpretation.

(a)   Son of Man

Any study of the expression 'Son of man', as used in the New Testament (mostly in the Gospels), is beset with complex problems. In

---

56.   See above, pp. 181–85.

57.   Cf. John 14:18–24, esp. verses 20, 23; 17:11, et al.

58.   So Hanson, Grace and Truth, pp. 73–74. See further below, pp. 276–82.

59.   New Testament christology cannot be elucidated purely by a study of the titles of Jesus. But, certainly as a means of understanding John's interpretation of the person of Christ, they are helpful markers. See also F. Hahn, The Titles of Jesus in Christology: Their History in Early Christianity (London: Lutterworth Press, 1969), esp. pp. 347–51, where the 'common traits' (p. 347) in the New Testament titles of Jesus are drawn out.

particular, we need to investigate the background to this term, in Judaism as well as Christianity, and try to decide whether Jesus himself used it, and if so of whom. Before a 'Son of man' christology is put together from John's Gospel, therefore, all the relevant critical issues should be carefully considered. However, this is not the place to reproduce a discussion of the Son of man problem in all its aspects, since material on this subject is already available, with reference to both the synoptic Gospels and John.[60] Instead, assuming the results of earlier enquiry,[61] we shall come straight to the theological significance of the Johannine Son of man sayings themselves.

If John's Son of man christology stems from a primitive tradition about Jesus, and indeed belongs as a result to the earliest christological stratum within the Fourth Gospel (and we submit that both of these suggestions are reasonable),[62] it is likely that the Son of man sayings in John will form an important and controlling witness to the evangelist's view of Christ's person. We find that in fact this is the case. The thirteen uses of the expression 'Son of man' in John's Gospel[63] – beginning with 1:51, which forms an introduction and guide to the meaning of the others[64] – are used to expound the central christological theme of the identity of Jesus, who is related intimately both to God and to humankind.[65]

The Son of man tradition in the Gospels generally associates the figure of the Son of man himself with the theme of vindication after suffering; and this is a theme belonging to the figure as he appears in Daniel, 1 Enoch and 2 Esdras.[66] In John the Son of man is similarly one who

60. See further I.H. Marshall, 'The Synoptic Son of Man Sayings in Recent Discussion', *NTS* 12 (1965–66), pp. 327–51; also Smalley, 'Johannine Son of Man Sayings' (and the literature cited in both articles).

61. My own view, set out in 'Johannine Son of Man Sayings', is that the expression 'Son of man' was taken over by Jesus from a Jewish, especially Old Testament, Son of man concept – the background to which is fundamentally Hebraic – and used of himself (so Moule, ' "Son of Man" ', p. 278) in preference to the explicit title 'Messiah'. The Son of man logia in John are indeed distinctive, and betray evidence of Johannine 'tinting' (*cf.* the element of pre-existence in John 3:13, *et al.*). But, with the possible exception of 9:35 (*pace* Maddox, 'Function of the Son of Man', pp. 198–200), I regard these sayings in the Fourth Gospel as dependent on a primitive christological tradition parallel to that behind the synoptic Gospels. For alternative views see Smalley, 'Johannine Son of Man Sayings', pp. 278–81. See also B. Lindars, 'The New Look on the Son of Man', *BJRL* 63 (1981), pp. 437–62, esp. 460–62 (the Son of man sayings in John are inauthentic, but based on tradition); *cf.* also Lindars, *Jesus Son of Man*, esp. (on John's theology), pp. 145–57.

62. See the previous note.

63. John 1:51; 3:13; 3:14; 5:27; 6:27; 6:53; 6:62; 8:28; 9:35; 12:23; 12:34 (*bis*); 13:31.

64. See further above, pp. 137–39.

65. *Cf.* Lindars, 'The Son of Man in the Johannine Christology' in *idem*, *Essays on John*, ed. C.M. Tuckett, SNTA 17 (Leuven: Leuven University Press and Peeters, 1992), pp. 33–50. See further above, pp. 183–85.

66. *Cf.* Mark 8:31 par. *et al.*

suffers and is then exalted; although in typical fashion most of the Johannine sayings include the two ideas of humiliation and honour in one expression: as, for example, when Jesus speaks of being 'lifted up' or 'glorified'.[67] John differs from the other Gospel writers, however, in that usually his sayings lack the synoptic emphasis on the vindication of the Son of man in future glory.[68] But this is because of John's particular eschatological outlook, which – as we shall be seeing later[69] – causes him to merge into one the chief historical moments involved in the salvation event: the incarnation, passion and parousia of Jesus, for example. As a result, it is difficult if not impossible to classify the Johannine Son of man sayings into the three groups – logia referring to the earthly ministry, the passion and the future return in glory of the Son of man – which are normally used by critics to describe the synoptic version of this tradition.

The Son of man figure in the Fourth Gospel, it may thus be argued, is not essentially different from his synoptic counterpart, even if he appears in different sayings. Moreover, there is another important point of contact, in that the Johannine Son of man is a real and representative figure, as in the tradition generally.[70] John's sayings, however, draw out the implications of this truth further. For him Jesus as Son of man is not merely the embodiment of the new and true Israel – he is the 'true vine'[71] – but also true *Man*: humanity as it should be, upon which God has set his seal. In line with John's normative christology, this is because the Son of man is one with both God and humankind. He ascends into heaven, having descended from it.[72] As such, he can establish a decisive link between heaven and earth, between God and his creation.[73]

We have reached the heart of John's Son of man christology. In the Fourth Gospel the Son of man is above all the one who because of his unique nature can bring heaven down to earth, and earth up to heaven. Moreover, John takes this christology one stage further by letting us glimpse the pre-existent character of the Son of man. He is one with God not only in time and beyond time, but also before time. He comes from God and is exalted to God. By 'descending from heaven', therefore, and undergoing a death which is at the same time glorification, he can be the Saviour of all believers.[74] Precisely because he *is* the Son of man, Jesus

---

67.   *Cf.* John 3:14; 8:28; 12:34 (using ὑψοῦν, 'to lift up'); 12:23; 13:31 (using δοξάζειν, 'to glorify').

68.   *Cf.* Mark 13:26 par.; 14:62 par., *et al.* But note John 5:27.

69.   See below, pp. 265–69.

70.   Note the 'Adamic' background to the expression, '(one like a) son of man' in Dan. 7:13–14 (also Psa. 8:4; Ezek. 2:1, *et passim*); *cf.* also Matt. 8:19–20 par., *et al.* See further Sidebottom, *Christ of the Fourth Gospel*, pp. 96–97.

71.   John 15:1 (1:47–51); *cf.* Psa. 80:8–19; Isa. 5:1–7, *et al.*

72.   John 1:51; 3:13; 6:62; 13:31.

73.   John 1:51.

74.   John 3:13; 12:23, 34; 13:31 (*cf.* 12:32; 4:42).

can bring God's judgment continually to the world, and enable the believer to live eternally.[75]

A final point of interest in connection with the Johannine Son of man logia is that the main statements of the kerygma in the Fourth Gospel are all given in terms of John's Son of man christology: as Son of man, Jesus comes into the world, dies, is exalted, and is given the authority to execute judgment.[76]

(b)   Logos

This is John's special christological title, which is used in the opening section of the Fourth Gospel (1:1–14), but not afterwards. At that point the title 'Son' seems to take over.

We have already discussed the background to the *Logos* terminology in the Johannine introduction, and noticed that the associations of the term are Jewish as well as Greek.[77] To this extent such a title as *Logos* would be intelligible and significant to all sections of John's readership as we have defined this: both Hebrew and Hellenistic. Similarly if, as we have suggested, the introduction to John were written last,[78] this means that the Johannine theology of the *Logos* belongs to the environment in which the Fourth Gospel was received, and not to its (Palestinian) background.

Given this title, then, what does it signify? Once more we find John's characteristic theology of the person of Christ asserting itself. Eternally and pre-existently, the Word is one with God, and even identified as God.[79] Like the figure of Wisdom,[80] the Word of God is always 'with God'. Yet, like Wisdom again, the Word of God is also and throughout time the faculty by which God is at work in the world, accomplishing his purposes.[81] God spoke in creation; and for purposes of salvation he also spoke through the prophets.[82] At the appropriate moment in time,

75. John 5:27; 6:27, 53.

76. John 3:13; 3:14; 12:23; 5:27. See further, on the Son of man in John, C.F.D. Moule, 'Neglected Features in the Problem of "the Son of Man" ' in J. Gnilka (ed.), *Neues Testament und Kirche: Für Rudolf Schnackenburg* (Freiburg im Breisgau: Herder, 1974), pp. 413–28, esp. 421–22 (the Son of man title is used by Jesus not only to refer to himself, but also to describe his vocation to be God's true people, suffering and vindicated). *Cf.* also F.J. Moloney, *The Johannine Son of Man*, 2nd edn., BDSR 14 (Rome: Libreria Ateneo Salesiano, 1978); and J.D.G. Dunn, *Christology in the Making: A New Testament Inquiry into the Origins of the Doctrine of the Incarnation*, 2nd edn., (London: SCM Press,1989), pp. 88–90.

77. See above, pp. 47–48, 62–63.

78. See above, p. 156.

79. John 1:1.

80. *Cf.* Prov. 8:22–31.

81. *Cf.* Isa. 55:10–11.

82. Gen. 1:3; Psa. 33:6, *et al.*; Jer. 1:4–5, *et al.*

moreover, the divine speech was given ultimate and fulfilled expression; for the Word became flesh.[83] This was no temporary conjoining; the Word actually – and for all time – *became* one with us, as with God. When that tabernacling was complete, and the glory of God could be fully seen, the purposes of God could be finally accomplished.[84]

Here again we are reminded forcibly, at the very opening of John's Gospel, of the evangelist's distinctive christology, with its two poles of the deity and the humanity of Jesus.

(c) Son (of God)

The christological title to which *Logos* seems to give place in the Fourth Gospel is that of 'Son of God'. It is probable therefore that John's use of 'Son' will include some of the theological ideas which we discovered behind his use of *Logos*. At the same time, the titles 'Son of God' and 'Son of *man*' in John are related. This relation is not, of course, in terms of the divinity as opposed to the humanity of Jesus. For John's 'Son of man' terminology, as we have seen, included both ideas; and we are about to see that the same is true of his 'Son of God' christology. The relation between 'Son of man' and 'Son of God' in this Gospel has rather and most obviously to do with the fact that in both cases the identity of Jesus is described in terms of the 'Son' image, which is used to represent his unique relationship to both God and the world.

Already we can see that we are dealing here with an immensely significant aspect of John's christology. This becomes even more apparent when we remember that the fourth evangelist declares that his main purpose in writing his Gospel is to make Jesus known as both Christ and Son of God.[85] Possibly, as we have suggested earlier,[86] the use of two titles for Jesus at this point indicates the 'double' nature of John's audience: Jewish, as well as Greek. But even if there is a Greek background to the *term* 'Son of God', associated particularly with the θεῖος ἀνήρ ('divine man') figure of the Hellenistic world, there is also an important Jewish background. Israel was chosen by Yahweh to be his 'son', and Israel's kings were 'sons' of God in the sense of being the representatives of Yahweh's people.[87] Similarly, in Hellenistic Judaism the expression 'son of God' could be used of a righteous man who was loyal to God's law.[88] In all these instances of the use of the term 'son of God' in Jewish literature, the sonship in question is determined not by blood-relationship but by obedience to God's covenant. 'If Israel, or the

83. John 1:14*a*; the Greek (ὁ Λόγος σὰρξ ἐγένετο, lit. 'the Word flesh became') is emphatic.

84. John 1:14*b*, *c*. For John's use of the title *Logos* see further *IFG*, pp. 263–85.

85. John 20:31; *cf.* 11:27.

86. See above, p. 181 n. 103.

87. *Cf.* Hos. 11:1; Psa. 2:7, *et al.*

88. *E.g.* Wisdom 2:18.

king of Israel, is the son of God, he is so by adoption, not by procreation.'[89]

The understanding of the sonship of Jesus in the Fourth Gospel builds essentially on these Jewish antecedents, but is carried further. Jesus proves his obedience to God, and therefore his true sonship, by accomplishing the work which the Father gives him to do.[90] He is 'sent' by God as revealer; and, in truly prophetic fashion, Jesus comes to the world in God's name and as his representative.[91] He arrives with the delegated authority of God himself, and is charged with the two essentially divine activities of bringing judgment and giving life.[92] In this work the Father and the Son are completely at one. Jesus speaks and acts not on his own initiative, but entirely in accordance with God's will and at his command. His dependent obedience, and therefore his sonship, are perfect.[93]

Once more the twin poles in John's christology are beginning to emerge. For the period of the incarnation, the relationship of Jesus to God may be described as that of 'Son' to 'Father'; and from his baptism onwards[94] he appears in one sense to be no more than a Son who – among us, and for our sake – is consistently obedient to God's will. But the sonship of Jesus is unique: because he is not only one with humanity, but also one with God. He moves among mankind as Son of man and Son of God. He does so as a Son who is *eternally* related to the Father. He is 'from the Father', and 'from above'.[95] His sonship is distinctive; and it is effective for us *in* time because it is *beyond* time. In every respect the Son is one with the Father, as well as being one with his creatures. Thus Jesus can baptise with the Holy Spirit, and dispense life, and (at the Father's charge) lay down his life and take it again.[96] Thus also the love of God is 'released in history', and people can be brought into the same unity among themselves as that which is typified in St John's Gospel by the relation of the Father and the Son.[97]

(d)   Christ (Messiah)

As we have noticed, the intention of the Fourth Gospel is primarily related to the identity and function of Jesus as both Christ and Son of

---

89. *IFG*, pp. 252–53. For a further account of the background to the Johannine 'Son of God' christology see *ibid.*, pp. 250–53.

90. John 17:4.

91. John 5:37, 43; 13:20; 15:23.

92. John 5:21–23 (*cf.* 5:17, 19–20).

93. John 5:30; 8:28; 12:49, *et al.*

94. John 1:32–34.

95. John 16:28; 8:23, 26–27.

96. John 1:33; 10:10, 18. Note in John 10:18 the ambivalence characteristic of the fourth evangelist's christology. Jesus acts on his own accord, but *also* by his Father's authority.

97. *IFG*, p. 262; *cf.* John 17:21–22, *et al.* For further discussion of the christological expression 'The Son (of God)' in John see Harris, *Prologue and Gospel*, pp. 155–72.

God.[98] John shares with the Synoptists the title of 'Christ' for Jesus; but the obvious difference is that the so-called 'messianic secret' of the first three Gospels does not appear as such in the Fourth Gospel. According to the synoptic tradition Jesus was only hesitantly confessed as Messiah, and he did not openly accept the title: presumably to avoid political confusion.[99] In the Johannine account of the ministry, however, the messianic nature of Jesus seems to be openly acknowledged from the beginning. The first disciples 'find' the Messiah,[100] Jesus tells the Samaritan woman that he is the Christ;[101] and people claim, even at the risk of excommunication, that Jesus and the Messiah may be the same person.[102]

When we were examining the relation between the synoptic and Johannine traditions, we considered this difference.[103] We argued then that the variation between John and the other Gospel writers in their presentation of Jesus as Messiah should not be exaggerated. For a start, John appears to have his own version of the 'secret' that Jesus was Messiah. For in the Fourth Gospel the eye of faith is still needed to 'see' the true messianic identity of Jesus; and the challenge 'if you are the Christ, tell us plainly' is still put to Jesus by the Jews.[104] Also, as in the other Gospels, those who have eyes to see can perceive the witness borne to Jesus by his works.[105]

Nevertheless, it is a fact that from this point of view John's portrait of Jesus has an individual appearance; and this may well be the result in part of John's theological interpretation. Further reflection on the person of Jesus, and an intense concern to demonstrate his true identity, caused John perhaps to 'historicise' what he came to realise was theologically always true: that the messiahship of Jesus, like his glory, was hidden from sight only by unbelief.

What, then, is the significance of John's use of 'Christ' as a title for Jesus? The background to the concept of 'Messiah' is obviously and intensely Jewish, and the Johannine portrait of Jesus as the Christ – like the synoptic – shares this fully. John is also aware, like any good Jewish person, of the kingly and triumphal implications of the figure of Messiah: whether these were by association political, or religious, or both. However, once more John's christology – while ultimately indebted to a Jewish-Christian tradition familiar to all the Gospel writers – is taken

98. Cf. John 20:30–31.
99. Mark 8:29–30 par., et al.
100. John 1:41–42, which may well be John's version of the 'confession' at Caesarea Philippi in Matt. 16:13–20.
101. John 4:25–26.
102. John 7:41–42; 9:22; 11:27, et al.
103. See above, pp. 28–29.
104. John 10:24.
105. John 10:25; cf. Matt. 11:2–6, et al.

further. To this end John interprets the messiahship of Jesus by linking it to the notions of 'derivation' and, in a developed sense, 'kingship'.

An abiding concern in the Fourth Gospel, as part of John's unfolding of the true identity of his central character, is the origin of Jesus. The question 'where are you from?'[106] is always in the air, and no more so than in connection with the potentially messianic nature of Jesus. The Jews at the Feast of Tabernacles (John 7), in response to the unhindered and authoritative teaching of Jesus, speculate about his possible identity as the Christ. Yet, they say, 'we know where this man comes from'; and – according to Jewish tradition – 'when the Christ appears, no one will know where he comes from' (verse 27). Again, we are presented with John's ambivalence. In one sense the Jews *did* know about the origin of Jesus; they thought he came 'from Galilee' (verse 41).[107] But in another sense they could not guess that the real origin of Jesus Christ was 'from God', who 'sent' him (verse 29), and that in truth he 'stays for ever'.[108] The Messiah, who was associated with Galilee, and descended from David (verse 42), also performed signs (verse 31) and discerned hearts[109] and elicited faith.[110] For Jesus is one with both humanity and God.

John also develops his presentation of the messiahship of Jesus in conjunction with the theme of 'kingship'. The confession in the introduction to the Gospel by Nathanael, that Jesus was both Son of God and King of Israel,[111] contains important messianic overtones. Jesus is the embodiment of the new and true messianic community, and its leader.[112] It is possible that similar implications about the identity and function of Jesus as victorious Messiah are also involved, but almost certainly not alone, in the announcement by John the Baptist that Jesus is the 'Lamb of God'.[113] Manifestly the Johannine account of the triumphal entry into Jerusalem,[114] also, underlines (even more than the synoptic account) the kingly nature of Jesus as Messiah; for only John reports that the crowds greeted Jesus as 'King of Israel'.[115] In the trial of Jesus before Pilate,[116] finally, the theme of kingship in connection with the origin, and by implication the messiahship, of Jesus receives – as we saw earlier – its clearest expression.[117]

106. *Cf.* John 19:9.
107. *Cf.* John 1:45–46 ('from Nazareth').
108. John 12:34.
109. John 4:29; *cf.* 2:25.
110. John 11:27.
111. John 1:49.
112. The whole passage, John 1:47–51, is a commentary on this point.
113. John 1:29, 36. Dodd (*IFG*, pp. 230–38) argues that 'Lamb of God' here is a messianic title, virtually equivalent to 'King of Israel' (p. 238). See below, pp.254–55.
114. John 12:12–19.
115. John 12:13. But see Matt. 21:9, which uses the proximate expression 'Son of David'.
116. John 18:33–19:22.
117. See above, pp. 151–52.

In what sense is Jesus a *kingly* Messiah? We have noticed John's ambivalence on this point already.[118] In one sense Jesus could be regarded, and even crucified, as a political pretender to the throne of Israel. The disciples themselves did not fully comprehend the implications of the triumphal entry, for example, which on the surface was so obviously open to a political and materialistic interpretation.[119] In any case, it needed the eye of faith to see that the figure who entered Jerusalem riding on an ass's colt, and not – in typically regal fashion – on horseback, was indeed the messianic king of Zechariah's prophetic vision. At one level, then, the kingship of Jesus could be understood and accepted in worldly terms. But at another level the kingship of Jesus was 'not from this world'.[120] He could not be made a King by force.[121] Although the King dies, he remains for ever.[122] Jesus as the Christ shares fully the natures of both God and humanity, so that now, through his final triumph on the cross, he is able to give life to those who believe in him.[123]

We have seen that John's major christological titles are all interpreted with reference to his basic understanding of the person of Jesus: as both divine and human. We have also discovered that John's christology is intimately related to his soteriology. As the revealing and glorified Son of man, incarnate Logos, Son of God and Messiah, Jesus, in whose flesh the spiritual is decisively communicated, becomes the final mediator of eternal life. We turn now to this further dimension of John's christology: the Word glorified, as well as the Word revealed and revealing.[124]

GLORIFICATION IN THE FOURTH GOSPEL

Only John among the Gospel writers sees the death of Jesus as his 'glorification' (using the verb δοξάζειν). When the evangelist comments,

118. See above, p. 246.
119. John 12:14–16.
120. John 18:36.
121. John 6:15.
122. John 12:34.
123. *Cf.* John 20:31.
124. For this section see further J.A.T. Robinson, 'The Use of the Fourth Gospel for Christology Today' in Lindars and Smalley, *Christ and Spirit*, pp. 61–78. See also W. Loader, *The Christology of the Fourth Gospel: Structure and Issues*, BET 23 (Frankfurt am Main: Peter Lang, 1989), which adopts a structural and theologically thematic, rather than traditional-historical approach, to the topic (note pp. 226–32); J.W. Pryor, *John: Evangelist of the Covenant People: The Narrative and Themes of the Fourth Gospel* (London: Darton, Longman and Todd, 1992), pp. 115–56; R.E. Brown, *An Introduction to New Testament Christology* (London: Geoffrey Chapman, 1994), pp. 196–213; R. Schnackenburg, *Jesus in the Gospels: A Biblical Christology* (Louisville: Westminster John Knox Press, 1995), pp. 219–94, esp. (for the balance in John's view of the person of Jesus), pp. 289–94; Smith, *Theology of John*, pp. 124–35.

for example, that 'the Spirit had not yet been given, because Jesus had not yet been glorified',[125] or that after Jesus had been 'glorified' his disciples applied to him Zechariah's prophecy about the triumphant arrival of the messianic king in Jerusalem,[126] he is referring to the crucifixion of Jesus: which at the same time he sees as his exaltation. By speaking of the cross in this way, John is beginning to interpret the death of Jesus according to his own developed understanding. What exactly does he mean by 'glorification'?

In the Old Testament the 'glory' of God refers to a visible disclosure of the divine presence and nature in significant actions. For example, the Israelites were promised a vision of God's 'glory' by Moses, when the manna was about to fall from heaven;[127] and they were made aware of God's presence and guidance when his *shekinah* 'glory' was disclosed in both cloud and fire during their wilderness wanderings.[128] In the Fourth Gospel Jesus, as the incarnate Word, reveals *fully* the real presence and nature of God; and he does so both generally in his life on earth, and particularly in his signs. As we have seen already, John's characteristic way of expressing what happened in the incarnation is to say that the 'glory' (δόξα) of God was to be seen in him; and that in the performance of his miracles Jesus manifested his glory, which was ultimately God's glory.[129] The pre-existent glory which Jesus shares with God because he is one in nature with him,[130] a glory which even before the incarnation was glimpsed by the prophets,[131] is now radiated by the life and actions of Jesus, and constitutes a decisive communication of the nature and presence of God himself to the world.

It is against this background of John's presentation of the life of Jesus that we must understand the Johannine interpretation of Christ's death as 'glorification'. Christology and soteriology cannot be separated in the Fourth Gospel. The life and death of Jesus – who he was, and what he did – are held together by John, and understood as one. When, therefore, Jesus in this Gospel refers to his approaching death by using the language of 'glorifying', or 'being glorified',[132] or when John describes the cross

125. John 7:39.

126. John 12:16 (referring to Zech. 9:9).

127. Exod. 16:7.

128. *Cf.* Exod. 16:10; 24:15–18.

129. John 1:14; 2:11; 11:40. In our view, John sees this disclosure as taking place in signs which were performed on either side of the resurrection; see above, pp. 129–32.

130. John 17:5, 24.

131. John 12:41 (referring to Isa. 6:10). See further on this passage Brown 1, pp. 486–87; Beasley-Murray, pp. 215–18; Carson, pp. 447–51, esp. 450. Carson thinks that the fourth Evangelist had the Servant Song of Isa. 52:13–53:12 in mind when he composed chapter 12.

132. *E.g.* John 12:23; 13:31–32; 17:1, 5.

in this way,[133] the meaning is plain: what began in the incarnation was completed in the crucifixion. In the words and actions of Jesus during his ministry, the life-giving presence of God was specially brought to earth. In a final act of self-giving on the cross, after which Jesus returns to the Father, the eternal life or 'glory' of God is made available to every believer for all time; although John does not in fact say how this happens.

In the life and death of Jesus together, then, the glory of God is to be 'seen'. But in neither case is the fourth evangelist saying that a 'revelation' was involved, and nothing more. In the life of Jesus, as the signs illustrate so clearly, the nature of God was really present and really given. Similarly, in the death of Jesus the salvific purposes of God reached their completion. Thereafter it becomes possible for those who have not seen Jesus in the flesh, but who have believed that he is the messianic Son of God, to live eternally.[134]

The death of Jesus is seen as his 'glorification' in John's Gospel, moreover, because the cross was not the end. Jesus rose again. The synoptic writers are also aware, of course, that the crucifixion of Jesus was followed by his vindication in resurrection.[135] But John, with characteristic 'telescoping',[136] sees that the risen Jesus – indeed, the ascended and exalted Jesus – is always alive and ever triumphant.[137] The glorification, like the glory, of Jesus is vividly apparent to John from the beginning, and not only (as in the synoptics) after the resurrection. When Jesus was 'lifted up' on the cross,[138] it was a movement of eternal triumph and exaltation. He ascended the tree always to reign from it.

Because of this, John can use the category of 'glorification' in a timeless way, and with subtle changes of meaning or even with double meanings. Thus, according to John, the name of God is glorified when the Son honours the Father by his obedience; and Jesus himself has been glorified, obtaining honour for himself with a triumphant glory not his own, even *before* the crucifixion.[139] Again, Jesus will be glorified, and glorify God, in his coming death and exaltation.[140] Finally, the Father will be glorified in the future by the discipleship of Christ's followers,[141] who are able through him to share the glory of God for themselves.[142]

133. John 7:39, *et al.*
134. John 20:29, 31; *cf.* 3:16–18.
135. Luke includes a probable reference to the ascension of Jesus (Luke 24:51, where the better MSS omit the words, 'and was carried up to heaven'; *cf.* Acts 1:9); and Matthew hints at this (Matt. 28:16; the disciples meet the risen Jesus on a *mountain*).
136. See further, on John's eschatological outlook, pp. 265–70.
137. But *cf.* John 20:17, where Jesus tells the Magdalene that he has 'not yet ascended'.
138. John 12:32, *et al.*
139. *Cf.* John 12:28; 13:31; 17:4 (note the use of the aorist tense, denoting a completed action in the past, in each passage).
140. John 12:28*c*; 17:1, 5.
141. John 14:13; 15:8.
142. John 17:22, 24.

All this is characteristic Johannine interpretation. The incarnate Word who reveals, is also the Word who is glorified.[143] Not surprisingly, John's presentation of the passion is affected by his understanding of its meaning. He shares with the synoptic Gospels, but independently of them, a common Christian tradition about the passion of Jesus: that he was arrested, tried, crucified and raised from the dead. But he treats this tradition in his own way, as we shall now see.

There are three directions in which John's account of the passion differs from the synoptic.

(a)   Omission

John does not describe as such the betrayal of Jesus by Judas Iscariot; although prior warning of this has been given.[144] He does not mention the agony of Jesus in the garden of Gethsemane,[145] or the mourning of the women who followed Jesus to Calvary.[146] The Fourth Gospel also omits any reference to the fact that Simon of Cyrene carried the cross of Jesus,[147] that Jesus was mocked while he was on the cross,[148] that in death he uttered a cry of dereliction,[149] and that when he died various portents occurred such as darkness, earthquakes and the tearing of the temple veil.[150]

(b)   Emphasis

On one or two occasions John seems to emphasise aspects of the passion tradition which he has received. Thus, using a different set of testimonies from the synoptists, he stresses that the death of Jesus was the inevitable fulfilment of scripture;[151] he enlarges upon the potential

143. It is possible, however, that John's theology of glorification has a kerygmatic background. At Acts 3:13 Peter says that God 'glorified (using δοξάζειν) his servant Jesus'. *Cf.* also Luke 24:26; and 1 Peter 1:11, where 'suffering' and 'glory' are linked. See the treatment of glorification in the Fourth Gospel by Smith, *Theology of John*, pp. 115–22. According to Smith (p. 122), John's concept of glory is both traditional and, because of the death and resurrection of Jesus, radical.

144. John 13:21–30 (*cf.* Mark 14:10–11 par.); note also John 18:2–3.

145. But there is a possible, traditional, version of this at John 12:17–28 (*cf.* Mark 14:32–42).

146. *Cf.* Luke 23:27–31.

147. Mark 15:21 par.

148. Mark 15:29–32 par.

149. Mark 15:34 par.

150. Matt. 27:45–54 par.

151. John 19:28, 36–37 (note esp. verse 36*a*). Although John's testimonia are unique to him, note that the Synoptic Gospels *allude* to Psa. 22:18, which John actually *cites* (*cf.* Mark 15:24; John 19:24). For the 'inevitability' of the cross, in both the synoptic and Johannine traditions, see Mark 8:31 par. (using δεῖ, 'must') and John 11:50 (18:14); 13:1, *et al.*

scope of the cross by mentioning the three languages in which the 'title' was written;[152] and he draws special attention to the anointing of Jesus for burial and the emptiness of his tomb on the resurrection morning.[153] But these are all traditional elements, even if John has underlined them, or presented them in a different light. As with the mention of Mary and the beloved disciple at the cross,[154] which would have an obvious and special interest for the fourth evangelist, we need not assume that John is redacting his tradition here for theological purposes. He is probably instead drawing on his own historical sources.

(c)   Addition

John's passion narrative includes features which are not only his own, but are also at times presented in characteristic Johannine language. 1. Jesus gives himself up to his captors at the time of his arrest.[155] 2. The comment at John 18:32 suggests that Jesus was handed over by the Jews to the Roman authorities so that he could be crucified (in Johannine terms, 'lifted up'), rather than stoned.[156] 3. During the Roman trial, Jesus engages with Pilate in a discussion about true kingship.[157] 4. According to John, Jesus is on the cross at the time of the preparation for the Passover, and therefore dies when the sacrificial lambs were being killed.[158] 5. Jesus carries his own cross to Golgotha.[159] 6. On the cross Jesus utters a cry not of dereliction, but of triumph: 'It is finished.'[160] 7. After his death a soldier pierces the side of Jesus, from which issue blood and water.[161] 8. In the discussion on Easter morning between the risen Jesus and Mary Magdalene, the language of 'ascent' is much in evidence.[162] 9. In the meeting between Jesus and Thomas after the resurrection, there is a discussion about the relation of 'seeing' to 'believing'; and Thomas confesses Jesus as his Lord and God.[163]

John's theology of the cross

On the basis of the special character which the fourth evangelist gives to his account of the passion, a character which becomes very clear (as

152.   John 19:20; but *cf.* Luke 23:38 in some versions.
153.   John 19:38–20:10.
154.   John 19:25–27.
155.   John 18:1–11.
156.   So *IFG*, pp. 426–27, 433–35; similarly, Carson, p. 592.
157.   John 18:33–38.
158.   *Cf.* John 19:42.
159.   John 19:17.
160.   John 19:30.
161.   John 19:34; *cf.* Exod. 12:21–22.
162.   John 20:17 (using the theological term ἀναβαίνειν, 'go up', 'ascend').
163.   John 20:26–29.

we have just noticed) when the Johannine tradition is compared with the synoptic at this point, we may now make the following observations about John's theology of the cross.

(i) Much more than the synoptic writers, John *has* a theology of the cross. He understands and interprets the death of Jesus from his particular point of view. The absorbing interest of the Fourth Gospel, as we have suggested, is (for the sake of its readers) the identity of Jesus; and the chief emphasis in its theology is therefore christological. This is not to say that John minimises the importance of the death of Jesus. But he does not concentrate on the cross in isolation from the person and life of Jesus. Instead, he views the cross christologically. His task is not to work out, as Paul attempts to do, *how* we are saved through the cross; but to show that because the death of Christ includes his exaltation, and reveals him as the Son who 'had come from God and was going to God',[164] we *can be* saved. As a result there is a sense in which St John's Gospel is 'one continuous passion narrative', in which the good news is proclaimed that the crucified Jesus is the glorified Son.[165]

(ii) Because for John the 'glory' of the cross is manifested at the moment of crucifixion, he reports that Jesus died with a word of victory and not defeat upon his lips. The work he had been given to do was 'finished'.[166] The miracles described in the other Gospels as accompanying the death of Jesus find no place in John. For him the crucifixion itself was a self-evident glorification: an enthronement, a 'lifting up', which carried with it exaltation. On the morning of the resurrection, therefore, Jesus can speak to Mary of his 'ascent' to the Father as both future ('I have not yet ascended') and present ('I am ascending').[167] At one level the 'descent' of Jesus to earth and to crucifixion is itself the beginning of his 'ascent' in glory.

(iii) John's distinctive christology emerges in his presentation of the death of Jesus, no less than elsewhere in the Gospel. During his passion, as throughout his life and ministry, the Johannine Jesus is seen to be at one with the natures of both God and humanity. His 'hour' is an hour of glory, not agony. He is in charge of the passion events: giving himself up to his captors,[168] baffling the procurator Pilate in theological argument, going voluntarily to the cross. As true King, he has the power not only to lay down his life, but also to take it again.[169] Yet his death was a real death. There was no need for the soldiers to break the legs of Jesus

164. John 13:3.

165. *Cf.* Fortna, 'Christology in the Fourth Gospel', esp. pp. 502–504.

166. John 19:30. Notice, however, that in the Marcan account of the passion, and its Matthean parallels, the Jesus who dies in dereliction is also recognised as 'a son (or the Son) of God'; *cf.* Mark 15:39 (Matt. 27:54).

167. John 20:17.

168. But note the 'control' implied in Matt. 26:53–54.

169. John 10:18.

on the cross because he was 'already dead',[170] so they pierced his side instead. Whatever symbolism may be read into the 'blood and water' which follow the spear-thrust,[171] the primary reference of this well-attested fact – John insists that the testimony of the witness is 'true' – seems to be physical. There was no doubt about the death, or indeed the burial, of Jesus. Similarly, after the resurrection Jesus was recognised as the man whose hands and side had been pierced on the cross; and he was also the man who shared a breakfast of bread and grilled fish with seven of the disciples by the sea of Tiberias.[172]

(iv)   The pattern of the death of Jesus, as understood by the fourth evangelist, is 'sacramental' in the Johannine sense of that word which we have already defined.[173] Here is the fulfilment of all the signs, by which the glory of God is not only revealed but also given, and given for eternity. In the incarnation of the Word, flesh becomes the carrier of spirit; in the glorification of Jesus, death becomes the carrier of life. Lazarus was raised to physical life, only (we must assume) to die physically again. But this sign was a pointer to the truth which was expressed in the glory of the cross: that for every believer the death and exaltation of Jesus mean life through death, and life beyond death. 'Happy are those who have not seen and yet believe.'[174]

(v)   Although John, as we have recognised, is not specific about the way in which salvation through the cross of Christ 'works' – what, for example, he would regard as the precise connection between the death of Jesus and the forgiveness of sin – there are elements in his account of the passion which suggest that he was familiar with the common Christian idea of Jesus dying 'for' our sin. (In 1 John the idea is explicit.[175]) In particular, the understanding of the death of Jesus as a vicarious sacrifice, a concept which has an important background in Judaism, may well be present to the fourth evangelist's mind. Thus it is not impossible that theological as well as traditional[176] considerations brought about John's chronology of the passion, whereby Jesus dies as the passover lambs are killed. As it now stands, John's dating of the crucifixion in any case reminds us of the description of Jesus by John the Baptist, which appears only in the Fourth Gospel, that he was '*the* Lamb of God'.[177] Varied as the background and meaning of that phrase may be,[178] it seems impossible to make proper sense of it without taking into account the prob-

---

170.   John 19:33.
171.   John 19:34–35; *cf.* 4:14; 6:55. That a reference to baptism and the eucharist is intended at 19:34 is very doubtful.
172.   John 20:27; 21:12–13 (15).
173.   See above, pp. 232–38, esp. 235–38.
174.   John 20:29–31.
175.   *Cf.* 1 John 2:2; 4:10 (using the term ἱλασμός, 'atoning sacrifice').
176.   See above, pp. 27–28.
177.   John 1:29, 36.
178.   See *IFG*, pp. 233-38; also Beasley-Murray, pp. 24–25.

ability that Jesus was regarded by the fourth evangelist as a sacrifice for sin – associated with the paschal lamb,[179] or the 'lamb' of Isaiah 53, the suffering servant, or both.[180] Certainly the idea of Jesus suffering for others vicariously is picked up at various points in the Gospel from John 1 onwards.[181]

Furthermore, the fact that Jesus is described by John alone as bearing his own cross to Golgotha[182] may be an allusion to the sacrifice of Isaac, who himself carried the wood upon which he was to be offered.[183] If so, the sacrificial aspect of the cross of Jesus may be in view here.[184] Equally, however, John may be emphasising that it was Jesus and no other (not Simon of Cyrene himself, for example, as the docetists were to say) who died on the cross which was carried; and that Jesus was all-sufficient and in control when he was glorified.[185]

(vi) We have pointed to John's christological interpretation of the cross, and noticed that – despite an awareness of the sacrificial nature of the death of Jesus – he does not work out a 'theology of atonement' as such. To this extent it could be argued that John was paving the way for an 'exemplarist' view of the cross.[186] According to this view, Christ's passion and death are seen primarily as revealing the truth that self-sacrificial love lies at the heart of God's dealings with humanity, and also as an example which Christians themselves are to follow in their own lives and relationships. Historically, Christians have found that such a view needs to be complemented with a more objective understanding of the death of Jesus, associated first with the theology of Paul. This interpretation sees the death of Jesus as making possible the removal of a barrier between a holy God and his sinful creatures.

Nevertheless, while it is true that John's theology of salvation leans in an exemplarist direction, it is not wholly exemplarist in character. For John shows us that through the incarnate and glorified Word of God

179. *Cf.* Exod. 12:1–27. The passover motif in John is in any case strong.

180. See further Schnackenburg 1, pp. 297–300; Carson, pp. 148–51; also S.S. Smalley, 'Salvation Proclaimed: VIII. John 1.29–34,' *ExpT* 93 (1981–82), pp. 324–29, esp. (on John 1:29) pp. 325–26.

181. *Cf.* John 3:14–16; 10:11, 15; 11:50–52; and note the reference to Exod. 12:46 in John 19:36.

182. John 19:17.

183. Gen. 22:6.

184. Although Isaac did not in fact die; and thus he is used by the writer of Hebrews as a type of the resurrection of Jesus (*cf.* Heb. 11:17–19).

185. See Barrett, p. 548. On the idea of 'liberation from sin' generally in John's Gospel see W.G. Kümmel, *The Theology of the New Testament: According to Its Major Witnesses – Jesus, Paul, John* (London: SCM Press, 1974), pp. 296–98, esp. 297–98. Forestell, *Word of the Cross*, pp. 58–102 (see also pp. 190–93) views the death of Jesus as integral to the Johannine understanding of salvation: but in terms of the culmination of the revelatory work of Jesus, and *not* as an 'expiatory sacrifice' for human sin (p. 101).

186. The stance of Forestell, *Word of the Cross*.

earth and heaven are finally conjoined; and that through him also exists for everyone the possibility of freedom from darkness and death. So even if John sees in the ministry of Jesus a pattern to follow, he also knows that eternal life ultimately depends on seeing who Jesus is, and – like Thomas – believing in him as the unique life-giver who 'came from God' and 'was glorified'.[187]

SPIRIT AND CHURCH IN THE FOURTH GOSPEL

We have been considering various aspects of John's particular theology of salvation. Related to this same theological area is the Johannine interpretation of the Spirit, with which may be linked the doctrine of the church in the Fourth Gospel. In his understanding of both Spirit and church we shall find that once more John makes a major contribution to the Gospel tradition.

The Spirit in John's Gospel is seen as the agent of regeneration, who brings believers into a dimension of new life which is shared by the whole church. An important commentary on the idea of spiritual regeneration is provided by the discussion between Jesus and Nicodemus in John 3:1–8, where Jesus tells the ruler of the Jews that entry into the kingdom of God is impossible 'unless one is born of water and the Spirit' (verse 5).[188] The background to this passage lies in the Old Testament (rather than in Hellenism),[189] where the gift of the Spirit – often in association with (cleansing) water – is promised to God's faithful people as a mark of the new age which will arrive in the 'last days'.[190] Jesus expounds this eschatological concept to Nicodemus in association with the theme, present but uncommon in Judaism,[191] of new birth. He says, in effect, that since the Word has become flesh the new age of the Spirit has been inaugurated. Now it is possible for the believer, who submits to God's kingly rule through the glorified Christ, to live eternally by being 'baptised with the Holy Spirit'.[192]

In general, such theology has a synoptic flavour;[193] although when, according to John, Jesus speaks of entry into the kingdom of God in

187. *Cf.* John 13:15, 34*b*, *et al.*; 20:26–29. See further, on John's soteriology, Kümmel, *Theology*, pp. 288–321; note also R. Newton Flew, *The Idea of Perfection in Christian Theology: An Historical Study of the Christian Ideal for the Present Life* (Oxford: Oxford University Press, 1934), pp. 92–117, esp. 116–17 (on 'the Johannine theology'). On 'glory', and the glorification of the Son of man in John, see further de Boer, *Johannine Perspectives*, pp. 176–217.

188. See also and esp. John 3:3–4, 6–8.

189. Schnackenburg 1, p. 371, points out the fundamental difference between the idea of 'rebirth' in the mystery religions, and the Christian doctrine of regeneration.

190. *Cf.* Joel 2:28–29; Isa. 44:3; Ezek. 36:25–27; note also 1QS 4. 19–21.

191. See Brown 1, pp. 139–41.

192. *Cf.* John 1:33.

193. *Cf.* Mark 1:8, 15, *et al.*

terms of birth 'from above',[194] this seems to be a distinctively Johannine idea which is being used in a new way. However, the fact that in John 3 'birth from above' and 'birth from water and the Spirit' are used by Jesus synonymously, does not necessarily mean that John is thinking exclusively or even at a 'second level' of rebirth in terms of regeneration through Christian baptism.[195] His theological individuality at this point arises in another way. For there is only one reference to 'water' (and the Spirit) in the whole of this discourse; so that presumably the speaker does not intend the subject of rebirth to be understood solely in the light of this single allusion. Moreover, the association between water and Spirit, as an eshatological gift, was (as we have noted) already present in Judaism.

Above all, John (we submit) was not primarily interested in the Sacraments as such. Even if a baptismal interpretation cannot be excluded altogether from the notion of regeneration in John 3, therefore, its immediate reference seems to be – as we have suggested – to the 'giving' of the Spirit to believers through Jesus when he has been glorified.[196] In this way, and only in this way, can we be created anew, and share – through the agency of the Spirit – in the life of God. John's doctrine of the Spirit in relation to the individual believer brings us back to his characteristic theology of salvation: from the incarnation onwards heaven and earth are decisively conjoined.

The Paraclete

In addition to being involved in the new birth of the individual, the Spirit is described by John as given to the church at large, in order to sustain the common life of Christian believers, as the promised Paraclete (Παράκλητος). This again is a distinctively Johannine category; and by looking at it carefully we shall once more be made aware of the considerable advance in the interpretation of New Testament Christianity which John's theology represents.

The term 'Paraclete' is confined – perhaps because of the writer's sources – to the farewell discourse in the Fourth Gospel; although within the few chapters concerned (John 14–16) there is a significant amount of material available to help us answer the two questions which will now occupy us. Who is the Paraclete, and what does he do?

Who is the Paraclete?

We have indicated already that we accept the identification of the Paraclete as the Holy Spirit; and indeed this is an identification which is

194. John 3:3, 7 (using ἄνωθεν, 'anew', or 'from above').
195. See further Brown 1, pp. 141–44, and the literature there cited.
196. John 7:39.

made by John himself, since he reports that Jesus spoke of 'the Counsellor (ὁ Παράκλητος), the Holy Spirit, whom the Father will send in my name' (John 14:26). Scholarly opinion, however, is divided on the exact nature of the Paraclete, and varies between regarding this as impersonal, or personal, or both. George Johnston, for example, challenges the common assumption that in John's Gospel 'paraclete' is the title of a person, and that it is proper to speak at all about 'the Paraclete'.[197] Johnston argues that the fourth evangelist saw the Spirit-Paraclete as the impersonal 'divine energy' which inspires certain Christian leaders, notably teachers, prophets and martyrs. For John, therefore, the church itself as a community of love can be the embodiment of the paraclete. The background evidence on which Johnston bases this interpretation is exclusively Judaistic. He suggests that John has combined the impersonal Jewish concept of a 'spirit of truth', derived from the Old Testament and Qumran, with the idea of a functional and representative spirit (paraclete) sent from the Father in the name of Jesus, or by Christ himself. John's reason for doing this, Johnston believes, was to refute heretical claims for an angel-intercessor (Michael) as the spiritual guide and guardian of the Christian church.[198]

On the other side Raymond Brown, who also locates the background to the Johannine Paraclete in Judaism, comes to the conclusion that we should view this figure in personal terms.[199] Brown regards three Jewish concepts as illuminating in this connection: the 'tandem' relationship of salvific figures such as Moses and Joshua, and Elijah and Elisha (compare also John the Baptist and Jesus); the prophetic spirit coming upon people to interpret God's activity to them; and late Jewish angelology: the angel figures of the later Old Testament period, who intervene actively in human affairs, and the Qumranic 'angel defender' figure. All these ideas, Brown claims, have been Christianised by the fourth evangelist, and drawn into his concept of the Paraclete as the *alter ego* ('other I') of Jesus: the spiritual presence of Jesus in the community of disciples.

The important work on this subject by Otto Betz represents a mediating position.[200] Betz points, among other issues, to the way in which

197. G. Johnston, *The Spirit-Paraclete in the Gospel of John*, SNTSMS 12 (London and New York: Cambridge University Press, 1970), esp. p. 81.

198. *Ibid.,* esp. pp. 119–48. See also A.R.C. Leaney, 'The Johannine Paraclete and the Qumran Scrolls' in Charlesworth (ed.), *John and Qumran,* pp. 38–61. Leaney maintains that the Fourth Gospel regards Jesus as paraclete because he was God incarnate, and as such the bestower of spirit (= the power of God). John's identification of the Paraclete as 'the Spirit *of truth*' may have been prompted by his realisation of the need for (christological) truth in his own community.

199. R.E. Brown, 'The Paraclete in the Fourth Gospel', *NTS* 13 (1966–67), pp. 113–32.

200. O. Betz, *Der Paraklet: Fürsprecher im häretischen Spätjudentum, im Johannes-Evangelium und in neu gefundenen gnostischen Schriften,* AGSU 2 (Leiden: E.J. Brill, 1963). For a summary of this work in English see Johnston, *Spirit-Paraclete*, pp. 80–83.

John's own descriptions of the Paraclete slide between the personal and the impersonal. Personally, the Paraclete is to stay with the disciples always; but the paraclete as 'power' is also sent to the disciples, and breathed into them.[201] Betz therefore concludes that the nature of the Johannine Paraclete is both personal and impersonal: a person who succeeds Jesus, the first Paraclete,[202] *and* a heavenly power.[203]

The evidence about the nature of the Paraclete in John's Gospel is thus open to different constructions, and is indeed apparently not altogether consistent in itself. We shall not be able to find a solution to this problem for ourselves without considering, as we are about to do, the *ministry* of the Spirit-Paraclete in John. Before that, however, two points should be made in connection with the views just summarised.

First, to interpret John's theology exclusively in terms of Jewish antecedents, and without reference to the person or teaching of Jesus, as Johnston does, is likely to result in odd conclusions. Similarly, to assume that the Jewish understanding of 'spirit' in any form was entirely imper-sonal, which is Johnston's starting-point, is unwarranted.

Second if, as Betz maintains, John appears to describe the Spirit-Paraclete as simultaneously a person and a power, this is perhaps because of a characteristic Johannine theological outlook. The view which John takes of the Paraclete's nature is, in fact, similar to his 'two level' understanding of the person of Jesus. For the Paraclete comes from God when Jesus goes away, and is 'sent' from both the Father and the Son.[204] The Paraclete is thus one with God and the glorified Christ, revealing their nature.[205] But he is also the agent of God and Christ among his creation, acting – as we shall discover – on their behalf in the church and in the world. In one sense, like the Father and the Son, the Paraclete *is* the truth and also instructs truthfully;[206] but in another sense he does not speak on his own authority.[207] Like the Father and the Son, again, the Paraclete indwells the church; but he is also 'sent' by both God and Jesus, and indeed 'given' by God at his Son's request, for this very purpose.[208] We conclude, therefore, that the Paraclete in John is by nature both one with God and 'at one' with the church.

201. *Cf.* John 14:16–17; 16:7; 20:21–22.
202. *Cf.* John 14:16, in which Jesus speaks of 'another' Paraclete; and note 1 John 2:1, where *Jesus* is referred to as Παράκλητος. John 14:16 can only with difficulty be interpreted to mean that the Spirit is 'another one, that is a Paraclete' (ἄλλον, Παράκλητον). The natural sense, as in 1 John 2:1, is that Jesus is the first Paraclete, and the Spirit is the second. So E. Frank, *Revelation Taught: The Paraclete in the Gospel of John*, ConBNT 14 (Lund: Gleerup, 1985), p. 38; similarly Carson, pp. 499–500.
203. See Betz, *Der Paraklet*, pp. 2, 159–64, *et al.*
204. John 15:26; 16:7*a*; 14:26; 16:7*b*.
205. *Cf.* John 16:14–15.
206. John 14:17; 16:13.
207. John 16:13.
208. John 14:17 (*cf.* verse 23); 14:26; 16:7; 14:16.

What does the Paraclete do?

A consideration of the Paraclete's ministry in the Fourth Gospel will throw further light on his nature.

The Greek associations of the term παράκλητος are to some extent legal;[209] but various *non*-legal functions are also ascribed to the Johannine Paraclete: for example, teaching and prophecy.[210] Furthermore, even the forensic duties of the Spirit-Paraclete need clarification. The usual interpretation makes the Paraclete an 'advocate', in the sense of counsel for the defence, as in the NRSV translation of Παράκλητος as 'Advocate'. But in the farewell discourse the Paraclete is essentially counsel for the *prosecution*;[211] and the only defence he makes, in the sense of 'witness', is of Jesus and not of the disciples.[212] Thus we must be on our guard against the search for a unitary definition of the function – or indeed the nature – of the Johannine Paraclete figure. His ministry is too varied to be interpreted against the background of a single (legal) image; and his person and work together are so many-sided that no one English translation of the Greek term Παράκλητος (not even the popular versions, 'Comforter' and 'Counsellor') can really be regarded as adequate. For this reason we shall continue to use the transliteration 'Paraclete'.

What, then, does the Paraclete do? He occupies two major roles: one in relation to the church, and one in relation to the world. In the church he indwells the disciples; he teaches them everything, and reminds them of all that Jesus said while he was with them; he bears witness to Jesus, which means that he reveals Jesus and interprets him to the disciples; and the Paraclete, as the Spirit of truth, guides the disciples into all the truth and declares to them 'what is to come'.[213]

In the world, the Paraclete again bears witness to Jesus, especially when the disciples are persecuted; and he also effects a ministry of discrimination, convicting the world of sin and of righteousness and of judgment.[214]

We can now begin to see that both the nature and the ministry of the Paraclete, as described in the Johannine farewell discourse, are consistent with the person and work of the (Holy) Spirit as presented elsewhere in John, and indeed elsewhere in the New Testament. Like the Paraclete,

209.   See further Brown 2, pp. 1135–39.
210.   John 14:26; 16:13. 'Comfort' (or 'consolation') is an idea in John associated with Jesus after the resurrection (*cf.* John 14:18, 27, *et al.*); but it is never stated directly in the farewell discourse that the Paraclete will comfort the disciples.
211.   John 16:7–11.
212.   John 15:26.
213.   John 14:16–17; 14:26; 15:26; 16:14; 16:13.
214.   John 15:26 (*cf.* verses 18–25); 16:8–11. On the meaning of the latter passage see B. Lindars, 'ΔΙΚΑΙΟΣΥΝΗ in Jn 16.8 and 10' in *idem*, *Essays on John*, pp. 21–31.

the Spirit in John outside the supper discourse is presented as intimately related to both God and Jesus;[215] and similarly Paul can speak of the Holy Spirit as both the Spirit of God and the Spirit of Christ.[216] Again, the Paraclete in John acts as the Spirit does in all parts of the New Testament – for example, he enables witness to be borne to the risen Jesus, and he teaches and defends the disciples, particularly in a situation of persecution.[217] We shall not be mistaken, therefore, if we identify the Johannine Paraclete with the Spirit himself.

But the Paraclete in John is not just the Spirit with another name, even if 'Paraclete' and 'Holy Spirit' appear together as synonymous in John 14:26. For the Johannine doctrine of the Paraclete adds to what we know of the Spirit from elsewhere. In particular, the Paraclete is not only (as we saw earlier) like Jesus in nature; he is also like Jesus in activity. Almost point by point, what can be said of the Paraclete after the resurrection can be said of Jesus during his ministry. Both Jesus and the Paraclete come into the world from God; they both stay with the disciples and – as the truth – teach them what they need to know; they both bear witness; as Jesus glorifies the Father, so the Paraclete glorifies Jesus; as believers 'see' the identity of Jesus, so the disciples will recognise the Paraclete; and as the world rejected Jesus, so it cannot receive the Paraclete.[218]

In other words, the Paraclete is indeed the *alter ego* of Jesus. He acts in the church and in the world *for* the risen Jesus, and *as* Jesus; he is the second ('another') Paraclete, as Jesus is the first.[219] For this reason it appears that the most obvious and illuminating way of understanding John's theology in this area is to interpret the Paraclete (with Brown) in thoroughly personal terms. John does not go as far as Paul, and identify the Spirit-Paraclete and the 'Spirit of Jesus';[220] but the implications of his pneumatology are the same.

It seems likely, then, that in view of the message of Jesus, the fourth evangelist brought together the concepts of 'Spirit' and 'Paraclete' in order to describe and interpret further what Jesus himself said – with or without the use of the term 'Paraclete' – about his intimate relation in the Spirit to the Father, and (after the passion) to the disciples and the world. If so, we can fully determine John's theology of the Spirit only by holding together what he says in his Gospel about both the Holy Spirit and the Paraclete. Then the picture becomes clear. Before the resurrection, the Spirit of God 'descends' upon Jesus at the start of his ministry,

215. *Cf.* John 4:24 ('God is Spirit'); 20:22 (Jesus says, 'receive the Holy Spirit').

216. *Cf.* Rom. 8:9.

217. Acts 5:32; Luke 12:12; Matt. 10:19–20.

218. John 16:28 (15:26); 12:35 (14:17); 14:6, Jesus is 'the truth' (14:17, the Paraclete is the 'Spirit of truth'); 7:14–17 (14:26); 8:18 (15:26); 17:4 (16:14); 1:41 (14:7b); 5:43 (14:17a).

219. John 14:16.

220. Phil. 1:19; see Gal. 4:6.

and 'remains' upon him.[221] He thus becomes the carrier of the Spirit. Jesus also *gives* the Spirit after his crucifixion (glorification). Possibly John believed that this happened at the moment of death.[222] But in any case, after the resurrection – and even before the ascension – Jesus breathes on the disciples and says, 'Receive the Holy Spirit.'[223] As promised in the farewell discourse, the Spirit-Paraclete now indwells the church until the parousia, and as the agent of God continues the ministry of Jesus to the believer.[224] In this capacity he provides the disciples with both the means for their worship, and the authoritative power for their mission.[225] The Spirit-Paraclete, who assists the disciples with their task of witness, also challenges the surrounding world of opposition.[226]

From the Fourth Gospel, it may be concluded, we learn more about the *nature* of God's Spirit, for the Spirit-Paraclete is also found to be the Spirit of Jesus (even if that is not John's language); and we learn more about the *activity* of God's Spirit, because the Spirit-Paraclete is also found to be the agent among believers of both God and the risen Christ.

A final point must be made about the Johannine theology of the Spirit-Paraclete. Possibly John's passionate interest in the identity of Jesus has influenced his pneumatology. We have already noticed a 'two level' dimension in John's view of the Paraclete's nature, echoing the Johannine two-level christology. It is worth noticing further that *the Spirit-Paraclete also bears testimony himself to the two natures of Jesus.* Part of the Paraclete's function is to 'glorify', or manifest, the real nature of Jesus, and interpret his person to the disciples.[227] He witnesses thus to the Christ of both earth and heaven: to the very words which Jesus spoke during his incarnate ministry, and to his exalted status with the Father.[228]

221. John 1:32–33.

222. *Cf.* Barrett, pp. 88–89, and (cautiously) 554. *Cf.* John 19:30. G. Bampfylde, 'John xix.28: A Case for a Different Translation', *NovT* 11 (1969), pp. 245–60, suggests that παρέδωκεν τὸ πνεῦμα in 19:30 means (Jesus) 'handed over the (Holy) Spirit'. Against her view see Schnackenburg 3, p. 285.

223. John 20:22.

224. John 14:16–17; 16:14.

225. John 4:23–24; 20:21–23.

226. John 16:8–11 (*cf.* 15:18–27).

227. John 16:14–15.

228. John 14:26; 15:26. See further on this subject H. Windisch, *The Spirit-Paraclete in the Fourth Gospel* (Philadelphia: Fortress Press, 1968); U.B. Müller, 'Die Parakleten-vorstellung im Johannesevangelium', *ZTK* 71 (1974), pp. 31–77; Schnackenburg 3, pp. 138–54; Franck, *Revelation Taught* (the Paraclete's role is multidimensional, but essentially didactic, pp. 145–47); J. Breck, *Spirit of Truth: The Holy Spirit in Johannine Tradition, 2* vols. (Crestwood: St Vladimir's Seminary Press, 1991 [vol. 2, forthcoming; vol. 1 of this work deals with the mostly Jewish *Origins of Johannine Pneumatology*]); S.S. Smalley, 'The Paraclete: Pneumatology in the Johannine Gospel and Apocalypse' in Culpepper and Black (ed.), *Exploring the Gospel of John*, pp. 289–300.

The Church

John's theology of the church is closely related to his theology of the Spirit. Indeed, we have already begun to consider the one with the other; for, as we have seen, the Spirit who brings the believer into the church is at work both in the Christian community and in the world at large.

The term 'church' (ἐκκλησία) as such is not used in the Fourth Gospel; but the idea and reality of the church are presupposed throughout. The company of the disciples, from the first moment of their-calling, forms the nucleus of a new and growing community of which Jesus is the head.[229] Significantly, Nathanael acknowledges Jesus from the beginning as 'King of Israel', the leader of the true messianic society.[230] And before his passion Jesus prays not only for his own disciples, but also for those who will believe in him through their word.[231]

In line with Old Testament imagery, and developing from it, the Christian fellowship in John is represented as the new Temple, the new Israel, the flock of the good Shepherd and the branches of the true Vine.[232] Ultimately, no limits are imposed upon its membership; Samaritans and Greeks, as well as Jews, belong to it.[233] So its missionary task is seen to be universal in scope.[234]

The doctrine of the church in John provides us with a good example of the many-faceted nature of Johannine theology. For the concept of ecclēsia in this Gospel involves a tension between the individual and the corporate.

The Fourth Gospel as a whole possesses a strongly individualistic character.[235] Many sayings of Jesus in John, for example, refer to the relation between individuals and himself.[236] Four out of the seven Johannine signs involve individual people,[237] and the most 'representative' of the pre-resurrection signs – in the sense that it points forward to the resurrection-life which Jesus brings to all mankind – concerns the raising of one individual, Lazarus (John 11). The same individualism characterises John's ecclesiology. To describe the Christ-Christian relationship, John uses distinctive ideas which appear to be thoroughly corporate: such as temple, shepherd and vine. But manifestly these images include an individual dimension; the temple is built of stones, the flock is made up of sheep and the vine contains branches.

229. John 1:35–51.

230. John 1:49.

231. John 17:11, 20.

232. John 2:13–22, esp. verse 21 (cf. Ezek. 37:27–28; also 1 Cor. 3:16–17); 8:31–58 (cf. Isa. 63:16); 10:14–16 (cf. Psa. 80:1; Ezek. 34); 15:1, 5 (cf. Psa. 80:8–19; Isa. 5:1–7).

233. John 4:39–42; 12:20–21 (cf. 1:35–37).

234. John 10:16.

235. So C.F.D. Moule, 'The Individualism of the Fourth Gospel', NovT 5 (1962), pp. 171–90.

236. E.g. John 4:13–14; 5:25–29; 6:43–51.

237. John 4 (the official's son); 5 (the sick man); 9 (the blind man); 11 (Lazarus).

At the same time, however, the corporate aspect of the church is also evident in John's Gospel. The images just mentioned, for example, are obviously collective in their primary reference. Furthermore, the Johannine theme of corporate belonging – to Christ and to other Christians – complements that of individual belonging. This theme is focused in the Twelve, who appear under that title on only two occasions in John,[238] but are present throughout as the seminal nucleus of a new community. The disciples are called to follow Jesus individually;[239] yet they believe in him together, and after the resurrection experience corporately the indwelling and activity of the Spirit-Paraclete.[240] In other words, the theology of the church in John is nicely balanced between the one and the many.[241]

John's balanced view of the church, as both individual and corporate in its character, forms an interesting parallel to the Pauline doctrine of the church as the 'body of Christ'.[242] Both John and Paul are concerned about the church's unity. But whereas Paul argues – at least in 1 Corinthians 12 – for unity in diversity,[243] John (and here his interpretation is markedly developed, certainly in relation to the ecclesiology of the synoptists) thinks of the church's diversity – in terms of its individual membership – as subordinate to its unity. Jesus prays that in the end the unity of the church may not only exist, but also be perfect; and, as such, reflect the unity and mutual indwelling of the Godhead.[244] The togetherness of the Christian community, moreover, is seen by John as evidence of God's love for the church and as a testimony to its risen Lord.[245]

Church and Spirit

The remaining point in this section ties together the doctrines of both the church and the Spirit in John which we have been considering. It is that the dimension of both is eschatological. The gift of the Spirit, to the church and to the individual believer, forms part of the parousia of Jesus, and points towards its final stage.[246] To that extent the church lives 'in

238. John 6:67, 70; 20:24. Significantly, perhaps, this title is used of the disciples on both sides of the resurrection.

239. John 1:43, *et al.*

240. John 14:16–17 (note the plurals in the Greek).

241. See further Smalley, 'Diversity and Development', pp. 282–83.

242. *Cf.* Rom. 12:4–5; 1 Cor. 12; Eph. 4:1–16.

243. So J.A.T. Robinson, *The Body: A Study in Pauline Theology*, SBT (London: SCM Press, 1952), pp. 58–67, esp. 59–60.

244. John 17:20–23 (note the phrase in verse 23, ἵνα ὦσιν τετελειωμένοι εἰς ἕν, 'may they be perfectly one').

245. John 17:21, 23. On the balance between the individual and the collective nature of John's church, as it appears in the Johannine corpus, see further Smalley, 'Johannine Community' in Bockmuehl and Thompson (ed.), *Vision for the Church*, pp. 98–102, esp. (for this balance in John's Gospel) 99–100. See also Schnackenburg 3, pp. 203–217.

246. John 14:18–19, 3.

the Spirit', anticipating the end in the present, and living in the light of the consummation. The disciples of Jesus exist as members of a community which has been inaugurated by the glorification of Jesus;[247] they worship and witness in the Spirit; they enjoy his presence and help; and they await the return of the church's Lord at the last day.[248]

Mention of the eschatological dimension of John's pneumatology and ecclesiology leads us, finally, to a consideration of his eschatology as such.

6. ESCHATOLOGY IN THE FOURTH GOSPEL

'Eschatology' in the strict sense means a description of what is to happen to the world and especially to humanity at the *end* of all things (at the *eschaton*). Traditionally this involves the study of death, judgment, hell and heaven. As the term has come to be used more recently in theology, however, 'eschatology' refers generally to the history of salvation at *any* point in time, even if inevitably salvation is related to the end (of the world) eventually. In this sense, eschatology can be considered from the point of view of both Christ and the Christian; and there is a connection, of course, between the two. For Christ makes eternal life available in time as well as eternity, and the believer is able by faith to share in it at any moment.

This broader understanding of eschatology is particularly relevant to the study of John, since the fourth evangelist has little to say about the 'last things' as such, and is much more concerned about the – to him – vital inter-relation between time and eternity.

Present eschatology

We have already noticed many times that John is deeply interested in the effect of history being invaded by that which is supra-historical. He perceives that since the Word has become flesh, history carries and can convey the life of God in Christ. The divine revelation is decisive, and apparently complete. In one sense, therefore, it is possible to claim that for John the climax of all salvation history – and all history, indeed – has been reached. Certainly the Johannine eschatological stress is on the past and present, rather than on the future; and 'what will happen' seems for John to be the *continuation* of 'what has happened', rather than its consummation.

It is this element in John's theology which has sometimes caused his eschatology to be described as more 'realised' than that of the synoptic

---

247. John 7:39, with its mention of the Spirit being 'given' when Jesus is glorified.
248. John 4:24; 20:21–22; 16:7; 6:39.

writers.[249] From the view-point of the believer, for example, there is a familiar emphasis in the Fourth Gospel on the present tense of both salvation and judgment. 'The one who believes in him (the Son of God) does not come under judgment. The one who does not believe is condemned already.'[250] Equally, the strong, future apocalypticism of the first three Gospels[251] disappears in John; and the Jesus of the Fourth Gospel says very little about his coming parousia in vindicated glory at the end.[252]

Furthermore, John 'telescopes' all the important moments which are included in the salvation event. By contrast, Luke – whose tradition otherwise reveals interesting points of contact with John's – lays out in an ordered, chronological line, the birth, baptism, transfiguration, death, resurrection and ascension of Jesus. John, however, in harmony with his characteristic view of history, draws this line together until those moments overlap. The death and exaltation of Jesus shade into one act of glorification;[253] Pentecost merges with the death of Jesus on the one hand and his ascension on the other;[254] and the gift of the Spirit becomes an immediate parousia of Jesus.[255]

What accounts for these features in John's eschatology? That question is sometimes answered in terms of the so-called 'delay of the parousia'. The imminent expectation of the end receded as time went on, it is argued, and this was one reason for John's concentration on a theology of the presence of Christ in the church and in the believer *now*.[256] But quite apart from the likelihood that this was not a serious problem for the early Christians,[257] it is much more probable that John's particular eschatology was determined and shaped by his christology.

We have already discovered that the pattern of 'descent and ascent' is an important part of John's christological perspective.[258] The fourth

249.   *E.g.* Brown 1, p. cxvii: 'In many ways John is the best example in the NT of realised eschatology.' Because of its ambiguity, the term 'realised' – although convenient – is probably best avoided, except when it is intended to signify the rigorous view that there is *no* future tense to salvation.

250.   John 3:18; *cf.* 5:24; 6:47; 9:40–41, *et al.*; and contrast John 1:12 (sonship as a present gift) with Luke 6:35 (sonship as a future reward; *cf.* Mark 10:30).

251.   *E.g.* in the eschatological discourse of Mark 13 par.

252.   *Cf.*, by contrast, Mark 13:26; 14:62, *et al.*

253.   John 7:39; 13:31–32, *et al.*

254.   John 20:22; *cf.* 19:30; 20:17. W.J.P. Boyd, 'The Ascension according to St John', *Theology* 70 (1967), pp. 207–211, goes so far as to regard John 17 as the fourth evangelist's version of the ascension.

255.   John 14:16–18; 16:16; *cf.* 14:3.

256.   *Cf.* Schnackenburg 1, pp. 159–60.

257.   See above, pp. 166–68.

258.   For a discussion of the centrality to the Fourth Gospel of the *katabasis – anabasis* ('descent–ascent') pattern, see W.A. Meeks, 'The Man from Heaven in Johannine Sectarianism', *JBL* 91 (1972), pp. 44–72; see also G.C. Nicholson, *Death as Departure: The Johannine Descent–Ascent Scheme*, SBLDS 63 (Chico: Scholars Press, 1983), esp. pp. 161–68.

evangelist is not alone in the New Testament, of course, when he speaks of a redeemer who descends to earth and ascends to heaven. This idea is already present in Judaism;[259] and it reappears in other parts of the New Testament – for example, in Paul.[260] But John develops this theological concept further by dwelling on the dimension of Christ's pre-existence. In the Fourth Gospel Jesus not only 'descends' to earth and 'ascends' to heaven; he is also represented as ascending 'where he was before'.[261] In other words, the ascension is built in to every part of John's theological line. The earthly life and life-giving ministry of Jesus presuppose, in John's view, both his divine origin (before the incarnation) and his exalted destiny (after the resurrection); and with all three – the origin, life and destiny of Christ – John is deeply concerned.

This is the reason for the theological overlapping in the Fourth Gospel of which we have taken note. For John, the act of revelation in Christ shades inevitably into his glorification. There is no mention in this Gospel of the transfiguration as a separate event, because the glory, the transfigured nature, of Jesus is to be seen – by the eye of faith – at all times. Likewise the cross, and indeed every part of the self-giving ministry of Jesus, constantly imply his exaltation as well as pointing towards it.

Thus we find that John's eschatology is directly related to his christology, and once more to the two balanced poles – the divine and the human – within that christology. The Jesus who in one sense is always exalted, and therefore not 'of the world', also and in reality is sent 'into the world'.[262] He has come from the Father, and is going to the Father;[263] but on earth his humanity is nevertheless genuinely manifested and visible.[264] His salvation and judgment are mediated in time as well as eternity.[265]

It is quite possible that John's preoccupation with the 'present' aspects of salvation reflects the thought of Jesus himself. This is the contention of C.H. Dodd,[266] who believes that Jesus proclaimed – without apocalyptic trimmings[267] – the complete and historical presence of the

259. See Meeks, 'Man from Heaven', esp. pp. 59–60. Meeks regards Hellenistic Judaism as the primary background to John's descent–ascent motif.

260. *Cf.* Eph. 4:8–10, where the 'descent' of verses 9–10 is likely to be a reference to the incarnation, rather than to the *descensus ad inferos* ('descent into hell'); Phil. 2:6–11, where Paul is evidently quoting an early Christian hymn.

261. John 6:62; *cf.* 1:1–3, *et al.*

262. John 17:16, 18.

263. John 13:3; 16:28.

264. *Cf.* 1 John 1:1–3.

265. *Cf.* John 3:16–21; 5:25–29, *et al.*

266. C.H. Dodd, *The Parables of the Kingdom,* 2nd edn. (London: Nisbet, 1936).

267. *Ibid.,* 187, *et al.* Dodd believes that these are part of the 'reconstructed eschatology' of the early church.

kingdom of God in his own person and ministry. Dodd supports his argument by analysing the synoptic parables of the kingdom, each of which (he maintains) is best understood when it is interpreted in terms of 'realised' eschatology.[268] Not all would subscribe to such a monochrome view of the message of Jesus; and indeed, Dodd himself modified it later.[269] But there is no reason to doubt that this was one element in the eschatological perspective of Jesus. According to *all* the evangelists, Jesus announces the arrival in himself of a decisive moment in God's salvific activity. The kingdom of God is at hand; the signs of the new age are apparent; the scriptures have been fulfilled; the glory of God has been fully revealed.[270] John has no parables of the kingdom as such; but, with the other Gospel writers, he knows that – in one sense at least – the harvest-hour has already come.[271]

Future eschatology

However, this is not the only aspect of John's eschatology; as we have begun to see, there is another.[272] In addition to an emphasis on the present tense of salvation, there are some passages in the Fourth Gospel which speak explicitly of what is to happen in the future. The note of consummation, the gathering up of all things in eternity at the end of time, is clearly sounded. For example, believers can share in the present the life of God through Christ; and they will also be raised up at the 'last day'.[273] Judgment for the unbeliever has already begun, here and now; and those who have done evil will also 'come forth' to the resurrection of judgment.[274] Jesus comes to his own in the world; and at the end he will also come and take them to himself.[275] The church continues in time its immediate task of worship and service; and the hour is coming when worship in spirit and truth will be shared by the church in eternity.[276]

Johannine eschatology, then, manifests an intriguing double perspective. Thus Jesus comes now, and he will also come again. Salvation is a possibility for the believer in the present, and also in the future. But John is too sophisticated an interpreter to place these two strands of

268. *Ibid.* Note the conclusions reached at pp. 195–210.

269. *Cf.* C.H. Dodd, *The Coming of Christ* (Cambridge: Cambridge University Press, 1951).

270. Mark 1:15; Matt. 11:2–5; Luke 4:16–21; John 1:14.

271. John 4:35–38; *cf.* Matt. 9:37–38; Luke 10:1–2. See further Dodd, *Parables*, pp. 186–87.

272. Against Bultmann, pp. 257–62 (on John 5:24–30), *et passim*, who finds in the original John only 'realised' eschatology.

273. John 6:47; 6:40*b* (note also the present tenses in verse 40*a*).

274. John 3:19; 5:28–29. Note the firmly apocalyptic tone of the whole passage, 5:25–29, in contrast to the 'present' emphasis of 5:19–24.

275. John 14:18, 23; 14:3.

276. John 14:12–14; 4:23.

eschatology, present and future, side by side in his Gospel without resolution. A creative tension develops between them – between what 'is now' and what is 'not yet'; and with consummate skill the fourth evangelist draws these two poles together until, as we discovered earlier with reference to his view of the life of Jesus, they blend. We can see this from John's distinctive use of the term 'hour'. For Jesus, the 'hour' of glorification has not yet arrived; but in one sense it has struck already.[277] For the individual, the 'hour' of true worship is here and not yet here;[278] and 'the hour is coming and now is' when those who hear the Son's voice will live.[279]

In this way the 'future tense' of John's eschatology is historically anchored, and given real content. Because of this, as Alf Corell has shown, the eschatology of the Fourth Gospel may be associated with the Johannine understanding of the church.[280] Church and eschatology are both concerned with salvation; and therefore it is possible to view them from the perspective of the past and present, as well as the future. Moreover, both are rooted not only in the death and resurrection of Jesus (as Corell suggests), but also – once again – in the total fact of his 'descent and ascent'. The Christian community on earth is headed by one who came from the Father, and who, after creating an entirely new situation by his glorification, returned to him. Jesus now indwells the church as Spirit-Paraclete. This church is therefore able in the present time to project the resurrection life of Jesus in the world, while awaiting the consummation of all things at the end. When that point is reached, the exalted Jesus, whose parousia is anticipated by his glorification, will take his disciples in the church to be with him: for the Christian also 'ascends', even if for the believer there is no 'descent'.[281]

Church and eschatology in John, like church and Spirit, are thus complementary ideas, tied to each other. Their content and meaning have a christological basis and a background in history. Once more we find in John a coinherence between the historical and the supra-historical.

Conclusion

John's eschatological perspective, with its built-in resonance between the present and future tenses of Christ's coming and the Christian's salvation, is not far from that which is attributed to Jesus himself by the synoptic writers. They also suggest that the teaching of Jesus contained a double polarity. Admittedly, as we noticed at the outset, their emphasis differs from John's by being markedly futurist.

277. John 2:4 and 7:39; (cf. 5:26–27).
278. John 4:23.
279. John 5:25.
280. Corell, *Consummatum Est*, esp. chapter 4; see above, pp. 264–65.
281. John 14:3.

But as well as referring to the parousia of Jesus and the eternal life of the believer as future possibilities, the synoptic Gospels preserve a tradition which implies that these are also present realities.[282] As in John, the present and future poles are on occasions brought very close together; so that in the same discourse Jesus appears to view the consummation as both imminent and distant.[283] Similarly, the very phrase 'the kingdom of God is at hand',[284] is – perhaps deliberately – ambivalent in its meaning, since the time of the kingdom's arrival may in this case be either present or future.[285]

It is possible, of course, that a redactor's hand has been at work: in the synoptic Gospels, adding present to future eschatology, and in John, adding future to present.[286] But in the light of the complex character of New Testament eschatology as a whole, which can seldom be pegged down in one direction and is inevitably varied in its perspective,[287] we do not need, for John at least, to resort to such an explanation. Those who do, must still reckon with the possibility that the future elements in John's eschatology, including their apocalyptic tinting, belong to an early stage in the development of Johannine interpretation, paralleled by the primitive stages in the transmission of the synoptic tradition, rather than to a late period.[288]

While John's eschatology may have increased its present emphasis as the Fourth Gospel came to birth, therefore – particularly in view of the pressures exerted by the evangelist's own theological and christological outlook – there is no real reason to doubt that the basic double polarity of his eschatological perspective is traditional. But while the eschatology of the Gospel is certainly in touch with other parts of the New Testament, it is also true to say that John handles this aspect of his material in a distinctive and seminally important manner. The theological effect of this is ultimately to bring together the 'times' of salvation, and to show that they are inter-related. The time of Israel, the time of Jesus, the time of the church and the time of the end overlap in the Fourth Gospel. All history is there; and so is all salvation history.[289]

282.   Cf. Mark 1:15; Luke 4:21; Matt. 10:40; 11:12, et al.
283.   Cf. Mark 13:28–31, 32–37; (note also, e.g., Matt. 10:23 and 28:19–20).
284.   Mark 1:15 par.
285.   See further Smalley, 'Delay of the Parousia', pp. 42–47, and the literature there cited.
286.   For the latter view see Brown 1, pp. cxx–cxxi.
287.   Note the shift in perspective from 1 Thess. to 2 Thess.
288.   So M.-E. Boismard, 'L'Évolution du Thème Eschatologique dans les Traditions Johanniques', RB 68 (1961), pp. 507–524, esp. 523–24; against Bultmann, p. 11, et passim.
289.   See further Barrett, pp. 67–70; also, for the balance in John's eschatological viewpoints, Brodie, pp. 248–50.

JOHN'S INTERPRETATION

We have been looking at the leading ideas in John's theology, and noticing the special interpretation of the Christian tradition which the fourth evangelist offers us in each case. On this basis we are in a position to see that John's presentation of Jesus as the Word, who reveals God to the world, and is glorified for the sake of the world, adds up to a specialised version of the biblical theme of fulfilment.

The Gospel of John is in effect an exposition of its opening statement, 'in him was life'.[290] In Johannine terms, as we have seen, the life of God is made available to the believer through Jesus and by the Spirit. John's theology involves God in all his fulness, as Father, Son and Spirit; it is trinitarian in character, if not yet in definition. Nevertheless John's particular purposes, which we have studied, cause the focus of his doctrine to be christological. It is *Jesus* in the Fourth Gospel who is brought to the centre of the stage as the one who is life and gives life;[291] although the Father and the Spirit share in this ministry.[292]

Thus Jesus, in John's view, makes possible the new creation;[293] he inaugurates a new Israel, and gives a new centre to Judaism;[294] he initiates a new Passover;[295] he institutes a new worship, and is responsible for the new sabbath;[296] he brings about a new Pentecost;[297] and he enunciates a new law of love.[298] In many ways Jesus in the Fourth Gospel is in fact a new Moses, who accomplishes a new Exodus.[299] So, for example, the manna of the wilderness wanderings is replaced by Christ, as the true and living bread, descending from heaven. Instead of the streams which came from the rock struck by Moses, Jesus offers the living water which he himself gives. As the light of the world, Jesus guides the paths of believers, in place of the pillar of fire which led the Israelites along their way.[300]

However, the Johannine Christ is not simply 'another' Moses. To be sure, the fourth evangelist is well aware that through Jesus an eternal 'promised land' is reached; and he was no doubt familiar with the Jewish tradition which connected Moses with the Messiah himself, so that to

290. John 1:4.
291. John 11:25–26.
292. John 6:44; 3:5.
293. John 1:1, 14.
294. John 1:49, *et al.*; 2:1–22 (*cf.* 1:4).
295. John 2:13; 19:31 (*cf.* 1:29), *et al.*; 6:47–51.
296. John 4:21–26; 5:15–18.
297. John 20:22–23.
298. John 13:34–35.
299. *Cf.* further Glasson, *Moses.*
300. (Exod. 16:1–36) John 6:26–58; (Exod. 17:1–7) John 7:37–39, where the context demands that the subject of the quotation in verse 38 should be regarded as Jesus himself; (Exod. 13:21–22) John 8:12. See further Glasson, *Moses*, pp. 10–11.

regard Jesus as a Mosaic/messianic deliverer would be natural.[301] But for John there is a real difference between Moses and Jesus, as well as a comparability. The law was given through Moses; but grace and truth in their fulness came through Jesus Christ. Moses' vision of the divine was incomplete; while Jesus, the only Son of God, was able uniquely and therefore fully to know the Father and to make him known.[302]

Despite the christocentric nature of John's Gospel, therefore, we find that in the end and above all the Johannine Jesus does just this. He draws attention to himself, in order to point people to God and lead them to him.[303] He is the way to God; while the truth about God and the life of God are to be known through him.[304]

301. *Ibid.*, pp. 20–26, and the literature there cited.

302. John 1:17–18.

303. John 14:6–7, *et al.*

304. *Ibid. Cf.* D.M. Smith, 'The Presentation of Jesus in the Fourth Gospel' in *idem, Johannine Christianity*, pp. 175–89. On John's theology in general see further G.E. Ladd, *A Theology of the New Testament* (Guildford and London: Lutterworth Press, 1975), pp. 213–308; also D. Rensberger, *Overcoming the World: Politics and Community in the Gospel of John* (Philadelphia: Westminster Press, 1988, and London: SPCK, 1989), esp. pp. 15–36 and (for contemporary application) pp. 135–54. See also Brodie, pp. 55–67; Smith, *Theology of John*; Witherington, III, pp. 18–27 (on John's sapiential language and teaching).

EPILOGUE

We are almost at the end of our study of John's Gospel. Before we conclude, however, some further comments may be in place. In this section we shall attempt to answer two questions which arise out of our investigations in the body of this book. First, we must pursue a little further the matter of John's relationship to the synoptic writers, and ask *why* he is so different from them. Second, we must enquire about the relevance of the Fourth Gospel for us today. Then we can draw together some final conclusions.

Inevitably, and as always with a Gospel like John's, we shall be raising new questions and opening up lines of further enquiry even as we try to face these immediate problems; and that is why a book such as this can never really be finished. None the less, we must not allow the difficulty of our task to dissuade us from attempting it.

WHY IS JOHN DIFFERENT?

We argued in the second chapter that the fourth evangelist neither knew nor used the other Gospels in their present form, although he shared with them a common Christian tradition which he drew upon independently. But if John begins at the same point as the other evangelists, why is the final result so different? There are many points of obvious contact, but there are also real differences. The presentation of Jesus in this Gospel – his actions and teaching, and even his character – seem far removed from its synoptic counterpart. Admittedly, Mark is different in many ways from both Matthew and Luke; but, even if he is not eccentric, John seems generally to be in a different league altogether. Rather than minimise the contrast, then, we may offer some suggestions to account for it. Why *is* John different?

(i) First, if John's tradition is ultimately independent, it follows logically that it should have been *treated* independently by those who were responsible for the composition of the Gospel.

(ii) By the time of its publication, as we suggested in chapter 7, the Gospel had gone through different stages of writing. At the second stage, we believe, the fourth evangelist himself recorded and developed the beloved disciple's ideas about Jesus in a determinative way, so that the essential character of the Fourth Gospel probably comes from him. But others were also involved; and in the end we have a document in which traditional Christian sources and their redaction are fused together into a remarkable unity and imprinted with a distinctively 'Johannine' character. In view of its literary and theological history, then, we should not be surprised if the Fourth Gospel now conveys a different atmosphere.

(iii)   A great deal of the basic Jesus tradition, apparent in the synoptic Gospels, seems to be assumed in John. The fourth evangelist probably knew, for example, that one tradition of the message of Jesus contained much information about his relation to the kingdom of God, but very little about his relation to the Father. In the Fourth Gospel the reverse is the case: Jesus speaks often about his relationship to God, and seldom about God's kingdom. This need not mean that John had no reliable knowledge from which to work, or that he was distorting what he knew. It could mean simply that he was assuming some parts of the basic Christian tradition, whether narrative or discourse, and emphasising other parts – or developing them theologically – in accordance with the aims of his Gospel.

(iv)   The main differences which appear to set John apart from the Synoptics are these: the Fourth Gospel's regard for historicity, its literary form, its vocabulary and its theology. But, as John Robinson has argued so persuasively, in none of these areas does John *conflict* with the witness of the synoptic Gospels; and in the matter of theological presentation, at least, he rather *draws out* to their fullest extent the implications of a common tradition.[1] In this way John is adding a new but legitimate dimension to the story of Jesus; he is not 'filling in', but 'filling out'.[2]

(v)   The basic tradition behind the Fourth Gospel, we have argued, is Palestinian; but its ultimate setting and audience were no doubt Asian.[3] If John's version of the Jesus tradition took shape eventually in the context of a Jewish-Gentile church in Asia Minor, as proposed in chapter 8, then it is understandable that the result should have been individual. We may compare the origin of the synoptic Gospels. Mark was probably written in Rome and for Roman readers; and even if Luke originated (as its anti-Marcionite Prologue[4] suggests) in Achaia, it is quite possible that the Third Gospel was also addressed to non-Christians in Rome. Matthew, on the other hand, may well have been written for a Jewish-Christian congregation in or near Palestine. The orientation of the first three Gospels, then, was broadly-speaking either Italian or Palestinian. John's orientation, however, was Asian; and even if Asia Minor in the first century belonged to the same general Graeco-Roman environment as

1.   Robinson, 'Place of the Fourth Gospel', esp. pp. 57–74.

2.   *Ibid.*, p. 74.

3.   See above, pp. 14–41, 180–85, *et passim*.

4.   For an English translation of this Prologue see E.E. Ellis, *The Gospel of Luke*, 2nd. edn., NCB (London: Oliphants, 1974), pp. 40–41.

the rest of the Mediterranean world, its distinctiveness should not be forgotten. Ephesus was not Rome, neither was it Jerusalem. If John's Gospel finally originated from Ephesus, therefore (and this seems likely), there is no reason why its outlook should not differ from that of the Synoptics, and no reason why it should not now possess a theological life of its own.

(vi) We have stressed in this book the extent to which the Gospel of John arose within the particular context of a community which had its own character (both Jewish and Hellenistic) and its own problems (debates about the true identity of Jesus).[5] There is no doubt, therefore, that the needs of the Johannine church itself, as much as the environment in which the Fourth Gospel was produced, affected John's treatment of the Jesus tradition and created a christological emphasis in its record of the teaching of Jesus. There is a sense, of course, in which all four Gospels are concerned with christology; in one way or another they all present the good news about Jesus as the Christ of God. But John wrestles more deeply than the other evangelists with this problem, and for the sake of his audience deals extensively with the exact relation of Jesus to God on the one hand, and humanity on the other. Not surprisingly, the outcome is a Gospel with a developed theological approach of its own.

(vii) In the past, the description of John as the 'Fourth' Gospel has sometimes reflected presuppositions about the character of this document as a secondary, theological version of the synoptic Gospels.[6] We have seen reason to question such presuppositions seriously.[7] But almost certainly the Gospel of John was in fact the fourth and last of the canonical Gospels to be written. As such, it testifies to a period of further reflection on the Christian tradition, during which characteristically Johannine ideas could develop and be given expression.

Thus, while we may take note of the very real differences between St John and the other Gospels, we do not have to conclude that they are unaccountable, or that they necessarily indicate John's unreliability as a witness to Jesus. John has treated the Christian tradition with freedom, and stamped it with his individual character. Nevertheless, his own faith and understanding have developed and heightened, rather than obscured or dismissed, the common historical tradition (even about the person of Jesus) from which he began. In the end, we submit, the difference between John and the synoptists is one of degree, not one of kind.[8]

5. See above, pp. 181–85.
6. *Cf.* Robinson, 'New Look', p. 95.
7. See above, pp. 6–13, 158–60. Other features in the background to the Fourth Gospel, such as a setting of worship and the Jewish-Christian conflict, may also have contributed to John's distinctiveness. But the extent of these factors cannot always be determined exactly; and in any case such influences were typical of life generally in the early Christian church, and therefore probably helped to shape the other Gospels as well.
8. *Cf.* Robinson, 'Place of the Fourth Gospel', p. 71.

JOHN FOR TODAY

Christians in the early church, as we have seen, approached the Fourth Gospel in very different ways.[9] In the second century, for example, some (such as the Alexandrian gnostics Basilides and Valentinus) used John in the interests of heresy; while others (like Irenaeus) used it to defend orthodoxy.[10] It was, indeed, a 'natural battle ground' for both sides;[11] since it appears at one and the same time to have favoured those who wished to support either a gnostic, or a non-gnostic, position. This ambivalence within John, combined with consequent doubt about the Gospel's apostolic origin, makes it easy to see why the church hesitated some time before recognising fully the authenticity and authority of such a document.[12]

However, there was a reason for the ambivalent attitude towards St John's Gospel which was adopted by early Christianity. This Gospel could be used in apparently contradictory ways, and in support of conclusions which seemed to be mutually exclusive, precisely because of its diversity: especially in its presentation of the person of Christ.

We discussed in chapter 8[13] the possible motivation behind John's theological and in particular christological diversity; and we suggested there that perhaps this is best accounted for in terms of the varied background, outlook and needs of those – Jews in the diaspora *and* Greeks – who belonged to the Johannine church. Such a situation might well have given rise to John's insistence that Jesus is both one with humanity *and* one with God. It is unlikely that in doing this John was consciously adopting a 'two natures' christology, or attempting to re-solve the problems associated with presenting Jesus as the God-man. Nevertheless, as Anthony Hanson says, Chalcedonian christology follows from this presentation.[14] By holding together the pre-existence and real manhood of Jesus, John was providing the materials from which, whether satisfactorily or not, traditional christology could be fashioned: both in the early church, and down to our own day.

John's balance

What relevance, therefore, does John's theology, and in particular his conception of the person of Jesus, have for us today? It may be answered at once that John's great contribution to the New Testament view of

9. See above, pp. 77, 91, 183; and *cf.* further Pollard, *Johannine Christology.*

10. See further Sanders, *Fourth Gospel*, pp. 47–84; also, carrying the survey forward into the third and fourth centuries, Wiles, *Spiritual Gospel*, pp. 96–128, esp. 112–28.

11. Wiles, *Spiritual Gospel*, p. 96.

12. *Cf.* Streeter, *Four Gospels*, pp. 436–42.

13. See above, pp. 183–85.

14. Hanson, *Grace and Truth*, pp. 73–74 (see 72–74); see also above, p. 183.

Jesus, and consequently to any understanding of the eternal life which is mediated through him, is to be summed up in the one word, balance.

First, the Fourth Gospel insists on the divine nature of Christ. John makes it abundantly clear that Jesus is from God and one with God; he reveals God's glory uniquely and – unusually, in the New Testament – is confessed as God.[15] But the Johannine Jesus is not *just* God; he is also one with humanity.[16]

Significantly, John's Gospel begins in heaven, but ends on earth. In the introduction we read of the pre-existent Word who was with God at the beginning of time.[17] It might be thought that John, of all evangelists, who was so aware of the glory of Christ, would end his Gospel in the same transcendental sphere. Matthew and Luke both do so; they end on a mountain, and hint at the exaltation of Jesus through his ascension.[18] Admittedly John includes a prospective allusion to the ascension in his resurrection narrative;[19] and at the close of his Gospel – as indeed throughout – he is conscious of the glorification and exalted status of Jesus.[20] But the Johannine epilogue finishes with the risen Lord still on earth; and if it be argued that John 21 is a later addition to the Gospel, the fact is that John 20 also concludes on earth. Perhaps, by this very means, the fourth evangelist wishes to remind us of the abiding relation between history and the Word who invaded history; between Jesus and us.

The Jesus of St John, then, is not *just* God. However, some early Christians, as we know, went to the Fourth Gospel expressly to find support for the docetic view that Jesus was divine but not human.[21] Is not this mode of thought also a modern, and dangerous, phenomenon? We have taken note already of at least one contemporary scholar who is ready to construe the Fourth Gospel in completely docetic terms.[22] Docetism is, moreover, one outcome of the 'new quest' for the historical Jesus, which we discussed earlier.[23] Emphasis on an existential encounter

15. John 13:3; 10:30; 1:14, 18; 20:28.

16. See Thompson, *Humanity of Jesus*, esp. pp. 117–28.

17. John 1:1.

18. Matt. 28:16; Luke 24:50–51 (not all MSS read, 'and was carried up to heaven' at Luke 24:51). Mark has a reference to the ascension only in the so-called Longer Ending, which was almost certainly added later.

19. John 20:17.

20. *Cf.* esp. John 20:19–23, 30–31.

21. There were varying forms of docetic error in the early history of Christianity. Cerinthus, for example, to whom the 'Alogi' ascribed both the Gospel and Apocalypse of John, taught that the Christ was sent by the Father to Jesus (a normal man) at his baptism, and departed from him before the crucifixion. Later gnostics, such as the Valentinians, adopted a more thoroughgoing docetism, in which the body of Jesus was regarded as visible, but without 'substance' from Mary.

22. *Cf.* Käsemann, *Testament of Jesus*, pp. 8–13, *et passim*.

23. See above, pp. 206–209.

with Jesus today through the kerygma (in all its forms) may preclude a real concern for the Jesus of history, the Word made *flesh*, or at least diminish the value of that figure. If logically pursued, such an approach is bound to lead to docetism: a preoccupation with the person of Jesus as exalted, but not incarnate; as divine, but not human.[24]

Even in present-day *evangelism*, moreover, it is possible to hear the claims of Christ presented in such a way as to suggest that in Jesus we are dealing with an unreal figure who only *appeared* to be human, and was not truly limited by material and temporal conditions.

One evangelist, for example, has described the incarnation in these terms:

> The angelic hosts bowed in humility and awe as heaven's Prince of Princes and Lord of Lords . . . got into His jewelled chariot, went through pearly gates, across the steep of the skies, and on a black Judean night, while the stars sang together and the escorting angels chanted His praises, stepped out of the chariot, threw off His robes, and became man![25]

The same evangelist can also say that when Christ died, he died voluntarily, and 'chose the exact moment' for his expiry.[26] The impression given here is that the birth, life and death of Jesus were invested with quasi-magical properties which excluded him from a proper involvement with humanity and the human situation. Admittedly, this impression can be balanced by other quotations from the same source which point out that Jesus on earth 'walked among men as a man'.[27] But the over-all picture of God's Son moving 'supremely, gloriously, and with great anticipation toward the mission that He had come to accomplish',[28] leans in fact in the direction of a docetic christology, and is to that extent capable of giving rise to an unbalanced view of the person of Jesus.

This danger is increased, of course, if preaching and teaching, including explanations of the person of Christ, are carried out on the basis of docetic-type texts drawn exclusively from the Fourth Gospel. It is therefore important to maintain a truly Johannine balance in these activities, insisting that Jesus shared fully in both natures, divine and human. He was not *just* God; he was also man.

Secondly, however, it is equally true that the fourth evangelist did not see Jesus as *just* a man. Adoptionism – the view that Jesus was a man of blameless life who became the adoptive Son of God – is today a more fashionable way of approaching christology, in fact, than docetism; and this view has affected modern theology significantly.

24. *Cf.* Martin, 'New Quest', esp. pp. 40–41. See also pp. 43–45, on 'The New Quest and the Fourth Gospel'.

25. W.F. ('Billy') Graham, *Peace with God* (Kingswood: World's Work, 1954), p. 78.

26. *Ibid.*, p. 82.

27. *Ibid.*, p. 80.

28. *Ibid.*, p. 81.

Scholars like Eric Mascall, who are still prepared to defend credal formulations of Christian doctrine such as the one preserved in the Chalcedonian Definition ('in the incarnate Lord ... two natures, a divine and a human, are inseparably and unconfusedly united in one divine Person'[29]), therefore find themselves right at one end of the theological scale. At the other end, wé find theologians who are dissatisfied with what they describe as the 'traditional orthodox supernaturalism' in which the Christian faith has in the past been framed, and who believe that the 'lay world' neither understands nor accepts this.[30]

Professor Maurice Wiles, for example, submits traditional Christian doctrine to a searching analysis, in the light of present-day thought and the 'doctrinal activity' which, he maintains, is being carried on within the church as a result of this.[31] In his treatment of the person of Christ,[32] Wiles accordingly opens up the subject of the uniqueness of Jesus – whether as man he is also God – and questions the aspect of Christian tradition which identifies absolutely 'all that has come to be implied by the term Christ with the figure of Jesus'.[33]

Similarly Professor Anthony Hanson, whose christological study we have noticed already,[34] sets himself the task of providing an account of the doctrine of the incarnation which will act as an alternative to the Chalcedonian solution, since he finds Chalcedon 'incredible'.[35]

Hanson's answer seems to lie somewhere between Käsemann[36] and Wiles, for he attempts to steer a middle course between docetism and adoptionism. Chalcedonian theology, he believes, is too heavily

29. E.L. Mascall, *Christ, the Christian and the Church: A Study of the Incarnation and Its Consequences* (London: Longmans, 1946), p. 20; see the whole chapter on 'The Incarnation of the Word of God', pp. 1–22. Professor Mascall reaffirmed the basic stance of this book in a subsequent study; see E.L. Mascall, *Corpus Christi: Essays on the Church and the Eucharist*, 2nd edn. (London: Longmans, 1965), p. xi.

30. So J.A.T. Robinson, *Honest to God* (London: SCM Press, 1963), p. 8; *cf.* the whole chapter on 'The Man for Others', pp. 64–83. See also J. Hick (ed.), *The Myth of God Incarnate* (London: SCM Press, 1977); J. Hick and P.F. Knitter (ed.), *The Myth of Christian Uniqueness* (London: SCM Press, 1987), esp. pp. 16–36, Hick's own contribution on 'The Non-Absoluteness of Christianity'. Similarly D. Cupitt, *Taking Leave of God* (London: SCM Press, 1980), p. 7, *et passim* ('we do not have sufficient evidence to justify objective theism'); and note the response by K. Ward, *Holding Fast to God: A Reply to Don Cupitt* (London: SPCK, 1982). *Cf.* also D. Cupitt, *After All: Religion without Alienation* (London: SCM Press 1994), where the author claims that the present age has become post-Christian and post-philosophical (esp. pp. 110–17). See further S.J. Smalley, 'Christological Developments in Response to Current Challenges', *The Franciscan* 18 (1975–76), pp. 159–67.

31. M.F. Wiles, *The Remaking of Christian Doctrine* (London: SCM Press, 1974).

32. *Ibid.*, pp. 41–60.

33. *Ibid.*, p. 58.

34. Hanson, *Grace and Truth*; also Hanson, *Prophetic Gospel*, pp. 347–71.

35. Hanson, *Grace and Truth*, p. 1.

36. See note 22.

dependent on the docetic picture of Christ presented in the Fourth Gospel.[37] Beginning from the assumption that, whatever else he may have been, Jesus was 'a real human personality',[38] Hanson therefore formulates his understanding of christology as follows: in the perfectly obedient life of Jesus Christ, God's 'self-revelation reached its climax'.[39] Hanson fails to make clear, however, how this divine *self*-disclosure (or *self*-giving) was possible, if (as he also argues) Jesus was not in fact 'of one substance' with the Father.[40] The result is a christology which seeks to acknowledge the self-manifestation of God in the life of Jesus, but leaves us in the end with Jesus as 'a completely human personality', about whom there was 'nothing superhuman'.[41] Hanson, when pressed, should probably admit to membership primarily of the adoptionist camp.[42]

Those who favour the view that Jesus was 'the man for others', but very little more, find it impossible to support their christological position from the Fourth Gospel. Indeed, as we have just seen, Anthony Hanson's position is precisely a reaction *against* what he regards as an unhistorical presentation in St John's Gospel of the person of Jesus as supremely divine.[43] Nevertheless, nothing in John allows us to conclude that Jesus is other than the *Word* made flesh. He is one with us, and shares fully the human condition; but he is also one with God.[44]

The Johannine Christ, we may conclude, was neither God alone, nor man alone. The christology of the Fourth Gospel is perfectly balanced between the two poles which are now labelled 'docetic' and 'adoptionist'. As a result, thirdly, John points the way forward to a resolution of the tensions within today's church over christology.[45]

Throughout the history of Christianity, there has been an inclination for thinkers in the church to begin at one end or the other: to emphasise the humanity of Jesus to the exclusion of his divinity, or the reverse; to say that if Jesus were really God he could not also have been really man,

37.   Hanson, *Grace and Truth*, p. 2. Hanson does not regard the Fourth Gospel as 'a straightforward historical record of the life and teaching of Jesus of Nazareth'.

38.   *Ibid.*

39.   *Ibid.*, p. 76.

40.   *Ibid.*

41.   *Ibid.*

42.   In *Prophetic Gospel* (pp. 309–310) Professor Hanson refers to my criticism in this present book of his *Grace and Truth*, that it makes no 'allowance for the divine substance' (p. 310), and rebukes me for (apparently) accepting 'the Chalcedonian christology without question' (p. 309)!

43.   Hanson, *Grace and Truth*, pp. 1–2. For an equally 'low' view of the fourth evangelist's christology see F. Watson, 'Is John's Christology Adoptionist?', in Hurst and Wright (ed.), *The Glory of God*, pp. 113–24.

44.   John 10:30; *cf.* 8:58.

45.   For a constructive christological survey and statement see J. Macquarrie, *Jesus Christ in Modern Thought* (London: SCM Press and Philadelphia: Trinity Press International, 1990); for John's (balanced) witness to the person of Jesus see esp. pp. 97–122.

and *vice versa*. We can see this very clearly in the christological variations which surfaced during the first Christian centuries.

The Alexandrians (for example, Clement[46]) stressed the doctrine of the *Logos* in an effort to bridge the gap between God and the world; but in so doing the way was prepared for docetic heresy. The Antiochenes, by contrast (for example, Diodore of Tarsus[47]), insisted on the true humanity of Jesus, and formulated their christology from that viewpoint; but in so doing they paved the way for an 'adoptive' understanding of Christ's person. Antioch produced Theodore of Mopsuestia[48] and Nestorius,[49] who accepted the two natures of Jesus, the God-man, but made them into two separate persons. In reaction to this heretical belief, the archimandrite Eutyches[50] went so far as to confuse the two natures in Christ, and to work out a 'monophysite' christology which held that in the person of the incarnate Christ there was only one nature, and that was divine. The Council of Chalcedon was convened in AD 451 to refute the errors of both Nestorius and Eutyches; and in the course of their deliberations the bishops drew up the now famous 'Definition'. This states clearly that Christ is 'acknowledged' in two natures, God and man, 'unconfusedly, unchangeably, indivisibly and inseparably'.[51]

The Chalcedonian Definition is the high-point of christological debate in the early church. It was an attempt to resolve the difficult problem of maintaining that in one person there were two distinct natures; and to this understanding, as we have discovered, the Fourth Gospel pointed forward and contributed. However, ultimately we have to agree that Chalcedon was a statement, not a solution. It is balanced, like John's christology. But no more than the Fourth Gospel itself does it show us *how* the human and the divine are related in Jesus; it merely places these truths side by side.

Can more be done? Is not John's balanced witness reasonable? For whenever one aspect of the person of Jesus is consistently emphasised at the expense of the other, the balance is upset. Patristic discussion about the person of Christ was all too often a history of one error trying to correct another. And modern contributions to the same subject – favouring, as in general they do, the Antiochene position – are similarly susceptible to imbalance. Therefore Käsemann needs Wiles; Wiles needs Käsemann; and both need Mascall! Let us continue to explore the mystery of the incarnation; but let us also continue to affirm, with John, that in Jesus we encounter the *Word* made *flesh*.

46. *c.* AD 155 – c. 220.

47. Died *c.* AD 390.

48. *c.* AD 350–428.

49. Died *c.* AD 451. He was probably a pupil of Theodore.

50. *c.* AD 378–454.

51. For the text see C.A. Heurtley (ed.), *De Fide et Symbolo*, 4th edn. (Oxford and London: Oxford University Press, 1889), pp. 23–28, esp. 27–28.

Fourthly and finally, a postscript may be added to our comments about the contemporary use of the Fourth Gospel. John's Gospel is often recommended to non-Christian enquirers, as an 'invitation to live', because it throws so much light on the central issue of the identity of Jesus. The christological concern of this Gospel is an obvious advantage to anyone who wishes to know more about the Christian faith and the Jesus tradition. But John is not an easy place at which to start! This is perhaps because the Gospel was written, as we have suggested,[52] for those *inside* the church who had a Christian background, rather than for complete outsiders. So, if the Fourth Gospel were not originally intended for outsiders in the first place, even if it did not exclude them, we may well ask whether today it is the best Gospel for the enquirer to read first?

CONCLUSIONS

Of the many conclusions which might be drawn from our study of John's Gospel in this book, four will be suggested.

(i)   The Fourth Gospel can no longer be considered in isolation from the other three. Recent research on John encourages us, among other things, to take all the Gospels together if we require a properly rounded view of Jesus, and the Christian tradition about him. It is no accident that we have all *four* Gospels. And John complements the others; not in the sense that he sets out to interpret them, but that he 'shows *us* how to interpret them'.[53]

(ii)   We have spoken much in this book about the historical nature of John's tradition, and the new evidence for this which has come to light. But, as we have seen, while the fourth evangelist is seriously concerned about the historical basis of faith, and appears to be writing against the background of reliable Christian tradition, he is not *just* concerned with 'history' in the sense of 'what happened'. He is also aware of its theological meaning and existential appeal for all time. The words of Jesus in this Gospel, therefore – even if some of these may be the words of the *risen* Jesus – can still be his words for us today.

(iii)   The rediscovered literary approach to this Gospel, among other biblical documents, allows us to interpret from its pages not only the carefully nuanced and dramatic story of Jesus himself, but also the history of a volatile community gathered around the beloved disciple. That history, traceable from Revelation to 3 John,[54] reveals a circle wrestling with the implications of the Jesus tradition for their own belief and behaviour; and we can learn from this struggle, and from the real experience of God in Christ to which John himself is laying claim in his evangel.

52.   See above, pp. 177–85.
53.   Sidebottom, *Christ of the Fourth Gospel*, p. 187, italics mine.
54.   See above, p. 93 n. 74; also Smalley, *Thunder and Love*, pp. 121–37.

(iv) Accordingly, we can and should listen in *full* to the Johannine literary interpretation of Christianity. Because it is historically grounded, it is not to be dismissed as an eccentric spin-off from the mainstream; and because it is theologically sophisticated, it is not to be ignored as an unacceptable variant of the Jerusalem gospel. We need John in the New Testament, just as we need Paul and Mark and James and Peter, and all the rest. For in John we have an unexpectedly traditional evangelist, and an unusually perceptive interpreter.

BIBLIOGRAPHY

Republished or translated works are cited in their most recent known form

Abbott, E.A. *Notes on New Testament Criticism. Diatessarica*, vol. 7. (London: A. and C. Black, 1907).

Aland, K. 'Neue Neutestamentliche Papyri II'. *NTS* 9 (1962–63), pp. 303–316.

Albright, W.F. 'Recent Discoveries in Palestine and the Gospel of St John', in W.D. Davies and D. Daube (ed.), *The Background of the New Testament and Its Eschatology. In Honour of Charles Harold Dodd.* (Cambridge: Cambridge University Press, 1956), pp. 153–71.

Appold, M.L. *The Oneness Motif in the Fourth Gospel. Motif Analysis and Exegetical Probe into the Theology of John.* WUNT 2.1. (Tübingen: Mohr-Siebeck, 1976).

Argyle, A.W. 'Philo and the Fourth Gospel'. *ExpT* 63 (1951–52), pp. 385–86.

Ashton, J. (ed.), *The Interpretation of John.* IRT 9. (London: SPCK and Philadelphia: Fortress Press, 1986).

—, *Understanding the Fourth Gospel.* (Oxford: Clarendon Press, 1991).

—, *Studying John. Approaches to the Fourth Gospel.* (Oxford: Clarendon Press, 1994).

Bacon, B.W. *The Fourth Gospel in Research and Debate*, 2nd edn. (London and Leipzig: T. Fisher Unwin, 1918).

—, *The Gospel of the Hellenists*, ed. C.H. Kraeling. (New York: Henry Holt, 1933).

Bailey, J.A. *The Traditions Common to the Gospels of Luke and John.* NovT Sup 7. (Leiden: E.J. Brill, 1963).

Baker, J.A. 'The "Institution" Narratives and the Christian Eucharist', in I.T. Ramsey *et al.*, *Thinking about the Eucharist.* (London: SCM Press, 1972), pp. 38–58.

Baldensperger, W. *Der Prolog des vierten Evangeliums: Sein polemisch-apologetischer Zweck.* (Freiburg im Breisgau: J.C.B. Mohr, 1898).

Ball, D.M. *'I AM' in John's Gospel. Literary Function, Background and Theological Implications.* JSNTS 124. (Sheffield: Sheffield Academic Press, 1996).

Bampfylde, G. 'John xix.28: A Case For a Different Translation'. *NovT* 11 (1969), pp. 245–60.

Barr, J. 'Which Language did Jesus Speak? – Some Remarks of a Semitist'. *BJRL* 53 (1970–71), pp. 9–29.

Barrett, C.K. 'The Old Testament in the Fourth Gospel'. *JTS* 48 (1947), pp. 155–69.

—, 'Stephen and the Son of Man', in W. Eltester (ed.), *Apophoreta: Festschrift für Ernst Haenchen*. (Berlin: Alfred Töpelmann, 1964), pp. 32–38.

—, 'John and the Synoptic Gospels'. *ExpT* 85 (1973–74), pp. 228–33.

—, *The Gospel of John and Judaism*. (London: SPCK, 1975).

—, *The Gospel According to St John*, 2nd edn. (London: SPCK, 1978).

Bauer, W. *Das Johannesevangelium*, 3rd. edn. HNT 6. (Tübingen: Mohr-Siebeck, 1933).

—, *Orthodoxy and Heresy in Earliest Christianity*. (London: SCM Press, 1972).

Beasley-Murray, G.R. *A Commentary on Mark Thirteen*. (London and New York: Macmillan, 1957).

—, *John*. WBC 36. (Waco: Word Books, 1987).

Becker, H. *Die Reden des Johannesevangeliums und der Stil der gnostischen Offenbarungsrede*. FRLANT ns 50. (Göttingen: Vandenhoeck & Ruprecht, 1956).

Becker, J. 'Wunder und Christologie: Zum literarkritischen und christologischen Problem der Wunder im Johannesevangelium'. *NTS* 16 (1969–70), pp. 130–48.

Benoit, P. 'Praetorium, Lithostroton and Gabbatha', in *idem*, *Jesus and the Gospel*, vol. 1. (London: Darton, Longman and Todd, 1973), pp. 167–88.

—, 'Qumran et le Nouveau Testament'. *NTS* 7 (1960–61), pp. 276–96.

—, 'Découvertes Archéologiques autour de la piscine de Béthesda', in P.W. Lapp (ed.), *Jerusalem Through the Ages*. (Jerusalem: Israel Exploration Society, 1968), pp. 48–57.

—, 'L'Antonia d'Hérode le Grand et le Forum Oriental d' Aelia Capitolina'. *HTR* 64 (1971), pp. 135–67.

Bernard, J.H. 'The Traditions as to the Death of John, the Son of Zebedee', in *idem*, *Studia Sacra*. (London and New York: Hodder and Stoughton, 1917), pp. 260–84.

—, *A Critical and Exegetical Commentary on the Gospel According to St John*, 2 vols. (Edinburgh: T. and T. Clark, 1928).

Betz, O. *Der Paraklet: Fürsprecher im häretischen Spätjudentum im Johannes-Evangelium und in neu gefundenen gnostischen Schriften*. AGSU 2. (Leiden: E.J. Brill, 1963).

—, *What Do We Know about Jesus?* (London: SCM Press, 1968).

Beutler, J. and Fortna, R.T. (ed.), *The Shepherd Discourse of John 10 and its Context*. SNTSMS 67. (Cambridge and New York: Cambridge University Press, 1991).

Black, C.C. ' "The Words That You Gave to Me I Have Given to Them". The Grandeur of Johannine Rhetoric', in R.A. Culpepper and C.C. Black (ed.), *Exploring the Gospel of John. In Honor of D. Moody Smith*. (Louisville: Westminster John Knox Press, 1996), pp. 220–39.

Black, M. *An Aramaic Approach to the Gospels and Acts*, 3rd edn. (Oxford: Clarendon Press, 1967).

Blinzler, J. *Johannes und die Synoptiker. Ein Forschungsbericht*. SBS 5. (Stuttgart: Katholisches Bibelwerk, 1965).

Böcher, O. *Der johanneische Dualismus im Zusammenhang des nachbiblischen Judentums.* (Gütersloh: Gerd Mohn, 1965).

—, 'Das Verhältnis der Apokalypse des Johannes zum Evangelium des Johannes', in J. Lambrecht (ed.), *L'Apocalypse johannique et l'Apocalyptique dans le Nouveau Testament.* BETL 53. (Gembloux: Duculot and Leuven: Leuven University Press, 1980), pp. 289–301.

Boer, M.C. de *Johannine Perspectives on the Death of Jesus.* CBET 17. (Kampen: Kok Pharos, 1996).

Boice, J.M. *Witness and Revelation in the Gospel of John.* (Exeter: Paternoster Press and Grand Rapids: Zondervan, 1970).

Boismard, M.-E. 'Importance de critique textuelle pour établir l'origine araméenne du quatrième évangile', in *idem et al., L'Évangile de Jean. Études et Problèmes.* Rech Bib 3. (Bruges: Desclée de Brouwer, 1958), pp. 41–57.

—, 'L'Évolution du Thème Eschatologique dans les Traditions Johanniques'. *RB* 68 (1961), pp. 507–524.

—, 'Saint Luc et le rédaction du quatrième évangile (Jn IV, 46–54)'. *RB* 69 (1962), pp. 185–211.

— et Lamouille, A. *L'Évangile de Jean.* (Paris: Edition du Cerf, 1977).

Bonsirven, J. *Palestinian Judaism in the Time of Jesus Christ.* (New York: Holt, Rinehart and Winston, 1964).

—, 'Les aramaismes de S. Jean L'Évangéliste?' *Biblica* 30 (1949), pp. 405–432.

Borgen, P. *Bread from Heaven. An Exegetical Study of the Concept of Manna in the Gospel of John and the Writings of Philo.* NovT Sup 10. (Leiden: E.J. Brill, 1965).

—, 'God's Agent in the Fourth Gospel', in J. Neusner (ed.), *Religions in Antiquity.* (Leiden: E.J. Brill, 1968), pp. 137–48.

—, 'Observations on the Targumic Character of the Prologue of John'. *NTS* 16 (1969–70), pp. 288–95.

—, 'The Use of Tradition in John 12:44–50'. *NTS* 26 (1979–80), pp. 18–35.

—, 'Philo of Alexandria', in M.E. Stone (ed.), *Jewish Writings of the Second Temple Period.* (Assen: Van Gorcum and Philadelphia: Fortress Press, 1984), pp. 233–82.

— and Neirynck, F. 'John and the Synoptics', in D.L. Dungan (ed.), *The Interrelations of the Gospels.* BETL 95. (Leuven: Leuven University Press and Peeters, 1990), pp. 408–458.

—, 'The Gospel of John and Hellenism: Some Observations', in Culpepper and Black (ed.), *Exploring the Gospel of John*, pp. 98–123.

Boring, M.E. 'The Influence of Christian Prophecy on the Johannine Portrayal of the Paraclete and Jesus'. *NTS* 25 (1978–79), pp. 113–23.

Bornhäuser, K. *Das Johannesevangelium: Eine Missionsschrift für Israel.* (Gütersloh: Bertelsmann, 1928).

Bornkamm, G. *Jesus of Nazareth.* 2nd. edn. (London: Hodder and Stoughton, 1963).

—, 'Zur Interpretation des Johannes-Evangeliums. Eine Auseinandersetzung mit Ernst Käsemanns Schrift "Jesu letzter Wille nach Johannes 17" '. *EvT* 28 (1968), pp. 8–25.

Bousset, W. *Die Hauptprobleme der Gnosis*. FRLANT 10. (Göttingen: Vandenhoeck & Ruprecht, 1907).

Bowker, J.W. 'The Origin and Purpose of St John's Gospel'. *NTS* 11 (1964–65), pp. 398–408.

—, *The Targums and Rabbinic Literature. An Introduction to Jewish Interpretations of Scripture*. (Cambridge: Cambridge University Press, 1969).

Boyd, W.J.P. 'The Ascension According to St John'. *Theology* 70 (1967), pp. 207–211.

Brandon, S.G.F. *The Fall of Jerusalem and the Christian Church*, 2nd edn. (London: SPCK, 1957).

Braun, F.-M. 'Hermétisme et Johannisme'. *RevT* 55 (1955), pp. 22–42, 259–99.

—, *Jean le théologien*, 4 vols. (Paris: J. Gabalda, 1959–72).

Breck, J. *Spirit of Truth. The Holy Spirit in Johannine Tradition*, 2 vols. (Crestwood: St Vladimir's Seminary Press, 1991; vol. 2 forthcoming).

Brodie, T.L. *The Quest for the Origin of John's Gospel. A Source-Oriented Approach*. (New York and Oxford: Oxford University Press, 1993).

—, *The Gospel According to John. A Literary and Theological Commentary*. (New York and Oxford: Oxford University Pess, 1993).

Brooke, A.E. 'John', in A.S. Peake (ed.), *A Commentary on the Bible*. (London and Edinburgh: T.C. and E.C. Jack, 1920), pp. 743–65.

Brown, R.E. 'The Paraclete in the Fourth Gospel'. *NTS* 13 (1966–67), pp. 113–32.

—, 'The Qumran Scrolls and the Johannine Gospel and Epistles', in *idem*, *New Testament Essays*. (London: Geoffrey Chapman, 1967), pp. 102–131.

—, 'John and the Synoptic Gospels: A Comparison', *ibid.*, pp. 192–213.

—, 'The Problem of Historicity in John', *ibid.*, pp. 143–67.

—, *The Gospel According to John*, 2 vols. AB 29 and 29a. (London: Geoffrey Chapman, 1971).

—, Donfried, K.P. and Reumann, J. (ed.), *Peter in the New Testament*. (London: Geoffrey Chapman, 1974).

—, *The Community of the Beloved Disciple. The Life, Loves, and Hates of an Individual Church in New Testament Times*. (London: Geoffrey Chapman and New York: Paulist, 1979).

—, *The Epistles of John*. AB 30. (Garden City: Doubleday, 1982, and London: Geoffrey Chapman, 1983).

—, 'Not Jewish Christianity and Gentile Christianity but Types of Jewish/Gentile Christianity'. *CBQ* 45 (1983), pp. 74–79.

—, *An Introduction to New Testament Christology*. (London: Geoffrey Chapman, 1994).

—, *The Death of the Messiah: From Gethsemane to the Grave. A Commentary on the Passion Narratives in the Four Gospels*. (London: Geoffrey Chapman, 1994).

Brown, S. 'From Burney to Black: The Fourth Gospel and the Aramaic Question'. *CBQ* 26 (1964), pp. 323–39.

Brownlee, W.H. 'Whence the Gospel According to John?', in J.H. Charlesworth (ed.), *John and Qumran*. (London: Geoffrey Chapman, 1972), pp. 166–94.

Bruce, F.F. *The Speeches in the Acts of the Apostles.* (London: Tyndale Press, 1944).

—, *The Acts of the Apostles. The Greek Text with Introduction and Commentary*, 3rd edn. (Grand Rapids: Eerdmans and Leicester: Apollos, 1990).

—, *New Testament History*, revised edn. (London and Glasgow: Pickering and Inglis, 1982).

—, 'Paul and the Historical Jesus'. *BJRL* 56 (1973–74), pp. 317–35.

—, 'The Speeches in Acts – Thirty Years After', in R.J. Banks (ed.), *Reconciliation and Hope: New Testament Essays on Atonement and Eschatology. Presented to L.L. Morris on his 60th Birthday.* (Exeter: Paternoster Press, 1974), pp. 53–68.

—, 'The History of New Testament Study', in I.H. Marshall (ed.), *New Testament Interpretation. Essays in Principles and Methods.* (Exeter: Paternoster Press, 1977), pp. 21–59.

—, 'The Trial of Jesus in the Fourth Gospel', in R.T. France and D. Wenham (ed.), *Gospel Perspectives. Studies of History and Tradition in the Four Gospels*, vol. 1. (Sheffield: JSOT Press ,1980), pp. 7–20.

Bultmann, R. 'Die Bedeutung der neuerschlossenen mandäischen und manichäischen Quellen für das Verständnis des Johannesevangeliums'. *ZNW* 24 (1925), pp. 100–146.

—, *Gnosis.* (London: A. and C. Black, 1952).

—, *Theology of the New Testament*, 2 vols. (London: SCM Press, 1952 and 1955).

—, 'New Testament and Mythology', in H.W. Bartsch (ed.), *Kerygma and Myth. A Theological Debate*, vol. 1. (London: SPCK, 1953), pp. 1–44.

—, *Primitive Christianity in its Contemporary Setting.* (London and New York: Thames and Hudson, 1956).

—, *Jesus and the Word.* (New York: Scribner's, 1934, 1958, and London: Nicholson and Watson, 1935).

—, 'Johannesevangelium'. *RGG* 3 (1959) cols. 840–50.

—, *The Gospel of John. A Commentary.* (Oxford: Basil Blackwell, 1971).

Burge, G.M. *The Anointed Community. The Holy Spirit in the Johannine Tradition.* (Exeter: Paternoster Press and Grand Rapids: Eerdmans, 1987).

Burkett, D. *The Son of the Man in the Gospel of John.* JSNTS 56. (Sheffield: JSOT Press, 1991).

—, 'The Nontitular Son of Man: A History and Crtique.' *NTS* 40 (1994), pp. 504–521.

Burney, C.F. *The Aramaic Origin of the Fourth Gospel.* (Oxford: Clarendon Press, 1922).

Burridge, R.A. *What are the Gospels? A Comparison with Graeco-Roman Biography.* SNTSMS 70. (Cambridge: Cambridge University Press, 1992).

—, *Four Gospels, One Jesus? A Symbolic Reading.* (London: SPCK, 1994).

Carmignac, J. 'Les affinités qumraniennes de la onzième Ode de Salomon'. *RQ* 3 (1961–62), pp. 71–102.

Carson, D.A. *The Gospel According to John.* (Leicester: Inter-Varsity Press and Grand Rapids: Eerdmans, 1991).

Charlesworth, J.H. 'A Critical Comparison of the Dualism in 1QS III.13 — IV.26 and the "Dualism" Contained in the Fourth Gospel'. *NTS* 15 (1968–69), pp. 389–418.

—, 'The Odes of Solomon – not Gnostic'. *CBQ* 31 (1969), pp. 357–69.
— (ed.), *John and Qumran*. (London: Geoffrey Chapman, 1972).
—, (ed.), *The Odes of Solomon*. (Oxford: Clarendon Press, 1973).
—, (with R.A. Culpepper), 'The Odes of Solomon and the Gospel of John'. *CBQ* 35 (1973), pp. 298–322.
—, *The Beloved Disciple: Whose Witness Validates the Gospel of John?* (Philadelphia: Trinity Press International, 1995).
—, 'The Dead Sea Scrolls and the Gospel According to John', in Culpepper and Black (ed.), *Exploring the Gospel of John*, pp. 65–97.
Coakley, J.F. 'The Anointing at Bethany and the Priority of John'. *JBL* 107 (1988), pp. 241–56.
Colpe, C. 'Mandäer', in *RGG* 4 (1960) cols. 709–712.
Colwell, E.C. and Titus, E.L. *The Gospel of the Spirit. A Study in the Fourth Gospel*. (New York: Harper and Row, 1953).
Corell, A. *Consummatum Est. Eschatology and Church in the Gospel of St John*. (London: SPCK, 1958, and New York: Macmillan, 1959).
Cranfield, C.E.B. *The Gospel According to Saint Mark. An Introduction and Commentary*. (Cambridge: Cambridge University Press, 1959).
Cribbs, F.L. 'A Reassessment of the Date of Origin and Destination of the Gospel of John'. *JBL* 89 (1970), pp. 38–55.
—, 'St Luke and the Johannine Tradition'. *JBL* 90 (1971), pp. 422–50.
Cross, F.L. (ed.), *Studies in the Fourth Gospel*. (London: A.R. Mowbray, 1957).
Cullmann, O. *Early Christian Worship*. SBT. (London: SCM Press, 1953).
—, 'A New Approach to the Interpretation of the Fourth Gospel'. *ExpT* 71 (1959–60), pp. 8–12, 39–43.
—, *Peter – Disciple, Apostle, Martyr. A Historical and Theological Study*, 2nd edn. (London: SCM Press, 1962).
—, 'L'Évangile Johannique et L'Histoire du Salut'. *NTS* 11 (1964–65), pp. 111–22.
—, *The Johannine Circle. A Study in the Origin of the Gospel of John*. NTL. (London: SCM Press, 1976).
—, *Prayer in the New Testament*. (London: SCM Press and Minneapolis: Fortresss Press, 1995).
Culpepper, R.A. *The Johannine School*. SBLDS 26. (Missoula: Scholars Press, 1975).
—, 'The Pivot of John's Prologue'. *NTS* 27 (1980–81), pp. 1–31.
—, *Anatomy of the Fourth Gospel. A Study in Literary Design*. (Philadelphia: Fortress Press, 1983).
—, *John, the Son of Zebedee. The Life of a Legend*. (Columbia: University of South Carolina Press, 1994).
—, 'Reading Johannine Irony', in Culpepper and Black (ed.), *Exploring the Gospel of John*, pp. 193–207.
—, *The Gospel and Letters of John*. IBT. (Nashville: Abingdon, 1998).
Daniélou, J. 'Odes de Salomon'. *DB*(S) 6 (1960) cols. 677–84.
—, *A History of Early Christian Doctrine Before the Council of Nicea*, vol.1: *The Theology of Jewish Christianity*. (London: Darton, Longman and Todd, 1964).
Daube, D. *The New Testament and Rabbinic Judaism*. (London: Athlone Press, 1956).

Dauer, A. *Die Passionsgeschichte im Johannesevangelium. Eine traditions-geschichtliche und theologische Untersuchung zu Joh 18,1–19,30.* SANT 3. (München: Kösel, 1972).

—, *Johannes und Lukas.* (Würzburg: Echter, 1984).

Davies, W.D. *Paul and Rabbinic Judaism. Some Rabbinic Elements in Pauline Theology,* 3rd edn. (London: SPCK, 1970).

—, 'Reflections on Aspects of the Jewish Background of the Gospel of John', in Culpepper and Black (ed.), *Exploring the Gospel of John,* pp. 43–64.

Denaux, A. (ed.) *John and the Synoptics.* BETL 101. (Leuven: Leuven University Press and Peeters, 1992).

Derrett, J.D.M. 'Water into Wine'. *BZ* NF 7 (1963), pp. 80–97.

Dibelius, M. *From Tradition to Gospel.* (London: Nicholson and Watson, 1934).

—, 'The Speeches in Acts and Ancient Historiography', in *idem, Studies in the Acts of the Apostles,* ed. H. Greeven. (London: SCM Press, 1956), pp. 138–85.

Dillon, R.J. 'Wisdom Tradition and Sacramental Retrospect in the Cana Account'. *CBQ* 24 (1962), pp. 268–96.

Dodd, C.H. *The Bible and the Greeks.* (London: Hodder and Stoughton, 1935).

—, *The Parables of the Kingdom.* 2nd. edn. (London: Nisbet, 1936).

—, *The Apostolic Preaching and its Developments,* 3rd edn. (London: Hodder and Stoughton, 1963).

—, *The Coming of Christ.* (Cambridge: Cambridge University Press, 1951).

—, *The Interpretation of the Fourth Gospel.* (Cambridge: Cambridge University Press, 1953).

—, 'The Framework of the Gospel Narrative', in *idem, New Testament Studies.* (Manchester: Manchester University Press, 1953), pp. 1–11.

—, 'Some Johannine "Herrnworte" with Parallels in the Synoptic Gospels'. *NTS* 2 (1955–56), pp. 75–86.

—, *Historical Tradition in the Fourth Gospel.* (Cambridge: Cambridge University Press, 1963).

—, 'The Portrait of Jesus in John and in the Synoptics', in W.R. Farmer *et al.* (ed.), *Christian History and Interpretation. Studies Presented to John Knox.* (Cambridge: Cambridge University Press, 1967), pp. 183–98.

—, 'A Hidden Parable in the Fourth Gospel', in *idem, More New Testament Studies.* (Manchester: Manchester University Press, 1968), pp. 30–40.

Drower, E.S. *The Mandaeans of Iraq and Iran. Their Cults, Customs, Magic Legends and Folklore.* (Oxford: Clarendon Press, 1937, and Leiden: E.J. Brill, 1962).

—, *The Haran Gawaita and The Baptism of Hibil-Ziwa.* Studi e Testi 176. (Vatican City: Biblioteca Apostolica Vaticana, 1953).

Duke, P.D. *Irony in the Fourth Gospel.* (Atlanta: John Knox Press, 1985).

Dunn, J.D.G. *Christology in the Making. A New Testament Inquiry into the Origins of the Doctrine of the Incarnation,* 2nd edn. (London: SCM Press, 1989).

—, 'Let John be John: A Gospel for Its Time', in P. Stulmacher (ed.), *Das Evangelium und die Evangelien: Vorträge vom Tübinger Symposium 1982.* WUNT 28. (Tübingen: Mohr-Siebeck, 1983), pp. 309–339.

—, 'John and the Synoptics as a Theological Question', in Culpepper and Black (ed.), *Exploring the Gospel of John*, pp. 301–313.

Eller, V. *The Beloved Disciple. His Name, His Story, His Thought. Two Studies from the Gospel of John.* (Exeter: Paternoster Press and Grand Rapids: Eerdmans, 1987).

Ellis, E.E. *The Gospel of Luke*, 2nd edn. NCB. (London: Oliphants, 1974).

Ensor, P.W. *Jesus and His 'Works'. The Johannine Sayings in Historical Perspective*. WUNT 2.85. (Tübingen: Mohr-Siebeck, 1996).

Evans, C.F. 'The Kerygma', *JTS* ns 7 (1956), pp. 25–41.

Filson, F.V. 'Who was the Beloved Disciple?' *JBL* 68 (1949), pp. 83–88.

Fiorenza, E. 'The Quest for the Johannine School: The Apocalypse and the Fourth Gospel'. *NTS* 23 (1976–77), pp. 402–427.

Flew, R. Newton. *The Idea of Perfection in Christian Theology. An Historical Study of the Christian Ideal for the Present Life.* (Oxford: Oxford University Press, 1934).

Forestell, J.T. *The Word of the Cross. Salvation as Revelation in the Fourth Gospel.* An Bib 57. (Rome: Biblical Institute Press, 1974).

Förster (Foerster), W. (ed.), *Gnosis*, ed. R.McL. Wilson, 2 vols. (Oxford: Clarendon Press, 1972 and 1974).

—, *Palestinian Judaism in New Testament Times.* (Edinburgh and London: Oliver and Boyd, 1964).

Fortna, R.T. *The Gospel of Signs. A Reconstruction of the Narrative Source Underlying the Fourth Gospel.* SNTSMS 11. (New York and Cambridge: Cambridge University Press, 1970).

—, 'Source and Redaction in the Fourth Gospel's Portrayal of Jesus' Signs'. *JBL* 89 (1970), pp. 151–66.

—, 'Christology in the Fourth Gospel: Redaction-Critical Perspectives'. *NTS* 21 (1974–75), pp. 489–504.

—, *The Fourth Gospel and Its Predecessor. From Narrative Source to Present Gospel.* SNTW. (Philadelphia: Fortress Press, 1988, and Edinburgh: T. and T. Clark, 1989).

Franck, E. *Revelation Taught. The Paraclete in the Gospel of John.* ConBNT 14. (Lund: Gleerup, 1985).

Freed, E.D. *Old Testament Quotations in the Gospel of John.* NovT Sup 11. (Leiden: E.J. Brill, 1965).

Fuller, R.H. *The New Testament in Current Study. Some Trends in the Years 1941–1962.* (London: SCM Press, 1963).

Gardner-Smith, P. *St John and the Synoptic Gospels.* (Weston-super-Mare: Readersoft, 1992).

Gerhardsson, B. *Memory and Manuscript. Oral Tradition and Written Transmission in Rabbinic Judaism and Early Christianity*, 2nd edn. (Uppsala and Lund: C.W.K. Gleerup, 1964).

Glasson, T.F. *Moses in the Fourth Gospel.* SBT1. (London: SCM Press, 1963).

—, 'The Speeches in Acts and Thucydides'. *ExpT* 76 (1964–65), p. 165.

Goguel, M. *Les Sources du Récit Johannique de la Passion.* (Paris: G. Fischbacher, 1910).

Goodenough, E.R. 'John a Primitive Gospel'. *JBL* 64 (1945), pp. 145–82.

Goodwin, C. 'How Did John Treat His Sources?' *JBL* 73 (1954), pp. 61–75.

Goulder, M.D. *Midrash and Lection in Matthew.* (London: SPCK, 1974).

Grant, F.C. *The Gospels. Their Origin and Their Growth*. (London: Faber and Faber, 1957).

—, 'Was the Author of John Dependent Upon the Gospel of Luke?' *JBL* 56 (1937), pp. 285–307.

Grayston, K. *The Gospel of John*. (London: Epworth Press, 1990).

Green, J.B. (ed.), *Hearing the New Testament. Strategies for Interpretation*. (Carlisle: Paternoster Press, 1995).

Grobel, K. (ed.), *The Gospel of Truth. A Valentinian Meditation on the Gospel*. (London: A. and C. Black, 1960).

Guilding, A.E. *The Fourth Gospel and Jewish Worship. A Study of the Relation of St John's Gospel to the Ancient Jewish Lectionary System*. (Oxford: Clarendon Press, 1960).

Guillaumont, A. *et al*. (ed.), *The Gospel According to Thomas. The Coptic Text Established and Translated*. (Leiden: E.J. Brill and London: Collins, 1959).

Guthrie, D. *New Testament Introduction*, 4th edn. (Leicester: Inter-Varsity Press and Downers Grove: Apollos, 1990).

Haenchen, E. 'Johanneische Probleme'. *ZTK* 56 (1959), pp. 19–54.

—, *John 1* and *John 2*, ed. R.W. Funk. HS. (Philadelphia: Fortress Press, 1984).

Hahn, F. *The Titles of Jesus in Christology. Their History in Early Christianity*. (London: Lutterworth Press, 1969).

Hammond, H. 'De Antichristo', in *Dissertationes Quatuor*. (London: J. Flesher, 1651), pp. 1–51.

Hanson, A.T. *Grace and Truth. A Study in the Doctrine of the Incarnation*. (London: SPCK, 1975).

—, *The Prophetic Gospel. A Study of John and the Old Testament*. (Edinburgh: T. and T. Clark, 1991).

Harris, E. *Prologue and Gospel. The Theology of the Fourth Evangelist*. JSNTS 107. (Sheffield: Sheffield Academic Press, 1994).

Harris, H. *The Tübingen School*. (Oxford: Clarendon Press, 1975).

Harvey, A.E. *Jesus on Trial. A Study in the Fourth Gospel*. (London: SPCK, 1976).

Hengel, M. *Judaism and Hellenism. Studies in Their Encounter in Palestine during the Early Hellenistic Period*, 2 vols. (London: SCM Press, 1974).

—, 'The Interpretation of the Wine Miracle at Cana: John 2:1–11', in L.D. Hurst and N.T. Wright (ed.), *The Glory of Christ in the New Testament: Studies in Christology. In Memory of George Bradford Caird*. (Oxford: Clarendon Press, 1987), pp. 83–112.

—, *The Johannine Question*. (London: SCM Press and Philadelphia: Trinity Press International, 1989).

Hennecke, E. *New Testament Apocrypha*, ed. R.McL. Wilson, 2 vols. (London: Lutterworth Press, 1963 and 1965).

Higgins, A.J.B. *The Historicity of the Fourth Gospel*. (London: Lutterworth Press, 1960).

—, *Jesus and the Son of Man*. (London: Lutterworth Press, 1964).

Hill, D. 'The Request of Zebedee's Sons and the Johannine δόξα-theme'. *NTS* 13 (1966–67), pp. 281–85.

Hooker, M.D. 'Christology and Methodology'. *NTS* 17 (1970–71), pp. 480–87.

—, 'On Using the Wrong Tool'. *Theology* 75 (1972), pp. 570–81.

—, 'Were There False Teachers in Colossae?', in B. Lindars and S.S. Smalley (ed.), *Christ and Spirit in the New Testament. Studies in Honour of Charles Francis Digby Moule.* (Cambridge: Cambridge University Press, 1973), pp. 315–31.

—, 'In his own Image?', in M.D. Hooker and C.J.A. Hickling (ed.), *What about the New Testament? Essays in Honour of Christopher Evans.* (London: SCM Press, 1975), pp. 28–44.

—, 'The Johannine Prologue and the Messianic Secret'. *NTS* 21 (1974–75), pp. 40–58.

Hoskyns, E.C. *The Fourth Gospel*, ed. F.N. Davey, 2nd edn. (London: Faber and Faber, 1947).

Hoskyns, E.C. and Davey, F.N. *The Riddle of the New Testament*, 3rd edn. (London: Faber and Faber, 1947).

Houlden, J.L. *A Commentary on the Johannine Epistles.* BNTC. (London: A. and C. Black and New York: Harper and Row, 1973).

Howard, W.F. *Christianity According to St John.* (London: Duckworth, 1943).

—, *The Fourth Gospel in Recent Criticism and Interpretation.* 4th edn. (London: Epworth Press, 1955).

Hunter, A.M. *Paul and his Predecessors*, 2nd edn. (London: Nicholson and Watson, 1961).

—, *According to John. A New Look at the Fourth Gospel.* (London: SCM Press, 1968).

Howard-Brook, W. *Becoming Children of God. John's Gospel and Radical Discipleship.* BAL. (Maryknoll: Orbis Books, 1994).

Jaubert, A. *The Date of the Last Supper.* (New York: Alba, 1965).

Jeremias, J. *The Eucharistic Words of Jesus*, 2nd edn. (London: SCM Press, 1966).

—, *The Rediscovery of Bethesda: John 5.2.* (Louisville: Southern Baptist Theological Seminary, 1966).

—, *The Prayers of Jesus.* SBT (2) 6. (London: SCM Press, 1967).

—, *New Testament Theology*, vol.1: *The Proclamation of Jesus.* NTL. (London: SCM Press, 1971).

Johns, L.J. and Miller, D.B. 'The Signs as Witnesses in the Fourth Gospel. Re-examining the Evidence'. *CBQ* 56 (1994), pp. 519–35.

Johnson, L. 'Who was the Beloved Disciple?' *ExpT* 77 (1965-66), pp. 157–58.

Johnston, G. *The Spirit-Paraclete in the Gospel of John.* SNTSMS 12. (London and New York: Cambridge University Press, 1970).

Jones, L.P. *The Symbol of Water in the Gospel of John* JSNTS 145. (Sheffield: Sheffield Academic Press, 1997).

Jonge, M. de *Jesus: Stranger from Heaven and Son of God. Jesus Christ and the Christians in Johannine Perspective.* SBLDS 11. (Missoula: Scholars Press, 1977).

— (ed.), *L'Évangile de Jean. Sources, rédaction, théologie.* BETL 44. (Leuven: Leuven University Press, 1977).

Jülicher, A. *An Introduction to the New Testament*. (London: Smith Elder, 1904).

Kaefer, J.Ph. 'Les discours d'adieu en Jean 13:31-17:26. Rédaction et théologie.' *NovT* 26 (1984), pp. 253–82.

Käsemann, E. 'Rudolf Bultmann: Das Evangelium des Johannes'. *VF* 3 (1942–46), pp. 182–201.

—, 'The Problem of the Historical Jesus', in *idem, Essays on New Testament Themes*. SBT. (London: SCM Press, 1964), pp. 15–47.

—, *The Testament of Jesus. A Study of the Gospel of John in the Light of Chapter 17*. NTL. (London: SCM Press and Philadelphia: Fortress Press, 1968).

Klein, H.von 'Die lukanisch–johanneische Passionstradition'. *ZNW* 67 (1976), pp. 155–86.

Knox, W.L. *Some Hellenistic Elements in Primitive Christianity*. (London: Oxford University Press, 1944).

Koester, C.R. *Symbolism in the Fourth Gospel. Meaning, Mystery, Community*. (Minneapolis: Fortress Press, 1995).

Kopp, C. *The Holy Places of the Gospels*. (Freiburg im Breisgau: Herder and London: Nelson, 1963).

Kuhn, K.G. 'Die in Palästina gefundenen hebräischen Texte und das Neue Testament'. *ZTK* 47 (1950), pp. 192–211.

—, 'Johannesevangelium und Qumrantexte', in *Neotestamentica et Patristica. In Honour of O. Cullmann*. NovT Sup 6. (Leiden: E.J. Brill, 1962), pp. 111–22.

Kümmel, W.G. *The New Testament. The History of the Investigation of Its Problems*. NTL. (London: SCM Press, 1973).

—, *The Theology of the New Testament: According to Its Major Witnesses – Jesus, Paul, John*. (London: SCM Press, 1974).

—, *Introduction to the New Testament*. (London: SCM Press, 1975).

Kysar, R. 'The Source Analysis of the Fourth Gospel – a Growing Consensus?' *NovT* 15 (1973), pp. 134–52.

—, *The Fourth Evangelist and His Gospel. An Examination of Contemporary Scholarship*. (Minneapolis: Augsburg Publishing House, 1975).

Ladd, G.E. *A Theology of the New Testament*. (Guildford and London: Lutterworth Press, 1975).

Lagrange, M.-J. *L'Évangile selon Saint Jean*. (Paris: Gabalda, 1948).

Leaney, A.R.C. 'The Johannine Paraclete and the Qumran Scrolls', in Charlesworth (ed.), *John and Qumran*, pp. 38–61.

Lee, D.A. *The Symbolic Narratives of the Fourth Gospel. The Interplay of Form and Meaning*. JSNTS 95. (Sheffield: JSOT Press, 1994).

Lee, E.K. 'The Drama of the Fourth Gospel'. *ExpT* 65 (1953–54), pp. 173–76.

Léon-Dufour, X. 'Bulletin de Litterature Johannique'. RSR 68 (1980), pp. 271–316.

Lietzmann, H. *The Three Oldest Martyrologies*. (Cambridge: Deighton Bell, 1904).

Lieu, J.M. 'Gnosticism and the Gospel of John'. *ExpT* 90 (1978–79), pp. 223–27.

Lightfoot, J.B. *Biblical Essays*. (London and New York: Macmillan, 1893), essays 1–3.

Lightfoot, R.H. *St John's Gospel. A Commentary*, ed. C.F. Evans. (Oxford: Clarendon Press, 1956).

Lindars, B. *New Testament Apologetic. The Doctrinal Significance of the Old Testament Quotations*. (London: SCM Press, 1961).

—, 'ΔΙΚΑΙΟΣΥΝΗΗΗn Jn 16:8 and 10', in *idem*, *Essays on John*, ed. C.M. Tuckett. SNTA 17. (Leuven: Leuven University Press and Peeters, 1992), pp. 21–31.

—, *Behind the Fourth Gospel*. Studies in Creative Criticism 3. (London: SPCK, 1971).

—, *The Gospel of John*. NCB. (London: Oliphants, 1972).

—, 'The Son of Man in the Johannine Christology', in *idem*, *Essays on John*, pp. 33–50.

—, 'Word and Sacrament in the Fourth Gospel', in *ibid.*, pp. 51–65.

—, 'The Passion in the Fourth Gospel', in *ibid.*, pp. 67–85.

—, 'John and the Synoptic Gospels: A Test Case', in *ibid.*, pp. 105–112.

—, 'The New Look on the Son of Man'. *BJRL* 63 (1981), pp. 437–62.

—, *Jesus Son of Man. A Fresh Examination of the Son of Man Sayings in the Gospels in the Light of Recent Research*. (London: SPCK, 1983).

Loader, W. *The Christology of the Fourth Gospel. Structure and Issues*. BET 23. (Frankfurt am Main: Peter Lang, 1989).

Lohse, E. 'Miracles in the Fourth Gospel', in Hooker and Hickling (ed.), *What about the New Testament?*, pp. 64–75.

Loisy, A. *Le quatrième Évangile*, 2nd edn. (Paris: Picard et Fils, 1921).

Luzarraga, J. 'La función docente del Messías en el Cuarto Evangelio'. *Estudios Biblicos* 32 (1973), pp. 119–36.

Maccini, R.G. 'A Reassessment of the Woman at the Well in John 4 in Light of the Samaritan Context'. *JSNT* 53 (1993–94), pp. 35–46.

—, *Her Testimony is True. Women as Witnesses According to John*. JSNTS 125. (Sheffield: Sheffield Academic Press, 1996).

MacGregor, G.H.C. *The Gospel of John*. (London: Hodder and Stoughton, 1928).

Macquarrie, J. *The Scope of Demythologizing. Bultmann and his Critics*. LPT (London: SCM Press, 1960).

MacRae, G. 'The Fourth Gospel and *Religionsgeschichte*'. *CBQ* 32 (1970), pp. 13–24.

—, 'The *Ego*-Proclamation in Gnostic Sources', in E. Bammel (ed.), *The Trial of Jesus. Cambridge Studies in Honour of C.F.D. Moule*. SBT (2) 13. (London: SCM Press, 1970), pp. 122–34.

Maddox, R. 'The Function of the Son of Man in the Gospel of John', in R.J. Banks (ed.), *Reconciliation and Hope*. New Testament Essays on Atonement and Eschatology. (Exeter: Paternoster Press, 1974), pp. 186–204.

Manson, T.W. *The Teaching of Jesus*, 2nd edn. (Cambridge: Cambridge University Press, 1935).

Marsh, J. *The Gospel of St John*. PGC. (Harmondsworth: Pelican Books, 1968).

Marshall, I.H. 'The Synoptic Son of Man Sayings in Recent Discussion'. *NTS* 12 (1965–66), pp. 327–51.

—, 'Palestinian and Hellenistic Christianity: Some Critical Comments'. *NTS* 19 (1972–73), pp. 271–87.

— (ed.), *New Testament Interpretation. Essays in Principles and Methods*. (Exeter: Paternoster Press, 1985).

Martin, R.P. 'The New Quest of the Historical Jesus', in C.F.H. Henry (ed.), *Jesus of Nazareth, Saviour and Lord*. (London: Tyndale Press, 1966), pp. 25–45.

—, *Mark: Evangelist and Theologian*. (Exeter: Paternoster Press, 1972).

—, *New Testament Foundations. A Guide for Christian Students*, vol. 1: *The Four Gospels*. (Exeter: Paternoster Press and Grand Rapids: Eerdmans, 1975).

Martínez, F.G. *The Dead Sea Scrolls Translated. The Qumran Texts in English*. (Leiden: E.J. Brill, 1994).

Martyn, J.L. *History and Theology in the Fourth Gospel*, 2nd edn. (Nashville: Abingdon Press, 1979).

Mascall, E.L. *Christ, the Christian and the Church. A Study of the Incarnation and Its Consequences*. (London: Longmans, 1946).

Mastin, B.A. 'A Neglected Feature of the Christology of the Fourth Gospel'. *NTS* 22 (1975–76), pp. 32–51.

McConnell, F. (ed.), *The Bible and the Narrative Tradition*. (New York and Oxford: Oxford University Press, 1986).

McDonald, J.I.H. *Kerygma and Didache. The Articulation and Structure of the Earliest Christian Message*. (Cambridge: Cambridge University Press, 1980).

Meeks, W.A. 'Galilee and Judea in the Fourth Gospel'. *JBL* 85 (1966), pp. 159–69.

—, *The Prophet-King. Moses Traditions and the Johannine Christology*. (Leiden: E.J. Brill, 1967).

—, 'The Man from Heaven in Johannine Sectarianism'. *JBL* 91 (1972), pp. 44–72.

—, ' "Am I a Jew?" Johannine Christianity and Judaism', in J. Neusner (ed.), *Christianity, Judaism, and Other Greco-Roman Cults*, vol. 1: *New Testament*. SJLA 12. (Leiden: E.J. Brill, 1975), pp. 163–86.

Menken, M.J.J. *Old Testament Quotations in the Fourth Gospel. Studies in Textual Form*. CBET 15. (Kampen: Kok Pharos, 1996).

Miranda, J.P. *Being and the Messiah. The Message of St John*. (Maryknoll: Orbis Books, 1977).

Mlakuzhyil, G. *The Christocentric Literary Structure of the Fourth Gospel*. AnBib 117. (Rome: Pontificio Instituto Biblico, 1987).

Moffatt, J. *An Introduction to the Literature of the New Testament*, 3rd edn. (Edinburgh: T. and T. Clark, 1918).

Moloney, F.J. *The Johannine Son of Man*, 2nd edn. BDSR 14. (Rome: Libreria Ateneo Salesiano, 1978).

—, 'From Cana to Cana (John 2:1–4:54) and the Fourth Evangelist's Concept of Correct (and Incorrect) Faith'. *Studia Biblica 1978* II. JSNTS 2. (Sheffield: JSOT Press, 1980), pp. 185–213.

Moore, S.D. *Literary Criticism and the Gospels. The Theoretical Challenge*. (New Haven and London: Yale University Press, 1989).

Morgan, R. 'Which was the Fourth Gospel? The Order of the Gospels and the Unity of Scripture'. *JSNT* 54 (1993–94), pp. 3–28.

Morris, L.L. *Jesus is the Christ. Studies in the Theology of John.* (Leicester: Inter-Varsity Press and Grand Rapids: Eerdmans, 1989).

—, *The Gospel According to John*, 2nd edn. (Grand Rapids: Eerdmans, 1995).

Moule, C.F.D. 'The Individualism of the Fourth Gospel'. *NovT* 5 (1962), pp. 171–90.

—, 'The Intention of the Evangelists', in *idem, The Phenomenon of the New Testament. An Inquiry into the Implications of Certain Features of the New Testament.* SBT (2) 1. (London: SCM Press, 1967), pp. 100–114.

—, 'Neglected Features in the Problem of "the Son of Man" ', in J. Gnilka (ed.), *Neues Testament und Kirche. Für Rudolf Schnackenburg.* (Freiburg im Breisgau: Herder, 1974), pp. 413–28.

—, 'The Meaning of "Life" in the Gospel and Epistles of St John', *Theology* 78 (1975), pp. 114–25.

—, ' "The Son of Man": Some of the Facts'. *NTS* 41 (1995), pp. 277–79.

Müller, U.B. 'Die Parakleten-vorstellung im Johannesevangelium'. *ZTK* 71 (1974), pp. 31–77.

—, *Die Geschichte der Christologie in der johanneischen Gemeinde.* SBS 77. (Stuttgart: Katholisches Bibelwerk, 1975).

Munck, J. 'The New Testament and Gnosticism', in W. Klassen and G.F. Snyder (ed.), *Current Issues in New Testament Interpretation. Essays in Honour of Otto A. Piper.* (London: SCM Press, 1962), pp. 224–38.

Neill, S.C. and Wright, N.T. *The Interpretation of the New Testament 1861–1986*, 2nd edn. (Oxford and New York: Oxford University Press, 1988).

Neirynck, F. 'John and the Synoptics', in de Jonge (ed.), *L'Évangile de Jean,* pp. 73–106.

— *et al. Jean et les Synoptiques. Examen critique de l'exégèse de M.-E. Boismard.* BETL 49. (Leuven: Leuven University Press, 1979).

—, 'John and the Synoptics: 1975–1990', in Denaux (ed.), *John and the Synoptics,* pp. 3–62.

Nicholson, G.C. *Death as Departure. The Johannine Descent-Ascent Scheme.* SBLDS 63. (Chico: Scholars Press, 1983).

Nicol, W. *The Sēmeia in the Fourth Gospel. Tradition and Redaction.* NovT Sup 32. (Leiden: E.J. Brill, 1972).

Nineham, D.E. 'The Order of Events in St Mark's Gospel — An Examination of Dr Dodd's Hypothesis', in *idem.* (ed.), *Studies in the Gospels. Essays in Memory of R.H. Lightfoot.* (Oxford: Blackwell, 1955), pp. 223–39.

Noack, B. *Zur johanneischen Tradition. Beiträge zur Kritik an der literar--kritischen Analyse des vierten Evangeliums.* (Copenhagen: Rosenkilde og Bagger, 1954).

Nock, A.D. 'Early Gentile Christianity and Its Hellenistic Background', in Z. Stewart (ed.), *Arthur Darby Nock. Essays on Religion and the Ancient World*, vol.1. (Oxford: Clarendon Press, 1972), pp. 49–133.

—, 'Philo and Hellenistic Philosophy', in Stewart (ed.), *Arthur Darby Nock*, vol.2, pp. 559–65.

—, 'Gnosticism', in *ibid.*, pp. 940–59.

Nock, A.D. and Festugière, A.-J. *Corpus Hermeticum*, 4 vols. (Paris: L'Association Guillaume Budé, 1945–54).

Norden, E. *Agnostos Theos. Untersuchungen zur Formengeschichte religiöser Rede.* (Stuttgart: Teubner, 1956).

Nunn, H.P.V. *The Authorship of the Fourth Gospel.* (Eton: Alden and Blackwell, 1952).

Odeberg, H. *The Fourth Gospel: Interpreted in its Relation to Contemporaneous Religious Currents in Palestine and the Hellenistic-Oriental World.* (Amsterdam: B.R. Grüner, 1968).

O'Grady, J.F. *Individual and Community in John.* (Rome: Pontifical Biblical Institute, 1978).

Olsson, B. *Structure and Meaning in the Fourth Gospel. A Text-linguistic Analysis of John 2:1–11 and 4:1–42.* ConBNT 6. (Lund: C.W.K. Gleerup, 1974).

Painter, J. *John: Witness and Theologian*, 2nd edn. (London: SPCK, 1979).

—, 'The Farewell Discourses and the History of Johannine Christianity'. *NTS* 27 (1980–81), pp. 525–43.

—, 'Christology and the History of the Johannine Community in the Prologue of the Fourth Gospel'. *NTS* 30 (1984), pp. 460–74.

—, *The Quest for the Messiah. The History, Literature and Theology of the Johannine Community*, 2nd edn. (Edinburgh: T. and T. Clark, 1993).

Pancaro, S. 'The Relationship of the Church to Israel in the Gospel of St John'. *NTS* 21 (1974–75), pp. 396–405.

—, *The Law in the Fourth Gospel. The Torah and the Gospel, Moses and Jesus, Judaism and Christianity According to John.* NovT Sup 42. (Leiden: E.J. Brill, 1975).

Parker, P. 'Two Editions of John'. *JBL* 75 (1956), pp. 303–314.

—, 'John and John Mark'. *JBL* 79 (1960), pp. 97–110.

—, 'John the Son of Zebedee and the Fourth Gospel'. *JBL* 81 (1962), pp. 35–43.

—, 'Luke and the Fourth Evangelist'. *NTS* 9 (1962–63), pp. 317–36.

Percy, E. *Untersuchungen über den Ursprung der johanneischen Theologie, zugleich ein Beitrag zur Frage nach der Engtehung des Gnostizismus.* (Lund: C.W.K. Gleerup, 1939).

Perkins, P. *Reading the New Testament. An Introduction.* (London: Geoffrey Chapman, 1988).

—, *Gnosticism and the New Testament.* (Minneapolis: Fortress Press, 1993).

Perrin, N. *Rediscovering the Teaching of Jesus.* (London: SCM Press, 1967).

—, *The New Testament. An Introduction.* (New York: Harcourt Brace Jovanovich, 1974).

Peterson, E. 'Urchristentum und Mandäismus'. *ZNW* 27 (1928), pp. 55–98.

Pfleiderer, O. *Primitive Christianity. Its Writings and Teachings in Their Historical Connections*, vol. 4. (London : Williams and Norgate, 1911).

Phillips, G.L. 'Faith and Vision in the Fourth Gospel', in F.L. Cross (ed.), *Studies in the Fourth Gospel.* (London: A.R. Mowbray, 1957), pp. 83–96.

Pollard, T.E. *Johannine Christology and the Early Church.* SNTSMS 13. (Cambridge: Cambridge University Press, 1970).

Porter, S.E. and Olbricht, T.H. *Rhetoric and the New Testament. Essays from the 1992 Heidelberg Conference.* JSNTS 90. (Sheffield: JSOT Press, 1993).

— and Evans, C.A. (ed.), *The Johannine Writings. A Sheffield Reader.* Biblical Seminar 32. (Sheffield: Sheffield Academic Press, 1995).

Potterie, I. de la *La vérite dans Saint Jean*, 2 vols. AnBib 73 and 74. (Rome: Pontifical Biblical Institute, 1977).

Powell, M. *What is Narrative Criticism? A New Approach to the Bible.* (London: SPCK, 1993).

Preiss, T. *Life in Christ.* SBT. (London: SCM Press, 1954).

Pryor, J.W. *John: Evangelist of the Covenant People. The Narrative and Themes of the Fourth Gospel.* (London: Darton, Longman and Todd, 1992).

Purvis, J.D. 'The Fourth Gospel and the Samaritans'. *NovT* 17 (1975), pp. 161–90.

Quispel, G. 'L'Évangile de Jean et la Gnose', in Boismard *et al., L'Évangile de Jean,* pp. 197–208.

Raney, W .H. *The Relation of the Fourth Gospel to the Christian Cultus.* (Giessen: A. Töpelmann, 1933).

Reicke, B. 'Traces of Gnosticism in the Dead Sea Scrolls?' *NTS* 1 (1954–55), pp. 137–41.

Reim, G. *Studien zum alttestamentlichen Hintergrund des Johannesevangeliums.* SNTSMS 22. (Cambridge: Cambridge University Press, 1974).

Reinhartz, A. *The Word in the World. The Cosmological Tale in the Fourth Gospel.* SBLMS 45. (Atlanta: Scholars Press, 1992).

Reitzenstein, R. *Das mandäische Buch des Herrn der Grösse und die Evangelienüberlieferung.* (Heidelberg: Akademie der Wissenschaften, 1919).

—, *Die hellenistischen Mysterienreligionen: Nach ihren Grundgedanken und Wirkungen.* (Darmstadt: Wissenschaftliche Buchgesellschaft, 1966).

Rengstorf, K.H. *Johannes und sein Evangelium.* (Darmstadt: Wissenschaftliche Buchgesellschaft, 1980).

Rensberger, D. *Overcoming the World. Politics and Community in the Gospel of John.* (Philadelphia: Westminster Press, 1988, and London: SPCK, 1989).

Reumann, J. *Jesus in the Church's Gospels. Modern Scholarship and the Earliest Sources.* (London: SPCK, 1970).

Rhoads, D. and Michie, D. *Mark as Story. An Introduction to the Narrative of a Gospel.* (Philadelphia: Fortress Press, 1982).

Richardson, A. *The Gospel According to St John.* TBC. (London: SCM Press, 1959).

Robinson, J.A.T. *The Body. A Study in Pauline Theology.* SBT. (London: SCM Press, 1952).

—, 'The Baptism of John and the Qumran Community: Testing a Hypothesis', in *idem, Twelve New Testament Studies.* SBT. (London: SCM Press, 1962), pp. 11–27.

—, 'Elijah, John and Jesus: An Essay in Detection', in *ibid.,* pp. 28–52.

—, 'The Parable of the Shepherd (John 10:1–5)', in *ibid.,* pp. 67–75.

—, 'The New Look on the Fourth Gospel', in *ibid.,* pp. 94–106.

—, 'The Destination and Purpose of St John's Gospel', in *ibid.,* pp. 107–125.

—, 'The Relation of the Prologue to the Gospel of St John'. *NTS* 9 (1962–63), pp. 120–29.

—, 'The Place of the Fourth Gospel', in P. Gardner-Smith (ed.), *The Roads Converge.* (London: Edward Arnold, 1963), pp. 49–74.

—, 'The Use of the Fourth Gospel for Christology Today', in Lindars and Smalley (ed.), *Christ and Spirit*, pp. 61–78.

—, *Redating the New Testament*. (London: SCM Press, 1976).

—, ' "His Witness is True": A Test of the Johannine Claims', in E. Bammel and C.F.D Moule (ed.), *Jesus and the Politics of His Day*. (Cambridge and New York: Cambridge University Press, 1984), pp. 453–76.

—, *The Priority of John*, ed. J.F. Coakley. (London: SCM Press, 1985 and Oak Park: Meyer-Stone Books, 1987).

Robinson, J.M. *A New Quest of the Historical Jesus*. SBT 4. (London: SCM Press, 1959).

Rowland, C.C. *The Open Heaven. A Study of Apocalyptic in Judaism and Early Christianity*. (London: SPCK, 1982).

Rowley, H.H. 'The Baptism of John and the Qumran Sect', in A.J.B. Higgins (ed.), *New Testament Essays. Studies in Memory of Thomas Walter Manson 1893–1958*. (Manchester: Manchester University Press, 1959), pp. 218–29.

Ruckstuhl, E. *Die literarische Einheit des Johannesevangeliums: Der gegenwärtige Stand der einschlägigen Forschungen*. (Freiburg in der Schweiz: Paulusverlag, 1951).

Sanday, W. *The Criticism of the Fourth Gospel.*(Oxford: Clarendon Press, 1905).

Sanders, J.N. *The Fourth Gospel in the Early Church. Its Origin and Influence on Christian Theology up to Irenaeus*. (Cambridge: Cambridge University Press, 1943).

—, *The Foundations of the Christian Faith. A Study of the Teaching of the New Testament in the Light of Historical Criticism*. (London: A. and C. Black, 1950).

—, ' "Those Whom Jesus Loved" (Jn xi.5)'. *NTS* 1 (1954–55), pp. 29–41.

—, 'Who Was the Disciple Whom Jesus Loved?', in Cross (ed.) *Studies in the Fourth Gospel*, pp. 72–82.

—, 'St John on Patmos'. *NTS* 9 (1962–63), pp. 75–85.

—, *A Commentary on the Gospel According to St John*, ed. B.A. Mastin. BNTC. (London: A. and C. Black, 1968).

Sanders, J.T. *The New Testament Christological Hymns. Their Historical Religious Background*. SNTSMS 15. (Cambridge: Cambridge University Press, 1971).

Schein, B.E. *Following the Way. The Setting of John's Gospel*. (Minneapolis: Augsburg Publishing House, 1980).

Schlatter, A. 'Die Sprache und Heimat des vierten Evangelisten', in K. Rengstorf (ed.), *Johannes und sein Evangelium*. WF 82. (Darmstadt: Wissenschaftliche Buchgesellschaft, 1973), pp. 28–201.

Schmidt, K.L. *Der Rahmen der Geschichte Jesu*. (Berlin: Trowitzch & Sohn, 1919).

Schmithals, W. *Gnosticism in Corinth. An Investigation of the Letters to the Corinthians*. (New York and Nashville: Abingdon, 1971).

Schnackenburg, R. *The Gospel According to St John*, 3 vols. HTCNT. (London: Burns and Oates, 1968–82).

—, 'Die johanneische Gemeinde und ihre Geisterfahrung', in *idem et al.* (ed.), *Die Kirche des Anfangs*. (Leipzig: St Benno and Freiburg im Breisgau: Herder, 1978), pp. 277–306.

—, *Jesus in the Gospels. A Biblical Christology*. (Louisville: Westminster John Knox Press, 1995).

Schniewind, J. *Die Parallelperikopen bei Lukas und Johannes*. (Hildesheim: G. Olms, 1958).

Schottroff, L. *Der Glaubende und die feindliche Welt. Beobachtungen zum gnostischen Dualismus und seiner Bedeutung für Paulus und das Johannesevangelium*. WMANT 37. (Neukirchen-Vluyn: Neukirchener Verlag, 1970).

Schulz, S. *Komposition und Herkunft der johanneischen Reden*. BWANT 5. (Stuttgart: W. Kohlhammer, 1960).

Schwartz, E. 'Aporien im vierten Evangelium', in *Nachrichten von der Königlichen Gesellschaft der Wissenschaften zu Göttingen. Philologischhistorische Klasse*. (Berlin, 1907), pp. 342–72; (1908), pp. 115–88, 497–560.

Schweitzer, A. *The Quest of the Historical Jesus. A Critical Study of Its Progress from Reimarus to Wrede*, 3rd edn. (London: A. and C. Black, 1954).

Schweizer, E. *Ego Eimi. Die religionsgeschichtliche Herkunft und theologische Bedeutung der johanneischen Bildreden*, 2nd edn. FRLANT ns 38. (Göttingen: Vandenhoeck & Ruprecht, 1965).

Scobie, C.H.H. *John the Baptist*. (London: SCM Press, 1964).

—, 'The Origins and Development of Samaritan Christianity'. *NTS* 19 (1972–73), pp. 390–414.

Scott, E.F. *The Fourth Gospel. Its Purpose and Theology*, 2nd edn. (Edinburgh: T. and T. Clark, 1923).

Seeburg, A. *Die Didache des Judentums und der Urchristenheit*. (Leipzig: A. Deichert/Georg Böhme, 1908).

Segovia, F.F. *The Farewell of the Word. The Johannine Call to Abide*. (Minneapolis: Fortress Press, 1991).

Servotte, H. *According to John. A Literary Reading of the Fourth Gospel*. (London: Darton, Longman and Todd, 1994).

Shellard, B. 'The Relationship of Luke and John: A Fresh Look at an Old Problem'. *JTS* (ns) 46 (1995), pp. 71–98.

Sidebottom, E.M. *The Christ of the Fourth Gospel: In the Light of First-Century Thought*. (London: SPCK, 1961).

Smalley, S.S. 'Liturgy and Sacrament in the Fourth Gospel'. *EQ* 29 (1957), pp. 159–70.

—, 'The Christology of Acts'. *ExpT* 73 (1961–62), pp. 358–62.

—, 'The Delay of the Parousia'. *JBL* 83 (1964), pp. 41–54.

—, 'New Light on the Fourth Gospel'. *TynB* 17 (1966), pp. 35–62.

—, 'The Johannine Son of Man Sayings'. *NTS* 15 (1968–69), pp. 278–301.

—, 'Diversity and Development in John'. *NTS* 17 (1970–71), pp. 276–92.

—, 'The Christology of Acts Again', in Lindars and Smalley (ed.), *Christ and Spirit*, pp. 79–93.

—, 'Johannes 1,51 und die Einleitung zum vierten Evangelium', in R. Pesch and R. Schnackenburg (ed.), *Jesus und der Menschensohn. Für Anton Vögtle*. (Freiburg im Breisgau: Herder, 1975), pp. 300–313.

—, 'Redaction Criticism', in I.H. Marshall (ed.), *New Testament Interpretation*, pp. 181–95.

—, 'The Christ-Christian Relationship in Paul and John', in D.A. Hagner and M.J. Harris (ed.), *Pauline Studies. Essays Presented to F.F. Bruce.* (Exeter: Paternoster Press, 1980), pp. 95–105.

—, 'What about 1 John?'. *Studia Biblica 1978,* vol. 3. JSNTS 3. (Sheffield: JSOT Press, 1980), pp. 337–43.

—, 'Salvation Proclaimed: VIII. John 1.29–34'. *ExpT* 93 (1981–82), pp. 324–29.

—, 'Johannine Spirituality', in G.S. Wakefield (ed.), *A Dictionary of Christian Spirituality.* (London: SCM Press, 1983), pp. 230–32.

—, *1, 2, 3 John.* WBC 51. (Waco: Word Books, 1984).

—, 'John's Revelation and John's Community'. *BJRL* 69 (1987), pp. 549–71.

—, *Thunder and Love. John's Revelation and John's Community.* (Milton Keynes: Nelson Word, 1994).

—, ' "The Paraclete": Pneumatology in the Johannine Gospel and Apocalypse', in Culpepper and Black (ed.), *Exploring the Gospel of John*, pp. 289–300.

—, 'The Johannine Community and the Letters of John', in M. Bockmuehl and M.B. Thompson (ed.), *A Vision for the Church. Essays in Honour of J.P.M. Sweet.* (Edinburgh: T. and T. Clark, 1997), pp. 95–104.

Smith, D.H. 'Concerning the Duration of the Ministry of Jesus'. *ExpT* 76 (1964–65), pp. 114–16.

Smith, D.M. *The Composition and Order of the Fourth Gospel. Bultmann's Literary Theory.* (New Haven and London: Yale University Press, 1965).

—, 'The Sources of the Gospel of John', in *idem, Johannine Christianity. Essays on its Setting, Sources and Theology.* (Edinburgh: T. and T. Clark, 1987), pp. 39–61.

—, 'Johannine Christianity', in *ibid.*, pp. 1–36.

—, 'The Milieu of the Johannine Miracle Source', in *ibid.*, pp. 62–79.

—, 'The Presentation of Jesus in the Fourth Gospel', in *ibid.*, pp. 175–89.

—, 'John and the Synoptics: Some Dimensions of the Problem', in *ibid.*, pp. 145–72.

—, *John Among the Gospels: The Relationship in Twentieth-Century Research.* (Minneapolis: Fortress Press, 1992).

—, *The Theology of the Gospel of John.* NTT. (Cambridge and New York: Cambridge University Press, 1995).

Smith, M. 'On the Wine God in Palestine (Gen. 18, Jn 2, and Achilles Tatius)', in *S.W. Barron Jublilee Volume.* (Jerusalem: American Academy for Jewish Research, 1975), pp. 815–29.

Smith, R.H. 'Exodus Typology in the Fourth Gospel'. *JBL* 81 (1962), pp. 329–42.

Solages, B. de *Jean et les Synoptiques.* (Leiden: E.J. Brill, 1979).

Spiro, A. 'Stephen's Samaritan Background', in J. Munck, *The Acts of the Apostles*, revised by W.F. Albright and C.S. Mann. AB 31. (Garden City: Doubleday, 1967), pp. 285–300.

Stanton, G.N. *Jesus of Nazareth in New Testament Preaching.* SNTSMS 27. (Cambridge: Cambridge University Press, 1974).

Stauffer, E. *Jesus and His Story.* (London: SCM Press, 1960).

Stibbe, M.W.G. *John as Storyteller. Narrative Criticism and the Fourth Gospel.* SNTSMS 73. (Cambridge: Cambridge University Press, 1992).

—, *The Gospel of John as Literature. An Anthology of Twentieth-Century Perspectives.* NTTS 17. (Leiden: E.J. Brill, 1993).

—, *John.* Readings. (Sheffield: JSOT Press, 1993).

—, *John's Gospel.* NTR. (London and New York: Routledge, 1994).

Stott, J.R.W. *The Epistles of John. An Introduction and Commentary.* TNTC. (Leicester: Inter-Varsity Press and Grand Rapids: Eerdmans, 1964).

Strachan, R.H. *The Fourth Evangelist: Dramatist or Historian?* (London: Hodder and Stoughton, 1925).

—, *The Fourth Gospel. Its Significance and Environment,* 3rd edn. (London: SCM Press, 1941).

Strack, H.L. and Billerbeck, P., *Kommentar zum Neuen Testament aus Talmud und Midrash,* 2nd edn. vol. 2. (München: C.H. Beck, 1956).

Streeter, B.H. *The Four Gospels. A Study of Origins,* 2nd edn. (London: Macmillan, 1930).

Sweet, J.P.M. 'Second Thoughts: VIII. The Kerygma'. *ExpT* 76 (1964–65), pp. 143–47.

Swete, H.B. *The Gospel According to St Mark. The Greek Text, with Introduction, Notes and Indices,* 3rd edn. (London: Macmillan, 1909).

Talbert, C.H. *What is a Gospel? The Genre of the Canonical Gospels.* (Philadelphia: Fortress Press, 1997, and London: SPCK, 1978).

—, *Reading John. A Literary and Theological Commentary on the Fourth Gospel and the Johannine Epistles.* RNT. (New York: Crossroad Publishing and London: SPCK, 1992).

Tasker, R.V.G. *The Gospel According to St John.* TNTC. (London: Tyndale Press, 1960).

Taylor, V. *Behind the Third Gospel. A Study of the Proto-Luke Hypothesis.* (Oxford: Clarendon Press, 1926).

Teeple, H.M. 'Qumran and the Origin of the Fourth Gospel'. *NovT* 4 (1960), pp. 6–25.

—, *The Literary Origin of the Gospel of John.* (Evanston: Religion and Ethics Institute, 1974).

Temple, W. *Readings in St John's Gospel,* 2nd edn. (London: Macmillan, 1945).

Thomas, J.C.T. *Footwashing in John 13 and the Johannine Community.* JSNTS 61. (Sheffield: JSOT Press, 1991).

Thompson, M.M. *The Humanity of Jesus in the Fourth Gospel.* (Philadelphia: Fortress Press, 1988).

Thyen, H. 'Aus der Literatur zum Johannesevangelium'. *TR* (NF) 39 (1974–75), pp. 1–69, *et seq.*

Tilborg, S. van *Imaginative Love in John.* BI 2. (Leiden, New York and Köln: E.J. Brill, 1993).

Titus, E.L. 'The Identity of the Beloved Disciple'. *JBL* 69 (1950), pp. 323–28.

Torrey, C.C. *Our Translated Gospels. Some of the Evidence.* (London: Hodder and Stoughton, 1937).

Trebilco, P.R. *Jewish Communities in Asia Minor.* SNTSMS 69. (Cambridge: Cambridge University Press, 1991).

Trites, A.A. *The New Testament Concept of Witness.* SNTSMS 31. (Cambridge and New York: Cambridge University Press, 1977).

Tuckett, C.M. (ed.), *Essays on John: by Barnabas Lindars.* (Leuven: Leuven University Press, 1993).

Underhill, E. *The Mystic Way. A Psychological Study in Christian Origins.* (London and Toronto: J.M. Dent, 1913).

Unnik, W.C. van 'The Purpose of St John's Gospel'. *SE* 1 (1959), pp. 382–411.

Van Belle, G. *The Signs Source in the Fourth Gospel. Historical Survey and Critical Evaluation of the Semeia Hypothesis.* BETL 116. (Leuven: Leuven University Press and Peeters, 1994).

VanderKam, J.C. *The Dead Sea Scrolls Today.* (Grand Rapids: Eerdmans and London: SPCK, 1994).

Vanderlip, D.G. *John. The Gospel of Life.* (Valley Forge: Judson, 1979).

Van Segbroeck, F. *et al.* (ed.), *The Four Gospels 1992. Festschrift Frans Neirynck*, 3 vols. BETL 100. (Leuven: Leuven University Press, 1992).

Vellanickal, M. *The Divine Sonship of Christians in the Johannine Writings.* AnBib 72. (Rome: Pontifical Biblical Institute, 1977).

Verheyden, J. 'P. Gardner-Smith and "The Turn of the Tide" ', in Denaux (ed.), *John and the Synoptics*, pp. 423–52.

Vermes, G. *The Dead Sea Scrolls. Qumran in Perspective*, 3rd edn. (London: SCM Press, 1994).

—, *The Complete Dead Sea Scrolls in English*, new edn. (Harmondsworth: The Penguin Press, 1997).

Wahlde, U.C. von *The Earliest Version of John's Gospel. Recovering the Gospel of Signs.* (Wilmington: Michael Glazier, 1989).

Watson, F. 'Is John's Christology Adoptionist?' in Hurst and Wright (ed.), *The Glory of God*, pp. 113–24.

Wellhausen, J. *Das Evangelium Johannis.* (Berlin: G. Reimer, 1908).

Wendt, H.H. *The Gospel According to St John. An Inquiry into Its Genesis and Historical Value.* (Edinburgh: T. and T. Clark, 1902).

Wenham, D. 'The Enigma of the Fourth Gospel: Another Look'. *TynB* 48 (1997), pp. 149–78.

Westcott, B.F. *The Gospel According to St John.* (London: J. Clarke, 1958).

—, *The Epistles of St John*, 4th edn. (Abingdon: Marcham Manor and Grand Rapids: Eerdmans, 1966).

Whitacre, R.A. *Johannine Polemic. The Role of Tradition and Theology.* SBLDS 67. (Chico: Scholars Press, 1982).

Whiteley, D.E.H. *The Theology of St Paul*, 2nd edn. (Oxford: Blackwell, 1974).

Wieand, D.J. 'John V.2 and the Pool of Bethesda'. *NTS* 12 (1965–66), pp. 392–404.

Wilcox, M. 'The Composition of John 13:21–30', in E.E. Ellis and M. Wilcox (ed.), *Neotestamentica et Semitica. Studies in Honour of Matthew Black.* (Edinburgh: T. and T. Clark, 1969), pp. 143–56.

Wiles, M.F. *The Spiritual Gospel. The Interpretation of the Fourth Gospel in the Early Church.* (Cambridge: Cambridge University Press, 1960).

—, *The Remaking of Christian Doctrine.* (London: SCM Press, 1974).

Wilkens, W. *Die Entstehungsgeschichte des vierten Evangeliums.* (Zollikon: Evangelischer Verlag, 1958).

—, 'Die Erweckung des Lazarus'. *TZ* 15 (1959), pp. 22–39.

—, *Zeichen und Werke. Ein Beitrag zur Theologie des 4 Evangeliums in Erzählungs – und Redestoff.* (Zürich: Zwingli Verlag, 1969).

Wilson, R.McL. 'Philo and the Fourth Gospel'. *ExpT* 65 (1953–54), p. 47–49.

—, *The Gnostic Problem. A Study of the Relations Between Hellenistic Judaism and the Gnostic Heresy.* (London: A.R. Mowbray, 1958).

—, *Gnosis and The New Testament.* (Oxford: Blackwell, 1968).

Windisch, H. *Johannes und die Synoptiker. Wollte der vierte Evangelist die älteren Evangelien ergänzen oder ersetzen?* UNT 12. (Leipzig: J.C. Hinrichs, 1926).

—, *The Spirit-Paraclete in the Fourth Gospel.* (Philadelphia: Fortress Press, 1968).

Wink, W. *John the Baptist in the Gospel Tradition.* SNTSMS 7. (Cambridge: Cambridge University Press, 1968).

Witherington, III, B. *John's Wisdom. A Commentary on the Fourth Gospel.* (Cambridge: Lutterworth Press and Louisville: Westminster John Knox Press, 1995).

Woll, D.B. 'The Departure of "The Way": The First Farewell Discourse in the Gospel of John'. *JBL* 99 (1980), pp. 225–39.

Wrede, W. *The Messianic Secret.* (London: J. Clarke, 1971).

Wright, N.T. *Christian Origins and the Question of God,* vol. 1: *The New Testament and the People of God.* (London: SPCK, 1992).

Yamauchi, E.M. *Gnostic Ethics and Mandaean Origins.* (Cambridge: Harvard University Press and London: Oxford University Press, 1970).

—, *Pre-Christian Gnosticism. A Survey of the Proposed Evidence.* (London: Tyndale Press, 1973).

Zahn, T. *Introduction to the New Testament,* 3 vols. (Edinburgh: T. and T. Clark, 1909).

Index of Modern Authors

Abbott, E.A. 46
Abrahams, I. 6
Aland, K. 32
Albright, W.F. 33, 38, 73
Argyle, A.W. 64

Bacon, B.W. 4, 194-5
Bailey, J. 11, 22, 42
Baker, J.A. 28
Baldensperger, W. 162
Ball, D.M. 226
Bammel, E. 27, 109
Bampfylde, G. 262
Banks, R.J. 138, 189
Barr, J. 66
Barrett, C.K. 10, 19, 26, 49, 60, 63,
    68-9, 71, 74, 79, 81, 84, 90, 92,
    99, 101, 138, 140, 148, 166-7,
    170, 181, 255, 262, 270
Bartsch, H.-W. 190, 206
Bauer, W. 50, 166, 183, 186
Beasley-Murray, G.R. 12, 16, 30, 66,
    73, 90, 99, 113, 140, 147, 150,
    160, 216, 220, 249, 254
Becker, H. 103, 104, 105
Becker, J. 13, 105, 107, 108, 171
Benoit, P. 25, 27, 39
Bernard, J.H. 18, 79, 90, 100, 214,
    216, 217, 224, 227
Best, E. 29
Betz, O. 209, 258-9
Beutler J. 69
Billerbeck, P. 71
Black, C.C. 13, 36, 42, 74, 121, 147,
    262
Black, M. 67, 111, 227
Blinzler, J. 13
Böcher, O. 72
Bockmuehl, M. 188, 264
Boer, M.C. de 79, 126, 256

Boice, J.M. 154
Boismard, M.-E. 12, 68, 270
Bonsirven, J. 65, 67
Borgen, P. 13, 64, 71, 110-11, 112,
    120
Bornhaüser, K. 177
Bornkamm, G. 61, 206
Bourke, M. 215
Bousset, W. 56
Bowker, J.W. 70, 71
Boyd, W.J.P. 266
Brandon, S.G.F. 189
Braun, F.-M. 53, 58, 69, 148
Breck, J. 262
Brodie, T.L. 17, 31, 108, 124, 128,
    178, 217, 270, 272
Bromiley, G.W. 151
Brooke, A.E. 7
Brown, R.E. 10, 15, 16, 19, 28, 29,
    32, 33, 34, 39, 44, 48, 55, 57,
    58, 59, 65, 66, 67, 70, 71, 72,
    83, 84, 85, 90, 97, 115, 116-17,
    118, 135, 136, 139, 145, 148,
    151, 152, 155, 178, 179-80,
    185, 214, 215, 216, 220, 222,
    226, 227, 232, 233, 248, 249,
    256, 257, 258, 260, 261, 266,
    270
Brown, S. 67
Brownlee, W.H. 186
Bruce, F.F. 26, 34, 38, 48, 189, 197,
    202
Bultmann, R. 10, 19, 49, 50, 51,
    56-60, 67, 86, 99, 100, 101-4,
    105, 106, 108, 109, 112, 114,
    119, 162-3, 164, 166, 170, 171,
    177, 186, 190, 206, 207-8, 209,
    213, 217, 218, 219, 222, 232,
    233, 270
Burkett, D. 21

Burkitt, F.C. 51
Burney, C.F. 6, 64, 67
Burridge, R.A. 15, 26, 97, 125-6,
     175, 205
Busse, U. 10

Carmignac, J. 57
Carson, D.A. 60, 69, 74, 81, 90, 95,
     129, 140, 179, 213, 249, 252,
     255, 259
Charlesworth, J.H. 36, 58, 72, 90,
     186, 258
Coakley, J.F. 1
Colpe, C. 60
Colwell, E.C. 166
Corell, A. 59, 86, 269
Cranfield, C.E.B. 195
Cribbs, F.L. 11, 90
Cross, F.L. 176
Cullmann, O. 29, 59, 73, 164-5, 182,
     213, 229, 232-3, 237, 238, 255
Culpepper, R.A. 13, 36, 42, 58, 74,
     81, 90, 121, 122-4, 127, 141,
     145, 147, 182, 262
Cuppitt, D. 279

Daniélou, J. 58, 184
Daube, D. 21, 25, 33, 71
Dauer, A. 112-13
Davey, F.N. 82, 211
Davies, W.D. 33, 74, 189
Dauer, A. 11
Denaux, A. 7, 13
Derrett, J.D.M. 215
Dibelius, M. 188, 201-2
Dillon, R.J. 215
Dodd, C.H. 7-8, 16, 19, 23, 29, 30,
     37, 40, 49, 51, 53, 61, 63, 67,
     69, 74, 79, 81, 96, 111, 112,
     129-30, 136, 137, 150, 152,
     153, 161, 179, 188-90, 192,
     193, 194, 195, 196-7, 204, 213,
     222, 224, 226, 227, 228, 232,
     235, 244, 245, 247, 252, 254,
     267-8
Donfried, P. 29
Drower, E.S. 51
Duke, P.D. 147, 151
Dungan, D.L. 13

Dunn, J.D.G. 13, 42, 126, 243

Ellis, E.E. 22, 274
Eltester, W. 138
Ensor, P.W. 30
Evans, C.F. 10, 43, 92, 190

Farmer, W.R. 29
Farrer, A. 174
Festugière, A.J. 52
Filson, F.V. 86
Foerster, W. 51, 61, 65
Forestell, J.T. 232, 255
Fortna, R.T. 69, 105-6, 107, 108,
     115, 119, 131, 171, 253
Foster, D. 126
Franck, E. 259, 262
Freed, E.D. 69, 70
Fuller, R.H. 57, 193
Funk, R.W. 10, 100, 147

Gardner-Smith, P. 4, 6-8, 14, 16, 18,
     19, 23, 32, 41, 42
Gerhardsson, B. 111
Glasson, T.F. 69, 202, 271
Gnilka, J. 243
Goguel, M. 112, 113
Goodenough, E. 7
Goodwin, C. 69, 70
Goulder, M.D. 172
Graham, W.F. ('Billy') 278
Grant, F.C. 11, 57, 170
Green, J.B. 15
Greeven, H. 201
Grobel, K. 54
Guilding, A.E. 71, 173-4
Guillaumont, A. 54
Guthrie, D. 74

Haenchen, E. 10, 16, 100, 122, 147
Hagner, D.A. 193
Hammond, H. 56
Hanson, A.T. 125, 210, 216, 239,
     276, 279-80
Harris, E. 126
Harris, H. 3
Harris, M.J. 193, 245
Harvey, A.E. 154
Hengel, M. 46, 81, 213

Hennecke, E. 1, 78
Henry, C.F.H. 207
Heurtley, C.A. 281
Hick, J. 279
Hickling, C.J.A. 203, 238
Higgins, A.J.B. 25, 41, 137
Hill, D. 227
Hooker, M.D. 56, 136, 203, 238
Hoskyns, E.C. 82, 130, 140, 143,
    150, 208, 210, 211, 213, 222,
    228, 236
Houlden, J.L. 56, 81
Howard, W.F. 162, 165-6
Hunter, A.M. 30, 33, 38, 41, 189
Hurst, N.D. 213, 280

Jaubert, A. 27-8
Jeremias, J. 28, 39, 226, 227
Johnson, L. 85
Johnstone, G. 258, 259
Jonge, M. de 13
Jülicher, A. 3

Kaefer, J.Ph. 113
Käsemann, E. 60, 61, 103, 171, 206,
    210, 277, 279, 281
Klassen, W. 55
Knitter, P.F. 279
Knox, W.L. 160
Koester, C.R. 235
Kopp, C. 39
Kuhn, K.G. 34, 36
Kümmel, W.G. 56, 255, 256
Kysar, R. 13, 86, 99

Ladd, G.E. 272
Lagrange, M.-J. 25, 148, 150
Lapp, P.W. 39
Leaney, A.R.C. 258
Lee, E.K. 149
Lidzbarski, M. 50, 51
Lietzmann, H. 79
Lieu, J.M. 58
Lightfoot, J.B. 65
Lightfoot, R.H. 10, 19, 81, 96, 151,
    159, 160, 232
Lindars, B. 10, 17, 19, 21, 22, 26, 32,
    38, 56, 68, 69, 71, 72, 73, 92,
    106, 108, 111, 128-9, 145, 146,

147, 148, 189, 214, 215, 220,
    241, 248, 260
Loader, O. 248
Lohse, E. 238
Loisy, A. 5, 86, 90, 213, 217, 222, 228

MacGregor, G.H.C. 81
Macquarrie, J. 206, 280
MacRae, G. 109, 181
Maddox, R. 138, 241
Mann, C.S. 73
Manson, T.W. 28
Marsh, J. 27, 228
Marshall, I.H. 15, 26, 42, 92, 122,
    203, 241
Martin, R.P. 29, 197-8, 205, 207, 278
Martinez, F.G. 33
Martyn, J.L. 106, 142, 143, 179
Mascall, E.L. 279, 281
Mastin, B.A. 239
McConnell, F. 126
McDonald, J.I.H. 190
Meeks, W.A. 34, 179, 234-5, 266, 267
Michie, D. 121
Mlakuzhyil, G. 141, 238
Moffatt, J. 3, 46
Moloney, F.J. 243
Moore, S.D. 121, 122
Morgan, R. 11
Morris, L.L. 74, 95
Moule, C.F.D. 14, 27, 29, 42, 137,
    175, 203, 209, 217, 237, 241,
    243, 263
Müller, U.B. 262
Munck, J. 55, 73

Neill, S.C. 6, 49, 206
Neirynck, F. 12, 13
Neusner, J. 71, 179
Newton Flew, R. 256
Nicholson, G.C. 266
Nicol, W. 106, 107, 108, 115, 171,
    184
Niebuhr, R.R. 29
Nineham, D.E. 41, 197
Noack, B. 95
Nock, A.D. 52, 55, 59, 64
Norden, E. 109, 110
Nunn, H.P.V. 90

Odeberg, H. 71
Olsson, B. 145, 214, 237

Pancaro, S. 154, 179
Parker, P. 11, 42, 84, 155
Peake, A.S. 7
Percy, E. 50
Perkins, P. 2, 61
Perrin, N. 122, 169, 200, 203, 204,
    209
Pesch, R. 139
Peterson, E. 51
Pfleiderer, O. 5-6, 64
Phillips, G.L. 176, 232
Pollard, T.E. 276
Powell, M. 95, 123, 127, 128
Preiss, T. 154
Pryor, J.W. 248
Purvis, J.D. 73

Ramsey, I.T. 28
Raney, W.H. 172-3
Reicke, B. 55
Reim, G. 70
Reimarus, H.S. 205
Reitzenstein, R. 49, 50, 51, 56
Renan, E. 206
Rensberger, D. 272
Reumann, J. 29, 206
Rhoads, D. 121
Richardson, A. 32, 217
Robinson, J.A.T. 1, 8-9, 25, 27, 30,
    36, 37, 42, 46, 65-6, 74, 92,
    140, 155, 178, 224, 248, 264,
    274, 275, 279
Robinson, J.M. 197, 201, 206, 207
Rowland, C.C. 34
Rowley, H.H. 25
Ruckstuhl, E. 95, 99, 105

Sanday, W. 5, 194, 195
Sanders, J.N. 78, 86, 148, 183, 186,
    217, 219, 221, 276
Sanders, J.T. 48
Schein, B.E. 39
Schlatter, A. 6, 64
Schmidt, K.L. 197
Schmithals, W. 56, 139
Schnackenburg, R. 10, 20, 23, 32, 49,

    51, 52, 57, 58, 60, 62, 83, 106,
    115-16, 117, 118, 134, 135,
    136, 139, 140, 148, 152, 164,
    179, 186, 227, 228, 248, 255,
    256, 262, 264, 266
Schniewind, J. 11
Schottroff, L. 171
Schulz, S. 109, 110, 119
Schwartz, E. 104, 115
Schweitzer, A. 206
Schweizer, E. 95, 99, 105, 109, 110,
    119
Scobie, C.H.H. 25, 36, 73
Scott, E. F. 160-1, 166, 169, 171, 195
Seeberg, A. 188
Servotte, H. 126
Shellard, B. 11
Sidebottom, E.M. 144, 242, 280
Smalley, S.'J. 279
Smalley, S.S. 13, 21, 35, 41, 55, 56,
    59, 60, 61, 78, 80, 89, 91, 93,
    122, 130, 131, 137, 139, 142,
    151, 156, 168, 169, 172, 182,
    183, 185, 188, 189, 193, 202,
    203, 227, 238, 241, 248, 255,
    262, 264, 270, 280
Smith, D.H. 26
Smith, D.M. 2, 3, 4, 5, 12, 102, 103,
    182, 233, 238, 248, 251, 272
Smith, M. 213
Smith, R.H. 69
Snyder, G.F. 55
Solages, B. de 13
Spiro, A. 73
Stanton, G.N. 203, 205
Stauffer, E. 225
Stewart, Z. 64
Stibbe, M.W.G. 65, 69, 86, 121,
    124-5, 154
Stone, M.E. 64
Stott, J.R.W. 81, 187
Strachan, R.H. 96, 99, 141, 162, 170,
    232
Strack, H.L. 71
Strauss, D.F. 3, 205-6
Streeter, B.H. 4, 42, 276
Stuhlmacher, P. 126
Sweet, J.P.M. 190
Swete, H.B. 196

Talbert, C.H. 124, 126
Tasker, R.V.G. 84, 89
Taylor, V. 2
Teeple, H.M. 72, 95, 99, 117-18, 119, 171
Temple, W. 114, 219
Thomas, J.C.T. 150
Thompson, M.M. 188, 198, 264, 277
Thyen, H. 13
Tilborg, S. van 126, 185
Titus, E.L. 87, 166
Torrey, C.C. 67
Trebilco, P.R. 141
Trites, A.A. 154
Tuckett, C.M. 241

Underhill, E. 237
Unnick, W.C. van 178

Van Belle, G. 108
VanderKam, J.C. 36
Verheyden, J. 7
Vermes, G. 33, 36
Vincent, L.H. 39

Wahlde, U.C. von 107-8
Ward, K. 279
Watson, F. 280
Wellhausen, J. 85, 104, 115
Wendt, H.H. 213
Wenham, D. 42
Westcott, B.F. 5, 95, 187
Whiteley, D.E.H. 190
Wieand, D.J. 38
Wilcox, M. 22
Wiles, M.F. 59, 232, 276, 279, 281
Wilkens, W. 115, 118, 119, 179, 222
Wilson, R.McL. 34, 51, 57, 58, 63
Windisch, H. 5, 158-9, 160, 262
Wink, W. 25
Witherington, III, B. 62, 92, 124, 129, 141
Wrede, W. 29
Wright, N.T. 6, 49, 199, 206, 207, 213, 280

Yamauchi, E.M. 51, 57

Zahn, T. 3

Index of Subjects

Abba 227-8
Acta Ioannis (Leucius Charinus) 1, 78-9
Acts
  history and tradition 201-3
  speeches in 188-9
adoptionism 172, 278-80, 281
Aenon near Salim 38, 40
Aesculapius, cult 38-9
Against Heresies (Irenaeus) 76
Alexandria 171
  as provenance for John's Gospel 186
allegory, Philo's use 63
Alogi 277
ambivalence 153
'Amen amen' formula 226
  ἀμήν (truly) 137, 139
Andrew (disciple) 40, 77, 87, 136
anointing at Bethany 17-19, 149
ἄνθρωπος (man) 144
anti-Marconite Prologue to Luke's Gospel 77, 274
Antioch (Pisidia) 197
Antioch (Syria), as provenance for John's Gospel 186
Antonia Fortress 39
Apocalypse (John), and Ephesus 77-8
aporias 97-8, 99, 100, 105, 107-8
apostolic tradition 188-200
  in Acts 201-3
  in the church's teaching 208
  historicity 200
  in John's Gospel 191-5, 197-9, 203, 204-5
  in Mark's Gospel 196-7
  in Paul 194-5
ἀποσυνάγωγος 91, 92

Aramaic 66-8
  use by Jesus 111
Aristion 80, 81
ἀρνία (lambs) 134
ἀρχή (beginning) 195-6
ascent, and descent, symbolism 234
Asia Minor, as provenance for John's Gospel 158
audiences 177-85
  Christian disciples as 180-1
  diaspora Jewish-Christians 179-80
  the Johannine community 181-3
  as unbelieving Jews 177-9
  as witnesses of the signs 131
authorship (*see also* John (Gospel)) 45, 75-93
  beloved disciple 82-4
  evidence external to John's Gospel 75-81, 90
  evidence from John's Gospel 82-90
  John (disciple) 75-80
  John the Elder 80-1

baptism 51, 103, 177, 233-4
  teaching about 164-6
Baptist community 162-4
Barnabas (apostle) 85, 92
Bartimaeus 218
Basilides 276
belief, encouragement 174-6
beloved disciple (*see also* John (disciple); John the Elder) 139, 152, 153, 155-6, 176
  first appearance 150
  identity 82-90, 182
  and Lazarus 217
  and Mary 216, 252
Bethany 218, 222

Bethany beyond the Jordan 38, 39, 136
Bethesda, pool 38-9, 40
Bethphage 40
Bethsaida 136
biography in the Gospels 125-6
blind man's healing (sign) (*see also* signs material) 129, 135, 136, 145, 146, 147, 155, 180, 217, 218, 220, 263
  and baptism 165
  belief 176
  dramatic character 143-4
  parallels to 214
Bodmer Papyri II and XV 32
Book of John 49, 50
book of signs 129-32, 134-5
bread of life discourse 71, 96, 110-11, 132, 135, 145, 147-8, 173
  and the eucharist 232

Caesarea Philippi 40
Cana 26, 40, 130
Carthage, Calendar, and John's death 79
catch of fish (sign) (*see also* signs material) 105, 130-1, 133, 134, 135, 139
  parallels to 214
  symbolism 236
Cerinthus 169, 277
Chalcedon, Council 240
Chalcedonian Definition 279-80, 281
χάρις (grace) 96, 135
Chenoboskion 50, 54, 59, 91
Christ (*see also* Jesus) 136, 138, 245-8
  and eternal life 265
  person 171
Christianity, and Judaism 215-16
christology (*see also* John (Gospel)) 28-9, 60, 61, 144, 171, 172, 182-5, 187, 210, 231, 238-56, 271-2, 282
  in Acts 202
  ambivalence in John's Gospel 183, 184-5, 245, 276

in apostolic kerygma 189, 190
  balanced nature 276-7, 280-1
  and eschatology 266-9
  glorification of the Word 248-50
  and the Johannine community 275
  in John's Gospel 187, 191-3, 210, 231
  Logos 243-4
  Messiah 245-8
  non-orthodox interpretations 277-80, 281
  in the passion narrative 251-6
  in Paul 193-4
  in Paul and Mark 198
  Son of God 244-5
  Son of man 240-3
  in the synoptic Gospels 28-9, 239
  two natures christology 240
chronology (*see also* John (Gospel)) 149
  in the Gospels 25-8
  in John's Gospel 197, 214, 220, 221
  in Mark's Gospel 196-7
church (*see also* Johannine community)
  and eschatology 268, 269
  and the Paraclete 257, 258, 259, 260, 262
  teaching, and the apostolic tradition 208
  theology 256, 263-5
Clement of Alexandria (bishop) 2-3, 76, 159, 232, 281
Clement of Rome (bishop) 78
coin in the fish's mouth 213
Colossae, church 184
Community Rule (Manual of Discipline) 33
composition criticism, definition 121-2
conflict 143, 154
corporateness and individualism in the church 263-4
creation, theme 237
criterion of dissimilarity 203
critical methods 98-9, 205

cross, theology 252-6
Cyprian of Carthage 232

Daniel, and Son of man 241, 242
darkness and light 176
    symbolism 234
De Regeneratione 52, 53
Dead Sea Scrolls (*see also* Qumran
    community) 33
    dualism 34-5, 72
    and John's Gospel 33-5
Decapolis 40
demythologising 206
descent-ascent (*katabasis-anabasis*)
    pattern 234, 266-7, 269
descriptive criticism *see* synchronic
    criticism
diachronic criticism 94, 95, 120,
    126
diaspora Judaism 177-80
Diodore of Tarsus 281
Dionysius of Alexandria (bishop)
    80
Dionysus cult 213
Diotrephes 185
disciples 153
    as dramatic characters 142
    life 134, 135
    and marriage at Cana 212, 215
    prayer for 228
discourse material (*see also* farewell
    discourse; 'I am' sayings; John
    (Gospel); Samaritan woman)
    19-22, 102-4, 108, 109-12,
    132-5, 142, 143, 145-9, 156
    context 96
    dramatic character 142, 143,
    145-9
    in the Gospels 19-22
    historicity 211-12, 214, 223-9
    overlaps 96
    and sacraments 165
    and signs material 119, 129-35,
    145-6, 148-9
displacement theories 119, 173
Dives and Lazarus (parable) 217,
    222
docetism 169, 171, 172, 277-8, 280,
    281

doctrinal references, introduced into
    John's Gospel 103
drama 123, 141-54
dramatic irony 146-7
dualism 34-5, 52
    in Dead Sea Scrolls 72
    in gnosticism 54
    in John's Gospel 57, 58, 72

Ebionites 184
ecclesiology 193
Egerton Papyrus 2 32-3, 91
eighteen Benedictions (*Shemoneh
    Esreh*) 179
elders, and Jesus' disciples 81
Elijah 136
    and John the Baptist 24-5
Emmaus 40
entry into Jerusalem 149
Ephesus 163, 274-5
    church 76
    Johannine community 156
    and John (apostle) 77-8, 93, 155
    as provenance for John's Gospel
    186
    site of John's tomb 80
Ephraim 40
epilogue (*see also* John (Gospel))
    130, 131, 135, 139-40, 152-3,
    156, 182, 277
    attestation to importance of the
    Gospel 182
    dramatic character 152-3
eschatology 166-8, 265-70
    and christology 266-9
eucharist (*see also* Lord's Supper)
    233-4
    and bread of life discourse 232
    placement 115
    as setting for discourses 148
    as setting for Jesus' Prayer (John
    17) 228
    tradition 111
Eusebius of Caesarea (bishop) 3, 76,
    80-1, 159, 198
Eutyches 281
evangelism
    in John's Gospel 188-229
    in Mark's Gospel 195-7

exemplarism, and the cross 255
existentialism, and study of the
    Gospels 208-9
exodus 110-11

faith, and sight 175-6
farewell discourse (*see also* discourse
    material) 96, 97, 99, 113, 133,
    150-1, 156
    historicity 223, 224, 226-9
    hymnody 173
    and the Paraclete 257
    themes shared with synoptists
    224
'Father' (Πάτερ, Πατήρ) 227–8
father and the apprenticed son
    (parable) 30
Father's house (parable) 30
feeding of the five thousand (sign)
    (*see also* signs material)
    15-17, 19, 31, 129, 132, 135,
    145, 146, 155, 173-4, 232
    and eucharist 165
    parallels to 214
feeding of the four thousand 15-16
fig tree, cursing 213
Footwashing (*Pedilavium*) 17, 30,
    150
    and sacraments 165
form (tradition) criticism 15, 98,
    205, 206
four-document hypothesis 4, 42
Fourth Gospel *see* John (Gospel)
fulfilment 271
future eschatology 268-9, 270

Galilee 136, 139
    sources associated with 146
    symbolism 234-5
Gamaliel II (Rabbi) 91, 179
Gentiles, as John's audience 181
geography, symbolism 234-5
Georgius Monachus (Harmatolus)
    (historian) 79
Gessius Florus 39
Gethsemane 40, 251
    agony in 84
    tradition 228
Ginza 49, 50

glorification 248-50
glory, theme 136, 217
gnosticism 34, 54-61, 102, 161, 164,
    167, 169-72, 276, 277
    in Asia Minor 184
    as background to John's Gospel
    102, 161, 164
    revelation speeches 109
γνῶσις (knowledge), not used in
    John's Gospel 53
God
    glory 249-50
    Kingdom in Acts 196
God the Father 96, 136
good shepherd (parable) 30, 69
Gospel according to Thomas, The 54
Gospel of Peter 91
Gospel tradition, as interpreted by
    John 230-72
Gospel of Truth, The 54, 91
Gospels
    critical studies 15
    definition 188
    genre 125-6, 175
    historicity 208-11
    nature 204-7
grace (χάρις) 96, 135
'Greeks' in John's Gospel 66
Gregory the Great (pope) 86
Grundschrift 104

haggadah 110
halakah 110
Hebrew 66, 68
Hebrews, author 72
Hellenism 110, 160-1, 244
    influence 74
Hellenistic Judaism (*see also*
    Judaism) 61, 64
    effects on John's Gospel 63
    terms from absent in John's
    Gospel 62
Hellenistic-Christians, and divinity
    of Jesus 184
Hellenists 72
heresy, and orthodoxy 171-2
Hermetica 52-3, 57
Herod Agrippa I 79
historic present, use 145

historical criticism *see* diachronic criticism
historical traditions (*see also* John (Gospel)) 252, 265-6, 267-8, 269, 270, 282
    in Acts 201-3
    in the apostolic tradition 197-8
    in the Gospels 204-7
    in John's Gospel 198-200, 204-5, 207-29
    sacramentalism 235-7
'history of religions' criticism 102, 110, 161
    view of gnosticism 56-7
Hodayoth 57
homilies 148
'hour', use of term 227, 269
house churches 155
ὑψοῦν (to lift up) 153
hymnody 172-3

'I am' sayings (*see also* discourse material) 31, 109, 129, 132-5, 214, 217, 218-19, 231
    dramatic character 142, 143, 144, 145-6, 149
    historicity 225-6
    symbolism 234
ideal disciple, as the beloved disciple 86-7
Ignatius of Antioch (bishop) 78, 91, 166, 186
individualism and corporateness in the church 263
intertextuality 125
Irenaeus of Lyons (bishop) 75-6, 77, 78, 82, 85, 93, 183, 186, 276
irony 124, 151-2
Isaac 113, 255

Jacob, vision 138
Jairus, daughter 219, 221
James (disciple) 80, 83
    martyrdom 79
Jamnia, assembly 179
Jerusalem 136
    emphasis on 85
    and John (disciple) 78
    symbolism 234-5

Jesus (*see also* Christ)
    arrest 117
    ascension 250, 253
    baptism 11, 138, 233
    betrayal 150
    character 142, 144, 147-8
    as Christ 130-1, 134, 144
    conflict with the Jews 132, 134
    death as glorification 248-50
    disciples called elders 81
    eschatology 168
    and eternal life 133-5
    expulsion from synagogue 92
    glorification 152
    humanity 170, 171
    as Isaac figure 113, 255
    as Lamb of God 27, 254
    life, in the apostolic tradition 197-9
    as light 132-3, 135, 151
    as 'Lord' 218
    Messiahship 23, 28-9
    ministry in Jerusalem 84
    nature 239-40
    as the new Moses 271-2
    and the Paraclete 258, 261-2
    passion 11, 23, 26
    portrayal in the Gospels 1-3
    prayer 61, 156
    prayer (John 17) 227-9
    relationship to God 274
    resurrection 11, 146
        and raising of Lazarus 221
    as shepherd 133, 135
    signs 23, 97
    teaching, and its authenticity 203
    teaching methods 23, 96, 223-4
    teaching style 29-30
    titles 136-8
    transfiguration 84
    trial 103
Jesus of history quest 204-10
Jesus tradition 199, 200
    origins 14-15
    redaction by John 230
Jewish Christianity, background to John's Gospel 161
Jewish sects 72-3
Jewish terms, translation 178

Jewish-Christians
  and divinity of Jesus 184
  excommunication 143, 174,
    179-80
  as John's audience 179-81
Jews
  conflict with Jesus 132, 134
  hostility 143, 239
  portrayal 178
  role in John's Gospel 66
  unbelief amongst 177-9
  understanding of Christ 247
  as witnesses of the signs 131
Johannine community 118, 187-8, 282
  affected by gnosticism 56
  as audience of Gospel 124
  christology 275, 276
  and compilation of John's Gospel
    155-6
  experiences reflected in John's
    Gospel 143, 144, 234-5
  John's Gospel directed to 181-5
  liturgy as setting for discourses
    148
  prayer for 228
Johannine literature
  background 282
  canonical and non-canonical 1
  date 91, 93
1 John, and docetism 169
John (Acts) 1, 78-9
John (author), pastoral character
    187-8
John the Baptist 2, 3, 23, 24-5, 27,
    72, 82, 96, 97, 102, 105, 111,
    136, 154
  as dramatic character 142
  and the Mandeans 49, 50-1
  messianic style 11
  ministry 196
  portrayal 161-4
  and the Qumran community 36-7
  sees Jesus as the Lamb of God
    247, 254
  traditions about 20, 156
John (disciple) (see also beloved
    disciple; John the Elder)
    155-6
  as author of Gospel 75-80

as the beloved disciple 83-4
and Ephesus 77-8
and Jerusalem 78
martyrdom 79
as priest 76
John the Elder (see also beloved
    disciple; John (disciple)) 188
  as author of Gospel 80
John (evangelist)
  as interpreter of Gospel tradition
    230-72
  redaction of Jesus tradition 230
  semi-docetism 169-70
John (Gospel) (see also authorship;
    christology; chronology;
    discourse material; epilogue;
    historical traditions; narrative
    material; passion narrative;
    prologue; purpose; signs
    material; synoptic Gospels)
  anti-docetism 115
  and apostolic tradition 191-3,
    194-5, 197-9, 204-5
  audience 177-85
  author's role 123-4
  authorship 1, 5-6, 9, 45, 65, 75-93
  as biography 125-6
  characterisation in 146
  chronology 25-8, 149, 214, 220,
    221
  composition 95-8, 155-7, 225
  core 114
  cultural background 5-6
  date 32-3, 35-6, 60, 90-3
  and the Dead Sea Scrolls 33-5
  displacement of contents 100-1,
    103
  as drama 123, 141-54
  dualism 35, 57, 58
  editorial method 99-100
  eschatology 58-9, 166-8, 265-70
  evangelism 188-229
  farewell discourse 133, 173
  geographical symbolism 234-5
  geography 97, 98, 100, 101
  Greek style and language 96
  Hebraic nature 65
  and Hellenism 46-8, 74, 160-1
  historical tradition 235-7

John (Gospel) (*continued*)
  historicity 41-2, 198-200, 204-5,
    207-17, 217-23, 223-9
  individualist character 263
  influences on 46-61
  interpretations 276
  Jerusalem ministry of Jesus 84
  John the Baptist 36-7
  and Judaism 64-74
  language 66-8
  literary analysis 117-18
  liturgical background 172-4
  and liturgy 232-3
  and Luke's Gospel 22, 85, 222-3
  and Mark's Gospel 16-18, 20, 21,
    22, 68, 85, 112, 219
  and Matthew's Gospel 17-18, 20
  and the Old Testament 68-70
  and Paul 193-5, 264
  personal names in 40
  place of writing 158
  postscript 156
  provenance 186
  purpose 158–85, 187-8
  and Qumran sectarians 72-3
  redaction 114-19
  religious influences on 48-61
  sacramental teaching 58-9, 164-6,
    232-8, 240
  and the Samaritans 72
  scope 132
  sources 14, 31-2
  southern traditions of 40
  speech material 103, 172-3
  structure 128-40, 142-54, 219-22
  style 105, 107
  symbolism 234-5
  and synoptic Gospels 101, 135,
    158-60, 161-2, 191-3, 195-9,
    246, 251-2, 265-6, 270, 282
    differences 273-5
    shared traditions 113, 219,
      221, 223-8
  and teaching style of Jesus 29-30
  theology 210-11, 216
  topography 37-41
  traditions about 14-44
  unity 95, 98, 99-101
  universal nature 180-1

John (Letters) 188
  and christological problems 185
  date 93
John Mark, as the beloved disciple
  85
John (Revelation)
  authorship 75, 78, 80-1
  christological problems 185
  date 93
  dramatic structure 142
  nature 65
Joseph of Arimathea 18, 152, 180
Joseph (father of Jesus) 136
Jubilees calendar 27
Judaising believers, controversy with
  111
Judaism
  and Christianity 215-16
  influence on John's Gospel
    110-12
  and John's Gospel 64-74
Judas Iscariot (disciple) 18, 19, 40,
  150, 228, 251
judgment 268
Jung Codex 91
Justin Martyr 78, 80, 166

katabasis-anabasis (descent-ascent)
    pattern 266-7, 269
kerygma (preaching) *see* apostolic
    tradition
Kidron valley 37-8, 39
King of Israel 136, 138
kingdom, parables 267-8

Lamb of God 136, 138, 247, 254
last judgment 103
last supper *see* Lord's Supper
Lazarus 18, 40, 104, 116
  as the beloved disciple 85-6
  raising (sign) (*see also* signs
    material) 129, 133, 135,
    143, 145, 146, 149, 155,
    237, 238, 254
  historicity 217-23
  parallels to 214
  as precursor of resurrection
    life 263
  resurrection 31, 32

Lazarus and Dives (parable) 18
Leucius Charinus 1, 78-9
life
    and light, theme 135-6, 231
    theme 133-5
light
    and darkness 176, 234
    and life, theme 135-6, 220, 231
    theme 132-3, 135, 217
Light of the World 151
literary (narrative) criticism *see*
    narrative (literary) criticism
liturgy 172-4
    and John's Gospel 232-3
'Lives of Jesus' 26
Logos (Λόγος) 96, 135, 136, 138,
    243-4, 281
    John's understanding 48, 62-3
    in Mandean literature 52, 53
    Philo's understanding 62, 63
    in Stoicism 47
Lord's Prayer 227, 228
Lord's Supper (*see also* eucharist)
    27-8, 103, 149-51, 177
    and feeding of the five thousand
    232
    teaching about 164-5
love, Greek verbs for 83, 86
Luke (evangelist)
    faithfulness to sources 202
    and John Mark 85
    and John's Gospel 20
Luke (Gospel) (*see also* synoptic
    Gospels)
    and anointing of Jesus' feet 17, 19
    anti-Marcionite Prologue 274
    date 92
    and John's Gospel 4, 10-11, 22,
    85, 191, 222-3
    and Mark's Gospel 2, 11
    and Matthew's Gospel 11
    place of origin 274
    place of writing 43
    view of history 266

Malchus 40
Manda d'Hayye 50
Mandean writings, 'I am' style 109
Mandeans 49-51, 57, 59, 102

manna, concept 110-11
Manual of Discipline (*Community
    Rule*) 33
Marcion 77
Mark (evangelist) 155
Mark (Gospel) (*see also* synoptic
    Gospels)
    evangelism in 195-7
    historical concerns 197-8
    and John's Gospel 2, 4, 10-11,
    16-18, 20, 21, 22, 68, 85, 112,
    159, 191, 195-9, 219
    and kerygma in Peter's speeches
    202
    Longer Ending 277
    and Matthew's Gospel 2
    prediction of John's death 79
    provenance 43, 274
marriage at Cana (sign) (*see also*
    signs material) 97, 129, 132,
    133, 135, 143, 145, 146, 155
    and eucharist 165
    historicity 212-17
Martha 11, 17-18, 32, 154, 217, 218,
    222
Mary of Bethany 218, 221
Mary (mother of Jesus) 82, 83, 84,
    152
    and the beloved disciple 252
    and marriage at Cana 212, 214,
    216
Mary Magdalene 152, 155, 250, 252,
    253
Mary (Martha's sister) 11, 18, 32
Matthew (apostle) 80
Matthew (Gospel) (*see also* synoptic
    Gospels)
    christology 29
    and Mark's Gospel 2
    place of origin 274
    place of writing 43
    traditions 155
Matthias (apostle) 87
Melito of Sardis (bishop) 80
μένειν (to stay) 153
Messiah 71, 245-8
    Jesus as 28-9
messianic secret 29, 246
messianic *testimonia* 68, 69

Michael (angel-intercessor for the
  church) 258
Midrashim 70, 110, 224
Miletus, excavations 141
miracles (*see also* signs material)
  at the crucifixion 253
Mishnah 70
misunderstandings 124, 147
monophysitism 281
Moses 69, 136
  in the person of Jesus 271-2
Muratorian Canon 77
mystery religions 49

Nag Hammadi 50, 54, 59, 91, 109
narrative (literary) criticism 15, 98,
  121-8, 128-32, 205
  advantages 127-8
  disadvantages 127
narrative material (*see also* John
  (Gospel)) 15-19, 108
  in the Gospels 15-19
  historicity 229
Nathanael 136, 137-8, 139, 154
  confession about Jesus 247
  and Jesus as King of Israel 263
Nazareth 136
  Jesus preaches in synagogue
  142
Nestorius 281
'new look' Gospel criticism 8-9
New Testament
  affected by gnosticism 56
  prophecy 223
Nicodemus 18, 40, 47, 96, 132, 147,
  152, 180, 231
  character 146
  misunderstands Jesus 224
  and regeneration 256-7
Nisan, lectionary readings 173
novel writing methods 121, 123

Odes of Solomon 57-8, 59, 80, 102,
  186
Offenbarungsreden 102
official's son's healing (sign) (*see also*
  signs material) 97, 129, 132,
  134, 135, 146, 155, 218, 263
  parallels to 214

'old look' Gospel criticism 8-9
Old Testament
  and 'I am' sayings 225
  and God's glory 249
  in John's Gospel 68-70
  lectionary readings 173-4
  proof-texts 202
  prophecy, fulfilment 189, 190,
  192
oral traditions 155
  used by John 116
Origen 3, 232
orthodoxy and heresy 171-2

P66 Tert, and John 21 139
Palestine 136
  as provenance for John's Gospel
  186
Papias of Hierapolis (bishop) 77, 78,
  79, 80-1, 85
papyri records of John's Gospel 32-3
parables 29, 30
Paraclete (Παράκλητος)
  identity 257-9
  ministry 260-2
paschal lambs, sacrifice 254-5
Passion Gospel 115, 119
passion narrative (*see also* John
  (Gospel)) 26, 103, 104,
  112-13, 125, 136, 156, 219-20,
  251-3
  chronology 27-8, 254
  the cross 252-6
  differences between John's
  Gospel and the synoptic
  Gospels 251-2
  dramatic character 141, 149-52
  logia in 20-1
  in Luke and John 11
Passover 252
  and last supper 27-8
  number of festivals 25
Πάτερ, Πατήρ (Father) 227–8
Patmos, John's connection with 76
Paul (apostle)
  apostolic tradition 194-5
  Areopagus speech 109
  arguments against pre-gnosticism
  55-6

Paul (apostle) (*continued*)
  at Miletus 78
  controversy with Judaisers 111
  the cross 253
  descent-ascent pattern 267
  doctrine of the church 264
  eschatology 168
  expulsion from synagogue 92
  and gnosticism 184
  and the historical Jesus 197
  and John's Gospel 4, 193-5
  and kerygma 189
  meets Baptist community 163
  speeches in Acts 201
  and the Spirit 261
  teaching supplemented by Mark 197-8
the Pavement 38, 39, 40
Pedilavium see Footwashing
pericope de adultera 100
personal names 40, 136
pesher (interpretative) techniques 71
Peter (disciple) 40, 80, 83, 85, 87, 97-8, 134, 136, 139, 147, 150, 152, 153, 155
  confession 28
  naming 20
  presence at miracles 219
  speeches in Acts 189, 201
  traditions about 43
φανερόω (reveal) 153
Philip (disciple) 40, 80, 136
Philip of Side (historian) 79
Philo of Alexandria 57, 61-4
  midrashic style 110
philosophy, influence on John's Gospel 46-8
Pilate, Pontius 11, 39, 151-2, 153, 247, 252, 253
place-names in the prologue 136
Platonism 47-8
  influence on Philo 61-2
πλήρωμα (fulness) 96, 135
Poimandres 52, 53
Polycarp of Smyrna (bishop) 75, 76, 78
Polycrates of Ephesus (bishop) 76
postscript 156
pre-existence 135

pre-gnosticism *see* gnosticism
preaching (kerygma) *see* apostolic tradition
present eschatology 265-8, 269, 270
πρόβατα (sheep) 134
prologue (*see also* John (Gospel)) 48, 61, 102, 116, 117, 130, 131, 135-9, 140, 156
  dramatic character 141, 142
  hymnody 172
  Jewish sources 111
  motifs 135-6
  names used in 136
  setting and form 135
  and Son of man tradition 137
prophecy in the New Testament 223
a prophet having no honour logia 21
proto-John 104
provenance, of John's Gospel 186
Pseudo-Clementine *Recognitions*, portrayal of Baptist community 163-4
Ptolemaeus (disciple of Valentinus) 77, 91
purpose (*see also* John (Gospel))
  and audience 177-85
  and encouragement of belief 174-6
  and Hellenism 160-1
  John and synoptic Gospels 158-60, 161
  in John's Gospel 187-8
  John's Gospel as apologetic 161-72
  liturgical background 172-4

Q (Quelle) hypothesis 108
Qumran community 25, 51, 92, 227
  calendar 27
  and John the Baptist 36-7
  and John's Gospel 72, 73
  and the Paraclete 258

rabbinic Judaism, influence on John's Gospel 70-1
reader-response criticism 122, 124
realised eschatology 266
recapitulation 146-8

redaction criticism 15, 98, 104-7,
    114-19, 205
  definition 121-2
redeemer myth 55, 57, 58, 60
regeneration 256-7
religious influences on John's Gospel
    48-64
Revelation *see* John (Revelation)
revelation speeches 102, 109
rhetorical criticism 121
RQ (*Reden-Quelle*) 102, 104
Rylands Papyrus 457 (P52) 32-3, 91

S (Nicol's) signs source 106, 107
sabbath observance 71
sacramentalism 240
sacraments 164-6
  and the cross 254
  and John's Gospel 232-8
  and signs 233
  and symbols 235, 236
Salome 83
salvation 231-2
  theology 252-6
Samaria 40
  origins of gnosticism 164
  symbolism 234-5
Samaritan woman (*see also* discourse
    material) 146, 147
  discourse with 132
  and messiahship of Jesus 246
  narrative 105, 145
  witness 176
school *see* Johannine community
Second Isaiah 225
Semeia Quelle (SQ) 102, 104, 107
semitising 218
Septuagint 68, 69, 70
Sermon on the Mount/Plain 30, 223,
    227
sermons 29, 30
Servant Song 249
SG (Fortna's) signs source 105-6,
    107
sheep gate (Jerusalem) 38
Shemoneh Esreh (eighteen
    Benedictions) 179
shepherd, theme 133, 134, 135, 147,
    220

sick man's healing (sign) (*see also*
    signs material) 97, 129, 132,
    134, 135, 145, 146, 147, 154,
    155, 218, 263
  and baptism 165
  parallels to 214
sight, and faith 175-6
sign at Cana 26
signs material (*see also* blind man's
    healing (sign); catch of fish
    (sign); feeding of the five
    thousand (sign); John
    (Gospel); Lazarus, raising
    (sign); marriage at Cana
    (sign); miracles; official's son's
    healing (sign); sick man's
    healing (sign)); 26, 30-1, 102,
    104-9, 114, 115, 116, 142-6,
    155-6
  book of signs 129-32, 134-5
  as correction of heresy 170-1
  and discourse material 119,
    129-35, 145-6, 148-9
  dramatic character 142-9
  Gospel 108, 115, 119
  historicity 211-23
  individualism in 263
  meaning 130-2, 134, 136
  parallels in synoptic Gospels 214
  and the purpose of John's Gospel
    182-3
  and sacraments 165, 233
  symbolism 236-7
Siloam, pool 37-8, 39
Simon of Cyrene 113, 251, 255
Simon the Leper 17
Simon Magus 164
Simon Peter (disciple) *see* Peter
    (disciple)
sins, forgiveness through the cross
    254-5
Solomon's portico 38, 40
son of destruction 150
Son of God 96, 136, 138, 244-5
  in the synoptic Gospels 253
Son of man 28, 71, 117, 136-8, 147,
    240-3, 244
  Jesus as 144
  logia 20-1, 41

soteriology 193
source criticism 15, 42, 98, 205
sources 94
  consistency 95-8
  displacements 100-1
  use 99-113, 114-19
spear-thrust 165, 254
speech material 103, 172-3
Spirit 136
  and the church 263, 264-5
  as the Paraclete 257-62
  regeneration through 256-7
  and salvation 231
  theology 256-62
SQ (*Semeia-Quelle*) 102, 104, 107
St Anne (church) 38
St Stephen's Gate (Jerusalem) 38-9
Stephen (martyr) 72, 138
  expulsion from synagogue 92
  speech in Acts 201
Stoicism 47, 48, 61, 62
structuralism 122
suffering servant 255
Sychar 40
symbols
  and sacraments 235, 236
  use 124, 234-5
synagogue
  exclusion from 91, 92
  liturgy 173
synagogue lections, use 71
synchronic criticism 94-5, 120, 121,
    126, 140
synoptic Gospels (*see also* John
    (Gospel); Luke (Gospel);
    Mark (Gospel); Matthew
    (Gospel))
  christology 28-9
  chronology in 25-8
  eschatology 167, 168, 269-70
  evangelistic strategy 192
  historical traditions 219
  and Jesus' vindication 250
  and John's Gospel 1-13, 31-3,
    41-3, 84, 91, 101, 135,
    158-60, 161-2, 191-3, 195-9,
    246, 251-2, 265-6, 270, 282
  differences between 23-30,
    30-1, 37-41, 273-5

  shared traditions 219, 221,
    223-8
  similarities between 14-23
Messiah 246
miracles 30-1
parallels with signs 214
passion narrative 251-2
sources 31-2, 42-3
teaching syle of Jesus 29-30
synoptic problem 42
synoptists, dramatic instincts 142
Syria, location for composition of
    John's Gospel 158

Tabernacles, Feast of 152, 247
Talmud 70
Targums 70
Tatian, *Diatessaron* 91
temple, cleansing 23, 25, 26-7,
    72, 115, 132, 215, 216,
    220, 221
Tertullian 183
Test Benediction 91-2
testimonia, about Jesus' death
    251
textual variants 175, 180
θεῖος ἀνήρ (divine man) 105,
    244
Theodore of Mopsuestia 281
theology, John's Gospel 210-11,
    216
Theophilus of Antioch (bishop)
    80
Thomas (disciple) 80, 139, 152, 154,
    175, 176, 219, 252
Thucydides 201-2
Tiberias (Galilee) 40, 139
To Florinus (Irenaeus) 75
'to lift up' (ὑψοῦν) 153
'to stay' (μένειν) 153
tradition
  in Acts 201-3
  and history 200, 203
  transmission 94-5
tradition (form) criticism 98
Trajan (Roman emperor) 76, 93
trial narrative 154
  dramatic character 151-2
trinitarian ideas 271

triumphal entry 220, 221
  and Jesus' glorification 249
  Jesus' messiahship 247,
    248
'truly' (ἀμήν) 137, 139
Tübingen school 3
the Twelve, as the church 264
Tyre and Sidon 40

Valentinus 276
Victor of Rome (bishop) 76
vine, theme 30, 69, 133, 135
visitation, theme 191-2

walking on the water 129-30, 173
*The War of the Sons of Light and the
  Sons of Darkness* 34, 35
water, theme 132, 135
widow of Nain, son 31, 219, 221
Wisdom 62
witness, symbolism 234
women, ministry 155
Word (Λόγος) 135, 136, 138
Word of God 130-1
world, and the Paraclete 260

ζωὴ αἰώνιος (eternal life) 231-2

Index of Ancient Sources

Old Testament

Genesis
1 48
1:1 111, 237
1:3 243
22:6 113, 255
28:12 138

Exodus
3:13-14 225
3:14-15 192
4:31 192
12:1-27 255
12:12-22 252
12:46 255
13:21-22 271
15 173
16 173
16:1-36 271
16:4 110
16:7 249
16:10 249
17:1-7 271
20:2-3 225
24:15-18 249

Numbers
11 173

Deuteronomy
18:18 34
32:39 225
32:46-47 48

Psalms
2:7 244
8:4 242
22:18 251
27:1 63

33:6 48, 243
41:9 21
80 137
80:1 134, 263
80:8 133
80:8-19 242, 263
80:17 137
107:20 48

Proverbs
8:22-31 48, 62, 243

Isaiah
5:1-2 133
5:1-7 242, 263
6 176
6:10 249
29:13 68
31:3 48
40:3 24, 25, 36
44:3 256
45:5-6 225
45:18 225
46:9 225
47:10 225
52:13-53:12 249
53 255
54-55 173
55:10-11 243
60:1-3 192
60:19-20 192
63:16 263

Jeremiah
1:4-5 243
2:13 63

Ezekiel
2:1 242
6:7 225

34   263
34:12   134
34:15   63
36:25-27   256
37:27-28   263

Daniel
7:13-14   137, 242

Hosea
11:1   244

Joel
2   189
2:27   225
2:28-29   256

Zechariah
9:9   249
12:10   70

Malachi
3:1   25
4:5   25

Deuterocanonical books

Wisdom
2:18   244
16:12   48
16:26   48

Sirach
24   62

New Testament

Matthew
1:1   195
3:1   23
3:7-10   111
3:11   20
5:48   227
5-7   30, 223, 224
6:9   227, 228
6:14   227
7:21   111
8:5-13   214
8:19-20   242

9:17   215
9:37-38   268
10:5-6   192
10:18   192
10:19-20   261
10:23   167, 270
10:39   22
10:40   270
11:2   36
11:2-5   268
11:2-6   246
11:11   24, 162
11:12   270
11:14   24, 162
11:27   227
13:28-31   270
13:32-37   270
13:57   21
14:13-21   15
14:28-31   44
14:33   29
15:23   212
15:24   192
15:28   192
15:29   16
16:13-20   246
16:17-19   44
16:18   20
16:19   20
16:28   168
17:10-13   24
17:11-13   25
17:24-27   44, 213
18:18   20
20:22   22
20:22-23   79
21:9   247
23:1   224
24:5   225
26:6-13   17
26:8   18
26:21   21
26:23   22
26:34   22
26:39   228
26:42   228
26:45   227
26:53-54   253
26:61   21

26:64   225
27:40   21
27:45-54   251
27:54   253
28:8   152
28:15   178
28:16   250, 277
28:18   227
28:19   234
28:19-20   168, 270

Mark
1:1   42, 195
1:2   195
1:2-13   195
1:3   24
1:4   23, 36
1:7   20, 162
1:8   195, 256
1:10-11   138
1:15   195, 256, 268, 270
2:1-12   214
2:18-20   213
2:22   213, 215
3:1-6   143
3:16   20
4:10-20   224
5:21-43   145
5:22-23   218
5:22-24   214, 219, 221
5:35-43   214, 219, 221
5:42-43   218
6:1   21
6:4   21
6:32-44   15, 31
6:34   16
6:34-45   214
6:35-44   16
6:36   214
6:37   16
6:39   16
6:41   17
6:44   17
6:45-46   17
6:50   225
7:6-7   68
7:15   224
7:17   224
7:18-23   224

8:1-8   16
8:14-21   97
8:22-26   214
8:23   144
8:27-30   20, 28
8:27-9:1   29
8:29-30   246
8:31   28, 241, 251
8:35   22
9:1   167
9:1-8   196
9:2   83, 84
10:21   86
10:30   266
10:33-34   196
10:38   22
10:39   79
10:46   218
10:46-52   214
11:1-10   196
11:1-18   220
11:10   195
11:12-14   213
11:15-19   26
11:20-21   213
11:30-32   27
12:1-11   195
13   30, 196, 202, 224, 266
13:6   225
13:26   167, 242, 266
13:26-27   195
13:28-31   270
13:32-37   270
14:3   18, 218
14:3-9   17
14:4   18
14:5   18
14:10-11   251
14:12   27
14:18   21
14:20   22
14:30   22
14:32-33   84
14:32-42   251
14:36   227, 228
14:41   227
14:47   155
14:49   195
14:50   83

14:58   21
14:61-62   167
14:62   20, 138, 225, 242, 266
14-16   224
15:21   251
15:24   251
15:27   67
15:29   21
15:29-32   251
15:34   251
15:39   253
16:1   18, 83
16:7   195
16:8   152

Luke
1:4   195
1:17   24, 25, 162
1:68   191
3:7-9   111
3:15   11, 24, 162
3:16   20
3:21-22   11
4:16   21
4:16-21   268
4:16-30   142
4:21   270
4:24   21
4:29   92
5:1-11   214
5:38   215
5:39   215
6:17-49   30
6:35   266
7:11-16   214, 221
7:11-17   31
7:11-18   219
7:15   218
7:16   191
7:20   23
7:28   24
7:36-50   17
7:38   17, 18
9:10-17   15
10:1-2   268
10:22   227
10:38-42   11, 218
11:2   227, 228
12:12   261

13:4   38
14:2   222
15:11   222
16   218, 222
16:19-31   217
16:31   222
17:33   22
19:37   220
19:39   220
21   202
21:8   225
21:38   100
22:34   22
22:42   228
22:53   227
22:67   225
22:70   225
23:4   11
23:14-16   11
23:22   11
23:27-31   251
23:38   252
24:12   152
24:26   251
24:36-43   11
24:50-51   277
24:51   250, 277

John
1   96, 105, 111, 117, 130, 131,
        135-9, 140, 142, 148, 235, 255
1:1   48, 135, 136, 193, 237, 239, 243,
        271, 277
1:1-2   57, 192
1:1-3   267
1:1-13   142
1:1-14   62, 243
1:1-16   102
1:1-18   63, 96, 111, 129, 135, 136, 156
1:1-2:12   129
1:2   34
1:4   50, 124, 133, 231, 271
1:4-5   135, 176
1:4-9   231
1:6   24, 82, 162
1:8   162
1:9   63
1:9b   216
1:11   21, 65, 139, 192

1:12 49, 139, 149, 266
1:14 49, 57, 130, 131, 135, 136, 138,
      142, 149, 191, 192, 193,
      198, 231, 235, 239, 244,
      249, 268, 271, 277
1:15 20, 154
1:16 135, 216
1:17 136, 154, 193
1:17-18 272
1:18 136, 138, 154, 191, 193, 236,
      239, 277
1:19 23, 37
1:19-23 162
1:19-51 135, 156
1:19-2:11 237
1:19-10:42 129
1:20 11, 24
1:21 24
1:23 24, 36
1:25 37
1:26 20, 29
1:26-27 36
1:27 20
1:28 37, 38, 97
1:29 27, 136, 181, 247, 254, 271
1:29-34 97
1:29-2:1 237
1:30 20, 162
1:31 20, 24, 37
1:32-33 262
1:32-34 11, 232, 245
1:33 20, 36, 245, 256
1:33-34 136
1:34 136, 138, 154, 191
1:35-37 263
1:35-42 87
1:35-49 102
1:35-51 263
1:36 27, 136, 247, 254
1:38 178
1:38-39 153
1:40-42 155
1:41 28, 87, 136, 178, 261
1:41-42 246
1:42 20, 28
1:43 84, 264
1:45-46 137, 247
1:46 138
1:47 138

1:47-51 137, 242, 247
1:48 138
1:49 28, 136, 138, 154, 247, 263, 271
1:50 138
1:50-51 136
1:51 20, 117, 136, 137, 138, 226,
      237, 241, 242
1-12 102
2 132, 135, 146, 155, 165, 215
2:1 130, 212, 214
2:1-2 145
2:1-11 26, 129, 212-13, 214
2:1-22 271
2:2 212
2:3 214, 215, 224
2:3-4 145
2:4 149, 212, 216, 222, 269
2:5 145, 212
2:6 212
2:6-8 145
2:7 212
2:8-9 212
2:9 145, 212, 215
2:10 212, 215
2:11 97, 102, 129, 130, 131, 133,
      136, 149, 212, 216, 239, 249
2:12 235
2:13 25, 149, 271
2:13-22 26, 73, 132, 216, 263
2:13-12:11 129
2:19 20-1
2:19-21 147
2:19-22 193
2:21 263
2:23 97, 102
2:25 247
2-11 130
2-12 142-9
2-21 139
3 40, 132, 135, 146, 148, 165, 166,
   172, 214, 224, 226, 257
3:1-8 256
3:1-21 132
3:2 191
3:3 49, 139, 224, 257
3:3-4 256
3:3-5 147
3:4 124, 224
3:5 49, 103, 132, 231, 232, 256, 271

3:5-8   224
3:6   47
3:6-8   256
3:7   257
3:8   231
3:9   224
3:10-15   224
3:11   226
3:13   50, 136, 153, 241, 242, 243
3:14   241, 242, 243
3:14-15   231
3:14-16   255
3:15   147
3:16   231
3:16-18   53, 250
3:16-21   96, 267
3:17   181, 231
3:18   103, 266
3:18-19   35, 59, 231
3:19   103, 268
3:21   33, 147
3:22   97, 153
3:22-30   37
3:23   37, 38, 164
3:25-30   97
3:27-30   96
3:28-30   162
3:31   47
3:31-36   96, 116, 124
3:33-36   34
3:35   239
3:36   231
4   105, 132, 134, 135, 146, 155, 214,
      224, 263
4:1-4   100
4:7-26   132
4:9   65, 178
4:10   63
4:11   145
4:12   145
4:13-14   263
4:14   34, 63, 134, 235, 254
4:20-25   73
4:21   168
4:21-24   73
4:21-26   271
4:22   231
4:23   168, 268, 269
4:23-24   134, 262

4:24   261, 264
4:25-26   183, 246
4:26   134, 147, 225
4:29   134, 145, 176, 247
4:34   224, 239
4:35-38   268
4:39-40   234
4:39-42   145, 176, 263
4:40   235
4:42   131, 181, 231, 242
4:43   146
4:44   21
4:45   146, 149, 234
4:46   132, 146
4:46-54   129
4:47   146
4:53   131, 149
4:54   97, 102, 146
4-7   97
5   100, 101, 132, 135, 146, 153, 165,
      214, 263
5:1   25, 149
5:1-7:52   143
5:1-9   97
5:2   38
5:2-9   129
5:2-9b   145
5:6   134
5:7   134
5:8-9   149
5:9-10   145
5:9b-18   71
5:10   134
5:15   131, 134
5:15-18   271
5:16   134
5:17   71, 130, 191, 239, 245
5:17-47   224
5:18   154, 191, 239
5:19-20   224, 245
5:19-20a   30
5:19-24   268
5:19-25   96
5:19-29   222
5:19-30   29
5:19-47   132, 136
5:21   231
5:21-23   245
5:22   154

5:24   149, 231, 266
5:24-25   176
5:25   137, 168, 269
5:25-29   168, 231, 263, 267, 268
5:26-27   239, 269
5:26-29   132
5:26-30   96
5:27   154, 241, 242, 243
5:28-29   103, 268
5:30   245
5:31-32   34
5:36   239
5:37   154, 245
5:37-38   134
5:39   154
5:39-40   124
5:40   132
5:43   192, 245, 261
5:46   34
5:46-47   147
5-8   145
6   100, 101, 110, 111, 115, 116, 132,
      135, 146, 153, 155, 156, 165,
      166, 173, 182, 214, 224, 232
6:1   16, 97
6:1-14   129, 145
6:1-15   15, 31
6:3   16
6:4   25, 149
6:5   16
6:5-9   40
6:7   16
6:9   16
6:10   16, 17
6:11   16, 17
6:12   17
6:13   17
6:14   34
6:14-15   17, 131
6:15   248
6:16   16
6:16-21   129, 130, 132
6:19   130
6:20   225
6:22-24   100
6:25-65   132
6:25-71   232
6:26-58   271
6:27   241, 243

6:27a   224
6:28   154
6:31   148
6:31-58   110-11
6:33   148
6:35   132, 133, 135, 148, 231, 234
6:35-50   96
6:36   176
6:39   265
6:39-40   193
6:40   268
6:41   133, 148
6:41-59   147
6:43-51   263
6:44   193, 271
6:45   71
6:47   266, 268
6:47-51   231, 271
6:48   133
6:51   49, 59, 133
6:51-58   96, 103, 116, 232
6:53   49, 117, 236, 241, 243
6:55   254
6:56   198
6:58   147
6:60-65   224
6:62   153, 191, 241, 242, 267
6:63   47, 236
6:67   264
6:68   147, 219
6:68-69   149
6:69   191, 219
6:70   150, 264
7   101, 135, 147, 247
7:1   101
7:1-2   235
7:1-38   132
7:2   132, 149
7:3-5   97
7:8   97
7:10   97
7:14-17   261
7:19-24   68
7:22-23   71
7:27   29, 247
7:29   247
7:30   149, 154
7:31   247
7:35   178

7:37-39   132, 271
7:38   271
7:39   136, 193, 249, 250, 257, 265,
     266, 269
7:40   34
7:40-41   238
7:41   247
7:41-42   246
7:42   192, 247
7:50   146
7:53-8:11   100
7-8   152
8   109, 112, 135, 136, 147
8:12   33, 57, 132, 133, 135, 144, 151,
     176, 231, 234, 271
8:12-59   132
8:17   71
8:18   133, 261
8:20   149, 154
8:23   47, 133, 245
8:24   225
8:26-27   245
8:28   183, 225, 241, 242, 245
8:31   97
8:31-47   111
8:31-58   111, 263
8:35   235
8:37   97
8:40   62, 144
8:44   72
8:51   226
8:55   72
8:58   132, 137, 147, 192, 225, 226,
     280
8:59   29, 176
8-10   100
9   132, 135, 136, 143-4, 146, 147,
     153, 165, 176, 214, 217, 220,
     221, 263
9:1-7   129, 143, 145
9:1-10:42   143
9:1-38   220
9:2   144
9:5   132, 144
9:6   144
9:7   37, 144, 176
9:8   145
9:8-12   143
9:9   144, 225

9:11   144
9:13-17   143
9:16   144, 238
9:17   144
9:18-23   143
9:22   91, 92, 144, 180, 246
9:22-23   116
9:24   144
9:24-34   143
9:29   144
9:33   144, 191
9:34   92
9:34-38   180
9:35   144, 241
9:35-38   143, 176
9:35-41   147
9:38   131, 149
9:38-39   144
9:39-41   143, 176
9:40-41   266
10   134, 135, 153, 173, 219, 220, 222
10:1   137
10:1-5   30
10:1-6   69
10:1-18   63, 133
10:3-4   134
10:5   134
10:6   30
10:7   134, 135, 234
10:9   134
10:10   133, 134, 222, 245
10:10-11   193, 231
10:11   133, 134, 135, 234, 255
10:14   134
10:14-15   134
10:14-16   263
10:15   133, 255
10:16   134, 181, 263
10:17-18   133
10:18   245, 253
10:23   38
10:24   29, 246
10:25   154, 246
10:27-28   176
10:30   172, 193, 239, 277, 280
10:33   147
10:36   191
10:37-38   147
10:38   239

10:39   220
10:40-42   97, 219
10:41   162
11   40, 104, 133, 135, 146, 149, 214,
      217, 220, 222, 263
11:1   222
11:1-16   222
11:1-44   11, 31, 129, 145, 217
11:1-46   217
11:1-12:50   129
11:2   218, 222
11:3   86, 218, 222
11:4   217, 221, 222
11:5   86
11:5-6   222
11:7-8   234
11:7-10   221, 222
11:9   217, 222
11:9-10   144, 220
11:11   86
11:11-13   217
11:11-16   222
11:14   217
11:16   219
11:17   217
11:20   218
11:25   133, 135, 147, 217, 218, 234,
        235
11:25-26   222, 231, 271
11:27   131, 149, 154, 191, 217, 222,
        244, 246, 247
11:28   218
11:33   218
11:35   218
11:36   86, 218
11:37   146, 217, 220
11:38-39   221
11:39   217
11:40   222, 249
11:41   222
11:41-42   217, 222
11:44   218, 221
11:45   131, 149, 222
11:47-57   220
11:49-52   192
11:50   251
11:50-52   255
11:51-52   178
11:54   198

11:55   25, 149
11:57   149
11-12   116
12   176, 220, 222, 249
12:1-2   40
12:1-8   11, 17
12:1-19   149
12:2   18, 218
12:3   17, 18, 218
12:5   18
12:6   150
12:7   19
12:9-11   220
12:11   178
12:12-19   247
12:12-19:42   129
12:13   247
12:14-16   248
12:16   249
12:17   154
12:17-28   251
12:18-19   220
12:19   220
12:20   149
12:20-21   66, 181, 263
12:20-50   149
12:21   192
12:23   84, 149, 241, 242, 243, 249
12:25   22, 23
12:27   22, 149
12:27-28   84
12:27-38   228
12:28   250
12:31-36   58
12:32   153, 181, 242, 250
12:34   235, 241, 242, 247, 248
12:35   261
12:35-36   33, 35, 144
12:35-46   176
12:35-50   220
12:36   29
12:37   102
12:37-43   97, 124
12:40   69
12:41   249
12:42   91, 180
12:44-46   176
12:44-50   34, 96, 147, 149
12:46   144, 176, 231

12:49   245
12:50   129, 147, 149
13   165, 234
13:1   57, 150, 231, 251
13:1-15   30
13:1-20:31   129
13:1-38   149
13:2   150, 228
13:3   144, 153, 191, 253, 267, 277
13:6   219
13:14-15   231
13:15   256
13:16   23
13:18   22
13:19   225
13:20   23, 245
13:21   21, 228
13:21-30   251
13:23   82, 139
13:23-26   150
13:24-25   82
13:26   22, 150
13:27   150
13:30   150
13:31   117, 130, 241, 242, 250
13:31-32   57, 249, 266
13:31-17:26   150
13:34   72
13:34-35   34, 271
13:34b   256
13:36   98
13:38   22
13-17   153, 226, 228
13-20   44, 149-52
13-21   130
14   96, 99, 116
14:2-3   30
14:3   153, 168, 193, 264, 266, 268,
        269
14:4-5   224
14:5   98
14:6   35, 50, 57, 62, 133, 134, 135,
        231, 234, 261
14:6-7   272
14:6-14   224
14:7b   261
14:8-9   40
14:9   191
14:9-10   176

14:9-11   71
14:12   226
14:12-13   236
14:12-14   268
14:13   250
14:16   259, 261
14:16-17   259, 260, 262, 264
14:16-18   266
14:17   72, 235, 259, 261
14:17a   261
14:18   260, 268
14:18-19   264
14:18-24   240
14:20   240
14:22   40
14:23   240, 259, 268
14:24   176
14:26   258, 259, 260, 261, 262
14:27   260
14:28   153, 172, 239
14:31   98, 99, 116
14-16   133, 135, 224, 257
14-17   156, 173
15:1   63, 133, 135, 234, 242, 263
15:1-2   30
15:1-6   192
15:1-8   193
15:4   235
15:4-5   193
15:4-10   231
15:4-11   153
15:5   133, 263
15:8   250
15:12   184
15:13   224
15:16   193
15:18-25   260
15:18-27   262
15:23   245
15:25   260
15:26   35, 154, 193, 259, 260, 261,
        262
15:27   154, 196
15-17   98, 116
16   96, 99, 116
16:2   91, 180
16:4   196
16:5   98
16:7   193, 259, 265

16:7-11 260
16:7a 259
16:7b 259
16:8-11 260, 262
16:13 35, 259, 260
16:14 260, 261, 262
16:14-15 259, 262
16:16 224, 266
16:17-18 224
16:19-24 224
16:25-27 34
16:28 151, 153, 172, 245, 261, 267
16:32 83
16:33 151
17 133, 156, 226, 227-9, 266
17:1 149, 228, 249, 250
17:1-5 228
17:1-10 130
17:2 227, 231
17:3 34, 35, 62, 231, 236
17:4 151, 239, 245, 250, 261
17:5 228, 239, 249, 250
17:6-19 228
17:7 227
17:8 144
17:11 184, 227, 228, 240, 263
17:12 150, 228
17:16 50, 267
17:18 267
17:20 263
17:20-21 134, 181
17:20-22 192
17:20-23 264
17:20-24 193
17:20-26 228
17:21 228, 264
17:21-22 245
17:21-23 184
17:22 250
17:23 264
17:24 228, 249, 250
17:25 228
18 113, 125
18:1 37
18:1-11 252
18:1-12 154
18:1-14 117
18:2-3 251
18:3 151

18:10 40, 155
18:11b 22
18:12 151
18:14 251
18:15 85
18:15-16 87
18:28 68
18:29-32 152
18:30-31 152
18:32 252
18:33 151
18:33-19:22 247
18:33-38 136, 151, 252
18:33-38a 152
18:35 65
18:36 151, 248
18:37 151, 176
18:37-38 50
18:38 11
18:38b-40 152
18:39-40 152
18-19 136, 154
18-20 151
19 103, 113, 125, 165
19:1-3 152
19:1-16 151
19:4 11
19:4-7 152
19:5 144, 151
19:6 11
19:6-7 152
19:8-12 152
19:9 151, 153, 247
19:12 152
19:12-16 151, 152
19:12-22 136
19:13 38
19:13-16 152
19:14 151
19:15 152
19:17 113, 252, 255
19:17-20:29 152
19:18 67
19:19-22 138, 151
19:20 252
19:23-37 152
19:24 192, 251
19:25 83
19:25-26 88

19:25-27   216, 252
19:26-27   82
19:27   83, 155
19:28   192, 251
19:30   152, 252, 253, 262, 266
19:31   271
19:33   254
19:34   88, 103, 252, 254
19:34-35   232, 254
19:34-38   180
19:35   56, 88
19:36   255
19:36-37   251
19:36a   251
19:37   70
19:38   180
19:38-20:10   252
19:38-42   152
19:39   40, 146, 180
19:42   252
20   98, 117, 131, 146, 277
20:1   18, 221
20:1-10   152
20:1-21:25   129
20:2-10   83
20:4   152
20:7   221
20:8   84, 176
20:8-9   192
20:11-18   152
20:16   178
20:17   152, 250, 252, 253, 266, 277
20:19-23   277
20:19-29   152
20:20   11
20:21-22   193, 259, 265
20:21-23   234, 262
20:22   261, 262, 266
20:22-23   271
20:23   20, 23
20:24   264
20:26-27   175
20:26-29   252, 256
20:27   254
20:28   154, 175, 239, 277
20:28-31   29
20:29   139, 175, 176, 250
20:29-31   131, 254
20:30   31, 102, 129, 175

20:30-31   139, 175, 246, 277
20:31   42, 53, 58, 136, 138, 154, 164,
       174, 175, 180, 181, 182,
       193, 195, 238, 244, 248, 250
21   44, 84, 96, 98, 103, 105, 106,
    116, 117, 130, 131, 132, 133,
    134, 135, 139-40, 152-3, 155,
    156, 214, 277
21:1   139, 153
21:1-14   130, 131, 139, 151, 153
21:1-25   129
21:2   82, 83, 130, 139
21:7   83, 131, 139
21:7-9   88
21:9-15   11
21:11   88
21:12-13   253
21:12-15   254
21:14   153
21:15   134
21:15-19   139
21:15-22   155
21:15-23   153
21:16   134
21:17   134
21:18   139
21:19   134
21:20   139
21:20-21   83
21:20-24   93, 139
21:20-25   139, 182
21:22   134, 168
21:23   88
21:24   82, 83, 84, 88, 182
21:24-25   88, 156

Acts
1:9   250
1:13   84
1:13-14   155
1:14   84
1:21-22   196
2:16-21   189
2:17-21   189
2:22   197
2:22-32   189
2:23   190
2:25-28   202
2:33   189

2:33-36   189
2:38   189
2:38-40   189
2-4   189
3:1   83
3:11   38
3:13   189, 251
3:15   189, 190
3:18-19   189
3:19-20   189
3:20-21   189
3:26   189
4:11   189
4:13   84
4:25   189
4:36   85
5:32   261
6:1   73
6:7   37
7:56   138
7:58   92
8:9-13   164
8:12   196
8:14-15   83, 155
10:36   190
10:37   196
10:39   197
10:42   189
12:2   79
12:12   85
13:16-41   197
13:25   20
13:26-27   192
13:46   192
13:50   92
13:55   202
14:1-6   92
15:14   190, 192
17   109
17:5-9   92
17:13   92
18:24-19:7   49
19:1   163
19:1-7   163
19:2   163
19:3   163
19:4   163
19:5   163
19:7   163

20:18-35   78
20:25   196

Romans
1:2   194
1:3   194
8:9   261
8:9-17   194
8:10-11   193
8:15   227
12:4-5   264

1 Corinthians
1:22-23   56
1:23   194
2:2   194
3:16-17   21, 263
6:19   21
8:11-12   56
12   264
15:1-2   194
15:1-3   194
15:3   189
15:3-4   194
15:3-5   189
15:51   167

2 Corinthians
4:4-6   193

Galatians
2:9   78, 155
2:20   193
4:6   227, 261
6:16   194

Ephesians
1:3-2:10   168
2:15   193
2:21   194
3:3-4   56
3:19   56
4:1-16   264
4:8-10   267
4:30   168

Philippians
1:19   261
2:6-7   193

2:6-11 267
3:8-9 193

Colossians
1:15-17 193
1:16 56
1:18 193
1:19-20 56
2:1-3 56
2:8 56
4:10 85

1 Thessalonians
4:1-12 168
4:13-18 168
4:15-17 167, 194
4:16-5:3 168

2 Thessalonians
1:5-10 168
2:1-12 168
2:3 150

Philemon
24 85

Hebrews
8:5 48
10:1 48
11:17-19 255

1 Peter
1:1 81
1:11 251
5:1 81
5:13 85

2 Peter
3:4 167

1 John
1:1-3 267
2:1 259
2:2 254
2:15-17 50
2:18-19 185
2:19 188

4:1-3 56, 168
4:10 254
5:20 239
7 56

2 John
1 81
1:3 75
7 185, 188

3 John
1 75, 81
9-10 185

Revelation
1:4 75
1:7 70
1:9 75
2:1-7 78
22:8 75

Other ancient literature

Clement of Alexandria

Quis dives 42.1-15 76

Clement of Rome

1 Clement
42 78
44 78

Clementine *Recognitions*
1.54.8 163
1.60.1-3 163

Eusebius

Historia Ecclesiastica
3.23.1-4 93
3.23.3 76
3.23.4 76
3.23.5-19 76
3.24.7-14 3
3.24.12 198
3.31.3 76

3.39.3-4   78, 80
3.39.5-6   80
3.39.7   80
4.14.3-8   76
4.14.7   76
5.20.4-8   75
5.20.5   75
5.24.2-3   76
5.8.4   76
6.14.7   2, 159

Georgius Monachus (Hamartolus)

Chronicle 3.134.1   79

Hermetic literature

De Regeneratione
13.2   52
13.10   52

Poimandres
1.5-6   52
1.6-32   53

Ignatius of Antioch

Ephesians 12.2   78

Magnesians
7.1   91
8.2   91

Philadelphians 7.1   91

Irenaeus

Adversus Haereses
2.22.5   76, 93
3.1.1   76
3.3.4   76
3.11.1   169

Josephus

Antiquities 20.9.7   38

Jewish War 2.14.8   39

Justin Martyr

Dialogue with Trypho
63   80
81   78

Melito of Sardis

Homily 95   80

Origen

Commentary on the Gospel of John
10.2   3
10.2-3   3
10.15-16   3

Philo

De agric 50-53   63

De conf 145   62

De fuga 197-198   63

De migr
1-6   62
40   63

De praem 45   62

De spec leg 4.14   62

Quod det 22   62

Qumran Community

CD (Damascus Rule)
6   73
9.23   92
B19.33-35   34

1QH (Thanksgiving Hymn)
9.23-24   34
17.26-28   34
18.29   33

1QM (War Rule) 1.1-17   34

1QS (Community Rule)
1.5   33
1.9   34
1.9-10   33
3.15   34
3.17-26   72
4.19-21   256
4.20-22   36
4.20-23   37
5.1-7   72
5.7-9   36
5.18   92
5.19-21   33

6.24-7:25   92
7.26-27   34
8.12-14   36
9.9-11   34
9.11   37

Theophilus of Antioch

ad Autolycum 2.22   80

Thucydides

Peloponnesian War 1.22   202